THE INSTITUTE FOR GOVERNMENT RESEARCH
OF
THE BROOKINGS INSTITUTION

STUDIES IN ADMINISTRATION
No. 43

THE BROOKINGS INSTITUTION

The Brookings Institution—Devoted to Public Service through Research and Training in the Social Sciences—was incorporated on December 8, 1927. Broadly stated, the Institution has two primary purposes: the first is to aid constructively in the development of sound national policies; and the second is to offer training of a super-graduate character to students of the social sciences. The Institution will maintain a series of co-operating institutes, equipped to carry out comprehensive and interrelated research projects.

The responsibility for the final determination of the Institution's policies and its program of work and for the administration of its endowment is vested in a self-perpetuating board of trustees. It is the function of the trustees to make possible the conduct of scientific research under the most favorable conditions, and to safeguard the independence of the research staff in the pursuit of their studies and in the publication of the results of such studies. It is not a part of their function to determine, control, or influence the conduct of particular investigations or the conclusions reached; but only to approve the principal fields of investigation to which the available funds are to be allocated, and to satisfy themselves with reference to the intellectual competence and scientific integrity of the staff. Major responsibility for "formulating general policies and co-ordinating the activities of the various divisions of the Institution" is vested in the president. The by-laws provide also that "there shall be an advisory council selected by the president from among the scientific staff of the Institution and representing the different divisions of the Institution."

DEMOCRACY, EFFICIENCY, STABILITY

An Appraisal
of American Government

BY

ARTHUR C. MILLSPAUGH

WASHINGTON, D.C.
THE BROOKINGS INSTITUTION
1942

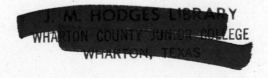

PREFACE

We are living in a time when philosophies and forms of government are being put to the supreme test. We are throwing into the present struggle our immense material resources. We are also bringing to it a renewed devotion to our historic political ideals and a fresh determination to vindicate democracy. Conscious of both right and power, we are confident of ultimate victory; and we are already discussing our hopes for the postwar world.

Recent economic conditions and the war now raging suggest that, if these hopes are to be realized, it is imperatively necessary that government should possess uninterruptedly and in larger measure than ever before the intellectual and moral capacity to do the right thing at the right time. In view of the trend toward increasing government controls we cannot risk anything short of maximum public efficiency; but we would not purchase efficiency, if it were possible to do so, at the price of democracy. Unless these two essential objectives are achieved and reconciled, we shall lack in large part the means and the stable conditions requisite for the realization of our economic, social, and international ideals.

This book differs in important respects from other studies of democracy. It is concerned with a proportioned analysis of government as a whole, endeavoring to show without burdensome detail or technical terms the various interacting factors that influence government and, along with the reactions of government, create our public problems. Since government, as well as the factors that act upon it, is dynamic, the book adopts a historical approach.

The present study also examines the various parts, operations, and trends of political life in their relation, not only to the realization of popular control, but also to the achievement of the two other basic essentials of satisfactory modern government—efficiency and stability. The term efficiency is used in a broad sense, meaning promptness, adequacy, and effectiveness in the determination of governmental policies, particularly those that affect national security. Stability means, not a static or stagnant condition, but a smooth, evolutionary process of political adjustment.

v

The three essentials of government are also standards or criteria, by which we may test the kind of government we have and locate its shortcomings and weaknesses. By undertaking this task of appraisal or diagnosis it is aimed to clarify and systematize public thinking and focus attention on the large, primary situations and issues. Obviously, these must be understood and kept steadily in view if we are to advance in an orderly way toward more democratic, more efficient, and more stable government.

The plan of the book is set forth in the Introduction. An attempt has been made to avoid the unconvincing "thinness" and the impression of dogmatism that often comes from excessive summarization. The result is a volume many may think too long. Of these, some are sufficiently familiar with the Constitution and with past history to dispense for the most part with the reading of Part I. Similarly, Part II, which deals with the period since 1929, may be passed over rapidly by those who must get the gist of the argument quickly. Part III is a restatement, review, rearrangement, and substantially a summary of the facts, interpretations, and conclusions set forth in preceding pages. This section is recommended to those who prefer a comparatively "short" treatment. In Parts I and II, an effort has been made further to assist the reader by providing him, not only with section headings, but also with key sentences; and the latter are also used liberally in Part III.

The contents of this book are derived from numerous publications, from varied personal contacts, and only in small part from what may be called original sources. In the collection and interpretation of facts, the author has put himself under obligation to many persons. A complete enumeration of them is impossible; a partial list might be misleading; but each may feel assured of the author's gratefulness.

Special acknowledgments are due Harold G. Moulton, president of the Institution, whose sympathetic counsel and thorough criticism from the inception of the project gave shape to much of the economic discussion and constructively influenced the book as a whole. Particularly valuable aid has also been rendered by Edwin G. Nourse and Laurence F. Schmeckebier.

ARTHUR C. MILLSPAUGH

April 1942

CONTENTS

Part III. The Situation Reviewed

INTRODUCTION

In a former revolutionary period, the emotions of aspiring and fighting men found expression in triplicate slogans. For Americans, the words were Life, Liberty, and the Pursuit of Happiness; for Frenchmen, *Liberté, Égalité, Fraternité*. These ideals and others were soon merged in the one term, Democracy; and democracy came to be no longer merely an inspiring hope but also and primarily a form of government.

From the American Revolution through the war of 1914-18, the trend of political development everywhere appeared to be toward the establishment and extension of popular government. Absolute and limited monarchies, aristocracies, and oligarchies seemed to have been outmoded, discredited, and drained of their early vitality. Military dictatorships, most common in Latin American countries, were viewed as symptoms of political immaturity which in time would give way to constitutional and stable self-government. Even in such countries as China and Persia, where at last monarchy had been overthrown or limited, it was confidently believed that, with experience, representative self-government could be made to work. Hope existed that the same happy outcome could eventually be brought to pass in dependent and semidependent regions, such as India, Egypt, and the Philippines.

To be sure, other so-called democracies and republics, ancient and medieval, had risen and fallen. Some were absorbed in empires; others supplanted by monarchies or dictatorships. It was held, however, either that these were not popular governments in the modern or true sense or that they lacked some element necessary to the success of democratic government and present in the modern world.

The growth of the spirit and forms of democracy had begun among Western peoples many centuries before the revolutionary era. Particularly in England, the simple customs that insured a measure of rudimentary self-rule to primitive communities and groups broadened from age to age and "from precedent to precedent," developing, by an almost uninterrupted process of accommodation, into the complex institutions and practices of modern popular government. The very slowness of the development gave to its results an appearance of solidity and proved worth. In France, the repeated perversions and reversals of the republican movement from 1789 to 1871 were considered to be evidences of Latin instability rather than of any inherent political weakness; and the Third Republic, persisting precariously through one crisis after another, was finally accepted as another testimonial to the inevitability of democracy. In America, the Civil War tested the ability of a democracy to remain united. The issue of that conflict seemed to provide a convincing demonstration that a nation "so conceived and so dedicated" could endure. The liberals of the seventeenth, eighteenth, and early nineteenth centuries, whatever their attitude toward popular rule might be, were convinced by first-hand experience of the theoretical and practical disadvantages of absolutism. Where the transition to principles of democracy was then making greatest headway, it was quite clear that autocracy, though it had played a large and vital part in the evolution of political institutions, had come to the end of its historic role.

After the democratic revolution had reached its climax in the Western World, its resulting institutions and habits of thinking gave every impression of strength and momentum. The World War was interpreted by President Wilson as a war to "make the world safe for democracy." Its outcome seemed to confirm the historical trend. Nations which were thought to be securely democratic had won the war; and the toppling of thrones round about them confirmed the general optimism. The society of nations, to be sure, continued to be essentially disorganized; but, in the League of Nations, many perceived the crude but hopeful beginnings of a world parliament, in which free nations through their representatives would meet to discuss and remove their differences. James Bryce, writing in 1921, noted as significant "the universal acceptance of democracy as the normal and natural form of government. . . . Men have almost ceased to study its phenomena because these now seem to have become part of the established order of things."[1]

[1] *Modern Democracies*, Vol. 1, p. 4.

It is true that many, during the last century and a half, have honestly questioned the desirability of democracy as a form of government. Perhaps still more have doubted its capacity to survive. Possibly an even larger number have been inclined to question whether the democratic ideal has ever been realized in practice or ever can be. The rise and spread since the First World War of dictatorships and of the dictatorial ideology seemed about to shatter finally the hopes of democracy's most confident devotees and to confirm the warnings of those who had doubted the durability of popular government.

DEMOCRACY FACES COUNTER-REVOLUTION

The aggressive dictatorships now attempting a world counter-revolution represent a reversal, let us hope temporary and partial, of a trend only recently thought to be impregnably established. This reversal, concurrent with and related to economic crises, has prompted a widespread re-examination of the foundations, validity, and prospects of democratic government; and, naturally, this re-examination has been concerned to a large extent with the international aspects of the crisis and with what has happened in other countries in the presence of dictatorial infiltration or aggression.

Until recent years, those who doubted the capacity of democracy to endure generally pointed to various internal causes of dissolution, such as concentration of wealth, corruption, paternalism, and popular ignorance or indifference. Confronted now by an external menace, we may assume that, during the next few months or years, humanity will eliminate German and Japanese aggression. By an extraordinary manifestation of wisdom, the victorious forces may contrive to prevent during a long future the reappearance of a similar world menace. Perhaps, one may hope, the ideal of international peace may be finally realized. But in any event, the American people cannot avoid the problems of government. They cannot ignore the counter-revolution; they have not been escaping it; and they can defeat it only through the process of government.

If the counter-revolution as it affects us is to be rationally controlled, it is appropriate and necessary that students of American government should, by clarifying the issues, prepare for the period of reconstruction. The discussion of democracy, now partially interrupted by the war, represents a highly significant movement in American life, a deepening and broadening effort to judge our institutions and ourselves by criteria appropriate to a technological and revolutionary era. Eventually this discussion may be comparable in comprehensiveness to that which our political system received in the period from 1776 to 1789.

The reconstruction that is now most discussed relates to the international system and to the essentials of permanent peace; but it is generally recognized that no new and more rational world order is likely to prove durable and effective unless it rests on a broad base of public acceptance, feeling, and support, and unless the institutions and policies of the great powers are in harmony with the requirements of international co-operation. International reconstruction itself requires, therefore, that we should look to our own attitudes, institutions, and policies.

Woodrow Wilson in 1885 denounced "the timidity and false pride which have led us to seek to thrive despite the defects of our national system rather than seem to deny its perfection." And he added:

When we shall have examined all its parts without sentiment, and gauged all its functions by the standards of practical common sense, we shall have established anew our right to the claim of political sagacity; and it will remain only to act intelligently upon what our opened eyes have seen in order to prove again the justice of our claim to political genius.[2]

The present study aims, by setting forth the facts and trends that are deemed significant, to indicate the situation of government in America from the standpoint of its democracy, its efficiency, and its stability. In short, where are we now? How have we got here? Are we reaching or falling short of our goals? Where do we go from here?

WHAT IS DEMOCRACY?[3]

We are dealing in this study with political democracy; and political democracy is partly a form and partly a process of govern-

---

[2] *Congressional Government*, p. 333.

[3] For definitions and concepts of democracy, see Edward McChesney Sait, *Democracy* (1929), pp. 3-7; Gerhard Leibholz, "The Nature and Various Forms of

ment. A functioning electorate seems to be the essential feature of the form; while the control exercised by public opinion over the governing authorities appears to be the essential feature of the process. In brief, the essence of political democracy is popular control.

Popular control is realized in a democracy through the expression of opinion. Opinion may be formally or informally expressed. It is expressed formally in elections where citizens generally are free to register their choices and where the majority decides. In a democracy an election is not a mere formality. The voters actually determine governmental policies; they choose the persons who are to be ultimately responsible for policy-determination; or they both determine policies and choose policy-determining officials. Democracy, fully realized, implies that all policies shall be subject ultimately to popular control.

If public opinion is to control policy-determination, the organs of government charged with the policy-determining function must be responsible to opinion. Government must be able and willing to function in the democratic way. It must translate the electoral mandate into terms of law and action and must reflect fresh manifestations of opinion that appear between elections. Government must be representative and responsive.

A study of political democracy must concern itself with conditions and influences, some of which may seem remote from the formal structure and mechanism of government. For government is a focus of social activity. It is the central social instrumentality. The state, according to Ascoli, "represents society and is derived from society; it is that section of the social structure wherein the loose ends of social organizations and habits are fastened together and knotted according to various styles. It is also that section of the social structure wherein choices are imperative and risks must be faced in making them."[4]

Democracy," in *Social Research*, Vol. 5 (1938), pp. 84-100; Ralph Adams Crain, *The End of Democracy* (1937), pp. 26-41; Charles A. Beard, "What Is This Democracy?" in American Association of Adult Education, *Adult Education and Democracy* (1936), pp. 1-6; R. Bassett, *The Essentials of Parliamentary Democracy* (1935), pp. 94-122; Marie Swabey, *Theory of the Democratic State* (1937), pp. 16-31.

[4] Max Ascoli, "Political Parties," in Max Ascoli and Fritz Lehmann, *Political and Economic Democracy* (1937), p. 206.

Government has in legal theory universal, decisive, definitive, and coercive power. But the way government acts, especially in a democracy or pseudo-democracy, is conditioned and controlled by forces which are to be found at any and every point in society. Government is doubtless where sovereignty resides; but sovereignty is here and there. In the determination of policy and in administration, public and private spheres overlap, influence each other, and to a large extent do each other's work. A complete reorganization of government would require a complete reorganization of society.

In a democracy, the people, if they are not actually *the* government, are at least a fundamental organ of government. The people may be dismissed, as Hamilton is reported to have dismissed them, as "a great beast"; but, now that we are measurably a democracy or at least desire to be, government can be usefully analyzed only by considering the popular mind and the multifarious forms of popular action. So the study of government necessarily includes within its scope: the political capacity of individuals, political philosophies and attitudes, social organization, social action, individual motivations, and leadership.

While our definition of political democracy has no visible economic content, no progress whatever can be made toward solving political problems without frank and understanding recognition of economic problems. At all times, the most concrete, pervasive, and potent features of the social environment are economic; that is, they are concerned with the production and consumption of goods and the distribution of wealth. Economic self-interest is, no doubt, one of the prime motivations of men in politics. Theories and forms of government have been economically shaped, usually without any contemporary appreciation of the real nature of the underlying influence. Moreover, the policies of government are predominantly economic, both in purpose and effect; and these policies in turn react on basic economic conditions.

The study of government is broadened still further by the time factor. Government is dynamic, not static. It is always in process of evolution. To see it as it is requires a moving-picture: a single photograph would be misleading. History does not repeat itself, and trends are not necessarily conclusive; but to know how government acted yesterday helps us to understand how it is acting today and how it may act tomorrow. Moreover, the institutions and the problems of government, particularly of an old government, are in large part deposited by the stream of history; and often the best place to get acquainted with these survivals is at their source.

Naturally, we must note the workings of government in the narrow sense: whether it is actually responsive and, if so, whether it responds to majority or minority opinions; whether government or some part of it manages or predetermines opinion; whether government is responsible or irresponsible; whether it has life, will, power, and momentum separate from the people; and whether within the forms of democracy, political authority is in fact paralyzed, a creature of accident or inertia, arbitrary, capricious, or personal.

WHAT IS EFFICIENCY?

This study is based on the assumption that any government, in order to endure, must function efficiently from the standpoint of those who possess actual sovereignty. The efficiency with which we are concerned is efficiency in policy determination. Such efficiency is ultimately measured by net results. In modern America, the primary concrete results expected, stated in the fewest possible words, are two: economic progress and national security.

It is not always clear to contemporary observers whether government is contributing to the attainment of these results. In many cases, it can be answered only by the historian and by him only with considerable uncertainty. In the present analysis, an effort has been made to avoid judging public policies and predicting their success or failure in the economic or international sphere. Nevertheless, efficiency may be inferred from the content of policies and their relation one to another. Policy-determining efficiency implies co-ordination and integration in the structure of policy, absence of internal contradiction and conflict. If the net result expected is economic progress, are the various policies and organs of government logically related to one another and to the central objective?

The efficiency of a government may be judged in part by the way it behaves. Does it possess or create the instrumentalities generally considered necessary for intelligent and effective action?

Moreover, in a democracy, the efficiency of a legislature or of a policy-determining executive or administrative authority depends also on its responsiveness and qualities of leadership. Democracy qualifies efficiency and efficiency qualifies democracy.

In efficiency, time is of the essence, and the time element provides an indispensable means of appraisal. Is government making measurable progress in the solution of its problems, or is it lagging? In judging the efficiency of a government, as of a machine, important facts relate to the quantity and nature of the work that it is expected to perform, the weight and character of its load. If the problems to be solved are increasing in volume and complexity and are changing in kind, and if the form and functioning of government appear no better adapted to their solution, then it may be presumed that government is farther below the desired standard of efficiency than it has been in the past.

Efficiency is an intangible quality, and for it there are no absolute criteria. The only instrument of measurement is candid, open-minded, common-sense observation. We do not assume that any human organization can be perfectly efficient or is likely to be completely inefficient. Efficiency or inefficiency is always a matter of degree and, in many cases, of opinion.

Democratic government, broadly viewed, includes individuals in the mass, sections and groups, private organizations and institutions, and political parties, as well as those offices and organs that are commonly termed governmental. In a democracy, therefore, the lowest common denominator of governmental efficiency is the public efficiency of the individual citizen. In the light of the problems that call for solution, one must ask whether the individual possesses the means of appraising and integrating policies. Does he have the requisite intelligence, information, and devotion to the general welfare? If not, does he have leadership that is intelligent, informed, and devoted to the general welfare? Is public discussion free, co-ordinated, integrated? Is the mandate transmitted to government through the opinion-expressing and electoral processes clear, reasonable, adequate? Thus, outside the formal structure of government, one must note the behavior of individuals and localities, the organization and nature of classes and groups, the character and functioning of political parties, the state of education, and the development and political applications of intellectual and scientific leadership.

Within the formal structure of government, one must examine the make-up, mental as well as organizational, of all the branches and agencies which determine policies or influence their determination.

WHAT IS STABILITY?

Stability implies predictability. It means, not changelessness, but peaceful, orderly change. Revolutions, violent upheavals, civil wars, widespread disorder, and the conditions that foreshadow such phenomena reflect instability. American government was unstable between 1854 and 1869. From the standpoint of international organization, Europe has never been stable. More specifically, Germany, quite obviously, has been internally unstable since 1918.

What are the factors that give stability to a democratic government? One would put first a general devotion to the concepts and ideals that make up the democratic philosophy. Next one would include those attitudes, habits, traditions, and moral standards that cause peoples to act in consistent and orderly ways. Closely related to these but of more direct political effect are constitutionalism and respect for law. All these things, however, change under the influence of economic, social, and political forces, both domestic and international. When these forces generate feelings of fear and insecurity and cause loss of confidence in government, increased instability may be presumed. Accordingly, one may say that all the factors that make for a governmental efficiency that is reconciled with democracy make also for stability.

The multifarious factors just mentioned have not all appeared at the same stage of our national development; and they have varied from time to time in nature, in strength, and in the direction of their influence. They are not all on the same plane. The position of the factors and their relationship to one another have not been constant. Consequently, any attempt to clarify the subject by a comprehensive and consistently applied classification or tabulation seems out of the question. Generally speaking, we shall be concerned with four major topics: fundamental influences, the governmental task, public opinion, and the governmental mechanism.

The study aims to make a dynamic rather than a static approach. Little value is perceived in merely describing government at any one moment, even the very latest moment. It appears more useful to show how government has evolved in relation to a changing environment and how the vital political organs have behaved and are behaving.

The book is divided into three parts. The first, entitled "Evolution and Experience," surveys American government in process of development from 1787 to 1929, the factors that acted upon it, and the problems that were presented to it and revealed by it. The second part, called "The Latest Time of Test," sketches in somewhat more detail the governmental situation with respect to democracy, efficiency, and stability from 1929 to the present day. Part III summarizes the discussion and indicates so far as possible the conclusions and implications that can be drawn from our political experiment.

It should be made clear at the start, however, that the author's conclusions do not take the form of a plan for constitutional reform, though they may suggest certain possibilities appropriate to such a plan. For the recovery or preservation of governmental health, the author has no final prescription to offer. He is concerned primarily with diagnosis.

PART I
EVOLUTION AND EXPERIENCE

America's political evolution does not begin with the framing of the Constitution. The political structure and mechanism as a whole are explained by habits acquired and institutions established over many centuries and by ideas and theories long in process of fruition, as well as by an immediately critical situation. In 1787, the thirteen colonies had accomplished a revolution by force of arms. Though they had won independence and nominal peace, they were handicapped by governmental inadequacies and disturbed by developing crisis. Fortunately, they were not set against the idea of political change, and they believed in the possibilities of human progress. The Constitution that they adopted made government more rigid in some important respects; but the political structure, along with the nation that came into being at the same time, contained the seeds of a remarkable transformation.

In Chapter I, we describe the fundamental features of American government as they took form in 1787-89. Chapter II describes the operation and adaptation of the system from 1789 to 1860, an era in which striking formative influences came from ruralism and expansion. In Chapter III, covering the years from 1861 to 1900, we make a similar description and appraisal, noting the influence of factors that tended at this time to be identified more with industrialism, emphasizing economic pressures, and sketching new political patterns. Coming then to the period from 1901 to 1929, Chapter V deals with underlying conditions and Chapter VI with government. In this period technological industry with its urban accompaniment sounds the dominant note.

CHAPTER I

THE CONSTITUTION

The government of the United States consists of national, state, and local institutions. In 1789, the state and local institutions were already in existence; the federal system and the national government were deliberately devised and formally adopted.

DEMOCRATIC AND ANTI-DEMOCRATIC ELEMENTS

The purpose of the federal constitution was not to establish national democracy, but to make government more efficient. Nevertheless, ideas and institutions of democracy were already firmly rooted in America. Equally significant is the fact that an influential group, though approving a republican form of government, was opposed to democracy as it was then or is now understood.

Many essentials of democracy were widely accepted in colonial and revolutionary America.

At the time of the American Revolution, the idea of democracy, in its relation to modern government, had long been in process of development and application. The idea appears to be attributable in the main to two species of revolt, one religious, the other politico-economic, but both at times closely interrelated.

A significant aspect of the religious revolt, exemplified by the Protestant Reformation, English puritanism, and various separatist movements, was its repudiation of theological authoritarianism and its emphasis on individualism, freedom of thought, and limitation of government in spiritual affairs. Religious liberty for the individual meant a large addition to his rights, responsibilities, and dignity in a domain of life that was then extensive and vital. In addition, congregational self-government was established in some of the new church organizations.

The politico-economic revolt grew out of that historic social transformation which was marked by the break-up of feudalism, the liberation of individuals from an agricultural-military regimentation, the unification of peoples into nations, centralization of political power in the hands of hereditary monarchs, and the rise of a merchant class. In the institution of representation, which reached its first and most vital national exemplification in the English Parliament, the merchant class had found a means to curb the king, originally in matters of taxation and, later, in the making of laws. During the seventeenth century, when the first English settlements were made in America, the struggle between Parliament and king, fundamental to the future development of popular government, resulted in a definitive limitation of autocracy, paving the way for the development during the eighteenth century of a responsible cabinet system.

The thinking of English, as well as French, liberals was concerned not only with freedom of thought and of speech and with legislative supremacy over the executive, but also with the problem of governmental power, especially its power to regulate economic life. It was accepted that government must have and exercise various economic functions, protective, promotive, and regulatory. Following the mercantile theory, however, governments were imposing numerous restrictions on domestic and foreign trade and were seeking to promote individual profits and national well-being by chartering trading and development companies and granting them monopolistic privileges. It was not wholly a coincidence that Adam Smith's *Wealth of Nations* should have been published in the same year as the American Declaration of Independence. His espousal of the purely police-state and of economic *laissez faire* fitted into the individualistic thinking of the time. The American Revolution was pre-eminently a revolt against the employment of economic controls, as well as taxation, by an imperial government in which, as the colonists thought, they were not represented.

In the colonies, a theory of representation had grown up different from that which had become accepted in the mother country. Here the intense localism of isolated settlements demanded that a legislator should actually come from the locality that he was supposed to represent. In England, on the contrary, a member of the House of Commons might be a resident of one place and elected from another, and, in any event, was held to represent, not a locality, but the entire nation.

To a large extent, English liberalism—religious, political, and economic—reflected the interests and the feelings of the middle classes. It was not a mass phenomenon. On the other hand, American conditions were such as to give to democratizing ideas a certain indigenous quality, greater intensity, and a wider diffusion among the masses.

In New England and the middle states, colonial America was predominantly a land of small farmers and agricultural pioneers, with a rising class of merchants and tradesmen and a goodly number of lawyers. It was a land, on the whole, of free private enterprise, of family and community self-sufficiency. The circumstances under which the colonists came and their manner of living in the new world called for independence of spirit, created conditions of equality, and bred a feeling for liberty and disrespect for authority. In New England, the character of the colonists found political expression in the town meeting. In all the colonies, the people received representation in the colonial assemblies, which endlessly squabbled with the governors over finance and prerogatives.

While the colonists in the mass were not given to political theorizing, from the very beginning democratizing ideas were being expressed and were receiving concrete application. Some of the settlements were consciously based on the doctrines that men were politically equal and that government rested on the consent of the governed.

During the next century and a half, radical doctrines propagated in England, France, and the American colonies were forecasting social reorganization, justifying revolution, and laying a philosophical foundation for popular government. These doctrines were given classical summary by Jefferson in the Declaration of Independence. They were more than mere political propaganda. They represented widely held aspirations and beliefs. They embodied an optimistic faith in the perfectibility, the dignity, and the rationality of man; and, on the foundation of this faith, men "could formulate the modern idea of progress: the idea that man, by deliberate intention and rational direction, can set the terms and indefinitely improve the quality of his mundane existence."[1]

The democratic doctrine so formulated was prepared to accept, through its far-reaching implications, the challenge of those who demanded efficiency in government, as well as of those who looked upon justice as the prime purpose of social control. To those who embraced this doctrine, the age of revolutionary democracy was the "age of reason"; and in the masses, ultimate wisdom and justice through good will were to be joined with ultimate power.

After independence had been declared, the revolutionary democratic theory was given various concrete embodiments in the early state constitutions. These were generally drawn up by representatives of the people, somewhat in accordance with the idea of the Social Compact. In some cases, the words of the Declaration of Independence were included almost word for word. In almost all cases the constitution contained a bill of rights designed to safeguard the fundamental liberties and rights of the individual. All states adopted the principle of separation of powers, intended to prevent the usurpation of authority by any branch of government and thus further to protect individual freedom. Despite their declarations in this latter respect, however, the state constitutions made the legislature practically supreme, and the state executive "a sorry figure."[2]

Moreover, at that time the administrative functions of the state were few, being largely delegated to the counties and towns; and the argument for centralized and integrated executive authority to promote efficiency would have carried no conviction in the local communities.

All of the constitutions eschewed hereditary titles and none established a nobility. In general, they reflected that hope and idealism which had made the American Revolution not merely a secession from the British Empire but a real social upheaval accompanied by an appropriate political reconstruction.

[1] Carl Becker, "Afterthoughts on Constitutions," in Conyers Read (ed.), *The Constitution Reconsidered* (1938), p. 393.
[2] Claude H. Van Tyne, *The American Revolution* (1905), pp. 144-45.

*Aristocracy, a critical situation, and political realism
produced an anti-democratic reaction.*

Colonial America had never been without its Tory element, derived in part from church authority and in part from a social aristocracy based on wealth. The church had separatist movements, but these were frequently intolerant.

In the South, democratic institutions and forces working toward democracy were almost nonexistent. Throughout the country, property was the basis of social and political privileges. As the colonies organized themselves into states, they put into effect the idea that the chief function of government was to protect property rights and that government, therefore, should be controlled by the owners of property. The new states, with one exception, included in their constitutions property qualifications for voters; and the privilege of holding office was also generally denied the poor.

By the time of the Revolution, the clericals had declined in power; and the exodus of Loyalists during and after the war, further reduced the number of those who possessed property or position. The growth of commerce, however, was increasing the number of those whose interests were allied with political, economic, and financial stability and with the promotion of economic enterprise. These, along with the great landholders, were in the minority; but they could exercise a political influence out of proportion to their numbers. In the minds of such men, the situation in 1787 had become extremely critical.

In the first place, America had not achieved that national unity which was the condition precedent to strength and security in international relations. The colonies had been parts of the British imperial system and had been protected against their external enemies by imperial power. But when independence had been won, geographical isolation was not then, as it later became, the central and reassuring factor in our international position. England, then both powerful and unfriendly, was on our northern and northwestern frontiers, and a number of disputes with her were still unsettled. We had fought the Revolutionary War in alliance with France. Spain hemmed us in on the south and southwest. The Indian tribes were troublesome. Commerce was then our chief source of wealth and an important part of it was foreign commerce; but it was seriously hampered by British restrictions. America was in fact thirteen sovereign nations, loosely leagued together under the Articles of Confederation and represented collectively by an impotent congress.

In the second place, the country in its domestic affairs was not well governed. The congress of the Confederation lacked power to collect revenue, borrow money, or pay its debts. The issues of Revolutionary currency had depreciated virtually to zero. National credit had sunk to its lowest ebb. Deficits were chronic; and the states were disinclined to impose taxes to support the central government. In the several states, the debtor class agitated for further issues of paper money; and other restless and discontented groups joined in the demand for inflation. Some of the states stood firm for sound money; but several yielded. In Massachusetts, discontent and disturbance led to the armed uprisings known collectively as Shays' Rebellion. A substantial interstate commerce had developed, but the states were raising commercial barriers against one another. Shipping regulation and a uniform tariff were needed but could not be supplied by state action.

Most of the basic prerequisites of increasing prosperity were present. The people were not in poverty. Population was increasing. The westward movement was gathering impetus; and the unsettled land beyond the Alleghenies offered an outlet to the unemployed, a living to the poor, and expanding markets to the commercial class. But the ownership of the western territory had been another matter of prolonged dispute; and the development of the west called for a national policy. The passage of the Ordinance of 1787 providing a political organization for the Northwest Territory was the outstanding achievement of the Confederation.

On the whole, ample reason existed to doubt the efficiency, honesty, and intellectual capacity of popular legislatures. During the fourteen years of war and confederation, the central government—if it can be called a government—was a legislature, charged with both the determination and the execution of policy. These tasks, to the extent that they were done at all, had been done with intolerable inefficiency. The behavior of the state legislatures had not been such as to enhance their prestige during a time when the need of the country was for constructive statesmanship. Indeed, before the federal constitution was framed, the executive had been largely reinstated in public esteem.

It was probably inevitable that as soon as representative government passed from the era of combat to the era of practice the prestige of the legislature should decline. When public opinion was ranged against an autocratic and unpopular monarch, or his representative the governor, the legislature, as the champion of the people, naturally became popular. When this struggle was won, neither the legislature nor the executive appeared to be more or less the servant and champion of the people.

Based on the alleged incapacity of the people for self-government in large affairs, anti-democratic opinion was controlling among the men of "substance" who dominated the Constitutional Convention of 1787. Though the conditions which caused alarm were created quite as much by the weakness of the national organization as by the democracy of the state governments, those who conceived it their duty to bring order out of chaos were inclined to view either popular rule or legislative absolutism as incompatible with the unity, wisdom, order, stability, and strength that they desired government to have.

Few were inclined to follow Hamilton in his monarchical leanings and in his condemnation of "mobocracy," but the majority went with him part of the way. In general, democracy meant to these men direct rule by the people, and it was believed to be workable at all only in very small states.

The means by which popular agitation was carried on and public opinion expressed were repugnant to those who were to determine the new governmental mechanism. They were aware that the Revolution had been initiated and kept going by groups and organizations, that it had been fed by propaganda, and that it was brought to success by a party. But after the Revolution, group manifestations—propaganda, agitation, and direct action—had been causes of alarm; and the parties then in process of formation, based on economic self-interest, seemed to preclude any possibility of national unity, stability, or prosperity. As Madison put it:

The instability, injustice, and confusion introduced into the public councils, have, in truth, been the mortal diseases under which popular governments have everywhere perished; as they continue to be the favorite and fruitful topics from which the adversaries to liberty derive their most specious declamations.[3]

The framers of the federal constitution feared "factions." A "faction," according to Madison, was "a number of citizens, whether amounting to a majority or minority of the whole, who are united and actuated by some common impulse of passion, or of interest, adverse to the rights of other citizens, or to the permanent and aggregate interests of the community."[4] It was Madison's view that "the latent causes of faction" were "sown in the nature of man,"[5] and therefore that "relief is only to be sought in the means of controlling its *effects*."[6] He thought that a republic or delegated government "promised the cure for which they were seeking";[7] and the Convention agreed that the mechanism must be contrived so as not to give free rein or quick response to popular impulsiveness. The idea was that the national government should be in the control of the "best" men, men who, because they were property-owners, would feel responsibility. These were also the men, it was felt, who possessed the requisite political capacity and emotional stability. In a sense, they were striving to identify national political leadership with economic leadership—with capitalism as it was then known. In another sense, they wished the federal government to be composed of and controlled by an intellectual aristocracy.

As a result, the Constitution is a mixture of democratic and undemocratic provisions.

Of the four organs of government set up in the Constitution, the House of Representatives alone was to be directly elected by

---

[3] *The Federalist*, Henry Cabot Lodge, ed. (1888), pp. 51-52.
[4] The same, p. 52.
[5] The same, p. 53.
[6] The same, p. 55.
[7] See George M. Dutcher, "The Rise of Republican Government in the United States," *Political Science Quarterly*, Vol. 15 (1940), pp. 199-216.

the people and, so far as numerical apportionment was concerned, equitably representative. As an additional concession to democracy, in line with the historically established idea that the people's representatives should control the purse strings, it was provided that "all bills for raising revenue shall originate in the House of Representatives. . . ."[8] On the other hand, the members of the Senate—two from each state, regardless of population—were to be selected by the state legislatures. Without the concurrence of this small and presumably aristocratic upper chamber, no law could be made; and the Senate was granted, to the complete exclusion of the lower house, substantial legislative and executive powers, the giving of advice and consent to treaties, and the confirmation of important appointments. The president was to be chosen by electors, who were not apportioned exactly according to population and who, like the senators, might be selected by the state legislatures. The fourth organ, the Supreme Court, was to be composed of justices appointed by the president with the approval of the Senate. In each of these four organs, moreover, the length of tenure was different. The representatives were to serve two years; the president four; the senators six; and the justices during good behavior. A popular majority might conceivably gain control of such a government; but no sudden or impulsive seizure of power appeared likely.

The amending process provided for in the Constitution is in keeping with the spirit and purpose of the instrument. It was designed to act more as a brake than an accelerator. It was not democratic in conception, yet provides alternative methods that may be made at least measurably democratic. No opportunity is afforded for direct popular initiative or a direct popular referendum. An amendment may be proposed in one of two ways: (1) by a two-thirds vote of both houses of Congress; or (2) by a convention, which must be called by Congress upon application by two-thirds of the state legislatures. An amendment, proposed in either of these ways, must be ratified (1) by the legislatures of three-fourths of the states, or (2) by conventions in three-fourths of the states. The procedure, in any event, was intended to be slow and difficult.

[8] Art. I, sec. 7.

Though the Constitutional Convention marked the flood-tide of anti-democratic reaction, it cannot be dismissed as merely a profiteering conspiracy. Regardless of economic motives, the obvious political need at that time was for union and for a central government equipped to deal with matters that could not be handled by thirteen separate and weak states. Political chaos meant economic chaos; and the political purposes of the Constitution were practical and appropriate irrespective of their economic motivation. It can be readily admitted that the protection of property and the encouragement of business were underlying and important purposes of the Constitutional Convention; but it was not in the long-run interest of the agrarians—though at the time they may have thought it was—that the states should severally regulate commerce, collect import and export duties, coin money, raise and support armies, or pass laws impairing the obligation of contracts. The men who drafted the Constitution and obtained its ratification were, above all, realists. They were undertaking a practical task. They were not formulating abstract principles: they were reorganizing government. The structure that they erected was founded in the main on two processes of thought: first, a rational appraisal of political experience, biased by class-feeling; and, second, consideration of expediency, leading to concessions and compromises—for the Constitution, before it could become effective, had to run the gauntlet of public debate and factional attack.

A "MORE PERFECT UNION"

England had failed to construct an imperial federation or commonwealth of nations able to reconcile national power with local interests and local feelings. The same problem on a smaller geographical scale was presented to the framers of the Constitution; and the way they sought to surmount its difficulties determined to a large extent the structure of the central government.[9]

[9] "In all our deliberations on this subject we kept steadily in our view that which appears to us the greatest interest of every true American, the consolidation of our Union, in which is involved our prosperity, felicity, safety, perhaps our national existence. This important consideration, seriously and deeply impressed on our minds, led each State in the Convention to be less rigid on points of inferior magnitude, than might have been otherwise expected. . . ." (Washington's letter of transmittal, Sept. 17, 1787.)

The problem of union was closely
related to that of democracy.

Pioneering and pioneer life had produced, along with individualism, an intense localism. The nation that adopted the federal constitution was predominantly agricultural and rural. The country was without railroads, the telegraph, or even good highways. In general, the roads were bad; in places almost impassable. Mails were infrequent and long delayed. The settlements in the back country were as much isolated from the seaboard as the northern states were from the southern; and the pioneering communities in the West took on the social characteristics of the colonies. Under these conditions it was the neighborhood center that was the chief, if not the only, headquarters for associational activity. To the people living in these isolated and self-sufficient communities any outside authority seemed more or less remote and superfluous, and it became positively objectionable when it interfered with their local interests. It was in the various communities that the idea of democracy was most keenly felt and most thoroughly practiced. If democracy depended on the closeness of government to the people, liberty would obviously be endangered were public functions and powers concentrated in the national government.

The thirteen independent states that emerged from colonial and revolutionary America had been given their geographical shape partly by the accidental location of the first settlements, partly by the physical features of the Atlantic seaboard, and partly by arbitrary decisions made in London. Each state had developed a fairly distinctive political individuality, derived not merely from its separateness but also from its special economic interests and social composition. At the close of the Revolution, the states were politically self-conscious and keenly jealous of one another. Afterward, self-centered nationalism seemed to be growing in each of them. State sovereignty was a generally accepted theory; it was specifically recognized by the Articles of Confederation; and, legally and practically, it was then a fact. Naturally, when it was a question of federation, the small states were jealous of the large. The economic difference between the South and the North opposed one section to the other. It was inevitable, therefore, that the states should remain as separate political units, responsible for exercising the functions that bore most directly on the people and free, within their respective jurisdictions, to preserve their own institutions and be as democratic as they wished.

The scheme of federalism provided for a
central government with limited functions.

Federalism required a division of the powers of government between the nation and the states. The division agreed upon represented a rough reconciliation of liberty and authority—of democratic institutions, ideas, and habits with the need of strong, adequate, wise, and prudent government. To these ends, the powers of the federal government were delegated and enumerated; all others, except those expressly prohibited, were reserved to the states or the people. For the most part, the federal government was given authority to deal only with those matters that experience had shown could not be handled satisfactorily or safely by the states acting separately.

Thus, conduct of foreign affairs, provision for the national defense, and the declaration and prosecution of war were included among the powers of the national government. Yet, standing armies were feared. The militia were expected to be the chief reliance for defense; and these forces, except when in the national service, were left partly under state control.[10]

Empowered to tax (within limits) and to borrow, the national government was to be no longer dependent on support from the states; and control of the currency was made a national function.

The manner and degree to which powers over economic life should be centralized were influenced by the strong agrarian feeling of the time and by the stage of industrial development then reached. The steam-engine had been invented more than 20 years before the Constitutional Convention; but the political implications of the Industrial Revolution and the economic and social transformations that were to accompany it were undreamed of by the founding

[10] Art. I, sec. 8.

fathers. Already there was some industrial specialization in America. The corporation was a recognized form of business organization; but the basic economic processes were in large measure directed by individuals and partnerships. There could be no conception at that time of the closely knit economic interrelationships and interdependencies which within a hundred years were to become national governmental problems of first importance. Commerce in its narrow sense, the exchange of goods, was practically the only economic activity that had anything but a local or community significance; and commerce for the most part followed water routes.

Several constitutional provisions equipped the central government to protect property interests and to regulate or encourage private economic activity. Such were the clauses relating to taxation, borrowing, the currency, patents, and bankruptcies. The power to establish post offices and post roads had its economic as well as social implications. In addition, the national government was given power to "regulate commerce with foreign nations, and among the several states, and with the Indian tribes." This was general phraseology, subject to broad or narrow interpretation. On the whole, the states appeared to retain a large field for economic functioning, being specifically deprived only of those powers that they had exercised with the most damaging effect.

On what are now known as the social functions of government, the Constitution was practically silent. A national postal service could, no doubt, be made a cultural instrument; the Constitution aimed "to promote the progress of science and the useful arts" through a national system of patents and copyrights; but nothing was said of education, public health, public safety, housing, or morals. A few international or national crimes were referred to; but the great body of private law, regulating the relations of individuals to one another and to the public, was left within the care of the states.

Because of the generality with which they were expressed, some of the powers granted to Congress were capable of extensions and ramifications that could not be foreseen at the time. There were, moreover, two general provisions that permitted the federal government to perform, incidentally to its own functions, the same functions as the states, and even to participate within the jurisdiction of the states in the exercise of admitted state functions.

To make all laws which shall be necessary and proper for carrying into execution the foregoing powers, and all other powers vested by this Constitution in the government of the United States, or in any department or officer thereof.

To lay and collect taxes, duties, imposts, and excises; to pay the debts and provide for the common defense and general welfare of the United States. . . .

Under a broad interpretation of this latter clause, many objectives might be included in the term "general welfare"; and much power was potential in the possession of money to spend.

In two provisions, the significance of which was to be largely ignored in future years, resided the possibility of an interesting development of national control over state governments and over the territorial layout of federalism. One concerned the obligation of the United States "to guarantee to every state in the Union a republican form of government"[11] and the other the power of Congress to admit new states into the Union.[12]

In working out the scheme of federalism, the makers of the Constitution did not interfere with the existing forms of state government or with state boundaries; but the Constitution made it difficult to effect regional readjustments, since no state could be partitioned or combined "without the consent of the legislatures of the states concerned, as well as of Congress."[13] Nor was any detailed arrangement set forth for the handling of interstate matters which were not within national jurisdiction. Provision was made, however, for "full faith and credit" among the states and for the extradition of criminals and fugitive slaves.[14] The states were permitted to make compacts with each other, but only with the consent of Congress.[15]

[11] Art. IV, sec. 4.
[12] Art. IV, sec. 3.
[13] Art. IV, sec. 3.
[14] Art. IV, secs. 1 and 2.
[15] A state could enter into an interstate or foreign compact without the consent

In the structure of the national government, the Senate was set up in such a way as particularly to safeguard federalism. The senators were to be chosen by the states; and the states, large and small, were to be equally represented in the Senate. This arrangement was presumably to be perpetual, since it was provided that no state, without its consent, should be deprived of its equal suffrage in the Senate. The localistic basis of representation was accepted in the requirements that the senators and representatives must be inhabitants of the states for or in which they are chosen.[16]

While the national government was equipped to maintain itself independently of the state governments and could bring its powers to bear directly on individuals, centralization was absent from the facts of American life, from the thinking of most Americans, and from the intention of the Constitution. The latter erected a federation, in which an attempt was made to separate and balance the powers of the whole and those of its parts. The scheme was structurally rigid; but it possessed a remarkable facility, later to be demonstrated, for the flow of power to the central government.

GENERAL STRUCTURE AND MECHANISM

In choosing between a complex and simple, between a mechanistic and an organic, form of national government, the framers of the Constitution were probably influenced by Montesquieu, or perhaps more directly by Blackstone, who erroneously believed that the British Government exemplified a system of separated and balanced powers. The theory supporting this system was attractive at that time and has since been steadfastly upheld by those concerned with the protection of individual liberty or with the safeguarding of selfish interests. A majority of the first state constitutions, framed before 1787, contained a declaration of adherence to this theory. Nevertheless, in Maryland, Virginia, North Carolina, and South Carolina, the executive was elected by the legislature, and in Georgia, by the lower house. In the Constitutional Convention a

---

of Congress, when actually invaded or in such imminent danger as would not admit of delay.

[16] Art. I, secs. 2 and 3. The Constitution did not require that the representatives be elected by districts or be residents of districts. They must only be residents of the states in which they are chosen.

proposal was made and received some support that the president should be chosen by Congress.[17]

The national governmental structure was based on the principle of separation of powers.

The Convention accepted separation of powers, it may be surmised, less as a theory than as a result of those practical compromises that satisfied the divergent viewpoints represented in the Convention. A president subordinate to Congress would not have satisfied those who wanted a strong central government. A congress subordinate to the president would have been equally unsatisfactory to those who were opposed to centralization. The independence of the Supreme Court would have followed as a logical conclusion even if judicial independence had not already been considered essential to justice. In the debate that preceded the ratification of the Constitution it was cogently argued that the federal government—since its power was cut into three slices—could not become stronger than it was intended to be.

The Constitution of the United States, unlike some of the state constitutions, does not in so many words declare a separation of powers. It does, however, provide that "all legislative powers herein granted shall be vested in a Congress . . ."; that "the executive power shall be vested in a President . . ."; and that "the judicial power . . . shall be vested in one Supreme Court, and in such inferior courts as the Congress may, from time to time, ordain and establish."

As a means of safeguarding the separation of the legislative and executive branches, two provisions require mention. According to one, no senator or representative or person holding an office of trust or profit under the United States can be appointed a presidential elector.[18] According to the other "no person holding any office under the United States shall be a member of either house during his continuance in office."[19]

[17] Woodrow Wilson, *Congressional Government* (1885), pp. 268-69; Gaillard Hunt and J. B. Scott (eds.), *Madison's Debates in the Federal Convention of 1787* (1920), pp. 38-49.
[18] Art. II, sec. 1.
[19] Art. I, sec. 6.

The independence of the judiciary was protected by the following: "The judges, both of the supreme and inferior courts, shall hold their offices during good behavior, and shall, at stated times, receive for their services a compensation, which shall not be diminished during their continuance in office."[20]

In still other ways, the Constitution aimed to keep each of the three great organs of government separate from the others.

Congress was divided.

There was warrant in experience as well as theory for a division of the legislative branch into two houses. The English Parliament had its two chambers. Some of the colonial assemblies had been single-chamber bodies, and after 1776 such bodies had been retained or adopted in Pennsylvania, Georgia, and Vermont; but as a rule the legislatures consisted of two chambers. Some of the states had a council, intended especially to advise and curb the executive. The framers of the Constitution wanted some such body. They also needed an upper house for the embodiment of federalism and aristocracy, and a lower house to represent the populace. The small states were held to be protected by the Senate as the large ones were by the House of Representatives. Under the circumstances that existed and the views held at that time, a two-chambered Congress, like separation of powers, was logical if not inevitable.

Power was to be kept separated and under control by checks and balances.

The framers of the Constitution were well aware that human beings are frequently motivated by a will to power. They entertained a well-founded fear of usurpation and abuse of authority by either the legislative or executive. As James Bryce said, the Constitution "is the work of men who believed in original sin, and were resolved to leave open for transgressors no door which they could possibly shut."[21] The system of separation of powers was therefore intermeshed with a system of checks and balances; and it was the latter system, in conjunction with the former, that

[20] Art. III, sec. 1.
[21] *American Commonwealth*, Vol. 1 (1888), pp. 299-300.

THE CONSTITUTION

seemed to provide effectual and durable safeguards against tyranny —tyranny of one man, of the legislature, or of popular majorities.

The fundamental balance, essential to the maintenance of legislative federalism, is found in the division of the field of law-making between the national government and the states. One can find in several quarters the anticipated means of preserving this balance; the size of the nation, which was believed to preclude centralization; the intense popular feeling for local self-government; the will to power and self-assertiveness of state and local politicians; the common sense and restraint expected from national statesmen; the amending process, in which the states were to participate; the composition of the Senate; and, finally, the Supreme Court, through the exercise of its power to review the constitutionality of federal and state enactments.

The most obvious effect of legislative federalism was to establish a multiplicity of legislatures;[22] and the general adoption of the two-house principle not only doubled the number of legislative bodies but also introduced a check within the legislative system that could produce anything from mere delay to absolute paralysis.

The Congress, divided within itself, was to be checked by the chief executive. So far as constitutional provisions go, the president participates in legislation in three ways. First, "he shall from time to time give to the Congress information of the state of the Union, and recommend to their consideration such measures as he shall judge necessary and expedient." Second, he may call both houses, or either of them, into special session, and he may adjourn them when they disagree on the time of adjournment. Third, he possesses a qualified veto over all acts of Congress: if he returns a bill, without his signature, within ten days after its passage, it can then become a law only by a two-thirds vote in each house.[23]

[22] "A more extensive plant than we have in America for the manufacture of statutes does not exist on the earth." Becker, *The United States: An Experiment in Democracy* (1920), p. 84.

[23] According to Hamilton, the primary purpose of the veto was to enable the president to defend himself. The secondary one was to protect the community against "the passing of bad laws, through haste, inadvertence, or design." Hamilton repeatedly stressed the "propensity of the legislative department to intrude upon the rights, and to absorb the powers, of the other departments." He had no fear of

While the veto is the only legally decisive check that the president has on the ordinary legislative work of Congress, the latter is supplied by the Constitution with a variety of means by which it may control, discipline, or subordinate the chief executive. Except for the presidency itself—powerless without assistance—the entire executive branch was to be dependent on Congress for its establishment, organization, and funds. His more important executive and judicial appointments were made subject to senatorial confirmation; and others could be likewise subjected by law. To any treaty that he negotiates, two-thirds of the senators must advise and consent before it can be ratified. He was made commander-in-chief of the military forces; but special provision was made to keep the army under legislative control.[24] Congress can remove a president by impeachment.

Then, too, the Supreme Court, as we shall see a little later, was to act as a check on the states and on the federal congress and the president; but the justices were dependent on the president and Senate for appointment and on legislation for much of the organization and some of the powers of the judicial branch.

Finally, the amending process was a check on all the powers and organs of government; and this process itself was compounded of checks and balances.

The conception of government embodied in the Constitution was structural and mechanistic, rather than organic; its purpose was negative, rather than positive. Legislation was expected to be slow, owing to the several organs engaged in it and the power of one to check the others; but slowness was considered to be necessary to deliberation, and, among fallible mortals, deliberation was and is still believed to offer one guarantee against the making of mistakes.[25]

---

executive domination and believed that the veto power would be used sparingly. Without a veto, absolute or unqualified, he contended, the president "would be absolutely unable to defend himself against the depredations" of the Congress. *The Federalist*, pp. 457-58.

[24] "The Congress shall have power . . . To raise and support armies; but no appropriation of money to that use shall be for a longer term than two years." Art. I, sec. 8.

[25] "Wise progress comes from conflict. Unanimity is always dangerous. An infinitude of human experience is behind the belief that discussion, criticism, oppo-

*The presidency was expected to introduce
energy, strength, and efficiency.*

That energy, strength, and efficiency which the country needed
and the framers of the Constitution desired were expected to come
chiefly from two constitutional accomplishments: union and the
institution of the presidency.

In the method of choosing the president, the Constitutional Convention devised an ingenious and pretty much an original scheme
to insure a deliberate selection of the best men without the intrusion
of party, "faction," group feeling, democratic emotionalism, office-
holders' interests, and control by Congress. This device, according
to Hamilton, was at the time "almost the only part of the system,
of any consequence, which . . . escaped without severe censure, or
which . . . received the slightest mark of approbation from its opponents."[26]

According to the words of the Constitution, the potentials of preponderant power were in the possession of Congress. Had that body
deliberately planned and consistently proceeded to reduce the
president to a figurehead, making the executive branch responsible
to the legislature, this object conceivably might have been attained.

According to the letter of the Constitution, the only area in which
the president could substantially determine national policies through
his own initiative was in the conduct of foreign relations. Here,
where vigor, consistency, secrecy, and dispatch were held to be necessary, he was given an unqualified initiative. Though a minority
of the senators might reject a treaty negotiated by him, he still
possessed an unplumbed reservoir of power to act decisively in
matters of utmost importance. From the nature of treaty-making,
it was considered an executive function; and, though the president
was made a participant in other forms of legislation, he was conceived of primarily as an executive, not as a legislator and not as
an officer who would exercise in his executive capacity a wide range
of discretionary administrative authority.

---

sition, conduce to sound conclusion. This alone would justify the balancing of the
powers, the offsetting of one against the other." Robert Luce, *Legislative Problems*
(1935), p. 239.
    [26] *The Federalist*, pp. 423-24.

It was not made entirely clear that the president should be the actual head of the federal administrative organization. The executive power was vested in the president; and the Constitution says that "he shall take care that the laws be faithfully executed, and shall commission all the officers of the United States." Yet, as we have seen, the life of the administration was at the mercy of Congress.

Though the executive departments were taken for granted—possibly because of this fact—the Constitution only incidentally dealt with them. Defense and diplomacy were important national administrative functions plainly indicated in the fundamental law. A treasury department was already in existence and was anticipated by the wording of the Constitution; but that it should be headed by an individual rather than a board or should be under any considerable degree of executive control was evidently not yet decided. A post office department was also necessary; and one had already been established under the Confederation. With the exception of the above-named functions and the agencies required to perform them, the Constitution suggests a national executive branch performing functions that were traditionally executive and having few responsibilities and no great size.

Under the Articles of Confederation, the administrative organization was closely dove-tailed with and controlled by the legislative body. For the direction of the administrative departments, such as they were, three types of setup were tried: the legislative committee, the board composed of persons outside the legislature, and the single administrator, likewise not a member of the Congress. The employment of the board or commission type of departmental control had been discredited in the minds of those who had observed its workings. The statesmen, exemplified by Hamilton, who were primarily concerned with vigorous administration, had no patience with the idea of plural heads and diffused responsibility.[27]

---

[27] "The actual conduct of foreign negotiations, the preparatory plans of finance, the application and disbursement of the public moneys in conformity to the general appropriations of the legislature, the arrangement of the army and navy, the direction of the operations of war—these, and other matters of a like nature, constitute what seems to be most properly understood by the administration of

The Constitution implies that the administrative departments are to be single-headed and that their heads are to be in at least an advisory relationship to the president.[28] Since laws affect a country only through administration, there is a faint significance, administrative as well as legislative, in the provision that "he shall from time to time give to the Congress information of the state of the Union."[29] The fact seems to be that the Constitution unquestionably placed the president in direct control of the military establishment and of any department entrusted with the initiative in foreign relations. In large part, however, control was to depend on authority to appoint and remove. Congress was empowered by the Constitution to vest the appointment of "inferior" officers "in the president alone, in the courts of law, or in the heads of departments."[30] All appointments not so vested were subject to confirmation by the Senate. Evidently, neither the Senate nor Congress as a whole could constitutionally appoint executive officers. Nothing was said in the Constitution about the removal of appointive officers, except that, in addition to the president and vice-president, "all civil officers shall be removed from office on impeachment for and conviction of treason, bribery, or other high crimes and misdemeanors."[31]

THE BILL OF RIGHTS

The framers of the Constitution included in the original document certain safeguards of private rights, guarantees against suspension of the writ of habeas corpus, against bills of attainder and ex post facto laws, against the granting of titles of nobility, against abolition of trial by jury in the federal courts, and against the misuse of impeachment and treason trials. The instrument, as drafted and submitted to the states for ratification, was held by

---

government. The persons, therefore, to whose immediate management these different matters are committed, ought to be considered as the assistants or deputies of the chief magistrate, and on this account, they ought to derive their offices from his appointment, at least from his nomination, and ought to be subject to his superintendence." Hamilton, in the *Federalist*, p. 450.

[28] "[He] may require the opinion, in writing, of the principal officer in each of the executive departments, upon any subject relating to the duties of their respective offices." Art. II, sec. 2.

[29] Art. II, sec. 3.

[30] Art. II, sec. 2.

[31] Art. II, sec. 4.

its framers to contain ample safeguards against oppression and injustice. They argued that it did not impair the traditional liberties or civil rights of the individual, which were intended to be left in the care of the states. Nevertheless, formulations of individual rights, wrested with difficulty from the king, had been embedded in the foundation of the British system; and bills of rights were already included in American state constitutions. An insistent demand arose that similar guarantees be placed in the federal constitution; and its ratification by the necessary number of states was obtained only on an understanding that the instrument would be amended by adding to it a bill of rights. This understanding was carried out when the first ten amendments took effect in 1791.

The Bill of Rights has significance and effect
from the viewpoint of democracy.

Demands for the addition of a bill of rights to the Constitution were actuated by something more than mere desire for a statement of principles. It was understood that the Constitution was to be law, enforceable in the courts, and it was felt that in this new law as in the old the rights of the individual should be distinguished and safeguarded from the rights and powers of government. The first amendment went to the essence of democracy, since it guaranteed religious liberty, freedom of speech and of the press, and the rights of assembly and of petition. The second guaranteed the right to keep and bear arms; the third had to do with the quartering of soldiers in private houses, and the fourth with security against unreasonable searches and seizures; and the aim of the next four amendments was to secure to the people the essentials of an impartial, humane administration of justice.

In the fifth amendment, we find that clause which was later to receive so much interpretation and arouse so much controversy: "No person shall . . . be deprived of life, liberty, or property, without due process of law." The original purpose of this clause was to secure to the individual, in courts of justice, those procedural safeguards which were deemed essential for his protection against a capricious, arbitrary, or tyrannical administration. It was this clause, perhaps more than any other, which, along with the general purpose and spirit of the Constitution and the Anglo-Saxon traditions of law and justice, made the government of the United States a government of law. It was intended to protect the individual against government itself. It meant that no officer of the government could be above the law. In short, none could become a personal dictator.

The ninth and tenth amendments read as follows:

The enumeration in the Constitution of certain rights, shall not be construed to deny or disparage others retained by the people.

The powers not delegated to the United States by the Constitution or prohibited by it to the States, are reserved to the States respectively, or to the people.

These latter amendments made federalism more explicit; but they also reflect the compact theory of government, that the people themselves are the original reservoir of rights and powers, that government obtains its powers only by popular consent, and that when certain powers have been delegated to government the entire residue remains with the people.

JUDICIAL POWER

In the United States, as Woodrow Wilson wrote, "constitutional government is *par excellence* a government of law"; and he added: "So far as the individual is concerned, a constitutional government is as good as its courts; no better, no worse."[32]

Judicial independence had become one of the historic safeguards of liberty. The justice dispensed by the British monarch had been necessarily capricious and frequently venal. Parliamentary judgments in private cases were inexpert and determined in many cases by political and personal favoritism. Courts had early appeared as separate institutions; but they had been until a comparatively recent date under the control of the political branches of government. Some of the judges, however, refused to be subservient; and their insistence on an impartial rule of law led those who were contending for Anglo-Saxon liberties to associate judicial independence with free government. At the end of the seventeenth century the principle was established in England that judges should hold office during

[32] *Constitutional Government in the United States* (1911), p. 17.

good behavior. In colonial America it was alleged that this principle had been violated; and one of the charges against the king in the Declaration of Independence was that he had "made judges dependent upon his will alone, for the tenure of their offices and the amount and payment of their salaries."

The prestige of the law and of the courts had been little affected by the American Revolution or by the chaotic years that followed it. The traditions of judicial administration that persisted in the new nation were those of Coke and the other great English judges who stood for impartiality and independence. A majority of the members of the Constitutional Convention were lawyers. It may be presumed that lawyers were numerous also in the state constitutional conventions and legislatures. As a class, their interests and attitudes are bound up with stability, especially stability of the law and of judicial institutions.

It was the necessary corollary of an effective federalism that the national government should have its own system of courts; and it followed from the doctrine of separated powers, as it was then understood, that the judges should be made substantially independent of the president and Congress.

The courts became the special guardians of the Constitution.

While the judiciary had become traditionally a distinct organ of government, its function was two-fold, being both executive (or administrative) and legislative. The more familiar function was to decide those lawsuits that came within its jurisdiction. So limited, its task was to apply, that is, to execute, the law. From this point of view, its work was and is executive or administrative.

Quite as clear was the fact that courts made law. Judge-made law long antedated statute law. The common law, inherited by the colonies, was judge-made; and, for most of the legal safeguards that the individual enjoyed before the nineteenth century, the Anglo-Saxon peoples were indebted to the judges, rather than to legislators and executives.[33] After the development of statute law-

[33] "[In] substance the growth of the law is legislative. And this in a deeper sense than that what the courts declare to have always been the law is in fact new.

making the process of judicial interpretation remained, in a sense and in a measure, a process of legislation, though judicial law-making became then, in theory, merely tentative, indispensable to the adjudication of controversies as they arose but always subject to repeal or correction by the statute-making authority.

The federal constitution was not conceived by its authors as a contract among states which could be obeyed in part, disobeyed in part, or abrogated altogether. It was not a series of pronouncements, like the Declaration of Independence, intended chiefly to influence and consolidate opinion. The Constitution was intended to be law. It says of itself:

This Constitution and the laws of the United States which shall be made in pursuance thereof, and all treaties made, or which shall be made, under the authority of the United States, shall be the supreme law of the land; and the judges in every State shall be bound thereby, any-thing in the Constitution or laws of any State to the contrary notwith-standing.

The legal authority of the Constitution was further buttressed by a provision that the president should take an oath or affirmation that he will, to the best of his ability, "preserve, protect, and defend the Constitution"[34] and by the additional provision that

the Senators and Representatives before mentioned, and the mem-bers of the several State legislatures, and all executive and judicial offi-cers both of the United States and of the several States, shall be bound by oath or affirmation to support this Constitution. . . .[35]

The judicial power of the United States, according to the Con-stitution, "shall extend to all Cases, in Law and Equity, arising under this Constitution, the Laws of the United States, and

---

It is legislative in its grounds. The very considerations which judges most rarely mention, and always with an apology, are the secret root from which the law draws all the juices of life. I mean, of course, considerations of what is expedient for the community concerned. Every important principle which is developed by litigation is in fact and at bottom the result of more or less definitely understood views of public policy; most generally, to be sure, under our practice and tradi-tions, the unconscious result of instinctive preferences and inarticulate convictions, but none the less traceable to views of public policy in the last analysis. . . ." O. W. Holmes, Jr., *The Common Law* (1881), pp. 35-36.

[34] Art. II, sec. 1 (7).
[35] Art. VI.

Treaties made, or which shall be made, under their Authority," as well as to a number of other classes of cases and controversies. In applying the Constitution as law to the cases that come before them, the judges necessarily must ascertain or determine the meaning of the Constitution's phraseology. In other words, they have to "interpret" the Constitution.

The Constitution did not expressly grant to the Supreme Court any power to declare acts of Congress unconstitutional. It has been asserted at times that the Court "usurped" this power and came to exercise a "veto" over legislation. The practice of the Court, however, was not a "usurpation" and it was not a "veto" in the accepted sense of the word.

The idea that the courts could declare a legislative act invalid was not invented by Chief Justice Marshall. It was implicit in colonial and revolutionary discussion. As McLaughlin says:

> The doctrine of what is now called "judicial review" is the last word, logically and historically speaking, in the attempt of a free people to establish and maintain a non-autocratic government. It is the culmination of the essentials of Revolutionary thinking and, indeed, of the thinking of those who a hundred years and more before the Revolution called for a government of laws and not of men.[36]

The doctrine of judicial review was accepted in the state courts both before and after the Constitution was adopted. The general trend of the discussion in the Constitutional Convention appears to indicate an assumption by many of the delegates that the power to declare legislative acts unconstitutional would be exercised by the courts in cases over which they had jurisdiction.[37]

The duty of the courts to disregard legislation reasonably believed to be contrary to the Constitution is inherent in the federal constitution itself. The Constitution allocated powers in three directions. First, it effected a division of powers between the federal government and the states. Second, it apportioned powers among the legislative, executive, and judicial branches of the federal government. Third, it imposed limitations on both the federal and

---

[36] Andrew C. McLaughlin, *A Constitutional History of the United States* (1936), p. 310.
[37] The same, p. 313. On this general subject, see the same, pp. 305-19.

state governments for the purpose of safeguarding the freedom of the individual. At the same time, the Constitution clearly prescribed the procedures by which it may be amended. Congress alone cannot amend the Constitution; nor can the states alone. The amendment procedure requires action by both Congress and the states. Were the courts to enforce acts of Congress contrary to or inconsistent with the Constitution, the power to amend the fundamental law would obviously pass to Congress. But that body was constitutionally limited and involved in the system of allocations and balances. To make Congress final judge of the validity of its own acts would have been in effect to abandon those limitations, distributions, and balancings of power that were essential characteristics of the American constitutional system.

While the Supreme Court was thus indicated as the special guardian of the Constitution, its opportunity to exercise judicial review of legislation was limited to justiciable cases. The initiative in constitutional interpretation belonged to Congress and the president; and they were to be left a broad field in which their initiative might be decisive.

It was inevitable that the powers to be exercised by the Supreme Court should force it into the field of political controversy. Certain terms used in the Constitution—for example, "general welfare"—were to retain through the years no commonly or constantly accepted meaning. What they might mean to any individual would depend on his conception of what is "socially desirable." The accepted meaning of the term "regulate" would depend very largely on the kind of governmental control that seemed to be needed in an emerging situation; and the meaning of "commerce" would expand or contract as the ramifications of economic activity were or were not comprehended. In these and other cases, the definition of a word would result in the determination of a policy; and the policy so determined might be a burning issue in a conflict between interests or ideals.

Possessing to all intents and purposes a life tenure, the justices of the Supreme Court would almost certainly be for the most part elderly men, representing not merely legalistic habits but also, in a changing world, the economic, social, and political opinions of the past. They would be, it was clear, a stabilizing and conservative element in government. Yet, they were to exercise a function which might be in effect indispensable to the preservation of whatever proportion of democracy the Constitution contained. Stability itself was deemed to be essential to free government. Then, as now, democracy was held basically dependent on a recognition of the rights of individuals; but constitutional guarantees of individual liberties were effective only when judicially enforced.

The government that has just been briefly sketched represented a compound of pregnant principles—constitutionalism, federalism, separation of powers, checks and balances, representation, executive authority, protection of individual rights, and judicial independence. Issuing from compromise, its form was complex. In certain critical features, it was experimental. Its democracy was limited; its efficiency unproved; and its durability doubtful. The founding fathers, as we have said, undertook a practical task and were largely guided by considerations of expediency. Those who framed the Constitution were not disposed to boast of their handiwork. Said Madison,

I never expect to see a perfect work from imperfect man. The result of the deliberations of all collective bodies must necessarily be a compound, as well of the errors and prejudices, as of the good sense and wisdom, of the individuals of whom they are composed. The compacts which are to embrace thirteen distinct States in a common bond of amity and union, must as necessarily be a compromise of as many dissimilar interests and inclinations.[38]

While the document was designed to meet an immediate situation, its authors were influenced by a belief that they were planning for posterity, for an unpredictable future in which government would require adaptation to changing conditions. In order to be adaptable it must be flexible; and in order to be flexible it must not only be capable of amendment but also provide room for interpretation and extension, for the filling in of details. For the most part, therefore, the provisions of the Constitution were confined to what seemed at the time the minimum necessities of national organiza-

[38] *The Federalist*, p. 548.

tion; and these were stated in general rather than specific terms, in some cases so general that their meaning could with equal plausibility be interpreted in contrary ways. Such flexibility and adaptability as the Constitution had were not derived in significant degree from the amending process, but from the lack of detail in the instrument and the interpretative function performed by the Supreme Court.

While the Constitution was being drafted and ratified, the new nation was feeling the impact of the outside world and was breeding fundamental conflicts of interests and of ideas and dynamic forces of unexampled volume. Expansive economic energies were about to be unleashed. The frontier was starting its mighty movement toward the Pacific. The "peculiar institution" of the South was about to assert a new vitality. Sectional interests, supported by legalistic and ethical theories, were soon to challenge the irrevocability of the Union. Localism retained a stout foothold. Individual liberty was not yet reconciled with public power. New values and ideals were capturing the minds of men. Other revolutions and counter-revolutions were in the offing.

CHAPTER II

RURALISM AND EXPANSION, 1789-1860

From the inauguration of the first president to the Civil War, the new nation was presented with unique opportunities, never before offered to any enlightened people. During approximately the biblical span of a man's life, the American people won and occupied a virgin empire of continental proportions and apparently inexhaustible wealth. They embraced the principle of democracy and devised means of giving it expression. Agriculture, the frontier, and pioneering dominated the period. An era of individual initiative, it witnessed numerous and significant experiments with public economic control. It was a time when the Constitution grew strong and the system established by it showed disturbing signs of weakness. Liberty seemed to be at its emotional flood-tide, but slavery and sectionalism were many-sided portents and for two-score years determining forces. Nationalism was most exuberant and most defiantly challenged.

STRENGTHENING OF CONSTITUTIONAL GOVERNMENT

When Washington became the first president, the problem was to give workability and durability to the constitutional scheme of government, in accordance with its purposes as he and his class saw them. Appropriately, the three branches of government were at the start largely composed of men of the same school of thought, who had helped to draft the Constitution and had supported its ratification.[1]

Under the leadership of Washington and Hamilton, the mechanism began to "work."

Congress proceeded to fill out the organization, to establish armed forces, to provide revenue, and to put into effect a far-

[1] Charles A. Beard and Mary R. Beard, *The Rise of American Civilization*, Vol. 1 (1927), pp. 336-38.

reaching fiscal program. The organization of the judiciary was completed.

In the executive branch, three departments were set up by law—State, Treasury, and War—with provision in addition for an attorney-general and the postal service. Each separate administrative agency was placed under a single head.[2] The four principal administrative officials were treated by the President as his special advisers. In the formation of his "Cabinet," Washington sought in the beginning to avoid partisanship and "factionalism." Jefferson, Secretary of State, and Hamilton, Secretary of the Treasury, represented, however, sharply opposing philosophies that were basic to the parties then in process of crystallization; and, in his second term, Washington made his official family exclusively Federalist, that is, Hamiltonian.

The economic task that government now assumed, represented and created by national policies, resulted in part from generally admitted needs, in part from the Hamiltonian philosophy and from the "economic predilections" of those who had framed the Constitution, and in part from what would now be considered political strategy, since these policies were calculated to enlist for the Constitution, the federal government, and the party in power the confidence and support of certain specially benefited groups—the financial, commercial, and manufacturing classes. Neither the Constitutional Convention nor the government of Washington and Hamilton accepted the principle of complete freedom or local autonomy in economic life. National economic problems existed; and, in their minds, these problems called for national governmental solution. In the main, the general welfare was to be promoted from the top down, through the encouragement of the propertied interests—the safeguarding and fostering of commerce, credit, and industry. A tariff act was passed, designed for protection as well as

[2] In 1798 a navy department was established; and control of naval affairs was transferred to it from the War Department. Congress provided in considerable detail for the internal organization of the Treasury Department, apparently, in the main, because of the traditionally close relation between financial administration and the legislative power.

On the history of the federal administrative organization in general, see Lloyd M. Short, *The Development of National Administrative Organization in the United States* (1923).

income. The federal government assumed at par the revolutionary debts of the Confederation and of the states. An excise tax was imposed on spirituous liquors. A law was passed for the chartering of a national bank. A mint was established. Shipping regulations were enacted.

Assertions of central authority by the executive branch served, on the whole, to fulfill the promise of vigor in foreign relations and order in domestic affairs.

How did the new legislative mechanism operate? The original expectation seems to have been that the House of Representatives would take a dominant position, and that the Senate would act as the President's privy council. From the very start, however, the upper chamber was aggressive in the initiation of legislation on a variety of important subjects[3] and thereafter easily maintained its position as a co-ordinate law-making body.

Both Washington and Hamilton desired close personal contact between the executive and the legislature. Yet, when the first president attempted to confer personally with the Senate on a question of foreign relations, he met with rebuff. Hamilton had the first two Congresses very much under his influence; and he was quite generally considered, as he was in fact, the President's first minister; but the Cabinet was not and did not become in any sense responsible to the legislative body, though, as early as Washington's first administration, the Senate had asserted its power to reject executive nominations, and the custom of "senatorial courtesy" was developing. Despite congressional jealousy of the executive power, it was imperative that some working relationship be established between Congress and the administrative departments. Nevertheless, a provision in the bill establishing the Treasury Department, authorizing the secretary to "digest and report plans," was opposed in Congress because it was interpreted to permit the secretary to present his program on the floor of Congress. The wording was changed; and thus, as one historian puts it, "the Secretary of the Treasury was shut out of the House and was condemned to work in the lobby."[4] When the Republicans gained control of the Third

[3] George H. Haynes, *The Senate of the United States; Its History and Practice* (1938), Vol. 2, p. 1021.
[4] Henry Jones Ford, *Washington and His Colleagues* (1918), p. 47.

Congress, the president, John Adams, was not of their party. Congress thereupon proceeded to demolish the Federalist system of executive leadership and administrative co-operation. A ways and means committee was set up to provide fiscal leadership in the House.

The Supreme Court solidified constitutionalism, furthered centralization, and protected the economic status quo.

John Adams, near the end of his administration, when Thomas Jefferson had already been elected president, appointed John Marshall chief justice of the Supreme Court. Marshall was a nationalist, of the same school of thought as Washington and Hamilton, quite out of sympathy with the triumphant public opinion which had put Jefferson in office. Yet, Marshall remained for more than a third of a century at the head of the Court. Great in statecraft, he put into action the doctrine of judicial review over acts of Congress, and extended the meaning of the Constitution by liberal construction so as to limit the states, and expand the scope and efficacy of federal powers. As a juristic statesman he had the vision of a unified nation with an adequate national government; but his somewhat inflexible mind was set against democracy and his sympathies were clearly with the "moneyed" interests.

With respect to the basic question of federalism, the commerce clause was to be the chief source of the Supreme Court's adjudications; and, so far as economic legislation and economic interpretation of the Constitution are concerned, the commerce clause was the key provision. Marshall's idea was that the power to govern must reside somewhere, and that in national affairs it belonged to the national government. He viewed the federal power to regulate interstate commerce as exclusive, holding that the states could not act on any matter involved in such regulation; and he gave broad scope to both regulation and commerce. His decisions appear to have led to the conclusion, or would have if they had been consistently followed, that the power resides solely in Congress to take any action which it deems advisable, not only to regulate but also to promote or prohibit any economic activity which produces an effect across state lines.

In the larger view, the special service of Marshall was to strengthen constitutionalism and nationalism at a time when judicial encouragement of disintegrating ideas and disruptive forces might easily have wrecked the great experiment. Nevertheless, constitutionalism, bound as it was to the ideas of nationalism and central power, was durably established only by the triumph of union in the Civil War.

THE JEFFERSONIAN REVOLUTION

The first of the major formative influences in American governmental development was personified by Washington, Hamilton, and Marshall; the second, by Jefferson. The latter marked our first major political reversal and the first significant democratizing movement that captured the national government.

Jeffersonian individualism embodied some, but not all, of the essentials of democracy.

The inauguration of Jefferson in 1801 did not mean the full realization of all the implications of popular government. Nor did the "Jeffersonian Revolution" involve a nominal acceptance of democracy. The Bastille had fallen on July 14, 1789, and subsequent events in France, and the excesses of the Democratic or Jacobin Clubs, as well as of French diplomacy in this country, had covered the term "democracy" with much the same kind of disrepute that the word "communism" was later to acquire.

While Jefferson's Republican Party of 1800 may have been "little more than a division of the governing class,"[5] it represented certain points of view sharply opposed to those of Hamilton, Marshall, and the commercial interests of New England. This second phase of the democratic movement—the first may be said to have ended with the Constitution—took its inspiration from Jefferson himself, whose political philosophy had been strongly influenced by French revolutionary thinking. Central to his philosophy were two ideas, both expressed in the Declaration of Independence—government by consent of the governed, and the right of revolution. Underlying

[5] Edgar E. Robinson, *The Evolution of American Political Parties* (1924), p. 75.

these ideas, belief in the dignity and rationality of the independent individual compelled logically a minimizing of the functions and powers of government.[6] Jefferson was more than an exponent of *laissez faire:* he was the philosopher of agriculture, holding that the only secure foundation of the republic was a population of free and self-supporting landowners. He disparaged industry and commerce, distrusted businessmen, feared cities, disliked industrial workers, felt that the functions and costs of government should be kept at the irreducible minimum, and advocated governmental retrenchment and lower taxes.

Individualism, equality, and localism rested on conditions as well as theories.

Not merely was individualism a philosophical tenet; it was becoming an American feeling and an American practice. Developing capitalism may have been operating against it in New England and elements making for its denial were present in the South; but in the West the individualistic spirit was bred and borne along on a tremendous wave of pioneering energy; and this spirit was continually to be renewed as the frontier advanced. The traits and the institutions of the frontier had their sources in the colonies; but the westward movement gave to these characteristics an amplitude, an apparent validity, and a durable quality.

Within three decades after the inauguration of Washington, eight new states had been erected in the West. The settlement of the West was in the main an unplanned and undirected multitude of private enterprises, selfishly motivated, and in considerable measure exploitative and speculative. Pioneering was not calculated to discourage that industry and acquisitiveness which already in the colonies had become motivating moral values.

In the frontier community, on the other hand, ideas of liberty and equality were natural and deeply felt. Prior to the ratification of the Constitution, the states had begun to relax their suffrage

[6] It was typical of the inconsistencies in Jefferson's position that twice he should have been identified with remarkable assertions of federal authority, once in the acquisition of Louisiana and later in the embargo on commerce. The embargo, moreover, showed a secondary aspect of inconsistency: it had the economic effect of a protective tariff.

restrictions; but on the seaboard these tended to persist where aristocratic leadership was strongest. In the pioneer West artistocracy was absent; and the new states generally adopted universal manhood suffrage. The older states followed.

Pioneers, like colonists, were in the habit of looking after their own needs; and the frontier settlements were real communities, homogeneous, isolated, and integrated.

Jefferson was, in the spirit of the times,
a "strong executive."

Jefferson as president was not a neutral or a coalitionist; under him, the president became what he has since remained, the recognized political leader of a like-minded portion of the electorate. But no definite organization existed by which persons of one opinion could determine what public policies they should collectively stand for and what candidates they should support. During this time, party meant a group of factional leaders, who might or might not work together.

Jefferson exerted a decisive influence over Congress; and his secretary of the treasury, Gallatin, taking up the role of Hamilton, worked closely with congressional committees. But from Jefferson to Jackson, the presidency lacked assertiveness and lost prestige. The executive, wrote Story in his *Commentaries*, "is compelled to resort to secret and unseen influences, to private interviews and private arrangements to accomplish its own appropriate purposes, instead of proposing and sustaining its own duties and measures by a bold and manly appeal to the nation in the face of its representatives."[7]

In a way, too, Jefferson stood for efficiency.

The governing class to which Jefferson belonged was never later, down to our own day, to find its counterpart in American politics. Largely centered in Virginia, its justification lay in its intellect and in its political dedication. If to the Virginia Dynasty we add Washington and the two Adamses, we find that all of the presidents from 1789 to 1829—a period of forty years—represented

---

[7] Quoted in Ford, *Washington and His Colleagues*, pp. 50-51.

on the whole a singularly high-minded experience in the art of government, and, for the most part, a personally thought-out or firmly adopted political philosophy.[8]

NATIONAL EXPANSION AND SECURITY

During the first quarter-century of independence, we were unable to avoid international entanglements. During the French Revolution and the Napoleonic wars, the national government tried to prevent the propagation of foreign ideologies in this country, as well as actual involvement in war through our commerce and shipping. The attempt was irritating to our domestic psychology and economy; but it was measurably efficacious.

The War of 1812, in which we in effect took sides with Napoleon, may be attributed in part to a sectional demand for the conquest and annexation of Canada. The expanding West, free of narrow provincialisms and commercial impediments, became jingoistic; and, later, the South, made even more consciously expansionist by its economic interest, took the nation into an essentially imperialistic war against Mexico.

National expansion brought a sense of power and resulted in national security.

Except for their failure in the War of 1812, the American people found it relatively easy to satisfy, by force or otherwise, a lusty appetite for territory. The Indians were dispossessed or segregated; and before 1860 Florida, the Louisiana territory, a large part of Mexico, and the Oregon country were acquired. The result of these occupations and annexations was both to expand the country and to isolate it. Spain and France were peacefully removed from our immediate boundaries; and the possibility of Mexico's becoming a powerful rival was eliminated. The British Empire, it is true, was left on our northern boundary; but our neighbor there was to be the autonomous Dominion of Canada, rather than a European-minded Great Britain.

Moreover, when the Latin American states won their inde-

[8] Of the five presidents between Washington and Jackson, two had been vice-president and four secretary of state. John Adams, Jefferson, and Madison take high rank as political scientists.

pendence, we endeavored through the Monroe Doctrine to transfer to the other nations of the New World, as a whole, the policy of isolation from and independence of Europe that we had adopted for our own protection; and, in this attempt to keep our Latin neighbors free from European aggression, we were protecting and simplifying our own international position.

Whether consciously or not, and whether scrupulously or not, we had adopted and more or less consistently followed a policy which seemed to provide adequately for our ultimate national needs: living space, natural resources, unity, power, and defense. This policy—or process—constituted a simple, easily understood, and rational program, consonant with imperialistic logic, with economic interest, and with the emotional drives of a colonizing and pioneering people. From 1815 until the twentieth century our international position appeared to be one of providentially arranged and impregnable security.

THE FRONTIER AND PUBLIC OPINION

National expansion, pioneering, and the frontier introduced into American political evolution certain fundamental influences of peculiar significance and, for the most part, of lasting effect. In connection with the Jeffersonian Revolution we have already spoken of some early effects in relation to the suffrage and localism.

Liberty of opinion, free association, and political-mindedness accompanied frontier individualism.

In spite of its practicality and certain sordid aspects, the expansive movement of the time, the glimpse of apparently inexhaustible resources and boundless opportunities, stimulated not only the taking of risks personal and financial but also the perception of romance, the fashioning of ideals, the envisioning of utopias, and the launching, always by private individuals, of daring social experiments.

The virile individualism of the soil, typical of frontier America, was sung by Whitman. A reading of Van Wyck Brooks suggests that it was an unspecialized and uninhibited individualism that most satisfactorily accounts for the "flowering of New England."

Individualism implied, and American life was breeding, self-reliant whole men, not specialists; and whole men can be sociable with one another. "In no country in the world," observed de Tocqueville, "has the principle of association been more successfully used, or more unsparingly applied to a multitude of different objects, than in America. Besides the permanent associations which are established by law under the names of townships, cities, and counties, a vast number of others are formed and maintained by the agency of private individuals."[9] The most numerous of these associations, it is believed, were concerned with broad purposes—religion, morals, peace, abolition, and politics. Organization and discussion expressed a general political interest and a growing consciousness of popular power. On this aspect of American life, de Tocqueville remarked:

The cares of political life engross a most prominent place in the occupation of a citizen of the United States, and almost the only pleasure of which an American has any idea is to take a part in the Government, and to discuss the part he has taken. This feeling pervades the most trifling habits of life; even the women frequently attend public meetings and listen to political harangues as a recreation after their household labors. Debating clubs are to a certain extent a substitute for theatrical entertainments: an American cannot converse, but he can discuss. . . .[10]

As time passed, the popular political consciousness became more and more national. Though the people were directly affected only slightly by the federal government, they were impressed by its power and increasingly intrigued by its large affairs.

Discussion was vigorous, dead in earnest, and frequently intemperate and intolerant. The newspapers, multiplying in number, were at first almost exclusively political pamphlets; and their vitriolic attacks on government officials, including the president, enlivened and embittered the history of the time. In turn, government became intolerant; and, in the Alien and Sedition Acts, the Federalist administration of John Adams made its short-lived and unpopular attempt to control public opinion. In later years, stimulated by economic sectionalism, nationalism, or group interest,

[9] Alexis de Tocqueville, *Democracy in America* (rev. ed., 1900), Vol. 1, p. 191.
[10] The same, pp. 254-55.

various forms of intolerance found expression and rather wide acceptance—ideas of racial superiority, hostility to immigrants, secret organized action, efforts to suppress the right of petition, and mob rule.

JACKSONIAN DEMOCRACY

Frontier democracy—its habits, its hopes, and its crude strength—found adequate representation in the personality and prejudices of Andrew Jackson. He was idolized, not because of his political principles or policies, for in the beginning he seems to have had none that were firmly held or widely known. That he was a military hero, a man of the West, a remarkable personality, and a champion of the masses was sufficient for the times.

Political parties crystallized into a party system,
democratizing the presidency.

Because of manhood suffrage and the addition of new states, the western agrarians were now numerous enough to place one of themselves in the presidency, provided they achieved working unity. In 1824 a multiplicity of candidates, among whom Jackson was the most popular, had thrown the election into the House of Representatives and a reputedly "corrupt bargain" between the "Puritan and the Blackleg" had placed John Quincy Adams in the presidency. In 1828, management, organization on a national scale, and a leadership that appealed to popular emotions resulted in the triumph of "Old Hickory." At this time, the national party convention was becoming a recognized feature of the electoral process; and no later than 1840, the political party had taken essentially its present form.

To the presidential electors, the party finished doing what factionalism had started; it made them rubber-stamps. The electoral scheme had overlooked two important facts: (1) that an economic interest or a political opinion, becoming preponderant, would insist on controlling the national government; (2) that of all national governmental organs, the presidency was the best calculated to become a symbol and embodiment of power. Any attempt to keep this glittering and substantial prize beyond the range of vital contention or group organization was foredoomed to failure.

That Jackson's organization and following should be frankly called the "Democratic Party" was significant of both its composition and state of mind. As an expression of democracy and as a democratizing influence, the Jacksonian idea of government, in many respects akin to Jeffersonianism, was more clearly a triumphant reassertion of the colonial and post-revolutionary economic radicalism of the agrarian group, acting within the framework of frontier localism. Jacksonian democracy presented a sweeping challenge to the Hamiltonian conception of centralization, control by a privileged class, and promotion by government of capitalistic enterprise. So undeviating and appealing seemed its economic and political creed to the agrarian majority, as well as to the workingmen of the cities, that the Democratic Party, except for eight years, had uninterrupted control of the presidency until 1861. From the accession of Jackson, the nation's political center of gravity lay in the Mississippi Valley.

The Whig opposition had great nationalistic leaders in Webster and Clay; but it was composed of various and almost irreconcilable elements; it was compelled to compromise; and it won only two presidential elections (in 1840 and 1848), both times without a program and with a military hero as candidate.

Jackson as a "strong" executive championed frontier agriculture against the "money power."

As champion of the masses, Jackson temporarily restored the prestige and asserted the power of the presidency. He did not defer to Congress; he fought it, and was applauded by the plain people for his boldness.

The United States Bank was the most spectacular object of his attack. Hamilton's program had included two principal means of insuring "sound money": the constitutional prohibition of paper money issues by the states and a national bank. The notes of the Bank were sound; but the institution's economic utility did not save it from attack. To the agrarian masses, now in the saddle, the institution was a symbol of the "money power." It was accused of political activity; and, finally, when the renewal of its charter was opposed by Jackson, the Bank used its political and financial weapons in an unsuccessful attempt to defeat the President.

After Jackson's victory in the election of 1832, he proceeded to withdraw federal funds from the Bank and distribute them among state institutions. When the Bank's charter came to an end in 1836,

the country under the inspiration of the new democracy entered an epoch of "wild cat" finance. The very next year, a terrible business depression fell like a blight upon the land, bringing as usual more suffering to farmers and mechanics than to the "rich and well-born"; but this calamity was likewise attributed by the masses to the machinations of the money power rather than to the conduct of their hero, President Jackson. Nothing would induce them to retrace their steps. For three decades a union of the South and West prevented a restoration of the centralized banking system. . . .[11]

States' rights, sectionalism, and oligarchy sustained at Washington the idea of minimized government.

Centralization now met attack along the whole line of governmental economic policies; and it was quickly evident that the constitutional significance of agrarian rule through the Democratic Party lay in an attempted holding of the federal balance by means of a restoration of functions and power to the states. In the case of Jackson himself, decentralization was not a matter of abstract theory. It was attributable, rather, to pioneer frugality, a settled dislike of debt, a feeling that central power was most amenable to control by selfish interests, and a well-founded conviction that national spending for local purposes would lead to log-rolling and accumulated extravagances.

We have noted how control over money and banking was substantially turned over to the states. The tariff could not be; but it was viewed as a gauge of battle between sectional interests and between the economically powerful and the economically weak, between industry and agriculture, and among various particular industrial and agricultural interests. At the end of this period, after many revisions, rates had been reduced to their lowest point.[12] On the question of ship subsidies sectional interests led to rapid

---

[11] *The Rise of American Civilization*, Vol. 1, pp. 570-71.
[12] See Leverett S. Lyon and Victor Abramson, *Government and Economic Life*, Vol. 2 (1940), pp. 534-63.

reversals of public policy. From 1817 to the outbreak of the Civil War the federal government levied no internal taxes.

The problem of developing the West was primarily one of transportation; secondarily, it involved the public land policy of the federal government. During the early period of transportation development, the federal treasury enjoyed a surplus. Jefferson proposed to devote it to the construction of national highways and canals; and in 1802 Congress earmarked certain of the proceeds from the sale of public lands for the building of roads across the Alleghenies. In 1817, Calhoun introduced a bill to create a fund for internal improvements; but Madison vetoed the bill on constitutional grounds. John Quincy Adams was keenly interested in western development and had his own comprehensive plan. In the meantime, Congress had begun appropriating money for river navigation and harbor improvements. Internal improvements became a party issue. Jackson used his veto power to prevent the appropriation of the federal surplus for the subsidizing of roads, canals, and railroads. Instead, the money was distributed among the states.

Generally speaking, three plans were advanced for dealing with the public lands. Hamilton's idea was that they should serve primarily as a source of federal revenues. John Quincy Adams proposed to use them for regulatory and social purposes, holding up the price, preventing speculation, and applying the proceeds to the endowment of education. Westerners represented by Benton wanted to dispose of the lands to settlers as rapidly and as cheaply as possible. No plan was definitely adopted or consistently followed.

The demand of the numerous "have-nots" for free homesteads was not satisfied, mainly because of the opposition of the southern planters and perhaps also of the northern manufacturers. Conceivably, the lands might have been given in their entirety to the states. In fact, portions of them were. In 1860 a compromise bill was passed by Congress which fixed a small price for homesteads and provided that, at the expiration of thirty years, any unsold land should be ceded to the states. The bill was vetoed by President Buchanan.

Before the Civil War no significant expansion occurred in the administrative functions or organization of the national government. The central government did not exercise all of the powers that it indubitably possessed. Certain functions were required expressly or impliedly by constitutional provisions;[13] others were in the main and in the beginning incidental to the constitutionally prescribed functions;[14] still others were undertaken by the federal government because it alone had the instrumentalities for their exercise.[15]

Federal administration revealed little of economic regulation or social service. Except for some efforts to encourage agriculture through tariff rates and public land administration, national promotion of agriculture was confined to the distribution of seeds and plants and the collection of agricultural statistics. Manufacturing statistics also were included in the census; but national administrative regulation of business was conspicuous for its absence. The census of 1840 included a greater variety of sociological and economic data, reflecting the humanitarian movement of the preceding years. Organized labor received some concessions from the federal government in the form of shorter hours for government employees. War veterans were pensioned. Washington's idea of a national university was not realized; but reservations of land were set aside for the educational purposes of the states.

Nor was the federal government extending to any significant extent its administrative contacts with individual citizens. These, for the most part, were those maintained by the United States marshals, the postmasters, and the land offices. The government at Washington made grants of land and money to the states; but it appears to have assumed no control or supervision over state legislation or administration not specifically provided for in the Constitution.

[13] For example, coinage of money, granting of patents, public land administration, supervision of Indian affairs, construction and operation of lighthouses, granting of copyrights, supervision of territorial governments, issuance of passports, taking a decennial census, steamboat inspection, marine policing to prevent smuggling, standardization of weights and measures, and operation of military schools.

[14] For example, maintenance of a naval observatory, and the provision of medical service for merchant seamen.

[15] For example, collection and dissemination of trade and general census statistics.

Because the country was growing, the work and the administrative personnel of the federal government were increasing; but during the 46-year period, 1816-61, federal expenditures were only about $33,000,000 a year.

SOUTHERN SECTIONALISM

Within the sectional agrarianism of Jackson's day, the special sectionalism of the southern planters, already a decentralizing force, was dividing the country rapidly and irreconcilably. Large-scale textile manufacturing in England had increased the demand for American cotton; the perfecting of the cotton gin in 1793 had made the production of raw cotton more profitable; and the acquisition of Indian lands in the South supplied more acres suitable to cotton culture and slave labor. South of the Potomac and the Ohio, the country became closely wedded to a one-crop agriculture and to a labor system which in effect excluded the small farmer, the immigrant from Europe, the capitalist, and the industrialist. When this economic system became exploitative and expansionist, southern leadership passed from Virginia to South Carolina, from the liberal philosophy of Jefferson to the defensive theories of John C. Calhoun.

The supremacy of the Constitution, the perpetuity of the union, and the absolute sovereignty of the federal government within its sphere had been brought into question from one angle or another by Virginia and Kentucky in their famous Resolutions and by New England Federalists in the Hartford Convention. The natural rights and compact theories, as well as the circumstances that surrounded the adoption of the Constitution, were now cited to support the idea that the instrument was a mere contract among states, in which sovereignty still resided. It was argued, further, that the constitutional checks were insufficient to prevent the setting-up of a centralized despotism: an additional check was necessary—the right of nullification or veto by the states.

With respect to democracy, southern thinking rejected the doctrine that all men were equal or that they all should be free. The democracy that it accepted was that of ancient Greece, in which labor was unfree and equality existed only within a politically privileged class.

The cleavage between southern agrarianism and northern industrialism was quickly evident; that between the southern plantation system and western free farming developed more slowly.

The inevitable decision among conflicting sectionalisms was postponed in three ways. First, an even balance was maintained in the Senate between the free and the slave states. Second, the southern element dominated the Democratic Party. In the operation of the convention system, party authority was subject to management; it was successively delegated; and it became at each step farther removed from the people and more and more amenable to minority control. Oligarchic control by southern leaders was facilitated by the "two-thirds rule," which was applied to presidential nominations in Democratic conventions. Third, a working combination of West and South was preserved through deep-seated agrarian prejudices, through policies that were broadly agrarian, and in general through the transfer to the states of issues, including slavery, which, if left in the national arena, might have hastened the "irrepressible conflict."

GROWTH AND CHANGES IN STATE GOVERNMENT

Jacksonian democracy shifted to the states nearly the whole burden of economic promotion, economic regulation, and social service.

The states undertook economic development,
not wisely but too well.

Economic promotion, specifically transportation development, appeared as the prior need. An expanding nation of scattered communities, with a range of mountains separating the old states from the new, created a tremendous demand for the large-scale development of transportation facilities.

Many of the state constitutions adopted during the early period contained either directions or permissions to the legislatures "to encourage internal improvements within the State." Viewing franchise seekers as public benefactors, the legislatures proceeded to grant charters of incorporation to private companies. As a rule, a separate act was passed for each particular case, the legislature acting in this respect as an administrative body. Several states were active in the promotion of canals, by direct construction on state account, by subscribing to the stock of private companies, by loans, or by subsidies.

While these developments were going on, the invention of the locomotive changed the transportation picture. Travel and transport now became relatively fast; and the new facility accelerated the growth and concentration of manufacturing. During the two decades before the Civil War railroad building proceeded rapidly westward. Before 1860 Chicago was an important railroad center, lines were already extending into Missouri and Iowa, and a railroad to the Pacific was in the promotional stage. But with the railroad came another phase of public spending and lending. In the states generally, the railroad business was promoted by direct construction, public ownership and public operation, subscription to stock, loans, money subsidies, and grants of land. For the most part, the states preferred to encourage private railroad construction, rather than undertake it directly.

Money was lent by the states to individual farmers and businessmen, and to local governmental units. Public funds were used to encourage banking, manufacturing, and agriculture. State banks, chiefly in the South and West, were established with capital contributed wholly or partly by the state governments. In some states, the boards of directors were entirely selected by the legislature; and in others, partly.

The spirit in which laws were enacted was one of speculative optimism and prevailing ignorance of economics and public finance. The sectional composition of the law-making body, the responsibility of individual members to their respective counties or districts, made it well-nigh inevitable that legislation should be piecemeal and framed from the standpoint of private and local interests. These interests, as well as political considerations, dictated to a considerable extent the location of projects and the different steps involved in their execution. Log-rolling and corruption ensued.

In general, the promotional experiments were financially disastrous, whatever may have been their economic benefits. While the federal government was extinguishing its debt and accumulating a surplus, the total amount of state and territorial indebtedness grew to exceed $200,000,000. A number of states defaulted. More-over, up to 1861 the states gave away more than 30,000,000 acres of their assets in public land.

Constitutional change shifted power from the legis-lature to the executive and the administration.

After the adoption of the Bill of Rights and until the Civil War, in spite of national expansion and rapid economic and social change, only two amendments were added to the federal constitu-tion, the eleventh and the twelfth. In the states, on the other hand, public opinion was aroused by what seemed to be disastrous legis-lative errors, and, through constitutional revisions and amend-ments, struck in several ways at the legislative mechanism. This development might be construed as a reaction from democracy, similar to that which had produced the system of brakes and side-tracks in the federal constitution; but the movement in the states is more correctly viewed as an attack on legislative supremacy, based on a widespread distrust of legislative honesty and compe-tence.

As constitutional conventions met, provisions were written into the fundamental law designed to curb the power of the legislature. These constitutional restrictions related both to legislative proce-dure and to the scope of the law-making function. Local and spe-cial legislation was either prohibited or severely limited. Restric-tions were placed on the manner of granting corporation charters. Prohibitions were laid on public aid to private corporate enter-prises, and on the direct or indirect lending of the credit of the state. Legislative powers over banking and public borrowing were special objects of attack. The principle of a popular referendum on certain bills, especially those having a fiscal purpose, was incor-porated into state constitutions.

The prevailing distrust of legislatures led to an increase in the authority of the executive. One by one the states gave the veto power to their governors. The executive received also a gradually increasing authority to remove state and local administrative offi-cers. Direct assertions of administrative authority by the legislature tended to diminish. Popular election of the older administrative officers was first substituted for election by the legislature. Many of the new officials and boards were also popularly elected; but, in the appointment of others, the governor was given increased participation. Yet, the practice of senatorial confirmation of executive appointments continued; and, when providing for the setup of new administrative agencies, the legislature, quite as a matter of course, made them by one means or another more or less independent of executive control.

In yet another way, steps were taken toward a reduction of legislative work and improvement of its quality. To the extent that local and special legislation was eliminated, it was necessary that general laws be enacted and that their application to specific cases be delegated to administrative agencies. Furthermore, the legislatures needed leadership and advice. They had their committees, which carried on during this period some useful investigations; but the committees required supplementation and guidance from permanent agencies continuously gathering information.

When the federal constitution was adopted, Pennsylvania and Georgia had single-chamber legislatures. When these states adopted new constitutions in 1790, each divided its law-making body into two houses. Vermont entered the union in 1791 with a single house; but it too changed in 1836. Afterward, until our own day, as Johnson says, "usage and tradition made bicameralism an established institution in the United States" and it "came to be considered essential to the process of law-making."[16]

The states turned from promotion to regulation;
and regulation was coming to be administrative.

Distrust of the legislature was accompanied by distrust and fear of the special interests. One of the fruits of the promotional epoch had been an increase in the number and size of corporations; and, with reference to them, especially to the monopolistic ones, it was now becoming apparent that the common law was not adequate for the protection of the public interest. Moreover, the machinery of local government was as unsuitable for the regulation of large-scale enterprises as it had been for their promotion.

[16] Alvin W. Johnson, *The Unicameral Legislature* (1938), p. 44.

The economic and political theories of the time were opposed to regulation; but the Supreme Court, under Taney, gave enlarged scope to state action. Taney not only favored the restoration of the states' sphere in the federal scheme, but he also feared the growing power of finance. The general effect of the Court's decisions was to recognize the right of the states to regulate corporations, including those incorporated by other states.[17] The state constitutions, moreover, placed direct limits on the promotional, rather than on the regulatory, powers of the legislatures.

In the beginning state regulation of the banking business sometimes took the form of constitutional or statutory prohibitions. It became speedily apparent, however, that simple prohibitions could not be applied to essential economic enterprises. The incorporation of such enterprises would seem to have offered a feasible means for their regulation; but piecemeal legislative regulation through the granting of charters and franchises was in no sense regulative in effect. Local and special legislation, as we have seen, was being proscribed by the state constitutions; and at the end of this period general incorporation laws were being enacted, with a measure of administrative control of banking and insurance.

In the case of the railroads, legislative regulation took for a short time the form of specific laws aimed at specific situations and specific abuses. Railroad combinations were not apparently included among the abuses. Nor was discrimination until after the Civil War; but railroad rates were regulated to some extent by statute law. A general railroad law was enacted by the New York legislature in 1848; and railroads were required to report to the state in 1850. Several states established railroad commissions before the Civil War. They were for the most part "merely fact-finding arms of the legislatures with no administrative powers;"[18] but some had

[17] It was not, however, the effect of the decisions during this period to turn the regulatory function entirely over to the states. To a very large extent, the Supreme Court, when passing on state legislation, determined the necessity for and the limits and direction of federal regulation. Thus, it may be said that the foundation structure of national governmental regulation was at this time being laid by the courts.

[18] G. Lloyd Wilson, James M. Herring, and Roland B. Entsler, *Public Utility Regulation* (1938), p. 13.

limited inspectional and supervisory authority.[19] With all their limitations, they contributed to legislative efficiency and somewhat to public planning and were a first step in the development of independent agencies charged with discretionary economic regulation.

Social welfare was a slowly expanding
field of state and local action.

Policies and administration in the field of social welfare—conceived to be almost entirely within state jurisdiction and locally exercised—were, in some respects, radically changing under the impact of industrialism, urbanism, and the democratic and humanitarian spirit of the times.

Certain hardships in the common law were ameliorated, with respect, for example, to inheritance, apprenticeship, and the rights of women and children.

Education was then, as it still is, the most important of the social welfare functions. It was held to be indispensable to a self-governing nation, and had a place in state constitutions from the beginning. It was close to the hearts of the people; and the common schools, wherever they were established by government, were kept jealously under the control of the local communities. While the school system was in the main administered by local districts, a small amount of state supervision was provided; and the practice of giving state grants-in-aid was started. In Michigan, perhaps in this respect fairly typical of the West, the territorial legislature planned a complete outline of education in 1817 and established the common school system in 1827. Massachusetts, as early as 1852, adopted the principle of universal attendance.

Before the Civil War, the public high school entered into competition with the private academies. Agricultural schools were also established. In the East, privately endowed colleges and universities predominated; and in the West and South small denominational seminaries and colleges dotted the country. In the new commonwealths, however, the state university, non-sectarian, tax-sup-

[19] Lyon and Abramson, *Government and Economic Life*, Vol. 2, pp. 758-59.

ported, and publicly controlled, was from the beginning a fixed and a highly significant feature of governmental policy.

Education was conceived to be liberating. Public health measures, in contrast, rested on the doctrine of the "police power," and restricted personal liberty to the end that the community might be protected. Public health regulations dealt largely with quarantines, particularly against small-pox and cholera, and with nuisances, sewers and drains, slaughterhouses, sale of spoiled foods, adulteration of milk, and the like. Local health authorities were organized in Baltimore and Philadelphia in 1793 and 1794, respectively, and in New York City and Boston before the end of the eighteenth century. Massachusetts in 1787 and Connecticut in 1805 prepared plans for a state-wide system of town boards of health. In 1849, a commission appointed in Massachusetts recommended the creation of a state board of health.

Due largely to the activities of Dorothea Dix, the period from the forties to the sixties was one of marked improvement in the care of the mentally ill. The reform movement included the transfer of these unfortunates from county almshouses to state institutions and the construction of additional state "asylums." State schools for the feeble-minded were established. In addition to the county jails, state penal and correctional institutions were constructed. During this entire period, those dependents who were unlucky enough to become "paupers" were provided for by private charitable organizations, the town, the township, or the county. The almshouses, like the jails, were locally administered with, generally speaking, no regulation by the state and no attention from the community.

In the early years of the nineteenth century, the hiring of children for factory work was advertised as a public benefit; but it was not long before considerable legislation had been enacted limiting the hours of employment for children.

Industrial wage earners were becoming a substantial part of the urban population. Organizations of skilled workers along craft lines were increasing in number and strength and were manifesting the modern characteristics and objectives of unionism. Among the first effects were elimination of imprisonment for debt and amend-

ment of the mechanics' lien laws. Laws were enacted limiting hours
of work for women and children and in a few instances establishing
a general ten-hour day.

Industrial unemployment appeared from time to time, as did also
agricultural unemployment; but the public land was viewed as a
form of relief. Near the end of this period a foreign traveler in the
United States wrote that the thing that impressed him most favorably was "the absence of pauperism."[20] Judged by the standards of
today, most of the population was badly housed and inadequately
served medically. Perhaps it was also "ill-clothed and ill-fed." Yet,
according to its standards, the country was prosperous and "progressing." It was then as now cursed by recurring panics and depressions; but such phenomena did not impair the basic confidence
of the people in themselves and their destiny.

FRONTIER DEMOCRACY IN RELATION TO EFFICIENCY

We have seen that the conditions of the time encouraged decentralization and that the states, retaining and increasing their share
of public functions and power, were assuming a more burdensome
and complex task. In the economic field, the states were clearly
inefficient, a fact that they recognized and took steps to remedy. In
general, these steps were four: (1) the curbing of legislatures, (2)
the increase of executive authority, (3) the tendency to regulate
economic enterprise rather than promote it, and (4) the assign-
ment of regulation to administrative agencies. It must not be
thought, however, that these steps signify any decline of faith in
democracy. Accordingly, taking our position at the end of this
period, let us now look back and note some of the fundamental influences, more or less closely identified with democracy, that were
affecting or were later to affect governmental efficiency.

*The influence of the frontier was ranged
against intellectual leadership.*

The pioneer was unaccustomed to dependence on cloistered
scholar or exotic expert. Since for his familiar tasks strength, common sense, and perseverence were usually adequate, he took pride

[20] Quoted in E. L. Bogart, *Economic History of the United States* (4th ed.,
1925), pp. 167-68.

in being "practical." Careless of political method and unconcerned with governmental efficiency, he was confident that all men were equal, not only in political rights, but also in capacity to hold public office. With the passing of John Quincy Adams and the triumph of Jackson, followed by the election of such men as Van Buren, William Henry Harrison, Taylor, Pierce, and Buchanan, American politics sank to a definitely lower plane.

Frontier democracy rejected intellectual leadership, but not leadership itself. The capture of government by the masses was not accompanied by any perfected system of rational popular discussion by which individual ideas were crystallized and imposed on political leadership. What frontier democracy appears in the main to have contributed was a means of mobilizing popular emotions and unreasoned conceptions of interest. Political leadership, whether individual or oligarchical, determined public policies under mandates that were broad and on the whole irrational and indefinite. The process of government became in its initial stage more democratic; but, in the succeeding stages, the complexity of the processes and mechanisms of government, as well as the complexity of the country itself and the shortcomings of the electorate, was in no way simplified or controlled by the democratic movement.

Nevertheless, signs of change were appearing. With the growth of industry, the spread of transportation and communication facilities, and the accumulation of wealth, the pioneer type of individualism and association tended to give way to more specialized, occupational, and technical organizations. Educational and learned societies appeared before the Civil War.[21] Considerable influence was exerted by academicians in the fields of economics and political philosophy. Federal administration was developing scientific and technical characteristics and feeling intellectual influences. Learned societies early co-operated with public administrators, notably in connection with the census.

[21] These included the American Philosophical Society, the National Education Association, the American Statistical Association, the American Association for the Advancement of Science, and the American Geographical Society. The American Medical Association was founded. Geologists and ethnologists were also organized on a national basis.

Other principles and practices of frontier democracy
bore directly on the problem of efficiency.

In contrast to national administration, state administration might be described during this period and for at least 50 years thereafter as fluid or organic. Subject to the molding power of custom and tradition but bound by no abstract rules, it was forced by the imminent pressures of need and function to grow luxuriantly, experimentally, and competitively, like a tropical forest. Its growth and its transformation were determined in the main by two expressions of democracy: local self-government and legislative primacy. Its more or less constant features were localism, election of administrative officers and judges, the use of boards, multiplicity of agencies, rotation in office, and statutory control. Almost unconsciously these features became firmly fixed in the institutional life and political habits of the people.

In most cases, counties or townships or both were provided for in the state constitutions; and thus the state government became in a sense federal. Local self-government, as it worked out, was in effect and in its limited area similar to state sovereignty in a larger sphere. It applied the idea of liberty to the community. Local self-government demanded further that the local officials should be locally elected, and, in order to be responsible to the people, should be chosen for short terms. The system, therefore, was in purpose almost wholly democratic. In a rural community at that time this form of decentralization was not inappropriate or impracticable. It was already a habit; and it speedily became one of the cardinal articles in the American democratic creed, second in importance only to individual liberty.

The tendency, however, was for local units to multiply; and, within or overlapping the counties and townships, other units appeared. With few exceptions, every city, town, and village became a self-governing entity, operating within territorial and functional limits fixed by the legislature. The cities had special problems, and they, too, were given their own frames of government, including a legislature (sometimes bicameral). More than that, school government was set apart from other local governments; and, since the schoolhouse had to be within easy distance of the children, school districts were exceedingly numerous. On top of these, special districts were created for road maintenance, drainage, and other purposes. Finally, in this complex scheme of local self-government, the courts were not sharply separated from the ordinary administrative agencies.

De Tocqueville, writing about 1830, thought that locally controlled administration was in some respects remarkably efficient. Because the administrative authorities were of the community, the people co-operated with them. In no other country, he said, "does crime more rarely elude punishment,"[22] and he remarked also the superiority of the schools and roads. He acknowledged the confusion of local budgets and accounts; but he thought "the end of a good government is to ensure the welfare of a people, and not to establish order and regularity in the midst of its misery and distress."[23]

Already before the Civil War, centralizing tendencies in state administration had become apparent, indicated by the establishment of state agencies to supervise certain aspects of local administration, inauguration of state grants-in-aid, and the assumption by the state of functions that could not or could no longer be exercised by the local units. Nevertheless, while the administrative work of the state expanded, the tasks of the local units also steadily increased.

Changes from appointment to legislative election, then to popular election, were taking place generally in the older states. The states that were admitted near the end of this period adopted at once the principle of elective administrative officers. Thus, under the influence of frontier democracy, state administration was not only decentralized; but also, locally and centrally, it was divided into separate compartments, each independent of the others and of the chief executive, each responsible only to the people.

The wave of democracy, especially in the West, likewise engulfed the courts. Judges were quite generally made elective for short terms. When the judiciary was thus "democratized," it remained

[22] *Democracy in America*, Vol. 1, p. 93.
[23] The same, footnote, p. 90.

independent of the other branches of government, but not independent of the people themselves or of the political parties.

In order to obtain, under these conditions, any degree of uniformity in administration, the statute law, as de Tocqueville remarks, "penetrates to the very core of the administration; the law descends to the most minute details; the same enactment prescribes the principle and the method of its application; and thus imposes a multitude of strict and rigorously defined obligations on the secondary functionaries of the state."[24] The state legislature, even more than the federal congress, was compelled to become an administrative supervisor.

As the state government increased its functions, the tendency was to add to the number of separate administrative agencies. Before the Civil War, however, there were signs that legislatures were perceiving the need, in some fields, of integrating these agencies; and, here and there, the governor was gaining some slight additional authority over them.

For the exercise of new functions, the state legislatures showed a decided preference for boards and commissions. This preference is explainable, at least in part, by the fact that the legislature, controlling the administrative setup and distrusting executive power, created that setup in the image of legislative committees. The conception had not yet taken root in the states that administration was within the executive, rather than the legislative, jurisdiction. Moreover, the idea of trusteeship doubtless had influence—the idea that when property was to be administered, money spent, or other responsible duties performed, safety dictated that one man should be watched and checked by others.[25]

The "spoils system" became entrenched
in national administration.

Federal administration, like the federal government as a whole, was during this period quite rigidly structural. The national government had adopted at the start and more or less consistently followed

[24] The same, p. 72.
[25] Other considerations entered in; for example, the idea of representing different groups and sections, and that of creating jobs for party workers.

three general principles of administrative organization: (1) centralization; (2) integration; and (3) (except for ultimate control) separateness from the judiciary. Without challenging these principles in their national application, frontier democracy and party organization extended their practices to the national administrative personnel. To the frontiersman, living in communities that had important but nontechnical functions, expertness was both unfamiliar and unnecessary, men were of substantially equal capacity, and democracy—keeping government "close to the people"—required short terms and rotation in office. Moreover, political party organization was immensely strengthened when it used appointive offices for the purchase and payment of party workers. The party thus built its strength on the frailties of human nature; and "politics," a matter of material interest as well as opportunism, became the normal method of operating democratic government.

Jackson is not to be personally blamed for the entrenchment of the "spoils system" in federal administration. In his time, however, the spoils system was fortified by its incorporation in democratic doctrine, by its consistency with the idea of local self-government, and by its concurrence with partisan and anti-intellectual trends. Patronage contributed to party cohesiveness and probably to the sense of party responsibility; but it brought in its wake a lowering of political as well as administrative standards.

LEGISLATIVE RESPONSIVENESS AND EFFECTIVENESS

The mechanism established for the determination of policies revealed during the period as a whole certain features of organization and functioning that seem from a common-sense standpoint to have indicated an unnecessary lack of essential democracy and probably a diminishing efficiency.

*Legislative bodies and the party system worked
neither responsively nor effectively.*

Congress was endeavoring through the committee system to supply leadership and control within itself and to provide channels for communication with and supervision of the administrative departments. These committees studied proposed legislation, conducted investigations, held hearings, and in some cases presented able reports. The caucus was used to enforce party unity and to expedite procedure. Nevertheless, the legislative body, lacking time and expertness, frequently called on administrative agencies for studies and reports; and, though presidents were more often than not weak men, Congress was unable to develop a durable national leadership. It was a crowd—two crowds—not a man. In Jackson's time, the House membership exceeded 200. To be sure, between 1820 and 1860 the Senate included Webster, Clay, Calhoun, Douglas, Seward, and Sumner. But the Senate, like the House, and unlike the presidency, was divided between the parties; and the responsibilities of its members were scattered territorially. Both houses early displayed, and thereafter maintained, a provincialism and sectionalism that precluded, in many important fields, a broad, unbiased, and expeditious comprehension of the general welfare. In the House, diffusion of responsibility was accentuated when, in the latter part of this period, the states generally adopted the district system for the election of representatives.

Theoretically, the party system should have harmonized the three legislative authorities. It did so only at times and then only partially. Constitutional provisions and defects in the party system itself stood in the way of complete and consistent co-ordination. Constitutionally, each legislative agency was elected in a different way, for a longer or shorter term, and from a larger or smaller territorial unit. When opinion was sectionalized and changing, there could be no assurance that all three of the agencies would be in accord. The party system was superficially a two-party system. Actually it was not. The Whig Party was a loose agglomeration of discordant elements. The Democratic Party, rendered more cohesive by organization and the spoils of office, was nevertheless an unstable compound. Third parties materialized, gained considerable strength, and then dissolved. At times, a third party or a dissident element of the majority held the balance of power in Congress. In the elections of 1856 and 1860, the successful presidential candidate, though winning a majority of the electoral votes, failed to obtain a majority of the popular vote.

Because of third parties, independents, and sectional groupings, it is difficult to say at certain dates which party was in the control of the Senate or the House. Once in the Senate and perhaps twice in the House, no party had a majority. Apparently, during six of the fourteen Congresses from 1833 to 1861, one party was clearly in control of the presidency, the Senate, and the House. Although the Whigs twice elected a president, they never got into their hands the whole of the legislative mechanism. They fell short first in 1840 when they lost the presidency through the death of Harrison and the non-Whiggishness of Tyler; and in 1848, when they again elected a president, they failed to win a majority either in the House or the Senate. Democratic administrations from 1833 to 1861 covered a total of twenty years. For a total of ten years—one-half the time—the Democrats lacked a majority in one or the other of the two houses.

The legislative mechanism, however, included also the numerous state legislatures and the governors, and in many major matters the courts and the amending process. The legislatures, during the period when they were constitutionally free to decide, did not approach within measurable distance of a clear-cut decision regarding the relations of government to private enterprise; and popular dissatisfaction with the law-making bodies left its indelible marks in distorted state constitutions. One may infer that no great amount of co-ordination was effected between national and state policies. The balance of federalism seemed to be subject to extreme fluctuations.

The Supreme Court became involved
in political conflict.

The assumption of judicial supremacy, probably essential to the establishment of stabilizing constitutionalism, inevitably drew the Supreme Court into the arena of philosophical and partisan conflicts. Jefferson distrusted the Court's power; Jackson defied it. In the fifties, as in the first decades of the century, the make-up of the tribunal was no longer to reflect changing public opinion. Just prior to the Dred Scott Decision, a resolution was introduced into the House of Representatives to reorganize the Court so as to give to the South greater "representation."[26] After that decision, Seward declared: "Whether the Court recedes or not, we shall reorganize the Court, and thus reform its political sentiments and practices, and bring them into harmony with the Constitution and the laws of nature."[27] The Republican platform in 1860, while making no direct attack on the Court itself, condemned the attitude of the judiciary on the slavery question and identified federal judges with the Democratic administration.[28]

The legislative mechanism as a whole failed to solve critical problems.

From the standpoint of democracy, one may perhaps justify legislative inefficiency by assuming that it faithfully reflected the sectional conflicts, clashes of opinion, and uncertainties among the people. But it can hardly be a legitimate purpose of any government, even a democratic one, to perpetuate popular deadlocks until national safety is imperilled and the general welfare irreparably injured.

If one man, supported by the majority and possessing its confidence, could "save" democracy or make it "work," Andrew Jackson assuredly was that man. Yet, the party system and party organization, developed to implement democracy, were quickly employed for its frustration.

The democratic movement that eventuated in the election of Jackson was stimulated by the effect produced on the agrarian debtor class by the depression of 1819-22. It was already assumed that it was a function of government to make the people prosperous; and it might well have been argued even then that the perpetuation of democracy depended on its economic effectiveness, its ability to promote the well-being of the people. Yet Jackson was hardly out of office before the depression of 1837-40 settled upon the land.

More serious and more significant was the failure of democracy to solve the problem of slavery. Perhaps, as the Beards say, "the

[26] Charles Warren, *The Supreme Court in United States History* (1923), Vol 3, p. 11.
[27] The same, p. 50.
[28] Kirk H. Porter, *National Party Platforms* (1924), pp. 56-57.

major portion of all those who in their hearts disliked slavery were bewildered by the complex character of every solution offered. . . . Practical men simply could not visualize the fiscal and administrative measures necessary to effect such an enormous social revolution. Perhaps most practical men gave little or no thought to the finalities of the issue. . . ."[29]

Here was unquestionably the basic difficulty—the incapacity of men in the mass to perceive in time the elements of fundamental crisis, to think hard toward the achievement of a distant objective, to put aside resolutely matters of lesser importance, and to remain united until the hour of complete accomplishment.

To say that the slavery crisis was unique, that it was settled in the end, and that it can have no lessons for our later democracy, appears to miss the point. Slavery constituted an economic and social system and represented what was deemed the vital interest of a section and a class. Now, the system is admitted to have been wrong; but, at the time, it was defended vigorously and cogently by those who benefited from it and by their intellectual retainers. It was justified on economic, social, moral, and religious grounds. To its aid came constitutional argument and political philosophy; and it was even supported in the name of democracy and liberty. When at last the democratic process, acting within the framework of constitutional nationalism, decided against the South, conflict of interests proved irreconcilable. It was not government through its normal processes, but war, that was to rebuild the shattered framework and enforce majority rule.

During this period of unique opportunity, the dominant influences were territorial expansion and the westward moving frontier. Nationalism and constitutionalism grew in strength. Democracy, typified first by Jefferson and later more thoroughly by Jackson, widened the suffrage, established a party system, subjected the presidency to more direct popular control, adopted decentralization, extended the elective principle in the states, and established the "spoils system" in both state and national governments. In many

[29] *The Rise of American Civilization*, Vol. 1, pp. 702-03.

respects, the influence of the frontier even at that time was opposed to efficiency.

Governmental policies had from the beginning economic objectives. These were first predominantly promotional; but the task of promotion, largely shifted to the states, was performed so incompetently as to lead to the curbing of legislatures, the strengthening of executives, and the beginning of administrative regulation. In the states, social services were gradually expanding. All these developments, including the character of legislative functioning as a whole, were strongly influenced by sectional cleavages, particularly that between North and South created by slavery, the latter presenting a problem that the governmental system of the time was unequal to solving. Events appeared amply to confirm Madison's view that "the causes of faction cannot be removed," and suggested that "the means of controlling its effects" were not at hand in the republic or delegated government originally established or in the democratizing features later introduced.

CHAPTER III

INDUSTRIALISM, ECONOMIC PRESSURES, AND NEW POLITICAL PATTERNS, 1861-1900

The outcome of the Civil War preserved the nation and destroyed slavery. So far as the territorial integrity of the United States was concerned, no new and possibly unstable international system was to exist in North America. A most important cause of sectionalism and challenge to democracy was removed. It was of enormous significance, too, that the central figure in the struggle should have been symbolic of the frontier and, though temporarily wielding dictatorial powers, devoted to democracy. Abraham Lincoln's faith in a democratic America rested on a belief in the freedom, dignity, reasonableness, and good will of the common people, on confidence in the long-run wisdom of the majority, and on the social desirability and political necessity of tolerance.

Lincoln's democracy was to exert its influence chiefly by example. Some of it was implicit in the Emancipation Proclamation and the thirteenth amendment; but his creed gained at the time little institutional embodiment. After his death, congressional reconstruction of the South added the fifteenth amendment to the Constitution, prohibiting any denial of the vote on account of race, color, or previous condition of servitude. Enfranchisement of the Negroes and disfranchisement of ex-Confederates produced in the southern states Negro and "carpet-bag" governments, ridiculously incompetent and corrupt. Southern whites, first by intimidation and later by legislation and administration, succeeded in practically disfranchising colored citizens. Thus political democracy, to the extent that it implied racial equality of voting rights, virtually disappeared in the South. Moreover, though the Civil War eliminated the most stubborn divisive factor in the nation, the South remained economically and politically sectional, with a heritage, proudly cherished, that largely insulated its people from democratizing currents.

For several reasons, the South was to remain committed to one party, thus inhibiting political discussion and political thinking among its own people and contributing to a partial paralysis of the party system in the nation.

ECONOMIC AND SOCIAL BACKGROUND

Joined with its instinctive and emotional elements, Lincoln's political philosophy contained obviously realistic ingredients—an acceptance of strong government as an instrument of social progress[1] and a perception of the change that was coming to America by way of industrial and population growth.

Between 1808 and 1840 small manufacturing and mechanical establishments had been developing throughout the country. After 1840 concentration and combination produced a steadily increasing number of larger plants. New inventions were improving machinery and reducing costs of production; the labor supply was plentiful and cheap; and increasing population provided a constantly expanding market. Before the Civil War, manufacturing already outranked agriculture in the value of its capital investment.

In 1860, the population of the country reached 31 millions. In the single decade from 1840 to 1850, Wisconsin's population rose from 30,000 to 300,000. In that decade migration began to the Oregon country; the Latter Day Saints settled in Utah; and the discovery of gold in California started a rush to that region. Between 1861 and 1890, eleven states were admitted to the Union. With the exception of West Virginia, all were in the new West. No less than six states were admitted in the two years 1889 and 1890; and only four more were then needed to round out the present 48: Utah, admitted in 1896, Oklahoma in 1907, and Arizona and New Mexico in 1912. After 1880, census reports no longer included a discussion of the frontier of settlement and westward movement because "the unsettled area has been so broken into by isolated bodies of settlement that there can hardly be said to be a frontier line."[2]

While the most impressive agricultural pioneering movement in

[1] Lincoln's conception of democracy was government *for* the people, as well as *of* and *by* the people.

[2] *Compendium of the Eleventh Census: 1890*, Pt. 1, pp. xlviii-xlix.

history was to take place after 1860, an acute observer in that year could have foreseen that the country was in the midst of a profound economic transformation, to be marked by the passing of the frontier and the assured primacy of industry.

America became industrial and was
becoming urban.

In the spirit of *laissez faire*, with boundless optimism and imagination, and with the assistance of the national government, American industrialists during and after the Civil War proceeded to realize the possibilities of machines and organizing genius applied to the exploitation of apparently inexhaustible resources.

From 1860 to 1900 national manufacturing increased in value of products from less than 2 to more than 13 billion dollars; in amount of capital invested, from about 1 billion to almost 10 billions; and in the average number of wage earners, from 1⅓ to 5⅓ million. The value of manufactured products per capita was about $60 in 1860. It rose to almost $200 in 1900. Railroad mileage in 1860 was 30,626; in 1900, 193,346. In 1860 there was about one mile of railroad per 1,000 inhabitants; in 1900, almost three miles. The population of the country more than doubled.

Urbanism accompanied industrialism. In 1900, the urban population[3] had increased to 40 per cent of the total. In New England, however, the percentage was 72.5 and in the Middle Atlantic states 65.2. In 1860 there were only 16 cities having a population of 50,000 or more;[4] in 1900 there were 77. In this period the population of New York City tripled; that of Philadelphia more than doubled; that of Pittsburgh increased almost six-fold; while Chicago grew from 109,000 to 1,699,000.

Industrial activities tended to segregate in the Northeast. In 1900, three-fourths of the manufacturing establishments were in the North Atlantic and North Central states; and these states had 83 per cent of the industrial capital and 81 per cent of the wage earners.

[3] Those living in incorporated places of 2,500 or more.
[4] What is now Greater New York is counted as one city.

*Social standards declined and political
capacity was diverted.*

The "gilded age" was by no means a period of uniform economic progress or prosperity. It suffered two major depressions. During much of the period, discontent among farmers and laborers constituted a major political factor. Yet, in the large, economic development was so visible and on so grand a scale as to intensify certain popular characteristics that had been previously evident. The general result of individual initiative and free enterprise, under the generous patronage of government, was the metamorphosis of a continent, through a process which, though generally unplanned and enormously wasteful, appeared to be providentially guided, miraculous in its swiftness, and pervasive in its tangible benefits. Competitive economic individualism seemed as democratic as it was effective. Opportunities for economic advantages and social position appeared to be within the grasp of the poorest and least well-born.

Perhaps a deterioration of social standards had begun earlier. Since the Revolution, the Church had been losing its control over the daily activities of men and over the education of the young, and the separation of Church from State had tended with other influences to isolate moral authority and the sanctions of the Bible from the primary centers of social control. Furthermore, America had no aristocracy of birth or governing class having special custody of social standards; and, with the passing of the "Virginia dynasty," the influence of the country gentleman had failed to grip the expanding West and the growing cities. The new America in its formative activities was neither Puritan nor Cavalier.

Out of the private purposes and qualities of the new era, given social reach by widened economic opportunities, grew deeply rooted in America what has been termed "a business man's civilization," in which purposes, ideals, and morals were in large measure fashioned by and harnessed to the making of money. Scholars seem to agree that "American history records no era more materially minded than the twenty-five years from 1865 to 1890."[5]

---

[5] Carl Becker, *The United States, An Experiment in Democracy* (1920), p. 314.

The successful businessman came to be universally admired; but he was usually too "busy" to be anything except a businessman; and at this time he was not apologetic about it. Andrew Carnegie saw nothing paradoxical in writing a book on "Triumphant Democracy" and saying in it:

Politics are but means to an end. When the laws of a country are perfect, and equality of rights and privileges reached, there is far more important work to be performed at home than in legislative halls. Hence the ablest and best men in the Republic are not found as a class trifling their time away doing the work of mediocrity.[6]

Bryce remarked that there had been, "till within the last few years, so great and general a sense of economic security, whether well or ill founded I do not now inquire, that the wealthy and educated have been content to leave the active work of politics alone."[7] During the greater part of this period, therefore, the country's resources in social leadership tended to be narrowly canalized and, so far as politics were directly concerned, partially wasted.

Increasing potentialities of leadership were joined with political indifference.

That capacity for leadership and co-operative effort which was to be found for the most part in the middle classes and among the intelligentsia and which was not absorbed in business was also in large measure either indifferent to politics or diverted from its main currents. The political "machine" derived its power to no slight extent from the fact that the "best people" did not vote in the primaries except during intermittent and usually short-lived "reform" waves.

It may be suspected that popular discussion was becoming less widespread, less spontaneous, and less political. The lyceum and the Chautauqua flourished, but their purposes were predominantly cultural. Contemporary writers remarked the indifference of the people to what government was doing. There was no excitement over fundamental questions. Freedom, equality, constitutionalism, nationalism, and democracy were taken for granted. The increasing

[6] *Triumphant Democracy* (1893), pp. 69-70.
[7] James Bryce, *American Commonwealth*, Vol. 2 (1894), p. 71.

complexity of society and accentuation of particular group interests rendered more and more difficult any generalized or integrated discussion of political questions. Industrial leadership was silent; governmental leadership was uninspiring if not depressing; and local self-government was losing vitality.

Discussion tended to break up into organized groups under specialized stimulation and direction. Local and state associations of all sorts were multiplying along specialized lines and many more of our present-day national organizations appeared.[8] Some of these associations reflected the increasing importance of technology in industry and municipal government; others the appearance of expertness and professionalization in private activities and in various branches of public administration. They represented in part the subordination of individualistic thinking to intelligent and expert leaderships that were in the main nonpartisan or nonpolitical.

Education, expected to sustain democracy, was by no means universal; but attendance in the public schools rose and illiteracy declined. Beyond the elementary schools, the educational plant expanded. During a time when government changed little, growth and changes in the field of higher education were almost revolutionary. Stimulated by the Morrill Act, the older state universities reorganized, and new technical institutions were established. Accumulations of private wealth contributed to the nation's educational plant.

Yet, in the main, professors were making no conspicuous effort to provide popular or governmental leadership. In the development of higher education, the physical sciences over-shadowed the social studies. History, economics, and public law were in college curricula before the Civil War; but as late as the seventies there was comparatively little instruction in economics, political science,

---

[8] To those already referred to (p. 68), one might add, as examples, the American Bar Association, the American Bankers Association, the American Forestry Association, the American Hospital Association, the American Institute of Mining and Metallurgical Engineers, the American Red Cross, the American Prison Association, the National Conference of Charities and Corrections (now the National Conference of Social Work), the National Congress of Parents and Teachers, the Women's Christian Temperance Union, the American Public Health Association, and the International Association of Chiefs of Police.

and sociology, even in the older and larger universities. Up to the turn of the century, the professors of public law who wrote books concerned themselves for the most part with theory, rather than with contemporary problems of political practice. Woodrow Wilson's *Congressional Government* marked a brilliant exception; but the ablest broad description and interpretation of American government came from an Englishman, James Bryce. The American Economic Association, founded in 1885, interested itself at once in questions of public policy; but the Association's Committee on Transportation observed in 1887:

It is rather a remarkable fact that in spite of the very great importance and significance of the railway, it is only within the last five years, with a single exception, that we have possessed in English any work on the social and economic aspects of the railway problem.[9]

When Lincoln Steffens was investigating municipal government in the nineties, he "did not find anybody with any intelligent plan for the reform of a city."[10]

THE PARTY SYSTEM

So far as the party system was concerned, government during practically all this period was either controlled by the Republican Party or divided between the two major parties. During the 40 years between 1860 and 1900, the Democrats had the presidency only eight years. This situation was due in part to underlying conditions, in part to accident, and in part to a strategy similar in general to that which had been adopted by Washington and Hamilton.

The Republican Party represented groups combined for national economic promotion.

The Republican Party started as a political expression of popular opposition to a sectionalism that was selfish, oligarchic, and, in the northern view, economically unsound and socially undesirable. The party, representing a minority in 1860, was composed of diverse groups; and these could be held together, after the slavery and

[9] Edmund J. James, "The Railway Question," *Publications of the American Economic Association*, Vol. 2 (1888), p. 275.
[10] *Autobiography* (1931), p. 249.

secession issues were decided, only by an unusually strong emotional appeal combined with a comprehensive satisfaction of different interests. After the war, the Republicans could assert that they had "saved the Union"; and as time passed the memory of the martyred Lincoln became an invaluable party asset. Armed with these sentimental properties, the party was further aided by the disfranchisement of the defeated states during the reconstruction period. It so happened that the Republicans won the contested election of 1876 and the Democrats were in power during the depression of 1893. The party thus escaped the consequences of crises. It early put into effect a program designed to benefit group interests, winning the support of the Union veterans, the bankers and industrialists, the middle classes in the North, the farmers of the West, and to some extent the labor group. This program, it should be noted, was both promotional and centralizing.[11]

Faced by a party that had captured prestige and seized sweeping initiative, the Democrats, still claiming lineal descent from Jefferson and Jackson, were reduced on the whole to a negative opposition. In the North they were, in the main, the party of the proletariat and the lower middle classes; but in the South they included almost the entire white population, practically the whole electorate.

The party system grew rigid and corrupt.

Exploitation of emotion and material interest gave to the party system a greater clarity of definition and more indications of immutability than it had ever shown before. In the minds of a majority of the voters, party loyalty and party regularity became habits and inherited qualities, which lent cohesiveness to party organization and facilitated the centralization and integration of party control.

The new conditions imposed unprecedented pressures on public

[11] Its significant features are illustrated by the protective tariff, veterans' pensions, encouragement of immigration, the national banking act of 1863, redemption of "greenbacks," "sound money," grants of land and loans to the Pacific railway companies, appropriations for river and harbor improvement, and benefits to farmers, such as the provisions of the homestead act of 1862, establishment of a federal department of agriculture, and grants of public land for the support of agricultural and mechanical colleges under the Morrill Act.

officials, who were in many cases morally as well as intellectually un-prepared to weigh or resist the pressures. As cities grew, their in-habitants demanded services, which involved the granting of lucra-tive awards and privileges to private business. Opportunities for making money out of public action or inaction were abundant also in the state and national governments. Industrial magnates during this era were not distinguished by a desire to maintain the purity of democratic processes. Partly in self-defense but largely because it was profitable to do so, they attempted, with considerable success, to control government. Political corruption was an essential by-product of an acquisitive and exploitative system.[12] This was the epoch of Black Friday, of the Whisky Ring, of the Credit Mobilier, of the Star Route scandals, of Boss Tweed and his wholesale looting of New York City, and of other equally malodorous episodes.

Business control of government was frequently direct. Lobbyists for business interests bribed and intimidated legislators, regardless of their party affiliations. Frequently, legislators solicited bribes and indulged in legislative blackmail. Probably more often, how-ever, the political "machine" acted as an intermediary between business and government. The "machine" controlled government; and either business controlled the "machine" or paid tribute to it.

Party organization ripened, becoming in this period distinctly over-ripe. It had long before taken on its peculiar features, includ-ing the professional politicians, the "machine," the "boss," and managed primaries and conventions.

The political "machine" is an autocratic or oligarchic develop-ment of party organization, resting on a materialistic foundation; and, while it may be forced to make concessions to public opinion in order to win elections, its purposes are in the main acquisitive, concerned only slightly or incidentally with emerging social needs and developing policies. The spoils system, enriched by an increas-ing number of administrative offices, supplied the candidate, the party leader, or the party manager with the tangible means to en-list active workers in his behalf. Assessments on candidates and

[12] Peter H. Odegard, "Political Corruption—United States," *Encyclopedia of the Social Sciences* (1931), Vol. 4, p. 454.

office-holders helped to finance party activities. Money came from businessmen in the form of campaign contributions and graft. Vice and crime were protected in return for money and votes.

"Machines" were strongest in the great cities; and their strength there was due, it may be surmised, not so much to the size of the cities as to their rapidity of growth, to the influx of immigrants, and to the constant need of more service and more public works, a need which supplied the organization not only with a real stake to fight for but with means to satisfy the appetites of the party workers. In the cities, too, there was the greatest demand for that personal charitableness which the "machine" could supply.[13]

"Machines" and "bossism" enforced party discipline, caused masses of ignorant men to function politically, in many cases provided social services which were neglected by the community, and to an extent co-ordinated a complex, cumbersome, and unpredictable system of government. Nevertheless, the "machine" was in essence a racketeering enterprise, an interest group, parasitic and corruptive. It was partially invisible, irresponsible, and usually uncontrollable by democratic processes. It represented a perversion of those processes. To make matters worse, it was appallingly expensive.

The "boss" was a local dictator operating under certain important limitations. He could employ force or terrorism but never to great lengths. He was unable to make himself the exponent of an ideology or the symbol of a cause. He could not go far toward suppressing free opinion. He could not do these things because he had not learned how to be national. His disabilities and limitations were local; and there the sword of democracy was always hanging over his head.

THE INTELLECTUAL IN POLITICS: CIVIL SERVICE REFORM

A few men, in the main outside either industry or the universities, were making diverse and in some cases unorthodox contributions to social criticism and economic and political discussion.[14]

---

[13] J. T. Salter, *Boss Rule: Portraits in City Politics* (1935), pp. 17-18.
[14] For example, Henry Demorest Lloyd, Henry George, Charles A. Dana, George Henry Evans, Horace Greeley, Peter Cooper, Parke Godwin, Wendell Phillips, Albert Brisbane, "Coin" Harvey, George William Curtis, Edwin L. Godkin, Edward Bellamy, and Ignatius Donnelly.

Intellectual leadership struck first
at partisanship and spoils.

One group, best represented by George William Curtis, taking its stand on ethical grounds, attacked corruption and machine politics, aiming to clear away those obstacles which, impeding the electoral process, were frustrating democracy. Australian ballot laws, generally adopted in this period, gave legal recognition to the party and established the principle of secret voting. Nonpartisanship and independent voting were advanced as moral standards and civic ideals. Municipal nonpartisanship was implemented by "citizens' unions," "good government clubs," "reform leagues," "municipal voters' leagues," and like organizations. In the national arena, occasional "bolts" from the major parties occurred. The Liberal Republican movement in 1872, which went down with Horace Greeley, was in large part a revolt of intellectuals against the low moral tone of politics. The legislatures passed a multitude of acts against bribery.

The "spoils system" was attacked, not so much because it was administratively wasteful as because it was one of the main supports of "machine" politics. Nationally, protests had been made before the Civil War against the prostitution of administration to party uses. The close connection seen between "politics" and fiscal waste is illustrated by the creation in 1866 of a Congressional Joint Select Committee on Retrenchment to consider ways of reducing the costs of government and of "withdrawing the public service from being used as an instrument of political or party patronage." The Committee, reporting in 1867, brought in a bill "to regulate the civil service and promote the efficiency thereof."[15] The New York City charter of 1873 prohibited the removal of policemen and firemen except for good cause. An abortive attempt was made in Grant's administration to apply executive rules and regulations to the admission of persons into the federal civil service. President Hayes urged adoption of the merit system. The National Civil Service Reform League was organized in 1881; and, since 1872, both parties had included civil service reform in their platforms. Finally,

[15] U. S. Civil Service Commission, *History of the Federal Civil Service, 1789-1939* (1939), pp. 46-47.

Congress in 1883, by a vote that cut across party lines, gave to the civil service reform movement its first decisive legislative victory. At the moment, little was accomplished beyond the establishment of principles and of a bi-partisan commission to supervise their application. The extension of the principles to a substantial percentage of federal employees was in the main the task of successive presidents. At first the classified service included only 10.5 per cent of the civil employees of the federal government; but 47.3 per cent had been brought under the act by 1901. New York enacted its first civil service law in 1883. Massachusetts followed in 1884; and Illinois, Wisconsin, and Indiana in 1895.

At the same time, the states and the federal government were in some measure eliminating politics from administration through the use of bi-partisan or nonpartisan boards.

AGRICULTURAL DISCONTENT

The group composition of the electorate, as Madison well knew, is a basic determining factor in the evolution of governmental forms, in the distribution of powers, in the alignment and programs of parties, and in the growth and nature of the governmental task. During most of the period under review, as in the preceding period, the agricultural group operated influentially in all of these directions, though, with respect to its immediate aims it was at this time largely frustrated.

This group did not retain the overwhelming voting power that it once possessed; but as late as 1900, in almost three-fourths of the states, the rural voters were numerous enough, if they stood together, to control the state governments; and in still other commonwealths they either held a small majority or were able because of the apportionment of legislative membership to control one house of the legislature, if not the whole of it. Incidentally, a majority of the United States Senate and of the House of Representatives was from rural states or rural districts. Moreover, to an extent the apparent interests of labor coincided with those of agriculture; and on the question of "free silver" the mining interests of the Rocky Mountain states were aligned with the farmers.

During this period, as at other times, agricultural grievances

were created primarily by the downward course of prices. The
farmers had enjoyed extraordinary prosperity due to high prices
during the Civil War; they had borrowed money at high rates to
buy land and expand production; during the postwar years they
were caught by declining prices that increased the weight of their
indebtedness; and they suffered also from two major depressions.
They were, of course, not the only sufferers, nor the only ones who
gave political voice to their grievances; but, because of economic
sectionalism and the voting power of agriculture, the political effect
of discontent was largely due to the farmers and, in its most intense and significant aspects, may be considered as of western origin.

Farmers demanded relief through currency inflation.

The decline in prices, which began immediately after the war,
produced a demand for the reissue of greenbacks and for an expansion of the total volume of government notes. The demand was
accompanied by protests against the "money power." This inflation movement waned during the prosperity of the late sixties and
early seventies; but it was resumed after the depression of 1873
and took the form of demands both for the expansion of greenback
currency and for the purchase of silver by the government. During
the early eighties, the movement again waned; but it revived and
attained its greatest strength in the Populist and free-silver movements. The free-silver issue was clearly stated and fought out in
the campaign of 1896; but it was not until prices began to rise in the
late nineties that the inflationary movement definitely subsided.

Another aim was national railroad regulation.

We have seen how transportation development, an early test of
federalism, was turned over to the states by Jacksonian Democracy,
how the states extravagantly promoted the building of canals and
railroads, and how, facing bankruptcy and in the grip of natural
monopolies, set up commissions with varying supervisory functions.
Except in New England, these commissions had little regulatory
power. Distrust of legislatures continuing, provisions regarding railroads were now inserted into some of the state constitutions, Illinois

leading the way in 1870. Some attempts were made to regulate rates by statute.

Faced on the one hand with the difficulties of the roads and on the other with the complaints of shippers, the legislatures began to admit their inability to handle the situation directly and, particularly in the West, proceeded to set up commissions with discretionary and enforcement authority.[16]

In the *Granger Cases,*[17] decided in 1877, the Supreme Court had given broad approval to state regulation of rates; but in 1886 these decisions were practically overruled,[18] and in effect state regulation was restricted to purely intra-state commerce. Moreover, the state commissions were too often controlled by the very corporations that were subject to regulation. On the whole, it appeared that if regulation was to be effective, it must be undertaken by the federal government.[19]

The farmers' protest was also
directed at monopoly.

The corporation went a long step beyond the individualism of Jefferson and of the frontier; but, after the disastrous consequences of public participation in transportation and banking, state governments encouraged almost unrestricted incorporation. The policy of government thus tended to freeze into the relations between government and industry the idea of private liberty, while fostering a form of economic organization which, along with its inevitability and efficiency, embodied concentration of economic power.[20]

[16] I. L. Sharfman, *The Interstate Commerce Commission* (1931), Pt. 1, p. 15.
[17] *Munn* v. *Ill.,* 94 U. S. 113.
[18] *Wabash, St. Louis and Pacific Ry. Co.* v. *Ill.,* 118 U.S. 557.
[19] The People's Party platform of 1892 went beyond regulation, and demanded government ownership and operation of the railroads.
[20] According to Henry C. Adams, ". . . the withdrawal of the States from the domain of internal improvements marks the rise of corporate power in the United States. As in 1830 the Federal government abandoned the thought of direct control over remunerative public works, so, during the years from 1842 to 1846, a revulsion of sentiment turned all this business over to individuals. So far from realizing the programme of Jacksonian democracy, according to which the States were to recover their administrative importance, this experiment resulted in the establishment of a new power, unknown to the founders of our government, yet intrusted with truly sovereign functions. . . . It thus appears that the financial crisis of the State treasuries was a turning point in the development of national

When, later, the states undertook regulation, the freedom of corporate enterprise was pretty consistently protected by the Supreme Court.[21] In the first place, the Court decided that the corporation was a person within the meaning of the due process clause.[22] The interpretation of the clause involved, further, a definition of the state's police power; and the Court in the early years was disposed to extend that power through the judicial concept of "public interest." On the other hand, the doctrine appeared and received in later years more and more emphasis that the individual possesses constitutional rights to economic liberty which cannot be infringed by legislatures and can only be determined by the courts. Thus the general effect of court decisions during this period was to limit the effectiveness of regulatory action under the commerce and due process clauses, but to recognize a large and undefined sphere for the exercise of national authority, as well as a sphere in which neither state nor national governments could encroach on individual or corporate liberty.

The corporation had proved its indispensability for the conduct of large-scale operations; but more significant from the point of view of concentrated control were the pools, holding companies, combines, and trusts. Socialistic writers believed that the concen-

---

life. . . . Illinois had undertaken both State banking and State improvements, and had failed in both. In her new constitution of 1848, she retained the clause that internal improvements should be encouraged, but with this significant modification —this was to be done by passing liberal laws of incorporation for that purpose." *Public Debts* (1893), pp. 338-41.

[21] In the seventies, the Court had in the main upheld the powers of the states; but, with the filling of three vacancies on the tribunal in 1881 and 1882, "a marked disposition to enhance the powers of the National Government by a liberal construction of the Constitution, and to widen the scope of the jurisdiction and powers of the National Judiciary became increasingly apparent; and this distinctly nationalistic era in its history continued for the next ten years." Charles Warren, *The Supreme Court in United States History* (1923), Vol. 3, p. 347.

[22] The fourteenth amendment provided that no state should "deprive any person of life, liberty, or property without due process of law; nor deny to any person within its jurisdiction the equal protection of the laws." In the passage of this amendment, according to Warren, the Republican leaders of Congress desired, not only to punish the South and to make the Negro equal in civil rights to the white man, but also "to centralize in the hands of the federal government large powers hitherto exercised by the States." (The same, pp. 261-62.) Some no doubt understood and intended at the time that "persons" would be construed to include corporations and that the effect of the amendment would be to curtail the power of the states to regulate corporate enterprises.

tration of control over industry was paving the way for the "dictatorship of the proletariat." A sober historian thought it possible that "the masters of industry may prove to be not so much an incipient aristocracy as the pathfinders for democracy in reducing the industrial world to systematic consolidation suited to democratic control."[23] The people, however, possessed an ancient prejudice against monopoly. Competition was held not only to be "the life of trade" and the best protection of the consumer, but it also appeared to be the logical expression in the economic sphere of the democratic ideas of liberty and equality. The forces of monopoly seemed to be entrenched in the East, in "Wall Street"; and the new industrial and financial combinations, like the railroads, exemplified to the economically discontented the "money power," "the predatory interests," and "special privilege," and, in view of the political influence of "big business," suggested the rise to power of another sectional oligarchy, this time a plutocracy.

It was widely held that these combinations constituted dangerous concentrations of irresponsible economic power and led to the unjust appropriation of wealth and income in the hands of the few at the expense of the toiling masses. Public criticism was directed as well at the methods used by "big business," such as discrimination, stock-watering, and rebates. In the eighties, anti-monopoly planks appeared in the more radical party platforms, and the states began to enact antitrust legislation; but New Jersey, Delaware, and Maine relaxed their laws. New Jersey became the chief breeding-place of combinations, which, when incorporated in that state, were free to operate throughout the nation.

A graduated income tax was demanded.

In general, the agricultural protest was directed at what was felt to be an unjust distribution of wealth and income. Taxation offered one channel through which government might aid in the rectification of that injustice. A graduated income tax seemed peculiarly suited to the purpose. Congress had enacted an income tax law during the Civil War; and it passed another such act in 1894. When this act was in the final stage of litigation before the Supreme Court,

[23] F. J. Turner, *The Frontier in American History* (1921), pp. 265-66.

counsel dwelt at great length on its socialistic character; and the Court by a 5 to 4 decision reversed itself and declared the tax unconstitutional.

The general purpose and effect were centralizing.

It may be noted that this new western agricultural-political movement was dominated neither by Jeffersonian individualism nor Jacksonian decentralization. National power was now an accepted fact. War and reconstruction were themselves unprecedented assertions of central authority. The Emancipation Proclamation achieved under the war powers of the president what could not have been accomplished constitutionally by peacetime federal legislation. The thirteenth, fourteenth, and fifteenth amendments placed new constitutional limitations on the states. The western commonwealths were creatures of the national government and were distant both in space and time from the former colonies along the Atlantic seaboard.

With respect to inflation and a graduated income tax, agricultural demands were for the most part resisted or circumvented. During the Civil War and later, however, the federal government adopted policies intended to promote directly the particular interests of the agricultural group. The Homestead Act and the Morrill Act were followed in 1887 by the Hatch Act, giving federal aid to experiment stations established in connection with the land-grant colleges. The federal department of agriculture was placed under a secretary and thus elevated to cabinet rank in 1889. Boards or departments of agriculture were created in the states. With respect to the railroads and monopolies, policies of special significance were adopted by the national government, not wholly because of the pressure just discussed and not entirely with the results that the discontented groups hoped for.

EXTENSIONS OF NATIONAL ECONOMIC CONTROL

We now turn from the major objectives of agricultural group pressure to two significant developments in national policy and equally significant additions to the national governmental task: (1) the Interstate Commerce Act of 1887, and (2) the Sherman Anti-Trust Act of 1890.

*The national government extended economic
control with confusion of principles.*

Previous to 1887, the policy of the national government with
respect to industry, when it was not a hands-off policy, was primarily
and almost exclusively protective and promotive. Regulation was,
in the main, either subsidiary to these purposes or incidental to other
national functions. The states, as we have seen, had attempted both
to regulate railroads and to prohibit monopolies; and, in the late
eighties, they were applying their developing police power to a
variety of other private enterprises.[24] The states, however, because
of limited jurisdiction, restricted constitutional power, and divergent
or conflicting policies, could not undertake successfully to control
any basic or large aspect of the economic system. Industry was national.

National policy, as we have seen, first encouraged and subsidized
the building of railroads. In the sixties and seventies, however, the
decline of river and canal traffic under railroad competition, as well
as agrarian opposition to the rates charged by the railroads, led to
demands for the restoration of competition through government
promotion of water transportation. First, canal tolls were abolished;
afterward, a movement was inaugurated for the improvement by
the government of inland waterways.[25] Late in the seventies, a
rapidly expanding railroad system, fighting for competitive business, caused a shift of interest to the problem of discrimination.

In the eighties, divergent points of view appeared in Congress;[26]
and the Interstate Commerce Act as finally passed in 1887 represented a compromise between the Senate and the House.

The Anti-Trust Act of 1890 was directed at monopoly. Designed
to remedy the deficiencies of the common law, it declared unlawful

[24] They were, for example, regulating saloons, hotels, factories, druggists, medicine, dentistry, money lending, banks, insurance companies, natural gas, plumbing,
nurseries, agriculture, dealing in futures, telegraph companies, gambling, cigarette
sales, sales of objectionable literature, lotteries, and labor.
[25] H. G. Moulton, "Fundamentals of a National Transportation Policy," *American Economic Review* (Suppl.), Vol. 24 (1934), pp. 34-35.
[26] Minor regulations of interstate railroads were enacted by Congress in 1866
and 1873. Beginning in 1868 presidential messages and congressional resolutions
called for committees to investigate the railroad problem. Such investigations were
made; and a number of railroad bills were introduced into Congress between 1878
and 1886.

and penalized any combination in restraint of commerce between the states and with foreign countries and also any monopoly or attempt at monopoly in interstate or foreign commerce.

The two laws were at certain points in striking contrast; and their contrasting features are indicative of the basic issues of principle and procedure that were involved.

The Interstate Commerce Act, restricted to the railroads, adopted the principle of segmentary economic control;[27] the Anti-Trust Act, whether intended to deal with the economic system or with commerce in the narrow sense, was not directed at any specific economic segment. The primary purpose of the former act was the correction of abuses; that of the latter was in effect the determination of private economic organization. The earlier legislation aimed, inconsistently, to regulate natural monopolies and also to enforce competition;[28] the later enactment embodied the traditional doctrine of individualistic competition. The Interstate Commerce Act, while including certain statutory prohibitions, also set up standards (for example, that rates must be "just and reasonable"); the Anti-Trust Act confined itself to statutory prohibitions.

The 1887 enactment set up an administrative agency essentially new to the national government—a bi-partisan Interstate Commerce Commission. In contrast, the legislation of 1890 relied exclusively

---

[27] The law, in fact, covered only a segment of the transportation problem. As we see more clearly today, either competition or systematization in the field of transportation involves not only the separate railroads but also those transportation media that compete with the railroads. In the early days the people had been interested, not so much in turnpike, canals, or railroads, as in transportation.

[28] It was already discerned by a few that the railroads constituted, not a multitude of separable small enterprises, but a system of transportation; and that the tendency of private competition was to make the system administratively unified, appropriate to a relatively simple type of public regulation. Charles Francis Adams in 1878 suggested that "regulated combination" was the ultimate solution of the railroad problem; and, writing in 1886, said:

"A confederation, or even a general combination among all the railroad corporations having some degree of binding force, might . . . not improbably prove the first step in the direction of a better and more stable order of things. But to lead to any results at once permanent and good this confederation must, in three respects, differ radically from everything of the same sort which has hitherto preceded it: it must be legal; it must be public; it must be responsible." Charles Francis Adams, Jr., *Railroads: Their Origin and Problems* (1886), p. 190. Much the same view was held by Henry C. Adams, "Relation of the State to Industrial Action," *Publications of the American Economic Association*, Vol. 1 (1887), p. 525.

on the traditional system of enforcement through a partisan attorney-general and the courts. In both cases, but especially in the case of the Anti-Trust Act, the general terms of the statutes called for judicial interpretation; and the courts, therefore, possessed wide opportunity to determine the meaning of the laws and to limit their effect.

THE LAST MAJOR DEMOCRATIZING WAVE

Having noted the causes and aims of agricultural discontent and the resulting public policies, we now point out the relation of this phenomenon to the democratization of government. "Jacksonian democracy" had been given form and force by western opinion and agricultural voting power. Now, the voters of the West were again discontented and, as in the past, along with pressure for specific policies they demanded a more representative, more responsive, more democratic government. The new democratizing movement was not wholly attributable to agricultural unrest; and it had supporters in all groups and sections. Its main sources of strength, however, were among those who were demanding an economic redistribution and who felt quite naturally that control of government had passed from the people to the "moneyed" interests. The movement concerned itself, in the main, with four features of political machinery: the party system, the suffrage, legislation, and the Supreme Court.

Agricultural pressure failed to realign
the party system.

Agricultural discontent in the West and South was first expressed by a number of organizations, chief of which were the Farmers' Alliance and the Grange. During the seventies, the Grangers and local farmers' groups won a number of state elections; and the Greenback Party polled over a million votes in the congressional campaign of 1878. However, the rigidity and opportunism of the party system, the strength of party organizations, the dominance of the tariff issue, and certain other political cross-currents divided both the farmers and the industrial workers and more or less neutralized their potential political effectiveness.

Spurred on by successes in 1890, the Farmers' Alliance early in

1892 held with the Knights of Labor a national conference and issued a call for a national convention. This convention organized the People's Party; and its candidate polled over a million votes in the presidential election of that year. Between 1892 and 1896— for the most part a period of depression—free silver became the central demand in the program of both the Populists and western and southern Democrats. The "silverites" controlled the Democratic Convention in 1896 and the Populists and Silver Republicans fused with the Democrats. The latter were in power during the depression and could not wholly escape blame for it. The Republican victory and economic recovery after 1896 disposed of the demand for inflation, and forestalled any possibility of a party realignment, such as that which had marked the birth of Jacksonian Democracy in 1828 or of the Republican Party in 1856-60. Thereafter, western radicalism, reinforced by labor unrest, was to work as Progressivism within the established framework of the two-party system.

The aim then was to broaden and strengthen popular control of parties and legislatures.

The new West, like the old, believed in political democracy and in the desirability of modifying political machinery so as to remove the obstructions that appeared to lie in the way of popular control. Whether or not the party system could be realigned, oligarchic or minority control of the system was scarcely consistent with the logic of democracy. It was proposed, therefore, to eliminate the convention system of nomination through the establishment of the direct primary. Also gaining favor was the idea of direct legislation, the initiative and referendum. This latter idea was not new; but it was now urged that it be given more extensive application.

These proposals rested on a reasonable belief that wealth and corruption had taken the party system and the legislatures from the control of the people. The people, therefore, were to be given the power directly to nominate and to legislate. Unlike previous attempts to correct legislative deficiencies, the new movement struck also at the national legislative mechanism. The continued strengthening of the governor was perhaps at this time a phase of the democratizing urge: the governor was looked upon as more representative than the legislature. "Weak executives," remarked Bryce, "frequently do harm, but a strong Executive has rarely abused popular confidence."[29]

President Johnson suggested to Congress a constitutional amendment providing for direct election of senators. The suggestion coming from him must have been maddening; but in 1893 the House of Representatives approved a similar proposal. The Senate was to "deliberate" on the matter another 15 years.

The woman suffrage movement also gained strength. As early as 1868 Wyoming gave the vote to women; and a constitutional amendment for woman suffrage was introduced in the House of Representatives in 1869.

The Supreme Court was again under attack.

A significant effect of the due process clause, like that of the commerce clause, was to enable the Supreme Court to become an important factor in the development of private economic enterprise and in the determination of the relation of government to the individual and the corporation, as well as in the shifting of governmental authority within the structure of federalism.

Despite growing dissatisfaction with government and with the economic conservatism of the Court, no movement for the reconstruction of the Court took form. It is true that after the Civil War, when it was feared that the justices would declare reconstruction legislation unconstitutional, attacks were leveled at the Court and proposals made to reorganize it.[30] In the heat of the controversy, Congress passed, and repassed over the President's veto, a bill divesting the tribunal of its appellate jurisdiction under the Habeas Corpus Act.[31] An act of 1866 reduced the Court to eight judges in order to deprive President Johnson of the opportunity to fill expected vacancies;[32] and it was proposed in 1867 in a bill reported by the Judiciary Committee of the House that two-thirds

---

[29] *American Commonwealth*, Vol. 1 (1888), p. 283.
[30] Warren, *The Supreme Court in United States History*, Vol. 3, pp. 168-69.
[31] The same, pp. 196-202.
[32] The same, p. 223.

of the justices must concur in any decision adverse to an act of Congress.[33]

During the ten years from 1873 to 1883, according to Warren, the Court "was substantially free from serious attack, either in Congress or in the press," though this was a period when few changes occurred in its membership.[34] After the income tax decision, the Court was publicly attacked by those representing the agrarian and labor interests. The Democratic platform in 1896 blamed the treasury deficit on the annulment of the income tax act and implied, as the People's Party declared, that the decision was a misinterpretation of the Constitution.[35]

In general, however, the Supreme Court's nationalism and its partiality to corporate enterprises, such as they were, reflected more or less faithfully the long-run public opinion of the time as it was expressed in the political processes. If the federal courts were lacking in vision, they did not stand alone; the state courts were inclined also to prevent what we now call social legislation. "Democratizing" the courts by making the judges elective had not made them, apparently, any more sensitive to social need; but the judges had been forced into politics and not infrequently into corrupt politics.

THE LABOR MOVEMENT

The second great voting group and likewise a discontented one comprised the industrial wage earners. These were steadily increasing in number.

Conditions accentuated industrial conflict and labor's power in group politics.

As we have just noted, one of the issues involved in public control of the economic system was whether private enterprises should be left free to organize into large units. Since the question was one of private economic power, it was also one of private economic responsibility. The cleavage between capital and labor reached down to the same basic question of power and responsibility. The worker

[33] The same, p. 188.
[34] The same, p. 285.
[35] Kirk H. Porter, *National Party Platforms* (1924), pp. 184, 197.

was no longer also an owner and manager. He had lost control of his tools. Likewise disappearing was that intimate relationship between master and servant, which identified both with a common undertaking and preserved a basis for mutual respect and understanding. As industrialism developed, those who were seeking, consciously or unconsciously, to organize the economic system failed to bring about the psychological and administrative adjustments necessary to a genuine peaceful partnership between capital and labor.

Proposals were made looking to the public or private co-ordination of the two forces. Labor organizations experimented with co-operatives, both productive and distributive. The Knights of Labor favored public ownership of railways, water works, gas plants, and other utilities; and an increasing number of municipalities undertook the ownership and operation of such enterprises. Socialism, long agitated, gained a considerable following. Nevertheless, as the Beards say, "the philosophy of schematic socialism— with its version of the 'down-trodden proletariat'—did not grip American workingmen."[36] Of the few national associations organized specifically for the purpose of bringing capital and labor together, probably the longest-lived and most important was the National Civic Federation, which started in Chicago in 1896 and became a national organization in 1900.[37]

On the whole during this period, middle-class opinion was opposed to unionism and to strikes. Those who disturbed the existing order either with violent action or radical ideas were likely to be classed as socialists, if not as anarchists. In general, public authority, especially the judicial power, was used against strikers. The attitude of the judiciary was based on legal concepts, such as freedom of contract and conspiracy, which no longer had much logical application to actual conditions. Arbitration of labor disputes was widely advocated; state acts were passed for the encouragement of voluntary arbitration; and Congress in 1888 enacted a law which created a federal commission for mediation in the field of interstate commerce. Nevertheless, some 24,000 strikes took place between 1881

---

[36] *The Rise of American Civilization* (1927), Vol. 2, p. 248.
[37] See Lewis L. Lorwin, *The American Federation of Labor* (1933).

and 1900,[38] frequently accompanied by destruction of property, rioting, and bloodshed.

Labor was now organized on a national scale, and thus the direction of labor was further isolated from plant and company management. In the early years, efforts were made to form a national labor party. Already there were two parallel movements in labor organization: one by crafts and the other by industries. The American Federation of Labor was on the whole a craft organization, while the Knights of Labor and its predecessor, the National Labor Union, were of the industrial type. Labor as a pressure group was growing in strength but it was not yet a major influence in either state or national government.

In general, labor organizations stood consistently for higher wages, shorter hours, and the right of collective bargaining. They demanded and to a slight extent obtained state legislation for shorter hours. The Massachusetts legislature established a bureau of labor statistics in 1869. Other states followed. Ohio in 1890 created the first public employment offices in the country. Congress in 1884 set up a bureau of labor in the Department of the Interior to collect and disseminate information on working conditions, and in 1888 labor was given the same recognition that agriculture had received in 1862: a separate department of labor under a commissioner was established.

In the early eighties, encouragement of immigration gave way to regulation and partial exclusion. Immigration from Great Britain, Ireland, Germany, and Scandinavia began to fall off, while the people of eastern Europe, largely of the poor, unskilled, and illiterate classes, were coming in ever-increasing numbers and for the most part congregating in the industrial cities and mining regions. From 1882 to the turn of the century different federal laws denied admittance to certain classes; and a head tax was placed on all immigrants.

In general, we may say that labor was now well advanced in the second stage of its role in the realization of popular control through the assertion of group power. The first stage was the winning of the suffrage; the second was organization and conflict. The approach

[38] E. L. Bogart, *Economic History of the United States* (4th ed., 1925), p. 429.

by labor to group or class consciousness and the employment of its collective strength is rightly represented as a major step in the spread of popular control and, more significantly, in the realignment of public opinion along the lines of group-composition. Labor was making ready to dispute and bargain in the sphere of party politics and government with the industrialists, the farmers, and the middle classes. Also, by consolidating its special position in the organization and management of industry and by impressing itself on public policy, labor was making governmental efficiency a more complicated problem.

LABOR, URBANISM, AND SOCIAL SERVICES

In the meantime, humanitarianism, long an ally of the economic interest of the wage earners, was producing that shift of definition by which legislation favorable to labor, such as that just mentioned, was to be known as "social" legislation, rather than as economic or industrial control. As a practical matter, urbanism in general, as well as labor in particular, required social services. The individual, the family, and the neighborhood were losing self-sufficiency.

Government was developing its power and expanding its functions.

The development of the regulatory powers in the states and federal government has already been referred to. An equally potent force in the evolution of government was the conception of the state as a service-state, expanding its services in accordance with industrial-urban conditions and the humanitarian ideal and under the pressures of particular groups. New or expanded functions and increased expenditure in the field of social welfare seemed to be putting into practice the ideal of government "for the people."

The protection of the health of mobile and congested populations required more varied techniques and more uniform enforcement. The first state administrative body having functions similar to modern boards of health was established in Massachusetts in 1869. The delinquent and the mentally deficient and diseased increased with the general population, demanding more institutions for their custody and treatment; and, as institutions grew in number, the need of overhead supervision and co-ordination became more pressing. State care of the insane in New York was completely shifted from the counties to the state in 1890. State boards of charities and state prison boards appeared.

To the urban populations, recreation and country life revealed new values, which, in part, could be realized only through government. Natural resources had dwindled under unregulated exploitation. Forestry conditions were investigated in several states; and in some a state forestry agency was established. Moreover, agricultural pursuits adjacent to the cities were becoming specialized, increasing the amount of traffic on the roads. Finally, the spread of population called for more roads; and the inauguration of rural free delivery emphasized to the farmer the desirability of passable thoroughfares. The industrial states took the first steps toward state control of highways. Massachusetts set up a state highway commission under acts of 1893 and 1894; and New York entered the field of highway construction in 1898.

In contrast to the decades of minimized government and states' rights from Jefferson to the Civil War, expansion of federal functions now proceeded without any effective popular or philosophical opposition. Possibilities of elaboration were seen in nearly every one of the specified constitutional powers. A number of these have already been noted. As a further example, the postal power, a rather definite grant, was used not merely to provide a money order system and rural free delivery, but also to suppress lotteries, a matter clearly within the states' police power. Marked expansion took place through the "necessary and proper" clause and by means of the spending power under the general welfare clause. The federal government interested itself in education, establishing in 1867 a department of education headed by a commissioner. Acts passed between 1870 and 1878 marked the beginning of the modern Public Health Service. The Office of Road Inquiry was set up in the Department of Agriculture in 1893. Informational, statistical, and scientific activities of the federal government greatly expanded. Older functions grew by specialization and division.

In England, John Stuart Mill and Herbert Spencer attempted to establish principles which might determine the extent and degree of governmental authority; and in this country Henry C. Adams, the economist, examined the phenomenon of increasing governmental functions. But as James Bryce observed,

... though the Americans have no theory of the State and take a narrow view of its functions, though they conceive themselves to be devoted to laissez faire in principle, and to be in practice the most self-reliant of peoples, they have grown no less accustomed than the English to carry the action of government into ever-widening fields.[39]

To be sure, voices were raised and presidential vetoes interposed against national paternalism; but these served to emphasize the tendency, rather than to check it.[40]

Centralizing trends appeared—clearly in the states,
less clearly in the nation.

In contrast to the dynamism, unrest, and experimentalism of the cities, rural government appeared artificial, static, stagnant, and neglected. In the counties and townships, the principle of local self-government retained its popularity; and few questioned its validity or its enduring quality. Not only administration but also policy-determination was still being delegated to the county. Prohibition of the liquor traffic, for example, was spreading through the application of the principle of "local option." But the rural county was obviously disqualified for the regulation of industry; it was unfitted to manage the larger institutions; and it proved in time to be incompetent to handle the jails and the almshouses. It lacked the professional leadership and technical ability to exercise final authority over educational and health activities.

Urbanization brought concentrations of population and wealth, increasing the inequality of tax-paying ability among counties. State grants-in-aid were increasingly used to relieve the local taxpayers and to equalize services. As in the case of the cities, statutory restrictions on taxing and borrowing were imposed on the counties.

---

[39] *American Commonwealth*, Vol. 2, pp. 540-42.
[40] *Messages and Papers of the Presidents* (1897), Vol. 11, p. 4708; Vol. 12, p. 5142.

Partly because of this financial assistance, partly because the local units lacked expertness, and partly because it seemed just that minimum standards should be applied uniformly throughout the state, more extensive provision was made for central supervision of local administration. The telephone, like the railroad and the telegraph, facilitated centralization; and in the nineties the automobile appeared, destined to make rapid transit a flexible, individual, and almost universal possession. The state was becoming the primary unit of rural government; the county, an anachronistic device for a semi-autonomous, uneconomical, and inexpert decentralization of administration.

Functional expansion and centralization were accompanied by an increase of state expenditure. Per capita costs of state government were also rising; and the tax burden was growing heavier. In New York State, the ratio of total taxes (federal, state, and local) to total income rose from 3.8 per cent in 1850 to 7.1 per cent in 1890.

In many respects the expansion of federal activities looked like centralization and was so interpreted at the time. Nevertheless, if the national government gained scope and power at the expense of the states, it was because of Supreme Court decisions rather than acts of Congress. Apparently, there was little if any intention on the part of federal legislators to set up central control over the states. The expansion of the national government is to be attributed in largest part to the fact that economic problems had become national and to the treasury surpluses that occurred almost continuously during this period. As a matter of fact, in some important fields of legislation and administration the federal government was following rather than leading. The states were pioneering and getting the hard knocks. The federal government was serving as a post-graduate department in the school of political experience, and serving laggardly.

ADMINISTRATIVE ORGANIZATION

The contrast between technological and political conditions has probably never been more striking than at this time. The importance of technical administration was scarcely perceived; the relation of certain administrative powers to the general problem of democracy was rarely commented upon; and the bearing of administrative organization on the efficiency of government was largely ignored.

Modern trends and problems were taking shape in the states.

The city, the most technological of governmental units, was emerging as a critical problem and a vital political force. Each urban center was a separate natural dynamic entity with a wide range of peculiar social problems. These problems reflected needs and desires that were generally local; and in the cities, particularly the larger ones, were concentrated a large share of the leadership, technical competence, and wealth of the state. The city, then, was basically and permanently an appropriate unit of government; and it had the resources to govern itself in all those matters that were of purely municipal concern. To democracy the cities obviously had much more than an administrative significance. If local self-government bore an intimate relation to the realization of democracy, the city must serve, in the new age, like the frontier community in rural America, as a nursery and testing-ground of democracy. Yet, how different was the urban community, with its specialization, its extremes of wealth and poverty, its technical functions, its dominating industrialism, and its aggregations of people who were in large numbers alien to the country and in still larger numbers alien to one another!

While the cities, governmentally, were creatures of the state legislature, their political organizations were modelled after the federal and state governments, embodying the principles of separation of powers and checks and balances.

It will be recalled that the excesses of state legislatures before the Civil War resulted in constitutional restrictions on their borrowing and lending powers. These restrictions shifted pressure for spending to the local governments. In any case, the cities had need of spending programs, for their physical growth outran their capacity to make fiscal adjustments. In consequence, the debts of municipalities rapidly increased.

In the larger urban centers during this period, maladministration, extravagance, corruption, and environmental degradation probably reached an all-time high. The "reform" movements of the time were for the most part generated by moral indignation rather than by applied intelligence. Various expedients were tried and mostly found wanting: state control of local police administrations; statutory limitations on municipal taxing and borrowing; reduction of the power of city legislatures; increase of the mayor's authority; reorganization of municipal boards and departments; and separation of municipal and state elections.

In the state governments, alongside the older offices, new agencies for regulation and service were constantly growing up and rapidly expanding. By 1880, in New York and probably in other states, the bulk of administrative work and public spending was no longer done by the traditional officials and departments.[41]

Administrative development reflected the decline of statutory-judicial control and legislative promotion-by-spending. While the legislatures and the public were perceiving the inadequacy of direct legislative action and of rural local self-government, they were inclined to look upon administrative agencies merely as arms of the legislature or as representatives of pressure groups. As administrative activities proliferated, each new branch seemed to have its separate identity, as it often had its separate clientele. Accordingly, as a rule each new activity was given a new agency to enforce it. As a result, the number of separate administrative agencies multiplied.

In part the old habit of election persisted. In some cases, ex officio boards were established. Quite generally, appointive boards were created and so arranged as to be substantially independent. Less frequently, administrative tasks were allocated to departments headed by appointive officials. Legislatures indulged in minor reorganizations and in some directions progress was made toward co-ordination. Nevertheless, while the foundations for administrative improvement had been laid by a more or less unconscious centralization, little thought had yet been given to integration at the top, to the requirements of economical and efficient operations, or to the proper balancing of centralizing with decentralizing principles.

[41] State of New York, *Report by Special Joint Committee on Taxation and Retrenchment*, Feb. 11, 1926, p. 34.

*Federal administration definitely entered
the policy-determining stage.*

In federal, as well as state, administration, the departure had already been made from the ministerial, routine, clerical stage of administration to the discretionary, policy-determining, sub-legislative stage. Before the Civil War, Congress had in many cases delegated legislative and discretionary authority to the president and to federal administrative agencies.[42]

Nevertheless, in the eighties, the president and the federal executive agencies were thought of as executive and their duties as ministerial. Woodrow Wilson in 1884 had written that the business of the president was "usually not much above routine," that "most of the time" it was "mere obedience of directions," and that administration was "merely the clerical part of government."[43] In an article on "The Study of Administration," published in 1887, he set forth a somewhat broader conception of the administrative function; but he nevertheless insisted that administration was "detailed and systematic execution of public law" and that, "while the administrator is not and ought not to be a mere passive instrument," his work was "a part of political life only as the methods of the counting-house are a part of the life of society."[44]

As Wilson wrote, however, Congress was creating a new type of administrative agency, and in this creation, as well as in delegations of legislative authority to the president himself, was suggesting the possibility of extraordinary alterations in the legislative mechanism and administrative structure.

The establishment of the Interstate Commerce Commission in 1887 added an essentially new organ—a "fourth branch"—to the national governmental structure; for the Commission was set up so as to be substantially independent of the executive and was expected to serve, not only for the execution of the law, but also as an instrument of Congress for the continuous development of policy. Moreover, the Commission was to act as a quasi-judicial body. It challenged the principle of separation of powers.

[42] See John Preston Comer, *Legislative Functions of National Administrative Authorities* (1927), pp. 50-72.
[43] *Congressional Government* (1913), pp. 253-54, 273.
[44] *Political Science Quarterly,* Vol. 2 (1887), pp. 210-12.

Likewise significant of trends was a provision of law, apparently enacted more or less by inadvertence in 1891, authorizing the president to set aside and withhold from sale public lands covered wholly or partly with timber. This legislation embodied, more broadly than in previous acts, the principle of delegating legislative details to the executive, as well as the principle of conservation. Both principles were to expand presidential power and opportunities for presidential leadership.[45]

Notwithstanding these developments, the federal government continued to adhere rather consistently to the original theory of departmental organization. Although several administrative establishments stood outside the Cabinet circle, the tendency was to absorb them or make them executive departments. The office which had developed under the attorney-general was formally made the Department of Justice in 1870. The Post Office Department acquired full legal status as an executive department in 1872. The Department of Agriculture was given a secretary and made coordinate with the other departments in 1889. Labor also had a department, but not of Cabinet rank.

The establishment of agencies for agriculture and labor—two of the great interest-groups—reflected the sectionalism and group composition of Congress, as well as the divisions in the nation. The older federal departments had been in purpose, in name, and, for the most part in fact, general-welfare agencies. The new departments were agencies in the main for particular interests.

THE LEGISLATIVE MECHANISM

Consideration of the responsiveness and effectiveness of the legislative mechanism requires reference to the relations between president and Congress—the actual working of separated and balanced powers—and to the operations of Congress.

[45] The bill was initiated by certain private organizations and by administrators in the Department of the Interior who won the support of some senators and representatives; but, if the Beards are correct, the majority of the members of Congress were "wholly unaware of the implications inherent in the bill." (*Rise of American Civilization*, Vol. 2, p. 590.)

In the assertion of public power, Congress
outweighed the president.

Lincoln had wielded unprecedented executive authority. His death and the coming of peace shifted party leadership to the Republican radicals in Congress. The most extreme manifestation of their dominating tendency occurred in the struggle with President Johnson. Impeached, he narrowly escaped conviction.

No other struggle of such violence was to occur between president and Congress. With the possible exception of Hayes and Cleveland, no chief executive between 1865 and 1897 was capable of either a dominating or a persuasive leadership. Both were handicapped. Hayes was Republican; but, during his administration, one house of Congress was Democratic. Cleveland was a Democrat; but during six of the eight years of his presidency at least one house was Republican.

The weakness of the presidents was in part due to a party system that emphasized availability rather than capacity. Grant was the most incompetent; but, in the beginning at least, he was the most popular. After Grant, three of the four successful Republican candidates were from Ohio. The other was from Indiana. From 1868 to 1892 inclusive, four of the five Democratic candidates[46] were from New York. The other was from Pennsylvania. Thus, in each party, the choice of a candidate was narrowly limited geographically. It may be noted, too, that after Grant left office in 1877 no other president was to be re-elected for a second consecutive term until 1900.[47]

Political leadership was either nonexistent or it was rendered impotent by the economic and political conditions of the time, or it was operating more or less under cover. When James Bryce wrote his *American Commonwealth* in 1888 he expressed the opinion that the president, except for the increase of his patronage, had gained little in dignity or power since Jackson. He could use patronage to influence members of Congress; but they, on the other hand, had largely

[46] Cleveland was a candidate three times and is counted only once.
[47] Cleveland was elected to a second term, but not a consecutive one.

arrogated to themselves the dispensing of federal jobs. In this way, they contributed substantially to the construction and maintenance of the local "machines." Patronage was, in fact, a two-edged sword: it could be used by the president on Congress or by Congress on the president.

Because the president was viewed in the main as a legislative leader, it was not illogical that the other member of the legislative team should consider itself equally if not better fitted to control administration. As Woodrow Wilson pointed out in the middle of this period, "The power of making laws is in its very nature and essence the power of directing, and that power is given to Congress.[48] And again, he said, "In legal theory the President can control every operation of every department of the executive branch of the government; but in fact it is not practicable for him to do so, and a limitation of fact is as potent as a prohibition of law."[49] The general theme of Wilson's interpretation was that Congress was "unquestionably, the predominant and controlling force, the centre and source of all motive and of all regulative power."[50] Bryce put the matter in these more measured terms:

Thus Congress, though it is no more respected or loved by the people than it was seventy years ago, though it has developed no higher capacity for promoting the best interests of the State, has succeeded in occupying nearly all the ground which the Constitution left debatable between the President and itself; and would, did it possess a better internal organization, be even more plainly than it now is the supreme power in the government.[51]

But the administration was never really subordinated to the legislature, so that responsibility could be located in one place. Members of Congress in general could hardly be expected to be competent supervisors of administration. By making them independent, observed Bryce, the Constitution "condemned them to be architects without science, critics without experience, censors without responsibility."[52]

[48] *Congressional Government*, p. 274.
[49] The same, p. 46.
[50] The same, p. 11.
[51] *American Commonwealth*, Vol. 1, pp. 223-24.
[52] The same, p. 224.

The national legislative mechanism appeared
neither democratic nor efficient.

Of the three legislative organs, the Senate, on the basis of numerical representation, was obviously and consistently unrepresentative. The presidency was occasionally so. In 1876, Tilden received more popular votes than Hayes; but this contested election, though acutely critical, was an exception. In 1888, however, Cleveland won a larger popular vote than Harrison; but the latter became president through the peculiar arithmetic of the Electoral College.

Of the two branches of Congress, the Senate lost popularity and the House failed to gain any. Though the Senate overrepresented the rural population and on occasion was over-responsive to agricultural and silver demands, it was steadily becoming more and more identified with big business and machine politics.

The House of Representatives was theoretically more directly and accurately representative and, to judge by the frequency with which its control shifted from one party to the other, it was more sensitive to changing public opinion. Its membership, however, increased at each census apportionment. In the sixties it was 241; in the nineties, 356. It became too numerous for debate and, if laws were to be enacted, it was necessary to curb the freedom of individual members. The strength of partisanship and of party organization made discipline possible; but control of the House passed to the Speaker and the chairmen of the standing committees appointed by the Speaker. The caucus enforced party unity. At the end of this period, "Czar" Reed exemplified the degree to which control of the House had become oligarchic, if not dictatorial. As Speaker, he not only ruled the House but in power and prestige stood almost equal to the president.

The committee system, with concentration of power in the Speaker, made it possible for the House to function. It obtained a modicum of efficiency by eliminating much that seemed democratic; but in fiscal matters, basic to the co-ordination of policies and the control of administration, the tendency was toward disintegration.[53]

[53] Until the end of the Civil War, the Ways and Means Committee of the House had charge of both revenue and appropriation bills. In 1865, the Appropriations

On large questions the tightened machinery of the House was used quite generally for obstruction. Although from 1865 to 1900 the country experienced profound economic and social changes with recurrent indications of tension and discontent, the federal legislative mechanism produced few major acts which seem to us now to have broad and enduring significance. Prolonged and repeated investigations by committees, even in the presence of pressure from conditions and opinion, failed to achieve timely or adequate legislation.[54]

Neither the Interstate Commerce Act nor the Anti-Trust Act seems to have represented much more than half-hearted acceptance of half-understood principles, and the principles of one were uncoordinated with those of the other. Both, as Justice Frankfurter remarks, had "only somnolent vitality."[55] With respect to the Interstate Commerce Act, a group of economists reported: "It is significant that there was no consensus of opinion whatever as to what the various provisions of the bill meant, or what they were intended to mean."[56] Much the same might be said of the Sherman Act. Until

---

Committee was created. Between 1865 and 1885, when expansion of functions and of administrative agencies was increasing the importance of appropriation bills, the handling of these measures was distributed among several committees each concerned with only a part of the administrative field. (See Daniel T. Selko, *The Federal Financial System* (1940), pp. 85-88.) To contemporary observers, so much power was exercised by these committees that they seemed to have become not only little specialized legislatures but also the actual heads of the executive departments. But, as Wilson observed, "To this new leadership, . . . as to everything else connected with committee government, the taint of privacy attaches. . . . It has only a very remote and partial resemblance to genuine party leadership." *Congressional Government* (1913 ed.), p. xi.

[54] The first income tax law, passed during the Civil War, was repealed in 1871; the second appeared about twenty years later and was annulled by the Supreme Court; but no constitutional amendment on the subject was proposed until years later. The legislation regarding withdrawal of public lands, referred to above, appears to have been suggested as early as 1867. The Sherman Art and the Interstate Commerce Act were preceded by decades of debate, committee investigation, and state experience. After 1887, the Interstate Commerce Commission repeatedly asked Congress for power to determine reasonable rates; but without result for some fifteen years. To cite a further example: A Senate resolution of Feb. 16, 1891 directed the Secretary of the Interior to report on the subject of a census bureau, and, if he found a permanent bureau expedient, to submit the draft of a bill on the subject. The Secretary reported favorably on Dec. 8, 1891, and submitted a draft bill. From this time on, bills were introduced and committees reported; but it was thirteen years before a permanent census office was established.

[55] Felix Frankfurter, *Mr. Justice Holmes and the Supreme Court* (1938), p. 19.

[56] James, *Publications of the American Economic Association*, Vol. 2 (1888), p. 272.

the turn of the century, the results of the Interstate Commerce Act were disappointing;[57] in part because the law itself was inadequate and was not substantially amended but largely because the courts refused to accept the Commission's findings and eventually decided in effect that the Commission had no mandatory power over rates. Similarly, the courts narrowed the application of the Anti-Trust Act so that manufacturing and production combinations were for the most part excepted.

A basic reason for legislative sluggishness or paralysis lay in the party system. The political party, as it developed in the Jacksonian period, was an instrument designed to permit majority control. It soon became oligarchically managed; and, in "machine" politics, another control system evolved that was essentially oligarchic or dictatorial. This system would have been more tolerable if it had been responsive and enlightened; but it was in the main politically unprogressive, intellectually bankrupt, and morally degrading. Both major parties trimmed their sails cautiously to catch the changing winds of opinion, but, by and large, they were much alike. Both tended to become fixed from time to time within a relatively narrow range of opinion, at points where neither was at the extreme right nor the extreme left. The social, economic, and political system of America was on the whole unquestioned, because it seemed to be "working." The general acceptance of constitutionalism, of democracy, of individualism, of economic expansion, of materialistic ideals, of quantitative standards, and of the idea that the interests and aims of all groups were fundamentally identical, made it possible for political contests to be fought within the limits of a common understanding. In such an atmosphere the compromising of extremes was natural, legislative advance was tentative, and "radicalism," when it raised its head, appeared to threaten the foundations of society. In general, the party system itself was immobile, unreceptive, and unresponsive.

In reality, there was sufficient variability of opinion in the North and West to swing general elections from one party to the other. This opinion, which represented a balance of power, was in part deflected into third parties; and, to the extent that it swung from

---

[57] The People's Party in 1892 demanded government ownership and operation of the railroads. Porter, *National Party Platforms*, pp. 168-69.

one major party to the other, it did not have enough strength, stability, or tenacity to bring all of the legislative organs under its control. From 1860 to 1900 the Republicans enjoyed uninterrupted control of the presidency except for Cleveland's two terms. Yet, after 1873-74, neither party was able to control the entire legislative mechanism for any considerable length of time. During the 25 years from 1875 to 1900 inclusive, the Republicans had the presidency and a working majority in both houses for only six years, and the Democrats for only two. The Senate was almost continuously Republican; but the House of Representatives was more often Democratic than Republican. The Democrats controlled the House about half the time when there were Republican presidents; and the Republicans controlled the Senate three-fourths of the time when the presidency was Democratic.

Thus, a rigid party system, acting on a government of separated, checked, and balanced powers, resulted in a substantial frustration of both majority opinion and intelligent leadership. But these were not all the difficulties.

Congress was basically localistic. The political fortunes and the material interests of its members impelled them to "do something" for their states and districts; and, to be immediately impressive, the "something" must be either tangible—a public building, a river or harbor improvement, a tariff favor—or personal—a pension or the payment of a claim. The tariff problem illustrates better than any other, except possibly the slavery question, the inability of a sectionally constituted legislative body, left to its own devices, to determine objectively and carry out consistently a general welfare policy. At its best, tariff legislation represented a combination and rough compromising of particular interests; but, as such, it could not be technically satisfactory. From 1865 on, futile attempts were made to place tariff-making on a rational and expert basis.[58]

Local interests cut across party differences, such as they were, and, with the pressure of the great interest-groups, made legislation largely nonpartisan. But it was not necessarily a nonpartisanship that upheld the general interest. On the contrary, local and group pressures prostituted the conception of the service-state—govern-

[58] James G. Smith, *Economic Planning and the Tariff* (1934), pp. 297-301.

ment "for the people"—to the plane of a paternalism that encouraged civic demoralization.[59]

The system was, to say the least, financially wasteful; but, observed Bryce, America was wealthy and had "the glorious privilege of youth, the privilege of committing errors without suffering from their consequences."[60] America's ship of state, he said, might not be well navigated; but "for the present at least—it may not always be so—she sails upon a summer sea."[61]

Little need be said of state legislatures during this period. In some respects they were more responsive to public opinion than Congress; but in the field of social legislation they were extremely dilatory.[62] They were more inclined than Congress to indulge in experimental, even "freakish" legislation; and intellectually and morally they were on a lower plane. Additional constitutional restrictions were imposed upon them; and, in all the rest of the states except North Carolina, the governor was given the veto power. The people were more and more looking to the executive to protect them from the legislative branch.

THE UNITED STATES AS A WORLD POWER

Territorial expansion, marked by the acquisition of contiguous territory, ended before the Civil War. Within the limits of this ex-

[59] "It cannot be denied that the selfish and private interests which are so persistently heard when efforts are made to deal in a just and comprehensive manner with our tariff laws are related to, if they are not responsible for, the sentiments largely prevailing among the people that the General Government is the fountain of individual and private aid; that it may be expected to relieve with paternal care the distress of citizens and communities, and that from the fullness of its Treasury it should, upon the slightest possible pretext of promoting the general good, apply public funds to the benefit of localities and individuals. Nor can it be denied that there is a growing assumption that, as against the Government and in favor of private claims and interests, the usual rules and limitations of business principles and just dealing should be waived." President Cleveland's Message of Dec. 3, 1888, *Messages and Papers of the Presidents*, Vol. 12, pp. 5361-62.

[60] *American Commonwealth*, Vol. 1, p. 179.

[61] The same, p. 303.

[62] The Industrial Relations Commission, created by Congress in 1912, reported various types of social legislation which had been passed only after decades of agitation, organization, and legislative miscarriages. The Commission pointed out, however, that "such a condition has not been the result entirely of the complacency or slothfulness of legislators, but that powerful influences have been at work to prevent such remedial legislation." *Final Report and Testimony*, S. Doc. 415, 64 Cong. 1 sess., pp. 39-41.

pansion, the country was approximately settled by 1890. The Civil War achieved unity and demonstrated military and economic strength. The subsequent growth of the nation in area, population, and wealth maintained the expansionist psychology and nourished a sense of power. The new industrial productivity led to a rapid increase of export trade. American industry looked abroad for markets and raw materials.

American missionaries joined in the process of peaceful penetration. United States naval officers had helped to "open" Japan. Alaska was purchased from Russia. We assumed with Great Britain and Germany the protectorate of the Samoan archipelago. We made jingoistic gestures toward Canada and Santo Domingo. We fought a war with Spain, ending with the acquisition of Porto Rico and the Philippines and the establishment of Cuba as an independent republic under our protection. In addition, at the end of this period, the United States possessed, in the Pacific, Tutuila in the Samoan group, the Hawaiian archipelago, and Midway and Wake Islands; and in the Caribbean, the harbor of Guantanamo, Cuba. After 50 years of discussion, we were on the eve of starting an isthmian canal. In the meantime, we had maintained the Monroe Doctrine with some reinterpretations.

In acquiring the Philippines we departed from the traditional policy of isolationism and integrated territorial development. In the 1900 presidential campaign, Bryan declared that "Imperialism" was the paramount issue and condemned it as un-American and a threat to democracy. The Republicans scorned the proposal to "haul down the flag"; and they won the election, probably in the main because of domestic prosperity.

The war with Spain, then, marked a logical climax of our policy of expansion and a radical departure from the policy of isolationism. Acquisitions in the Pacific and the Caribbean indicated a new conception of our manifest destiny and of our future role as a world power. Our international position became superficially stronger; but, at the end of this period, it was losing some of its traditional elements of security.

Between 1861 and 1900, constitutionalism, nationalism, and the principle of majority rule survived a crisis created by economic sectional cleavage; but politics and governmental evolution were still to be strongly influenced by the group and sectional make-up of the nation. The following groups were operating with more or less effect: agriculture (West and South), industry (North-East), labor (North-East), and the intellectuals (still quite limited in action). Urbanism was a growing factor.

Party politics were characterized (1) by Republican pre-eminence, based in part on economic promotional policies with manipulation of interest-groups, (2) by resistance to realignment, and (3) by corruption. Responding in part to agricultural unrest, to the labor movement, and to urbanism, the task of government was shifting from economic promotion to economic regulation and social service. Centralizing trends appeared. The national government now followed the states in the development of administrative power, most significantly in the form of commission regulation. With respect to administrative organization, modern trends and problems were now clearly sketched in the states. In the federal government, civil service reform made encouraging inroads on the spoils system. So far as the legislative process was concerned, executive authority continued to increase in the states; but, nationally, Congress was dominant; while in nation and states democracy and efficiency were not yet assured. Largely owing to agricultural unrest and western feeling, a new democratizing movement was under way. The United States assumed its position as a world power, losing thereby some of its traditional aspects of security.

CHAPTER IV

UNDERLYING CONDITIONS IN TECHNOLOGICAL
AMERICA, 1901-29[1]

At the turn of the century, in spite of frustration and reaction, allegiance to the democratic ideal seemed unimpaired. Its emotional roots were two—love of liberty and faith in humanity; but it also had concrete practical aims—political change and economic and social policies. Concerned in later years more with the possession than the curbing of political power, the majority groups, like the minority, aimed to use government for the promotion and protection of special interests. It was felt that faith was not enough; jealousy of power was not enough: democratic government must have also its positive economic and social function. Thus, the democratic aspiration was shifting from confidence in the individual to confidence in government; and, because community self-sufficiency, like individual independence, was disappearing, functional democracy identified itself with centralization. Other conditions—notably urbanization and the passing of the frontier—accelerated the transition from the minimized police-state to a state with constantly expanding functions of social service and economic regulation.

The coincidence of developing governmental supervision over the "Great Society" with efforts to extend mass control over political power emphasized more than ever before the twin questions of popular capacity and governmental efficiency. The first question, if it were to be answered, called for an understanding of Americans, individually and collectively, in their political relationships—their mental and emotional limitations, their nonpolitical preoccupations, their ability to resolve increasingly complex issues, the quality and adequacy of their leadership, the machinery through which indi-

[1] To call America from 1901 to 1929 "technological" is not to imply that technology began and ended in this period. Technology began long before, and, so far as one can foresee, an undetermined future belongs to it. In this period, it was simply the overshadowing characteristic and influence.

vidual and group opinions were brought to bear on government, and the ability of government to respond to such opinions. The second question required an equally searching analysis of government—its power to develop responsible leadership, its structural and mechanical adaptability to changing conditions, its ability to act with reasonable promptness and intelligence, and its capacity to respond and to lead in such a way as to resolve vital issues without undue confusion. A review of conditions and events from 1901 to 1929—so unlike the early years when constitutionalism and democracy began—may help further to clarify these questions.

The problem is complicated by the fact that the United States was not alone in the world. Its relationships to an unstable society of nations constituted then, as was later to become clear, a primary, perhaps a decisive, influence in its political development.

The analysis pertaining to this period falls, therefore, into three parts, dealing with (1) the international situation of the United States, with the First World War as the central fact; (2) the changing conditions in the country that were basic to democracy and governmental efficiency; and (3) movements concerned with policies, with the governmental task, with the realization of democracy and efficiency, and with developments in the form and functioning of government. The first two parts make up the present chapter; the third part, the chapter following.

INTERNATIONAL INVOLVEMENT

Throughout Europe nationality had never become a final, perfect, and stabilized accomplishment. Because unsatisfied, it continued dynamic, and, backed by military power, perennially threatened the peace and intermittently brought on war. Conditions precluded a total and lasting equilibrium. Some of the smaller nations came to rest; but the "great powers," largely because they were great, remained jealous and suspicious of one another, constantly preparing to fight, and grouped in opposing alliances.

In the meantime, industrialism had developed, first in England, later in the United States, still later in Germany and Japan. Industrialism stimulated growth of population and wealth, increased national power, demanded raw materials and markets, and turned to the exploitation of weak and uncivilized regions. In this process, nationalism became imperialism. British imperialism was most extensive and successful; but France, Belgium, and the Netherlands, to say nothing of the United States, also acquired colonies and dependencies.

Germany likewise shared; but its nationalism and imperialism were both unsatisfied. The Germany of the first decade of the century showed certain characteristics, not all peculiar to her but, in her case, markedly accentuating both nationalism and imperialism: propagation of doctrines of racial superiority; a widely held philosophy, long in preparation, that exaggerated the role of leadership (the idea of the superman); exaltation of war and acceptance of the policy of aggressive and ruthless war; theories that nationalistic and military ends justified the means, taking precedence over morals, international law, and treaty obligations; increasing armaments; a militaristic régime and a dominant military caste; a docile people; a government having parliamentary institutions but remaining essentially an autocracy; and, withal, extraordinary capacity for organization and administration.

After the war with Spain, the United States was evidently a world power and repeatedly asserted and sought to increase its diplomatic and military strength. It suppressed insurrection in the Philippines; "took" the Canal Zone and built the Panama Canal; intervened in Cuba, Nicaragua, and Mexico; established financial supervision over the Dominican Republic; purchased the Virgin Islands from Denmark; occupied and in effect governed Haiti; increased the Navy; supported the "open door" policy in China and joined with other powers in military measures at the time of the Boxer uprising; mediated to bring peace between Japan and Russia; and participated in the Algeciras conference on the Moroccan question. In the meantime, our relations with Great Britain were growing friendlier, while, a decade before the First World War, we were becoming distrustful of the saber-rattling Kaiser.

Disturbed by the piling-up of armaments in Europe, the United States participated in the two Hague Conferences and in the London Naval Conference, and led in the establishment of a Permanent Court of International Arbitration. Under Roosevelt and

Taft, arbitration treaties were signed with a number of nations; and in the first Wilson administration Secretary of State Bryan negotiated about thirty bilateral agreements known as "wait-a-year" or "cooling-off" treaties.

Politically and commercially, our policy was internationalist; but isolationist and exclusive tendencies were evident in the protective tariff and immigration restrictions. Quite consistently, the United States made clear its intention to avoid European entanglements and to maintain the Monroe Doctrine.

The eventual entrance of the United States in the World War demonstrated how far we were practically involved in the outside world. The defeat by the Senate of Wilson's proposal that we join the League of Nations brought to the fore in this country a fateful conflict of ideas. Wilson proposed that we recognize the facts of international interdependence and entanglement, which the World War had demonstrated, and that we endeavor to achieve security by asserting our power and influence with or against the power and influence of other nations. Wilson's opponents contended that American entrance into the League would mean further entanglement and diminished national security.

In the relations among the nations and in their domestic affairs, the potentialities and effects of war had been amply demonstrated in its monopolization of economic and social life, the killing and maiming of millions, destruction of property, creation of vast debts, economic maladjustments, disintegration of law and morals, suspension of democratic processes, regimentation of opinion by propaganda, and stimulation of unreasoning hate. The peace movement gained strength. In America the dominant idea seemed to be security through nonentanglement. At least this was the idea that appeared uppermost in Congress, expressed in rejections of presidential recommendations that America join in the World Court. But isolation was not achieved. We were a part of the international system, more so than ever because of loans, investments, and export trade.

Secretary of State Hughes embodied in the economic policy of the State Department the principle of equality of opportunity. The Washington Conference of 1921-22 agreed on a plan for limiting naval armaments and a treaty guaranteeing the integrity of China. Another disarmament conference in which the United States participated was held at Geneva in 1927. Finally, the United States played a leading part in bringing about the almost universal acceptance of the Kellogg-Briand Pact, by which the nations renounced war as an instrument of national policy. When the United States accepted the pact, however, it added a reservation to the effect that it was not obligated to join in coercing an offending nation. Neutrality was still a difficult problem; and an "arms embargo" resolution was introduced in the Senate.

In the meantime, problems left by the World War had not been solved. The question of reparations remained. Since the Russian Revolution, one of the great world powers was communistic; and the United States, alarmed by its propaganda, refrained from according official recognition to its government. Less fear was aroused by smaller but equally significant events in Italy—the march on Rome by the Fascists and the establishment under Mussolini of a dictatorship that renounced the ideologies both of democracy and peace.

For the most part, American suspicions were now directed toward Japan. American policy in the Orient was aimed at the preservation of the territorial integrity of China; but Japan was autocratic, militaristic, and imperialistic, and Japanese aggression at the expense of China was clearly foreshadowed.

INDUSTRY

It has been made sufficiently clear in preceding chapters that, except in times of national danger, and to an extent even then, the evolution and functioning of democratic government are primarily determined by two basic factors: (1) the economic condition of the country, and (2) the group composition of the population. During the period under review, private industry was the dominant element in the first factor and the most important influence over the second. It is, therefore, necessary to recall briefly how industry was organized and functioning and what were the resulting impressions and theories.

Between 1900 and 1929, American industry grew at an accelerated pace, with a corresponding augmentation of national wealth and income. To this progress technology made constantly more important contributions, though other factors were present.

The central fact of technological industry is the cumulative power of mechanical invention, physical discovery, and organizing ability to diversify and increase the production of goods, a fact brilliantly illustrated by the development of the automobile industry.[2] The motor vehicle, making its appearance during the nineties, resulted primarily from the invention of the internal combustion engine; but, later, a multitude of mechanical inventions and physical discoveries contributed to its improvement. Organizing ability produced research, standardization, mass production, and stimulation of sales. In the course of this development, the automobile became a better vehicle, a cheaper one, and an almost universal possession. Incidentally, the automotive industry contributed to the expansion of older economic activities and created new and subsidiary enterprises. Profits accrued and fortunes accumulated; but the improvement and cheapening of production achieved an increase and a fairly wide distribution of real income. This development resembled in some respects the railroad expansion after the Civil War. Along other lines, technological advances had much the same wealth-creating and income-distributing effect.

On the whole, however, industry proved more efficient in the creation of wealth than in the distribution of income. While "big business" was in part still competitive, over large areas the rigors of competition were mitigated by price agreements; and, even without such agreements, a common tendency existed to maintain prices at the customary level rather than to make prompt reductions in accord with increases of operating efficiency. Consequently, consumer purchasing power did not always keep pace with the capacity of industry to produce.[3]

Moreover, it was becoming apparent that all was not well with industrial employment. The census of 1930 showed that population growth was slowing, the birth-rate falling, and the number of aged relatively increasing. A tendency was already evident to impose

[2] See S. C. Davis, "Automobiles Go Ahead," *The Atlantic Monthly*, Vol. 167 (1940), pp. 23-32.

[3] For an analysis of this problem, see Harold J. Moulton, *Income and Economic Progress* (1935).

age-limits on employment, thus swelling the number of the unemployed aged. The average rate of unemployment in the manufacturing, railroad, building, and mining industries was close to 10
per cent during the prosperous years 1923-29.[4] In 1921 about 4
millions were thrown out of work.[5] In the ranks of labor, skilled
workers were giving way to the unskilled; and technological
changes produced rapid shifts in employment opportunities. The
idea was gaining currency not only that technological unemployment was increasing in amount but that this condition was chronic
and irremediable.

From 1926 to 1929, a "boom" developed. Political, economic,
and moral controls were insufficient to check the tide of speculation,
financial manipulation, and inflation. Stocks and bonds skyrocketed
to unbelievable heights; fantastic financial creations, some of them
fraudulent, contributed to the general disequilibrium. In the spring
and summer of 1929, the foundations of economic progress were
still sound; but the superstructure was unstable.

*Private economic power was
in general diffused.*

In the course of its development, industry and the economic system in general had become more complex and more delicately
adjusted. For the system as a whole, the American people had
accepted the principles of freedom and competition; but, from the
beginning, especially during depressions, the system had worked
in such a way as to raise the question of private economic power.
This question had been more clearly defined and more consistently
agitated as industrial management lost more and more its direct
and local association with agriculture and labor.

The trend in manufacturing was toward large-scale mass-production enterprises. In manufacturing and mining, and in transportation and other public utilities, the corporation was dominant and
growing; but the large corporations were still far from monop-
olizing the business of the country. Nevertheless, mergers were

---

[4] *Recent Social Trends* (1933), Vol. 2, p. 856.

[5] Don D. Lescohier, "Working Conditions," in John R. Commons, *History
of Labor in the United States* (1921), Vol. 3, p. 133.

numerous, even in the retail business, which had been highly individualistic. From some points of view, therefore, the American scene was now dominated by "big business"; while, from others, individualism was still a substantial reality.

Thousands of commercial and industrial associations were exercising a variety of functions. Chief of these organizations were the National Association of Manufacturers, organized in 1895, and the Chamber of Commerce of the United States, established in 1912. While a meeting of either national organization might bear the semblance of a "congress of industry," the views there expressed were neither binding on businessmen nor formulated in terms concrete enough to be enforced.

The corporations were, in appearance, democratically controlled joine enterprises. As time passed, most of the large ones came to be owned, not by a few individuals, but by thousands or even hundreds of thousands of stockholders. In several conspicuous instances, no single stockholder owned more than a small fraction of the stock. Actually, however, the large body of stockholders did not control the enterprise which they nominally owned. Control was largely separated from ownership.[6] In many cases, the management had no real responsibility to anyone except the board of directors, and the latter had no real responsibility to those who should have been, but usually were not, most interested in the enterprise.

"Finance capitalism" or "banker control" represented another highly significant factor in the organization and administration of private enterprise, particularly in the railroad and steel industries. This form of control was more or less hidden from the public; and it also tended to concentrate, thus giving rise to the popular conception of a "money trust." This phenomenon was made the subject of congressional investigation early in this period and also figured in legislation. Banking control not only was a form or phase of private economic power, but it also exercised an influence over industrial policies, an influence which on the whole tended to conserve assets rather than encourage technological innovations and managerial initiative. In this aspect of the matter lies much of the

[6] Adolf Berle and Gardiner C. Means, *The Modern Corporation and Private Property* (1933), pp. 47-118.

explanation of Henry Ford's determination to keep himself independent of the bankers. In the popular mind, the role that the banks played in industrial reorganization and financing appeared to be a piratical one—that of a small wealthy group profiting enormously and unjustifiably, if not immorally, from the manipulation of "other people's money."

With respect to the organization of the productive process, a number of industrial concerns sought to give labor a voice in industrial management, or at least an incentive to act with understanding and moderation. Most, if not all, of such efforts occurred in the operating departments; and no attempt was made on any important scale to give to labor authority in the determination of corporation policies.[7]

The political significance of class feeling was problematical.

In spite of the foregoing, it is impossible to say that the private holders of economic power and their retainers had definitely crystallized into a politically significant class. Such crystallization had been prevented or postponed by the peculiar social and economic conditions of American life, along with the growth and influence of political democracy. That there were classes and that class conflict was inevitable was recognized in the beginning and thereafter was repeatedly made clear by events. It was difficult, however, to identify by any simple rules those who constituted any particular class.

The "upper," "capitalist," or "plutocratic" class was evidently a small minority.[8] It may be inferred that the leaders of this class were likely to be the directors and salaried executives in industry, rather than the investors and owners. An analysis made in 1932

[7] On co-operation between industrial management and labor, see Louis Aubrey Wood, *Union-Management Cooperation on the Railroads* (1931); Earl J. Miller, *Workmen's Representation in Industrial Government* (1922); W. Jett Lauck, *Political and Industrial Democracy* (1926); Sumner H. Slichter, *Union Policies and Industrial Management* (1941).

[8] There were in 1929 about 2 million "income recipients" who were not reported as gainfully employed. Some of these derived their livelihood from pensions and family contributions; but most of them were presumably living on income from investments. The number deriving either the whole or a part of their incomes from investments is of course much larger, including a substantial portion of all those gainfully employed.

of several thousand business leaders indicated that vertical mobility of persons between classes was decreasing.[9] A slightly lessened ability to rise from the bottom to the top may have been due in part to the fact that industry was no longer expanding in the same way as formerly; but it may also have been due in some measure to a reduced supply within the laboring class of those qualities which formerly won economic advancement.[10] It would seem, moreover, that urban industrialism was placing the majority of laboring class families in an environment that discouraged the development of those qualities and the obtaining of that kind of education which won business success.

Industrial leadership revealed deficiencies.

One cannot doubt that among the industrialists and the wealthy there was in this period an insufficient realization of social responsibility and a lack of desire to understand the viewpoints of laborers, farmers, politicians, or consumers in general. The thinking, like the social life, of those who possessed economic power tended to be, in too great measure, exclusive, in-growing, and arrogant. They seemed to be, however, far from possessing a consensus of feeling regarding their economic interests and just as far from an uncompromising attitude regarding their relations with other classes and with the government. Partly because of law and partly because of an aroused civic conscience in the country, standards of business ethics tended, in certain respects, to improve; and the relations between industry and government became less corrupt. The exploitative, robber-baron type of industrial leader tended to be supplanted by the administrative or managerial type.

The development and effective expression of private economic statesmanship were retarded by diffusion of power and responsibility, as well as by other conditions. When applied to the office or the plant, American genius for organization, allied with technical invention and skills, introduced remarkable efficiency into manage-

[9] F. W. Taussig and C. S. Joslyn, *American Business Leaders* (1932), pp. 39-40.
[10] On the possible draining away of talent from the lower classes, see Edward McChesney Sait, *Democracy* (1929), pp. 18-21.

ment and operations. Undoubtedly, the ablest executives and administrators, as a rule, were still in the business world; and, when they had the incentive and the power to organize and could deal with tangible things, they did an admirable job. Industry was developing its own subordinate intelligentsia in the form of research departments; but these were largely technical. An increasing proportion of business leaders were college graduates; but, for the leadership and control of industry, a university or professional education was not yet considered indispensable. Industrial leadership remained in too great measure technical, financial, or manipulative.

Relations between government and industry
tended toward a higher plane.

With respect to the working relations between industry and government, businessmen still in general held aloof from politics; governmental controls were extended but not for the most part in a hostile, punitive, or demagogic spirit; and during and after the First World War a substantial co-operative relationship existed between government and industrial leadership.

A change in the political activities of business interests came about as a result of the muckraking campaign of the early years of the century, the attacks made by Theodore Roosevelt on "malefactors of great wealth," the constitutional amendment providing for direct election of United States senators, and the enactment throughout the country of direct primary laws and other laws concerned with electoral and legislative practices. Increasing governmental regulation of industry, promoted by organized groups, also helped to convince industrial leaders that the old under-cover methods were no longer sufficient or safe. Individual corporations and trade associations, representing sections of industry, propagandized, as well as lobbied, but usually within the narrow field of a particular interest and for the purpose of protecting or increasing profits. A striking example of business propaganda and pressure was provided by the activities of electric and gas utilities. According to the Federal Trade Commission, this campaign, "measured by quantity, extent, and cost, . . . was probably the greatest peace-time propaganda campaign ever conducted by private interests in this country."[11]

A general absence of antagonism between political and economic power, especially during the latter part of this period, is not to be explained simply by saying that "big business controlled government." The dominant sections of public opinion were reasonably well satisfied with the workings of the private enterprise system.

OTHER GROUPS

Other groups that call for discussion include labor, agriculture, the middle classes, cities, sections and regions.

Labor lost militancy.

The number of industrial wage earners continued to increase; and, partly as a phase of industrial conflict and partly because of friendly governmental policy, trade-union membership more than doubled between 1910 and 1920.

Early in 1918 the American Federation of Labor and the National Industrial Conference Board,[12] called into conference by President Wilson, agreed on a set of principles to govern industrial relations during the war. War orders increased the demand for labor; and favorable factors in the war situation continued until the depression of 1920-22. Afterward, industrial expansion brought rising wages. Great corporations established personnel departments, which cultivated good relations with the workers. In the twenties, according to Lescohier, the doctrine of the "economy of high wages" became "respectable, even orthodox." This doctrine was that as industry became more productive through technological improvements and greater efficiency wages should be raised.[13]

Organized labor turned from militant policies to less spectacular activities. Through the development of various services to its members, it became to some extent a well-to-do business enterprise; and it continued, but more conservatively, to work as a nonpartisan

[11] *Utility Corporations*, S. Doc. 92, 70 Cong. 1 sess., Pt. 71-A.

[12] The National Industrial Conference Board, organized in 1916, included in its membership representatives of industrial associations, certain business executives, and some educators, scientists, and financiers.

[13] Commons, *History of Labor in the United States*, Vol. 3, pp. 88-92.

pressure group for social and economic legislation. After the war, aroused by the revolutionary communism of Soviet Russia, reacting from the emotionalism of the war period, and lulled by prosperity, Americans generally set their minds against "radicalism." Organized labor shared and expressed this general feeling. The American Federation of Labor, with which about 80 per cent of union members were affiliated, was organized in the main on the craft basis; and the large mass of unskilled laborers had comparatively little representation in its councils. Union membership steadily decreased.

If labor was a class, it was, like capital, a highly amorphous one. Its members did not possess or feel a clear identity of economic interest. Labor was neither completely unionized, psychologically homogeneous, nor politically unified. The philosophy of skilled labor was middle class.

Agriculture prospered, then declined.

During the years from 1896 to 1914 agricultural prices rose. Industrial expansion and urbanism produced a steady improvement in the condition of the farmer, with the result that in 1914 he had attained a more satisfactory economic position than ever before in time of peace. The First World War greatly increased the demand for and the prices of farm products and raised farm income to unprecedented levels. But this enhanced prosperity was short-lived. With the return of European lands to agricultural productivity, exports of American farm products declined. War prices, joined with other factors, had led the farmer to incur further indebtedness; and postwar price deflation once again increased the burden of his debt. Expanding functions and costs of government imposed on real property a tax burden that was growing constantly heavier. Mortgage foreclosure and tax delinquencies increased. In 1929 a substantial portion of the low-income group was found among the farmers.

Mechanized farming increased the output per farm worker; and a substantial absolute decline took place in the farm population, with a considerable abandonment of farms or their diversion to nonagricultural uses. The proportion of farms operated by tenants increased from 35.3 per cent in 1900 to 42.4 in 1930; and the influence of urbanism produced a marked development of agricultural specialization.[14]

A drastic change had taken place in the fundamental conditions of American life. An economic development based on territorial expansion and on a speculative and exploitative utilization of soil resources was no longer possible. The flowering of industrialism and the fading of the frontier marked the passing of the economic self-sufficiency of the rural family and the rural community. Increase of tenantry and migration of young people from the farms to the cities sapped at the wholesomeness and integrity of farm and rural life. Those who continued to depend on agriculture were now, more than ever before, caught in the toils of a system which became constantly more complex and obscure. That individualism which had traditionally characterized the American farmer was not only being undermined but it was also becoming increasingly inappropriate. Not only was the farmer feeling the impact of industry, but agriculture, in a sense and to an extent, was becoming industrialized; and it was revealing, like industry, the need of organization and external controls.

Adopting corporation techniques, farmers experimented on a fairly large scale with co-operative marketing. National organizations, such as the American Farm Bureau Federation, the Grange, and the Farmers' Union, served to some extent as channels for co-operative activity and generally as means of carrying on discussion, as vehicles of leadership, and as pressure groups. A large number of technical agricultural associations appeared. In addition, a number of organizations were bringing intellectual and scientific leadership to the problems of agricultural and rural life.[15]

But private action was not sufficient. The agricultural problem, as it appeared to those who felt its direct effects, was one of extreme and baffling complexity, interwoven with the whole economic problem, and dependent for its solution on many factors that were not strictly agricultural. The traditions of economic freedom, individual

[14] See Leverett S. Lyon and Victor Abramson, *Government and Economic Life*, Vol. 2 (1940), pp. 864-904.
[15] Examples of these were the American Country Life Association, the American Farm Economics Association, and the Rural Sociological Society.

initiative, and personal independence had been nourished by pioneer life. Now, the conditions that surrounded agricultural enterprise caused the farmers to think more of security than of liberty, more of immediate and tangible relief than of ultimate adjustments to be brought about by economic "laws."

But the farmers did not feel as a class either separate, allied to labor, or in conflict with capital. The man who was both owner and operator was capitalist and manager as well as laborer. Sometimes his larger interests seemed to be identical with those of the urban worker; but more often they were antagonistic. The tenant and the "hired man" were more analogous to the industrial wage earner; but their thinking was conditioned by a different environment and a different employer-employee relationship.

*America became more than
ever middle class.*

More important than industry or labor were the middle classes— traders, small businessmen, many of those engaged in the service industries, professional men and women, "white-collar" workers, artists, public employees, and others devoted to scientific, cultural, and informational activities. The middle classes were always and everywhere numerous enough to constitute a balance of power, if not an actual majority. Most of the farmers and a substantial number of skilled workers were properly included in these intermediate groups.[16]

In the urban middle classes thrift was still a practicable virtue. As investors, their interests would tend to be identified with "big business," at least so long as dividends and interest were paid and savings protected. On the other hand, a considerable portion of the middle classes might be aligned either with labor or capital, depending on interests, sympathies, or contacts.

The urban middle classes now represented in large measure the sources of American leadership. Generally speaking, the children of middle-class families grew up in a relatively wholesome environment. They escaped both great riches and extreme poverty. Educa-

---

[16] For instructive and stimulating essays on the role of the middle classes in American political history, see Arthur N. Holcombe, *The Middle Classes in American Politics* (1940).

tional advantages were open to them; and they could exercise wide freedom in the choice of a career. On them, adaptation and adjustment worked most fruitfully. There was a time when the potential leader was a farm boy or a worker's apprentice; but after 1900 it was evident that the production of intellectual, social, and political leadership had become much more largely a function of the urban middle classes.

The middle-class attitude apparently characterized a substantial majority of the population. It was a balanced attitude. As a rule it was inclined to see both sides of the question. It tended toward viewing things whole. It made an effort at least to consider the general welfare. On political and economic matters it was, in the main, progressively conservative.

Urbanization proceeded, with significant shifts in population.

The census of 1920 revealed that the nation had become more urban than rural. The urban population, however, was not uniformly distributed over the country; and the rural states outnumbered the urban. Rural predominance remained a sectional characteristic of the South and the West.

The shifting of population just referred to represented in large part a migration from the farms to the cities primarily and to villages and small towns secondarily.[17] The migration from farm to city was selective, though not in the same sense as the colonizing or pioneering movements. Many migrants from the farms swelled the ranks of unskilled labor in the cities. On the other hand, it appeared that those who were leaving the farms included, in relatively large number, those young people who were equipped by intelligence, character, and education to exercise economic and political leadership. This same type of selective migration was also intersectional, moving from West to East and from South to North. Thus, the cities seemed to be either producing or attracting the best of the potential leadership in the country.

On the other hand, the labor element bulked large in the indus-

---

[17] The rural nonfarm population, found chiefly in villages and small towns, increased about 18 per cent. O. E. Baker, "Rural and Urban Distribution of the Population in the United States," *The Annals*, Vol. 188 (1936), pp. 264-79.

trial cities; and this element, in part alien to the ways of rural America, possessed doubtful political qualities and attitudes. Of the 14 million gainful workers in the manufacturing and mechanical industries, more than half were in seven states.[18] Of the 13 million white gainful workers in these industries, more than 25 per cent were foreign born; and the bulk of the foreign-born workers were from southern and eastern Europe. Immigration from that part of the world had virtually been stopped for several years, but the percentage of foreign born in 1930 was high in all of the industrial states, as well as in Montana, Arizona, Nevada, Washington, and California. Generally speaking, it was low in the agricultural states of the West and it was practically negligible in the South.

The city harbored all elements of society—except the immediately agricultural—in all aspects, extremes, and relationships. Social maladjustments, conflicts, stresses, and strains were both congenital and acquired in urban life. The personalities, interests, and attitudes of city residents were diverse. They were herded in an artificial and mechanized environment that accentuated individualistic competition but demanded at the same time adaptation and co-operation.

The city was a section as well as a group. In states and regions appeared a recognized divergence or conflict between urban interests and rural interests, as well as a contrast between the manners, attitudes, and morals of the city and the country. This differentiation, by no means new, had certain political consequences; but, in some respects, previous distinctions between the rural and the urban were becoming blurred. Some of the formerly characteristic aspects of the urban way of living had now become in a measure the possession of the countryside, thanks to rural free delivery, the telephone, paved roads, the automobile, the radio, and the consolidated school.[19] On the other hand, the city was endeavoring to capture

[18] Mass., N.Y., N.J., Pa., Ohio, Ill., and Mich.

[19] This assimilation of rural to city life should not be treated as an accomplished fact. It was only a trend. In 1930, more than one-third of all farms in the United States were located on unimproved dirt roads and only about 3 per cent on concrete roads; slightly more than one-third of all farms reported telephones; only 15.8 per cent reported water piped into dwelling house; only 8.4 per cent reported water piped into bathroom; and 13.4 per cent reported dwelling house lighted by electricity.

some of the advantages of country life, through the use of the automobile, better planned suburbs, better housing, parks and playgrounds, elimination of slums, and provision of more space, more privacy, more quiet, and more beauty. Perhaps, in the things of most value city and country were becoming more alike. Certainly, they were intermingling.

Sectionalism receded and regionalism emerged.

Either sectionalism or regionalism is an expression of population reacting to geography.[20] After the Civil War, the reactions had more complex causes and more complex and varied objectives. Since 1900 it has become more necessary than before to distinguish between the two terms. The term "sectionalism" may be used to describe a particularistic political attitude that has territorial bounds, while "regionalism" refers to a geographically bounded set of problems. Sectionalism looks at government; government looks at regionalism.[21]

Broadly speaking and without any attempt at fine distinctions, one might have divided the United States in 1929 into four sections, which roughly coincided with regions: the Northeast, the Southeast, the West, and the Pacific Coast or Far West.[22] No section or region had a monopoly of any one characteristic or interest.

[20] On regional geography, see Isaiah Bowman, *Geography in Relation to the Social Sciences* (1934), pp. 144-99.

[21] On the distinction between "regionalism" and "sectionalism," see National Resources Committee, *Regional Factors in National Planning and Development* (1935), p. viii and footnote; Howard W. Odum, *Southern Regions of the United States* (1936), pp. 253-59. Sectionalism may be defined as a regional state of mind opposed to complete national solidarity. Sectionalism may or may not be one of the common characteristics of a region of uniformity.

[22] On this basis, the Northeast would include all states north of the Potomac and Ohio and east of the Mississippi; the Southeast, all south of the Potomac and Ohio and east of the Mississippi, with Arkansas and Louisiana; the West, everything west of the Mississippi, except Arkansas, Louisiana, and the Pacific Coast region; and the latter, Washington, Oregon, California, and Nevada. Odum found six great regions of comparative uniformity. Bryce classified the states into five groups: the Northeastern or New England states; the Middle states; the Northwestern states; the Southern states; and the states of the Pacific slope. In distinguishing regional types of opinion, he selected four groups: the East, the West, the Pacific slope, and the South. James Bryce, *The American Commonwealth* (new ed., 1921), Vol. 2, pp. 311-20.

Each might be broken up into subsections or subregions which resembled outside areas more than the territory in which they were located.

The result of the Civil War and the subsequent gradual unification of the nation, along with governmental centralization, made persons with common interests and common demands more disposed to act through organizations that were more or less national than through admittedly sectional representatives, though political representation was still in effect sectional. On the other hand, specialization and technology increased the need of regional administration, as in the case of electric power development.

CONSERVATION

The American spirit applied to America's resources had produced amazing material developments. On the other side of the ledger appeared results and by-products that as time passed became more clearly perceptible and more thoroughly disturbing. The nation's capital resources—its forests, minerals, soil, wild life, and scenery—were being recklessly depleted. Man's outstanding creations—the great cities—were distinguished less by convenience, health, and beauty than by disorder, ugliness, and disease. The consciousness of nationality made Americans think more comprehensively of their country. Transportation and communication facilities extended the area of acquaintance and lessened provincialism. Social and economic research gave publicity to facts previously concealed or overlooked. Humanitarianism extended its range to embrace, not only the income of the people but also their assets, not only their individual well-being but also their physical and cultural environment and their responsibility to the future.

The opinion created by a converging of several forces had appeared intermittently and sporadically over many decades. The conception of order, conservation, protection, and organization and the desire for these things appeared as soon as a class or section acquired position and property. As the "ordered fringe" on the Atlantic coast widened westward, the demand for social thrift became more vocal. The kind of urbanism that had developed stimulated a new interest in country life, in travel, recreation, and outdoor sports. Moreover, agricultural conditions in the West compelled attention to such problems as soil exhaustion, aridity, forestry, and grazing.

THE STATE OF OPINION

When society was rural and economic life simple, when government attempted to do little and did much of that locally, the individual citizen, himself an all-round person, could to a considerable extent experience and see his own and the community's problems, and appraise personally the responsiveness and effectiveness of government. Times had now changed.

Public problems, more complex and remote,
baffled the individual.

Familiar conceptions expanded beyond the grasp of the ordinary individual. Property was taking on intangible forms and becoming a bundle of legal rights rather than a physical possession. Thrift was still an understandable maxim; but means of saving were no longer intimately related to ends. Taxation was increasingly indirect, making it more difficult for the individual to measure his tax burden or to trace the ramifications of tax policy.[23]

The equipment and opportunity of the individual were inadequate "to deal with so much subtlety, so much variety, so many permutations and combinations."[24] The individual tended more and more to be a specialist.[25] For adult citizens in general, occupation and recreation left little time for reading, study, or reflection. Getting a living not only took time and strength but exacted its

[23] "The world that we have to deal with politically is out of reach, out of sight, out of mind. It has to be explored, reported, and imagined. Man is no Aristotelian god contemplating all existence at one glance. He is the creature of an evolution who can just about span a sufficient portion of reality to manage his survival, and snatch what on the scale of time are but a few moments of insight and happiness." Walter Lippmann, *Public Opinion* (1922), p. 29.

[24] The same, p. 16.

[25] "[The] more you specialize people, the more power you can obtain over them, the more helpless and in consequence the more obedient they are. . . .

"The ideally 'free man' would be the man *least* specialized, the *least* stereotyped, the man approximating to the *fewest* classes, the *least* clamped into a system—in a word, the most individual. But a society of 'free men,' if such a thing could ever come about, which it certainly could not, would immediately collapse." Wyndham Lewis, *The Art of Being Ruled* (1926), p. 172.

nervous toll. In large numbers, the people were almost totally diverted from the consideration of public problems. To traditions, prejudices, "stereotypes," symbols, and other more or less non-rational responses and habits, the individual was conditioned by his parents and environment; and these compensated for his inadequacy while sustaining it.

Social organization, elaborating, tended to specialization.

It was obvious from the start that individuals needed and craved leadership and that popular government, in order to function, had to have it. The political party had been looked upon as an effective and decisive intermediary between individuals and the government. But the party was a transformer rather than a generator. It had to follow rather than lead.

Notable features of associational activity during this period were the rapidity and extent of its organization on a national basis. A considerable majority of the national organizations in existence in 1930 had been established after 1900. Associational development, therefore, was concurrent with that of industrial organization, increase of population and of urbanism, growth of governmental functions, and the elaboration of research and of more extensive as well as more specialized study in general. Some of the associations had general and broad objectives;[26] others were restricted but non-technical in purpose;[27] while others, also in the main nontechnical, were organized for the promotion or combating of some idea or condition.[28] Yet the majority of the new associations were technically or intellectually specialized, representing in some cases subdivisions or new branches of old professions, and, in other cases, the appearance of new technical specialties.

To a considerable extent, associations grouped themselves according to classes. In the middle classes, however, and largely under middle-class control, were found most of the associations that performed services, stimulated discussion, encouraged and supported

---

[26] For example, the National League of Women Voters.

[27] For example, the American Civil Liberties Union.

[28] Varied examples were the Ku Klux Klan, the Anti-Saloon League, the League to Enforce Peace, and the National Security League.

study of public problems, and otherwise aimed to promote social progress. While associations as a whole pointed to the incompleteness of social stratification, there was little associational overlapping between capital and labor.

Some groups focused, accentuated, and perpetuated non-rationality. Other groups were able, by pooling the resources of individuals, to command the services of experts, conduct research, and disseminate both objective information and reasoned conclusions. Associations were not as numerous as were individual diversifications. In the aggregate, however, they gave a fair picture of the special interests, the special skills, and the special aspirations of individuals. By pooling the resources of its members and contributors, or by obtaining a grant from a foundation, an association equipped itself within its special field to make that part of the environment understandable to those who were seeking understanding.

A considerable portion of the population, however, received little or none of this expert guidance. Many were associated only with certain primary or "natural" groupings, such as the family, neighborhood, or "gang," while no individual could really "belong" to or participate in a sufficient number of specialized associations to give him a comprehensive and balanced understanding of public problems.

Nationally, as well as locally, the multiplying of organizations seemed to spell not merely disintegration but also a considerable amount of overlapping and duplication. The situation was in a measure corrected by conferences, co-ordinating bodies, and federations. Generally speaking, however, each association or conference brought into relief only one part or aspect of the social environment. The problems they severally attacked were interrelated and could only be solved by some form of integrated thinking, in which the pros and cons of each relevant question were brought together and considered.

Local discussion, if not decreasing, was
losing ability to integrate opinions.

Some writers of the time wished to create or re-create in modern

America conditions in which thinking and discussion might be active, integrated, and purposive on the local level.[29] In many localities discussion groups were active, taking the form of community centers, citizens' associations, and forums, but their total effectiveness appears to have been limited. In general, the trouble was that America no longer had many neighborhoods or small communities that were themselves integrated, in which the main occupations, interests, and points of view were all resident. Was it possible to find anywhere in one neighborhood skilled and unskilled workers, farmers, professional men, small businessmen, and corporation executives? If such a neighborhood could be found, would each of its residents have a similar stock of facts?

*Expansion, diversification, and commercialization
of communication facilities continued.*

Mail was now delivered daily to practically every urban and rural home. Air mail service began in 1918. To the telegraph system was added commercial wireless communication. The number of telephones per thousand of population increased almost ten times between 1900 and 1930.[30] Two other technological developments, the moving picture and the radio, were showing even greater possibilities as instruments of mass communication.

In the large-scale formation of opinion, the newspaper remained the most important medium. Its editorial influence was apparently declining, but not its potentialities as a purveyor of facts and a carrier of publicity. The newspaper was a commercial undertaking; and, while aggregate daily circulation rose, the number of newspapers tended to decrease, mainly through consolidations, producing more local newspaper monopolies. While avowedly partisan organs were fewer, the press tended to reflect the interests and ideas of business, big and little, and of the middle classes.

Whatever partiality and standardization existed in the daily press was to some extent counterbalanced by an increasing number of weekly, monthly, and quarterly periodicals. In addition, technical journals and scientific reviews were, or attempted to be, dispas-

---

[29] For this view see M. P. Follett, *The New State* (1918).
[30] *Recent Social Trends*, Vol. 1, pp. 192-98.

sionate and impersonal. An enormous volume of publications issued from specialized organizations.[31]

Propaganda revealed
special problems.

The inadequacy of local face-to-face discussion was being partially compensated for by mass-communication means that were quick and practically national in scope. These served a clear need. When the community expanded, when its members could no longer meet for face-to-face discussion, when their problems became complicated and confused, when difficult alternatives presented themselves, then the opportunity came for varied, multiplied, and accelerated communication of facts and ideas. Publicity became more intense as the occupations and interests of individuals diverged, as specialization increased, as classes developed, as political, economic, and social privileges became unequally distributed, as tensions appeared, and as demands for readjustments pressed. The multifarious organizations just referred to and their voluminous, often conflicting, and frequently misleading propaganda were ways of adapting discussion to a large and heterogenous society, controlled by popular elections, but handicapped by individual inadequacies.

Organization, propaganda, and pressures were increasing, not only because the requisite communication facilities were available, but also because democratic government in the United States was vastly extending its scope and functions. It was expected to solve all manner of social problems and to resolve the more critical social conflicts. Another important cause was the existence of an economic surplus, available in part for the expenses of publicity, of group organization, and group representation. Another factor was publicly supported education, which had made the population almost universally literate. The United States had highly developed propaganda and pressures because it was huge, literate, dynamic, wealthy, complex, highly governmentalized, and, at least in form, democratically governed.

[31] See *Recent Social Trends*, Vol. 1, p. 204; Malcolm M. Willey and Stuart A. Rice, *Communication Agencies and Social Life* (1933).

Propaganda,[32] that is, large-scale publicity, was not a new or an evil thing. It had been from the beginning an important aspect of political life. It was now developing increased volume and apparently greater influence; but there was no reason to think that, in volume or energy, popular discussion in the form of propaganda or otherwise was excessive. Moreover, propaganda could not be conducted on a high intellectual and moral plane, for the reason that people in the mass had not yet risen to that plane.

Yet, certain aspects of propaganda, as it was carried on during this period, revealed dangers. The authors and sources of propaganda could now, more easily than in the past, hide their identities and motives. The commercial ownership and operation of media of propaganda presented the possibility of intentional and self-interested restrictions on freedom of discussion; and the spatial and mechanical limitations of the facilities made a measure of suppression and discrimination unavoidable. The expense of large-scale publicity discouraged its use except by those having ample financial resources, including those having special interests to serve. Finally, it was more than ever possible, through modern propaganda, to work on mass suggestibility.

Propaganda was a means of pressure,[33] and pressure the ulti-

---

[32] Propaganda, as the term is here used, means publicity designed to influence public opinion or public action. For other definitions, see Frederick E. Lumley, *The Propaganda Menace* (1933), p. 44; Leonard W. Doob and Edward S. Robinson, "Psychology and Propaganda," *The Annals*, Vol. 179 (1935), p. 88; Edward L. Bernays, *Propaganda* (1928), p. 20; Institute for Propaganda Analysis, Inc., *Propaganda: How to Recognize It and Deal with It* (1938), p. 3; George E. Gordon Catlin, "Propaganda as a Function of Democratic Government," in Harwood L. Childs (ed.), *Propaganda and Dictatorship* (1936), p. 127; Childs, "Pressure Groups and Propaganda," in Edward B. Logan (ed.), *The American Political Scene* (1936), pp. 205-42; Marie Swabey, *Theory of the Democratic State* (1937), p. 120.

On propaganda in general, see Lasswell, "The Study and Practice of Propaganda" in Harold D. Lasswell, Ralph D. Casey, and Bruce L. Smith, *Propaganda and Promotional Activities: An Annotated Bibliography* (1935), pp. 3-27.

[33] Pressure, if it is to be distinguished from propaganda, may be viewed as a systematic attempt by an individual or individuals to enforce his or their will directly upon the government or upon some private group. Pressure communicates will, rather than opinion; its primary purpose is to compel, rather than persuade. Pressure, thus viewed, attempts to bind the individual with little or no regard for the merits of the question. While its purpose at times may be to force consideration of both sides of a question, its aim is usually one-sided and its effect frequently is to estop discussion.

mate purpose of propaganda. The specialized and interest groups were, in general, pressure groups. Lobbying, the spearhead of pressure, was, like propaganda, an old and unavoidable, even democratic, phenomenon. When lobbying first became a conspicuous and malodorous influence, it was largely in the hands of representatives of industrial corporations; and the methods used at that time were generally corrupt. With the organization of other interests and aims, lobbying rose to a somewhat higher moral plane. In time, most groups lobbied, whenever the practice seemed necessary.

Propaganda and pressure, as they were practiced, did not counteract either particularism or materialism. The people wanted leadership; and to meet the requirements of efficient democracy, their leadership needed to be balanced, integrated, and concerned with the co-ordination of ideas and demands with ideals and principles and with the implications of the general welfare. Outside government and the party system, the American people had so many specialized leaders that, in the most fundamental and important matters, they were practically leaderless. Yet public opinion, in whatever partial or distorted form it might appear, had gathered enormous force and worked a correspondingly profound effect on the intelligence and morals of the government that bowed to that force.[34]

*America developed its institutional sources
of intellectual leadership.*

To the conditions just described education was widely held to offer the surest corrective; and, in any event, it was expected to supply a high quality of leadership.

Transformation and extension of educational facilities, noteworthy after the Civil War, now gathered momentum.[35] Means were devised to bring education to larger numbers.[36] The locality

---

[34] *The American Commonwealth* (new ed., 1921), Vol. 2, p. 365.

[35] Characteristics of this development were: more institutions of all kinds; increased diversification and specialization in courses of study and among teachers; improved equipment; greater attention to vocational training; shifting of emphasis from classical studies to scientific and "practical" courses; application of new scientific techniques to the understanding of children, guidance of young people, and evaluation of methods and subjects; and, in general, among educators and in the schools, a reorientation toward the ideal of social service.

[36] For example, parent education, evening classes, adult education, correspondence

and the layman were still educational forces; but the system was falling more and more under specialized and professional control, a control that increasingly emanated from state and national centers, both public and private.

Between 1900 and 1930 a remarkable increase occurred in the enrollment of students in educational institutions, particularly in the high schools, colleges, and universities. Graduate work in the institutions of higher learning expanded in scope and the number of doctors of philosophy multiplied. Correlated with teaching and graduate study, research came steadily to occupy a more important place among the university's functions.

It appeared that education was becoming, on the one hand, more democratic and, on the other, a more potent force in the realization and functioning of democracy. From the social and political points of view, educational progress in the true sense of the word was undoubtedly taking place; but it was accompanied by a swelling chorus of criticism directed at educational purposes, policies, and methods. The schools were dominated by the spirit of the age, indeed very largely by the spirit of a preceding age. Apart entirely from the influence of the teachers, the attitudes of students were more or less fixed by the environment; and the school was only one, and probably not the most potent, of the environmental influences. At a fairly early stage in the process the attention and training of the student was directed to a specialty, and, in a majority of cases, to an occupational rather than a cultural one, to private rather than public duties. Finally, the educational process was to such a degree formalized and standardized that many questioned the reality as well as the extent of its effect on either the individual mind or citizenship in general.

The development of universities, as well as of the specialized associations previously discussed, represented a considerable use of national wealth and income for the creation and implementing of intellectual leadership. Financial support not provided by taxation took the form of a vast number of contributions from private individuals. Technological productivity seemed sufficient to sustain

---

and extension courses, vacation and summer schools, classes for the handicapped, and the like.

an increasing class of intellectual workers, devoted to solving the problems and controlling the society that technology had created. If the intellectual resources of society were adequate to the task, and if the system by which funds were organized and administered resulted in a genuine utilization of those resources, then technological society might indeed be pulling itself up by its own bootstraps.

Outside the universities and institutions appeared the foundation, fund, or trust, concerned in the main with the making of grants from funds entrusted to it. Concurrently with the development of social research and social action by the universities and fund-granting foundations, independent organizations were established for research and public service.[37]

Science offered a spirit and a method
for improving public leadership.

Accompanying the educational advances just referred to and strongly influencing them, the scientific spirit and method were becoming a significant factor in government. Until the nineteenth century those who practiced science were in the main isolated individuals whose achievements were exceptional; and the scientific way of learning and thinking ordinarily met with distrust or condemnation from intellectual and political authorities and from the people. Only during the relatively brief span of years measured by the constitutional history of the United States were the spirit and method of science generally accepted as safe and salutary; and it was only during a shorter and more recent period that science became a major social influence.

Science—in its broadest sense, a will to be mentally free—spelled the rebirth in a new form of the spirit of liberty. In this broad sense, it was also a moral standard compelling intellectual honesty. Science was also a method, a way of handling and treating facts, a procedure for finding and validating the truth. Whether engaged in experimentation or observation, the scientist attempted to keep

[37] Familiar examples of these were the Russell Sage Foundation, the New York Bureau of Municipal Research (later the National Institute of Public Administration and now the Institute of Administration, affiliated with Columbia University), the Brookings Institution, and the National Bureau of Economic Research.

his own mind, like his microscope or his test-tube, an untainted instrument of truth-seeking, free of prejudices and unwarranted assumptions.

Science, pure and applied, was a tremendous stimulant of industrial technology. The resulting industrial transformations were so extensive and so rapid as to produce a profound psychological impression throughout the whole structure of society. Because the most impressive inventions and discoveries were those that could be seen and used and because technological improvement led to industrial development, the effect was to make industry continually more attractive to those with ability and ambition, including those with talent for scientific work. Of the impressive sum spent on research during this period, the greater part went to technical, physical, and biological studies, though the trend was to give relatively more to social projects.

Then, too, as science became influential and symbolic, it ran the risk of becoming the servant rather than the master of social leadership; and the garb of science was worn by an increasing number of charlatans and self-seekers.[38]

Scientific leadership in government showed
possibilities and limitations.

The method and spirit of science were being taken over with enthusiasm by those who devoted themselves to social studies. While private associations, such as those already mentioned, were conducting research into certain social, economic, and political problems, and an increasing amount of such research was being carried on by government, the universities accounted for the greater part of it; and their position in the field was strategic and commanding. Their scholars were united professionally and their work was to some extent standardized, co-ordinated, and guided by

[38] The public function of science, said Wyndham Lewis, was "to conceal the human mind that manipulates it, or that manipulates, through it, other people. For in its impersonality and its 'scientific detachment' it is an ideal cloak for the personal human will. Through it that will can operate with a godlike inscrutability that no other expedient can give. It enables man to operate as though he were nature on other men. In the name of science people can be almost without limit bamboozled and managed." *The Art of Being Ruled*, p. 44.

organizations.[39] The American Political Science Association was organized in 1904; and various specialized organizations were established, such as the National Tax Association and the American Municipal Association (in addition to the National Municipal League). Altogether, the period witnessed remarkable expansion, stimulation, and systematization of research in social, economic, and governmental problems.

Moreover, encouragement was to be found in the increasing personal activity of university and other scientific men in government and in public discussion and in the rapid development of agencies for the diffusion of economic and social information. Illustrations of this latter trend appeared in the greater number and activity of college presses, of associations, foundations, and institutions that disseminated scientific findings, and of agencies through which social scientists exchanged views on public problems.

All these developments indicated a relative as well as absolute growth in the quantity and improvement in the quality of intellectual leadership. One might easily have come to the conclusion at the end of this period that the quantity and quality were sufficient and that, if public opinion and governmental action were inefficient, the causes were inherent in the people and in the nature of public problems. To a large extent, the difficulties were inherent and certain to be of long standing. Democracy itself requires that general policies shall be determined by the people, not by an intellectual élite, even though it be assumed that an intellectual élite is always right. But public problems, especially those calling for governmental action, are of such a nature that the most competent of political scientists cannot be sure of his correctness, or sure in time.

[39] First among these organizations were the learned societies. These in turn were represented in and to some extent co-ordinated by the Social Science Research Council. Individuals working in different social sciences were also meeting in other organizations; for example, the American Association for the Advancement of Science and the American Council of Learned Societies. A measure of co-ordination and standardization, in administration if not in research, was achieved also by the national and regional associations of universities and colleges, by the Association of University Professors and similar organizations, as well as by certain foundations, notably the Carnegie Foundation for the Advancement of Teaching and the General Education Board.

*Attacks on freedom of speech and
of thought persisted.*

Intolerance was nothing new in America. During the Revolution, the Tories had been intimidated. Afterward, popular action had been taken against both "Democrats" and "Jacobins." Still later, extra-legal measures had been used to deny Abolitionists their rights of assembly, petition, and free speech. The Know-Nothing party before the Civil War had demonstrated the strength of feeling against Catholics and aliens.

Between 1900 and the depression, the existence of popular intolerance was again manifested on a number of occasions and on an extensive scale. For several years the Ku Klux Klan, in its second materialization, enjoyed in a number of states substantial political power. It was secret, intolerant, irrational. Its activities were directed at specific groups of the population—Negroes, Jews, and Catholics. Other examples were the religious issue in the campaign of 1928, the war hysteria, and concerted efforts to suppress "radicalism" after the war.

CHANGING IDEALS

The agrarian democratizing movement mentioned in the preceding chapter did not run its course until the middle of this period; but the democratic ideal seemed to be already in partial eclipse.

From various intellectual sources came influences that affected political thinking. Karl Marx had stated many years before the ideas of economic determinism, class conflict, and proletarian dictatorship, ideas that subordinated the role of individualism in social change. While his doctrines were not necessarily anti-democratic in the political sense, they were quite contrary to the American conception of democracy. Moreover, when historians examined the process by which American institutions and policies had been created, these were found to be predominantly of economic origin. Later, a "debunking" literature proceeded to destroy many cherished illusions about American historical figures. This rewriting of history and biography may have been desirable; but its immediate effect on many minds, one may suspect, was to promote a cynical attitude toward some of our political habituations.

The influence of Darwin had been concurrent with that of Marx. Darwin's work failed to provide a complete or final explanation of biological phenomena; but he gave tremendous impetus and volume to realistic thinking, emphasized the part played by forces beyond human control, and contributed to the destruction of the ideal or theoretical man.

The theories and ideals of democratic government began their conquests in the political world at a time when man was generally viewed as a special creation. For man, in this view, the universe had been created and around him it revolved. His obvious imperfections were explained by an original "fall"; but he was held capable of redemption, and, regardless of creed, there was a general belief in his adequacy and dignity. The theory of evolution did something to impair that belief. Yet, the process of evolutionary adaptation was one of change; and, however unconscious it might be, it seemed on the whole to indicate progress. While the immediate effect was widespread skepticism of former beliefs regarding the origin and destiny of man, the more significant and durable results may have been a refashioning of the doctrine of perfectibility and a reconfirmation of the apparently limitless possibilities of human beings.

The theory of evolution, identified with a ruthless struggle for survival, was applied to peoples and institutions as well as individuals. Applied to peoples, it led to the glorification of the power-state and the rationalization of war, as exemplified in the prewar Prussian philosophy of the state and soon to be even more evident in the rampant egotisms of Fascist Italy and Nazi Germany. Applied to institutions, the theory of evolution put democracy to the test of competition with other forms of government. If, on the competitive plane, it failed to survive,[40] no tears need be shed over it, since its failure to survive proved its unfitness.

Further inroads on the intellectual and moral supports of democracy were made at the turn of the century by the Viennese physician, Freud. From the Freudian school and other sources proceeded a comprehensive examination of all those hidden forces that condi-

[40] Compare Jacques Barzun, *Darwin, Marx, Wagner* (1941).

tion human behavior.[41] Considerable light was thrown on the nature of human beings, not only by psychology and psychiatry, but also by anthropology, physiology, medicine, and sociology. The general result was a conviction that human beings are not naturally or pre-eminently reasoning animals. It followed that the people might be right or wrong, depending on the stimuli applied to them and the strength and distribution of their own nonrational impulses, and that democracy as a means of focusing individual opinions was theoretically impossible since individual opinions were not independently formed except by a small minority.

Quantitatively, reasonableness and mental freedom are limited by intelligence or intellectual capacity. Ingenious tests seemed to indicate that a high percentage of the population was low in intelligence. This impression found its way into realistic fiction, exemplified in Sinclair Lewis's *Main Street*, and in the less realistic but allegedly factual representations of the "Bible Belt" contained in the *American Mercury*.

The "new psychology" struck another blow at the dignity of man. It led individuals to question, even to parade, their own inhibitions and to throw off the traditional moral sanctions and question anything that seemed to have purely traditional or moral support. On the other hand, progress toward emancipation from moral and traditional controls in large measure pointed in the direction of individual freedom and contributed to the release of intellectual energies. This effect was heightened by the influence of industrial technology, science, materialism, and realism. Social liberalism, however, tended to be undiscriminating, and all outworn traditions were not overthrown.

Breaking-down of moral sanctions appears to have been hastened by the First World War. Apart from the individual unsettlements that resulted, the general emotional let-down that followed victory

[41] In the introduction that he wrote in 1908 to his *Human Nature in Politics* Graham Wallis pointed out that for the moment "nearly all students of politics analyse institutions and avoid the analysis of man," and he felt that "many of the more systematic books on politics by American university professors are useless, just because the writer dealt with abstract men, formed on assumptions of which they were unaware and which they had never tested either by experience or by study." Pp. 14, 16.

favored a sharp reaction from an idealism that had invoked the democratic spirit. At the same time, the fact that in Europe forms of democracy generally replaced those of autocracy served to strengthen the popular feeling that democracy was at last secure and was no longer an ideal to be fought for with spiritual dedication and personal sacrifice.

Popular ideals shifted from political democracy to social justice.

In the early days, political ideals had been entangled with economic aims; but the political ideals had their own emotional, ethical, and philosophical supports. The latest movement to "let the people rule" was also a product of economic and social conditions; but it was motivated as a means to an end, not as an end in itself. Governmental power was no longer popularly distrusted: it was something to be seized for the people's material benefit. The ideal end was "social justice," concretely a broader distribution of the national income.[42] Social justice, so conceived, was represented as essentially democratic, in line with the pioneer tradition, a restoration of equality of economic opportunity. Frequently, this objective was called "social democracy" to distinguish it from the political democracy which appeared to be mainly engaged in futile tinkering with electoral and governmental machinery. It was beginning to be felt that the cure for democracy was not more democracy of the latter kind. We were adopting a more practical, a more utilitarian, and a less emotional attitude toward political panaceas. We were coming to think that social justice—social democracy—could be more quickly and more fully realized by developing economic regulation and social welfare programs through the existing political machinery, faulty as it might be. Continued concern with the problem of economic power tended also to shift

[42] "Democracy has become, all over Europe and to some extent even in North America also, desired merely as a Means, not as an End, precious in itself because it was the embodiment of Liberty. It is now valued not for what it is, but for what it may be used to win for the masses. When the exercise of their civic rights has brought them that which they desire, and when they feel sure that what they have won will remain with them, may they not cease to care for the further use of those rights?" Bryce, *Modern Democracies* (1921), Vol. 2, p. 603.

emphasis from the organization of government to the organization of industry.[43]

Emphasis shifted also from the concepts of liberty and political equality to the concept of security. Men had so long taken liberty for granted, it was so long since it had been a vital issue, and the word had been so often taken in vain by the politicians, that it had seemingly lost its power to appeal either to the emotions or interests of men.[44] The self-sufficient individualism which had given vital meaning to the concepts of liberty and equality had disappeared. Individuals now seemed helpless to cope with the complex system that ordered their lives. Not only its complexity but also its speed and its strains produced emotional as well as economic unsettlement. Steadily the concept of security became more familiar and, to an increasingly large number, more attractive, gradually overshadowing those ideas which had originally given emotional nourishment to the democratic spirit.

The conception of a social conscience ranged itself against legalism.

The significance of lawyers in technological America lay not so much in their distinctiveness or power as an organized group but more in their identification with all groups and in their occupation of strategic points in society. To the large extent that social control was expressed in the law, lawyers were the mediators between the individual and society. As politicians, legislators, and executives, lawyers accommodated themselves, in the fashion of their profes-

[43] This shift of emphasis appears in Louis D. Brandeis' testimony before the Industrial Relations Commission, during which he said:

"We are as free politically, perhaps, as it is possible for us to be. . . . And the main objection, as I see it, to the large corporation is that it makes possible—and in many cases makes inevitable—the exercise of industrial absolutism. . . .

". . . We are committed not only to social justice in the sense of avoiding things which bring suffering and harm and unequal distribution of wealth, but we are committed primarily to democracy, and the social justice to which we are headed is an incident of our democracy, not an end itself. It is the result of democracy, but democracy we must have. And, therefore, the end to which we must move is a recognition of industrial democracy. . . ." *Final Report and Testimony*, S. Doc. 415, 64 Cong. 1 sess., pp. 63-64.

[44] The opposition to prohibition appealed to "personal liberty"; but the narrowness of the appeal robbed it of any vital meaning.

sion and with a fair degree of flexibility, to the demands of those who played the role of employers and clients. As attorneys and judges, they were not only makers but also custodians of the law; and they were commonly criticized for their conservatism, their propensity to quibble over technicalities, their dialectical over-shrewdness, their lack of imagination, their devotion to the letter rather than the spirit of the law, and their resistance to the intrusion of sociological concepts into legal administration. Law, it was said, looked to the past. It tended to be static, while society was dynamic.

Behind the policies of government were pressing the classes that were economically unsatisfied but conscious of political power. Joining with and leading them were many representatives of intellectual and scientific groups, of the professions, and of the middle classes. These were the "socially conscious." What came to be termed the "social conscience," or "social consciousness" was in part humanitarianism, in part a sense of fairness, in part a revolt from shocking conditions, and in part a desire to deal efficiently with matters that had been neglected or wastefully handled. The movement was in large part a scientific and practical attempt to organize and accelerate social progress. It was handicapped to some extent by sentimentalism; and it suffered or profited from emotionalism, from intolerance of those who seemed hard-headed or legalistic, and from an indifference to the taxpayers' viewpoint.

The school of sociological jurisprudence, already making itself felt, concerned itself both with the making and interpretation of the law and called upon both legislators and judges to take more account of the social facts from which law was to be derived and to which it was to be applied. The sociological conception of law, according to Roscoe Pound, "conceives of the legal ordering of society as a practical process of eliminating friction and waste in the attainment of human desires."[45] From this point of view, law was pictured "as continuously more efficacious social engineering, satisfying, through social control, as much as is possible of the whole body of human wants."[46]

[45] *Criminal Justice in America* (1930), p. 3.
[46] Jerome Frank, *Law and the Modern Mind* (1930), p. 243.

The conception introduced a salutary corrective into public and legal thinking; but all lawyers who believed that they were "socialized" or called themselves "socially minded" were not necessarily well equipped to interpret the law or to determine governmental policies. When "social-mindedness" became an impractical idealism, it might be quite as incompatible with the ultimate good of society as was an unimaginative and unsympathetic legalism. The truly "social-minded" person gave proper weight to the value of discipline, to the restraints of law, and to the application of its strict letter.[47]

The fundamental law was, in a sense, what the judges declared it to be; and the judges felt bound, not only by the letter of constitutions, but also by the precedents that they and their predecessors had established. To depart suddenly and radically from the body of basic law which had been created in the past would have been to deny or destroy constitutionalism. The concept of a written constitution, of a government itself subject to law, demanded that the past should bind the present. For the judges, a social conscience alone was not quite adequate; their obligations implied a legal or judicial conscience as well. Yet, the Constitution had to be adapted to situations undreamed of in the past, to which the literal terms of the instrument might appear almost wholly irrelevant.

Intellectual leadership emphasized efficiency.

Some intellectuals, reviewing the ideals and practices of democracy, were growing skeptical, as James Russell Lowell and Godkin had in the previous century.[48] Few went so far as Mencken, who spoke of democracy as a "self-limiting disease, like measles";[49] but

[47] "A menace [to the Supreme Court] that is perhaps more serious than . . . open hostility may be defined as a sort of 'boring from within.' This phrase seems to fit the professors in our law schools who are departing from the traditional standards of the law in favor of 'social justice.' Social justice, it is well to remind these 'forward-looking' professors, means in practice class justice, class justice means class war and class war, if we are to go by all the experience of the past and present, means hell." Irving Babbitt, *Democracy and Leadership* (1924), pp. 307-09.

[48] Vernon Parrington, *Main Currents of American Thought* (1927-30), Pt. 3, pp. 138, 166-67.

[49] H. L. Mencken, *Notes on Democracy* (1926), p. 209.

the reaction of many scholars was that the times imperatively demanded intelligence and that, unless democracy could be made intelligent, it was fated to lose in its race with catastrophe.

It was pointed out that physical science and the machine were not sufficient. Repeated warnings were issued that scientific and technological progress in the material world was creating forces which men did not yet understand, much less know how to control.[50]

Accordingly, the intellectual activists and practitioners of applied political science emphasized efficiency. The apparent success of technological industrialism, the development of functionalism, the popular shift to social justice and the intellectual shift to efficiency were, as we shall see, intimately related. The efficiency movement was inextricably tied in with governmental evolution, and, in that connection, the movement will be discussed in the next chapter.

[50] The following is typical of these warnings: "The time has come when the people of the United States must bring all their intelligence and all their idealism to the consideration of the subtler realities of human relations, as they have formerly to the much simpler realities of material existence: this at least they must do if America is to be in the future what it has been in the past—a fruitful experiment in democracy." Carl Becker, *The United States: An Experiment in Democracy* (1920), p. 333.

CHAPTER V

GOVERNMENT IN TECHNOLOGICAL AMERICA,
1901-29

The conditions and concepts mentioned in the preceding chapter created or magnified problems calling for governmental solution, and, at the same time, constituted forces which were influencing political institutions and public policies. To aid the solution of emerging problems, the individual was offered various types of private leadership: the essentially selfish, the specialized, the educational, the intellectual, and the scientific. These leaderships were activated by different ideals and concepts: nationalism, internationalism, democracy, liberty, equality, security, legalism, constitutionalism, intellectual honesty, social justice, and social conscientiousness. Some of these were waxing; others, waning.

Private organization, private leaderships, private opinion-formation, and private ideals and concepts were engaged, as we shall now see, in controlling and remaking government; but government was also both a force and a problem, a growing force and a growing problem. Was expanding political power resolving private complications and providing new assurance of social progress? Was democratic government solving its own problem? Was it becoming more efficient and at the same time more responsive?

DEMOCRATIZATION

Theodore Roosevelt typified and speeded the transition from one era of American politics to another; and it was an interesting commentary on the workings of the American governmental system that he should have become president by the accident of an assassination. The western farmers' movement had been a revolt against the "money power" and the supposed instrumentalities of that power—the great corporations, the unresponsive party system, the "bosses," corruption, and the congressional oligarchy. At the turn of the century, fuel was being added to the fire by the revelations of the "muck-rakers." Roosevelt gave virile leadership to some aspects of the revolt; and he was at one also with the intellectual movement for civil service and political reform. During his administrations, other "fighting" leaders were rising in the states and cities. The national movement as a whole, however, was probably more indebted to a group of congressional leaders from the West, men who had already fought the corporations and bosses in their states and were continuing the attack in the United States Senate.[1]

The "Progressives" carried on the "Populist" democratizing movement.

The "Progressive" movement had its changing phases, and all progressives were not united on one program or in one party. Woodrow Wilson, as well as Theodore Roosevelt, belonged to the movement, though the two men differed in many important respects. Progressivism dominated American politics from 1901 to 1914, though not without constant struggle and some setbacks. Its democratizing aim appears to have reached its high-water mark in the Progressive platform of 1912, which proposed not only the recall of judicial decisions but also an easier method of amending the Constitution. The movement lost name, identity, popularity, and power during and after the First World War; but some of its essential attitudes and objectives continued to figure in politics and policies.

Its democratizing accomplishments up to the great depression may be briefly summarized. Independent voting and nonpartisanship gained in scope and practical results. During the first half of this period the direct primary almost universally supplanted the convention system of making nominations for state and local offices and for the national House of Representatives. The presidential primary was adopted in a number of states. By 1912 three-fourths of the states were using the direct primary to nominate candidates for the United States Senate. The initiative and referendum were widely adopted; and the recall was applied to many elective officers, in some cases including judges. By 1915 women had the right to vote in a number of states; and Congress in 1919 proposed a consti-

[1] Foremost among these were LaFollette of Wisconsin, Beveridge of Indiana, Cummins of Iowa, Clapp of Minnesota, and Bristow of Kansas.

tutional amendment providing for woman suffrage which was ratified in 1920.

Probably during no other period in American history was so much progress made toward purifying the ballot and eliminating election frauds. "Corrupt practice" acts became the order of the day. Corporations were forbidden to contribute to party funds, and publicity for campaign contributions was legally required.

Democratization through extensions of the franchise seemed to be partially nullified by the absence of voters from the polls. Abstention from voting may have been no greater than it had been in the past;[2] but, in an age of supposed democracy, its significance gained emphasis. A number of legislatures made provisions for absent voting.

An effort was made further to democratize Congress. The upper house was dominated by a small group of senators who were bosses of their states. The House of Representatives was practically controlled by Speaker Cannon, who agreed in most matters with the Senate oligarchs. In 1912, Congress finally proposed a constitutional amendment for direct election of senators; and in 1913 it was ratified by three-fourths of the states. The changes that were made in the procedure of the House need not be described in detail; but their net result was to deprive the Speaker of his control and transfer it to an elected rules committee.

Having briefly indicated the results of a movement that may be said to have come to an end in the middle of this period, we shall now turn to the development of policies and to the enlargement and complication of the governmental task. Our discussion in this connection will deal with (1) social welfare, social justice, and labor, (2) agriculture, (3) conservation, and (4) economic control.

SOCIAL, LABOR, AGRICULTURAL, AND CONSERVATION POLICIES

In the early decades of the Republic, family and community life were such as to render impracticable or unnecessary any elaborate

[2] See Charles A. Beard, *Economic Origins of Jeffersonian Democracy* (1915), p. 99; Charles H. Titus, *Voting Behavior in the United States* (1935), p. 68; Edward McChesney Sait, *American Parties and Elections* (1927), p. 555. For a comprehensive analysis of the problem of non-voting, see Charles E. Merriam and H. F. Gosnell, *Non-Voting* (1924).

governmental activity in behalf of the health, safety, and morals of the individual. These conditions tended to disappear as industrialism and urbanism advanced. Along with an apprehension of unsatisfactory social conditions[3] and growth of private philanthropies appeared specialized associations and new professions, notably the social workers and the public health physicians. Interest in child welfare continued to develop and was given national expression in conferences which met at Washington in 1909, 1919, and 1930. The federal Children's Bureau was established in 1912; and the Sheppard-Towner Act passed in 1921 provided federal aid for promoting the welfare and hygiene of maternity and infancy.

The concept of social justice was variously and substantially translated into public policy.

State social welfare functions increased; and, on the eve of the depression, the federal government had expanded or established activities in the fields of public health, education, child welfare, recreation, and vocational education and rehabilitation, and was administering educational, penal, and correctional institutions and hospitals for the physically and mentally ill. It is probable that the desire for social services was fairly uniform among the classes; and it was given practical propulsion by middle-class organizations financed in large measure by the wealthy, strengthened by the voting power of labor, and proselytized in general by the "socially conscious."

Included in social welfare policies were some that involved direct money payments to individuals; for example, mothers' or widows' pensions[4] and old-age pensions.[5] War veterans had been pensioned from the beginning of the national government. Civil

[3] Theodore Roosevelt, in his annual message in December 1904, called attention to the overcrowding of cities, draining of country districts, housing, mortality, slums, the youth problem, child labor, child health, juvenile courts, and public playgrounds.

[4] Beginning in 1911 in the states. The federal Maternity and Infancy Act of 1921 provided federal aid to the states for maternity relief.

[5] The old-age pension movement began in 1923 with the enactment of laws by Nevada and Montana. Arizona passed an old-age pension law in 1914 but it was voided by the state supreme court. By 1931 thirteen state old-age pension laws were in operation.

War pensions had widened in scope and increased in amount not entirely because the veterans were in need or because the government was "generous." The voting power of the "old soldiers" was an important consideration. In the case of the World War veterans, a federal law enacted on October 6, 1917 constituted a radical departure from the old system, since it sought to establish principles and standards which would be of general application and which, it was hoped by many, would obviate individual and group pressures on the legislators. It was not long, however, before the veterans were bringing pressure on Congress to extend and increase the benefits provided by law; and finally the demand was made that certificates maturing after a term of years be paid immediately at their full maturity value. In the meantime, the veterans had obtained from the states various favors and exemptions, including payments of cash. These benefits included partial or complete exemption from certain taxes.[6]

With the exception in part of veterans' pensions, social welfare policies were distributive, since they involved the levying by government on the incomes of individuals and the spending of the money thus obtained for the benefit of the public or of an under-privileged group.[7]

The concept of social justice had a wider, and for this analysis a more interesting, application. It was applied to the demands of the industrial wage earners and to public labor policies when these were in the workers' interest. Such policies were also distributive since, in large part, they resulted from a struggle for the economic output between the "haves" and the "have-nots;" and the latter, because of their voting strength, were gaining ground. Agriculture and labor comprised the articulate "have-nots"; but it was labor legislation that first became assimilated to social justice.

[6] From 1790 to June 30, 1932, the total expenditures for veterans' relief amounted to 16 billion dollars, of which 7 billions were on account of the World War. For a complete history of veterans' legislation and description of its administration, see Gustavus A. Weber and Laurence F. Schmeckebier, *The Veterans' Administration* (1934).

[7] Specific illustrations of the distributive tendency were provided by the public general hospitals, free clinics, milk stations, free distribution of biologics, vocational courses in the schools, free textbooks, school health work, free school lunches, adult education, public health nursing, extension work in home economics, "small claims" courts, and public defenders.

From 1900 until after the depression of 1920-22, the states and the federal government made many investigations into labor conditions. Legislation fell into three divisions: (1) that which was intended to ameliorate the condition of all the lower-income groups, labor among them; (2) that which was directed at labor conditions in particular; and (3) that which sought to regulate the controversial relationships between employer and employee. Much legislation of the first class and practically all of the second and third classes was termed indiscriminately "social legislation"; though most, if not all, of the legislation in the two latter categories involved directly or indirectly the regulation of industry and intervention in its management.

Social legislation of the first class, having to do with the general welfare of all lower-income groups, included certain types of taxation—such as the income tax and the inheritance tax—and services, such as the postal savings bank system, established in 1910, and others already mentioned.

Legislation directed at labor conditions in particular included state laws fixing maximum hours; minimum-wage legislation for women and minors; laws prohibiting child labor; restrictions on immigration; the federal law enacted in 1908 limiting the hours of certain railway employees working on interstate lines and the Adamson Act passed in 1916 prescribing an eight-hour day for all interstate trainmen; and state laws concerned with employment exchanges, night work, company stores, prison labor, and "sweating." The most extensive development of legislation, as well as of administrative regulation, occurred in the field of industrial safety and hygiene. Beginning about 1910 the states passed workmen's compensation acts, providing for the insurance of the workmen and for their compensation under state administrative supervision.

Legislation regulating the controversial relationships between employers and employees included laws passed in most of the states providing for mediation by state officials and voluntary arbitration under their guidance and laws regulating the issuance of injunctions by the courts.[8] In laws passed in 1920 and 1926 Congress set up

---

[8] Kansas in 1920 set up a Court of Industrial Relations for the compulsory settlement of labor disputes; but it was declared unconstitutional by the Supreme

machinery for the adjustment of railway labor disputes.

The limits of labor legislation fixed at that time were indicated by the fact that, during this period, labor organizations were opposing the idea of compulsory unemployment insurance; and the Industrial Relations Commission, reporting in 1916, declared that "the fixing of the wages of adult workmen by legal enactment is not practicable nor desirable as a general policy, except for public employees."[9] This commission viewed the public lands as a major means of relieving industrial unemployment.[10]

Agriculture now received additional aid
and regulatory protection.

Public agricultural policy before the Civil War was primarily concerned with the great questions of land, transportation, money, credit, and tariffs. Between the Civil War and 1900, the questions of homesteading and transportation development receded into the background. Money, tariffs, and the regulation of transportation came to the fore; and the federal government gave greater emphasis to agricultural promotion as an administrative function.

Financial aid and administrative stimulation through experimentation, education, and demonstration continued until and beyond the great depression. To carry on demonstration work, local farm bureaus, drawing together into state and national farm bureau federations, were made a part of a vast agricultural extension organization, financed by federal, state, and county funds, promoted and supervised by the Department of Agriculture at Washington, centered in the states in the land-grant colleges, and working locally through county agents in close personal contact with farmers and their families.

Tax equalization became a means of giving relief to the farmer. Income, inheritance, and corporation taxes, federal grants-in-aid to the states, and state grants-in-aid to the counties were introduced

---

Court. South Carolina in 1922 and Colorado in 1915 also applied the principle of compulsory arbitration. Leverett S. Lyon, Myron W. Watkins, and Victor Abramson, *Government and Economic Life*, Vol. 1 (1939), p. 201.

[9] *Final Report and Testimony*, S. Doc. 415, 64 Cong. 1 sess., p. 68.

[10] The same, pp. 36-38.

or extended. The tariff remained an issue. Reclamation acts sought to extend the area of cultivable land. Agricultural producers' associations were exempted from the prohibitions of the Sherman Anti-Trust Act. The Federal Farm Loan Act of 1916 was designed to ease the agricultural credit situation. Regulation of transportation was continued and extended; and, in addition, waterway development was underwritten and vast sums went to the construction of paved roads.

Regulation also extended to other industries with the primary purpose of promoting agriculture or protecting the farmers' interests. For some purposes and for his own protection, the farmer himself was regulated, as in the combating of animal and plant diseases. In the interest of consumers and of public health, regulation was applied to foods and drugs and to packers and stockyards. Legislation concerned with trading in "futures" was also conceived to be in the special interest of farmers.

The depression of 1920-22, from which agriculture did not recover, marked the beginning of new activities in behalf of agriculture. Seed loans began. The Department of Agriculture inaugurated crop forecasts with the idea that voluntary increases or decreases would be made in acreage. The Bureau of Agricultural Economics made surveys and reports designed to discourage surpluses and acted in general as a research and planning agency in the field of agriculture. Farmers' co-operative marketing associations were encouraged. New types of banks were established to provide agricultural credits. Finally, in the Agricultural Marketing Act of 1929 the Federal Farm Board was created and provision made for the acquisition by the federal government of crop surpluses. Under agrarian pressure, North and South Dakota between 1919 and 1933 made a number of excursions into state socialism, most, if not all, of them disastrous.[11]

Limits were seen, if not definitely set, to public agricultural policies. Theodore Roosevelt in 1909 thought that it was

not within the sphere of any government to reorganize the farmers' business or reconstruct the social life of farming communities. It is, how-

---

[11] On public agricultural policy during this period, see Lyon and Abramson, *Government and Economic Life,* Vol. 2 (1940), pp. 864-904.

ever, quite within its power to use its influence and the machinery of publicity which it can control for calling public attention to the needs and the facts.[12]

A Joint Commission of Agricultural Inquiry, which reported in December 1921, declared that a readjustment of prices could "not be brought about by legislative formulas but must be the result for the most part of the interplay of economic forces." The Commission pointed out that "the jurisdiction of the Federal Government is limited and that it can not directly regulate production, marketing, or transportation, not the subject of interstate commerce."[13] Nevertheless, several states in the twenties passed marketing laws that placed the individual farmer under a considerable measure of control; and various schemes were proposed in Congress looking to a comprehensive solution of the farm problem through national legislation.

Government undertook to conserve natural resources.

The conservation problem had both economic and social aspects. It carried the principle of equitable distribution of wealth. It involved promotion and regulation, both of agriculture and of business. It struck decidedly at the doctrines of individualism and *laissez faire*. It forced the acceptance within its self-imposed limits of the idea that the national government should exercise economic functions that could not be performed in the public interest by a free enterprise system or by the states.

Reference has already been made to the act of 1891 which permitted the president to reserve certain areas of public lands. These powers were exercised by Cleveland and more vigorously and extensively by Theodore Roosevelt. During the latter's administration, the federal government gave definiteness, direction, and range to its activities in the fields of forestry, reclamation, electric power, flood control, wild life, national parks and monuments, and the social aspects of rural living. During or following his administra-

[12] Special Message, Feb. 9, 1909.
[13] *Agricultural Crisis and Its Causes*, H. Rept. 408, 67 Cong. 1 sess., p. 11.

tion federal legislation provided for the reservation of sub-surface mineral rights in agricultural lands of the public domain and initiated the leasing system. An act of 1916 made sweeping provision for the reservation to the United States of all such rights. Water power sites were withdrawn from entry. The development of the Tennessee River at Muscle Shoals had received more or less engineering study from the time of Washington; and in 1917, as a war measure, the Wilson Dam was started. The building of dams for irrigation, flood control, and power development prior to the depression culminated in the great Boulder Canyon project.

In the meantime, remarkable development of motor vehicle traffic vastly increased the consumption of petroleum products; and these were finding other new and varied applications. While the United States led the world in petroleum resources, its supplies evidently had a limit. Though this limit, for obvious reasons, was not precisely ascertainable, petroleum geologists predicted that the domestic sources would be exhausted within a relatively short period. Efforts of the federal government to increase or conserve supplies took the form mainly of encouraging the acquisition by American capitalists of petroleum concessions abroad and demanding equality of economic opportunity in the British, French, and Dutch possessions and in the mandated territories.

ECONOMIC CONTROL

Labor and agricultural legislation might be advanced under the name of social justice or agricultural promotion; but it had its influence, its incidental effects, and its repercussions throughout the economic system. Labor legislation in particular struck close to the central problem of industrial organization and management. The essential unity of the problem of economic control was not widely appreciated, or, if it was, was not adopted as a political approach. Agriculture and labor were separate political pressure groups, and the concessions they won were always those that seemed closest to the immediate and particular interests of these groups. Moreover, when government looked directly at aspects of industry other than agriculture and labor, its affirmative actions were likely to be dictated in large part by agricultural and labor demands. As for industrial leaders, their primary concern was with governmental assistance, not control. The pressure for regulation came from those who had the most votes but the least familiarity with the broad problems of industrial production and distribution.

When the Sherman antitrust law was enacted in 1890, monopoly was the immediate object of attack; but the use of statutory prohibitions to destroy concentrated economic control did not prove conspicuously successful. The Interstate Commerce Act of 1887 made no clear choice between competition and monopoly, although efficiency and economy seemed even then to demand that the railroads be treated as natural monopolies. The Supreme Court decided that the Anti-Trust Act applied to the railroads; and thus, in legal theory, these enterprises, in so far as they were already competitive, must remain so. In practice, the enforcement of the Interstate Commerce Act was about as ineffective as that of the Anti-Trust Act. The two statutes, however, were administered by separate agencies, and on quite different theoretical and practical bases. In the absence of further legislation, whatever co-ordination and direction existed came in the main from the courts and the president. Judicial control was largely negative and restrictive. The president's political control was extensive with respect to prosecution under the anti-trust law. It was less evident and certainly much less decisive over the semi-independent Interstate Commerce Commission.

While monopoly was under attack and competition was looked upon as an automatic restorative, it was seen that either competition or concentration required regulation to prevent undesirable business practices.

Government faced general issues without clear-cut decision or a consistent and co-ordinated program.

Theodore Roosevelt saw society as a whole, stressed the interdependence of classes, and urged co-operation and mutual respect. Fundamentally, he said, welfare rested on "individual thrift and energy, resolution, and intelligence." Legislation and administration could not take the place of individual capacity; they could only give it scope and opportunity. He condemned demagoguery and the preaching of hate;[14] and warned that the "mechanism of modern business is so delicate that extreme care must be taken not to interfere with it in a spirit of rashness or ignorance." Publicity, he declared, is "the only sure remedy which we can now invoke." The federal government should, he thought, without interfering with the power of the states, assume supervision over all corporations doing an interstate business through a "Secretary of Commerce and Industries," who should "deal with commerce in its broadest sense; including among many other things whatever concerns labor and all matters affecting the great business corporations and our merchant marine."[15]

In 1903, the Department of Commerce and Labor was established. To it was assigned a number of existing bureaus most of which had some relation to the physical operations of commerce but practically none to that broad and integrated supervision of the economic system which seemed to be envisioned by the President. To these were added, however, a Bureau of Manufactures and a Bureau of Corporations. The latter, a continuation of the Industrial Commission, embodied Roosevelt's idea of an administrative agency engaged in economic research and economic publicity, acting as adviser to the President and Congress and helping to develop a comprehensive and presumably co-ordinated system of regulatory legislation.

Following the establishment of the Department of Commerce and Labor, Roosevelt's proposals regarding economic regulation took more specific form. In his message of December 5, 1905, he said:

What is needed is not sweeping prohibition of every arrangement, good or bad, which may tend to restrict competition, but such adequate supervision and regulation as will prevent any restriction of competition from being to the detriment of the public—as well as such super-

---

[14] "To preach hatred of the rich man as such, to carry on a campaign of slander and invective against him, to seek to mislead and inflame to madness honest men whose lives are hard and who have not the kind of mental training which will permit them to appreciate the danger in the doctrines preached—all this is to commit a crime against the body politic and to be false to every worthy principle and tradition of American national life." Annual Message, Dec. 3, 1901.

[15] The same.

vision and regulation as will prevent other abuses in no way connected with restriction of competition.

His annual message in December 1907 recommended the federal regulation of all interstate corporations through chartering or licensing by a federal board or commission. In his special message of March 25, 1908, he proposed that "some proper governmental authority" should be given discretionary authority to approve or disapprove contracts or combinations in restraint of interstate commerce.

In 1908, the Democratic Party, not the Republican, proposed in its platform the federal licensing of interstate corporations; but Taft, a Republican president, recommended a federal incorporation law.[16]

In 1912, the Progressives believed that "the concentration of modern business, in some degree, is both inevitable and necessary"; and they urged "the establishment of a strong Federal administrative commission of high standing, which shall maintain active supervision over industrial corporations engaged in interstate commerce."[17] The Republicans thought that a federal trade commission would be desirable, and favored clarification of the antitrust law.[18] The Democrats declared that "a private monopoly is indefensible and intolerable" and favored a "declaration by law of the conditions upon which corporations shall be permitted to engage in interstate trade." The abuses to be remedied included holding companies, interlocking directorates, stock watering, price discriminations, and "the control by any one corporation of so large a proportion of any industry as to make it a menace to competitive conditions."[19]

A majority of the people voted in 1912 for the Progressive or the Republican candidate; but the Democrats came to power. In power, their policy was to break up monopolistic structures and to suppress those business methods which stifled competition or were otherwise morally reprehensible. The Clayton Act and the Federal

[16] Annual Message, Dec. 5, 1911.
[17] Progressive Platform, 1912.
[18] Republican Platform, 1912.
[19] Democratic Platform, 1912.

Trade Commission Act represented an effort to embody these general policies in legislation. The former supplemented the Sherman Anti-Trust Act and prohibited certain specific practices when the effect might be "to substantially lessen competition or tend to create a monopoly."[20] The Federal Trade Commission Act prohibited "unfair methods of competition in commerce" and established the Federal Trade Commission to enforce the law. The Bureau of Corporations was abolished and its personnel transferred to the new commission. These acts, though they embodied in principle the conception of individualistic competitive business, were not free of confusion and cross-purposes; and they furthered the tendency toward divided or segregated economic control.[21]

Moreover, before the Federal Trade Commission was created, the Department of Commerce and Labor had been divided and a separate Department of Labor established. The Department of Commerce retained miscellaneous functions relating to economic life, but had no unifying policy.

The Federal Trade Commission, under the act creating it, had two basic functions: investigation and regulation. As a regulatory body, its orders were enforceable by the courts. The Commission tended to become practically ineffectual with respect to the destruction or prevention of monopoly but was useful to some extent as an investigatory agency, though it fell far short of becoming an economic planning body or a legislative council in economic matters. It contributed, however, to the establishment of an ethical "plane of competition."

During the postwar Republican administration, the Federal Trade Commission developed a procedure of co-operation with industry, or of industrial self-rule under the Commission's supervision. The Commission declared in its annual report for 1928: "Never in the history of American business has there been a time when 'self-regulation' has received more intensive considera-

---

[20] Lyon, Watkins, and Abramson, *Government and Economic Life*, Vol. 1, p. 285.
[21] The Clayton Act exempted agricultural producers' associations from the operations of the antitrust law. The Export Trade Act of 1918 provided that the Sherman law and the Clayton Act should not apply to associations established solely for the export trade.

tion."[22] At that time national policy in general again emphasized promotion rather than regulation. The Department of Commerce undertook, with the co-operation of trade associations, to standardize products and otherwise to eliminate waste from American industry. Its representatives abroad searched for and reported opportunities for trade and investment; but probably the chief stimulation of the export trade came from American loans to foreign governments and nationals.

At the same time the government interposed obstacles to the repayment of the foreign loans by maintaining a high tariff on imports. Steps were taken, nevertheless, toward so-called scientific and nonpartisan tariff-making. A fair measure of agreement was reached on the untenable proposition that protective tariff rates should be so fixed as to cover the difference between the cost of production abroad and at home; and an independent tariff commission was established in 1916 to make continuous studies.[23]

Control expanded in specific fields.

Federal regulation of electric power began in 1920 and the Federal Power Commission was established; but its function was limited to the licensing of projects on streams within federal jurisdiction and the purpose was as much developmental as regulative.[24]

A national banking system had been established in 1863; but, prior to the passage of the Federal Reserve Act in 1913, both public and private control of credit was limited.[25] The Federal Reserve Act set up twelve Reserve banks and over them a Board of Governors of the Federal Reserve System. The new system was a compromise between centralization and decentralization; but its authority was much wider than the established forms of bank

---

[22] Pp. 5-6. On business regulation and promotion in general, see *Investigation of Executive Agencies of the Government*, S. Rept. 1275, 75 Cong. 1 sess., pp. 667-811.

[23] For the historical antecedents of the Tariff Commission, see James G. Smith, *Economic Planning and the Tariff* (1934), pp. 297-301.

[24] Lyon and Watkins, *Government and Economic Life*, Vol. 2, pp. 650-51.

[25] Lyon, Watkins, and Abramson, *Government and Economic Life*, Vol. 1, p. 175.

regulation. This instrument of control went beyond the correction of abuses and the redistribution of privileges. Operating at a key point in the economic mechanism, it was designed to influence the workings of the mechanism itself.

Federal prohibitions, restrictions, regulations, or controls were applied to various other subjects. Methods and objectives varied according to the commodity or activity concerned. Miscellaneous regulatory laws were to a large extent designed to protect or promote agriculture or to protect consumers;[26] and their administration was for the most part assigned to the Department of Agriculture, rather than to separate commissions. It should be noted, however, that in these cases administration involved, in large measure, merely the application of concrete technical standards to physical commodities and not the development of policies.

The field of transportation particularly
illustrated lack of co-ordination.

Developments in the field of transportation were also illuminating. The Interstate Commerce Act of 1887 had been restricted to railways; and until the administration of Theodore Roosevelt the powers of the Interstate Commerce Commission were limited. A series of enactments between 1903 and 1930 extended the Commission's jurisdiction to express and sleeping-car companies, pipe-lines, industrial railways, private car facilities, and terminal facilities; and in 1910 telegraph and telephone companies were brought within its jurisdiction. Congress empowered the Commission to fix rates and to pass on issues of railroad securities.

During the Great War, a competitive railroad system appeared unequal to a situation in which all the nation's economic elements had to be integrated in a single unified effort; and the federal government took over operation of the railways. Partly because of this experience, Congress passed the Transportation Act of 1920, which indicated to some extent a reorientation of federal policy. This act recognized the desirability of maintaining an adequate transportation system, as well as of regulating it. The

[26] For example, the Food and Drugs Act of 1906 and the meat inspection law of 1907.

government had first encouraged the building of duplicating facilities and the overbuilding of the system generally. Now, extensions and branch lines were to be built only with the approval of the Commission; and consolidations and combinations were to be encouraged, provided they did not unduly restrict competition. The Commission was thus given a limited responsibility for the general promotion and organization of the transportation system. With respect to the railroads, therefore, the federal government was passing beyond the sphere of regulation, as the term was generally understood, and was taking over from private hands some of the powers and duties of industrial management.

The opinion brought to bear on the railroad problem represented in part a conflict of interests—those of the financiers, stockholders, and managers, the workers, and the shippers. Progress toward a solution of the problem was retarded by this conflict, as well as by the preoccupation of large sections of opinion with other public problems and with old prejudices. The Interstate Commerce Commission was not given the administration of laws relating to railroad labor; and new or amendatory railway labor acts were frequently passed.

The government, moreover, was promoting systems of transportation that were to become competitive with the railroads. Through the Bureau of Public Roads in the Department of Agriculture, and through state highway commissions separate from the state public service and utility commissions, the federal and state governments spent huge amounts for the improvement of roads, which were used not only for the transportation of passengers but also for the carrying of freight.

The federal government continued to disburse very considerable sums for improvement of inland waterways; and the completion of the Panama Canal in 1915 gave to the federal government the operation of a business enterprise. Incidentally, the government acquired ownership of the Panama Railroad; and the Panama Canal Act of 1912 gave the Interstate Commerce Commission jurisdiction over transportation by rail and water through the Canal Zone. In 1924 Congress created the Inland Waterways Corporation, financed and managed by the federal government, to operate a fleet of barges on the Mississippi and Warrior Rivers. The Corporation was in part an outgrowth of defense measures taken during the war; and it operated under the supervision of the Secretary of War.

During the long history of shipping policy, legislation had been advanced or opposed by several interest groups: those directly affected—the ship builders, ship owners, and the seaman's unions— and those indirectly affected—the Navy, the iron and steel industry, shippers, travelers, and the general public. Due in the main to differences among the interests concerned, frequent deadlocks occurred between the president and Congress and between the Senate and the House. It was found difficult to harmonize shipping policy with tariff policy and with general foreign policy. Beyond technical regulations and services designed for health and safety, the main concern was with promotion. But no single objective was ever accepted as controlling and no one method as more efficacious than another.[27]

After 1910 the regulatory aspects of shipping policy received more attention; and the war introduced still another phase. The Shipping Act of 1916 established the United States Shipping Board, which in turn created the United States Shipping Board Emergency Fleet Corporation. This act not only launched a huge shipbuilding and operating program but also initiated the regulation of shipping rates, fares, charges, and services. The Shipping Board was made the regulatory agency. Postwar legislation in 1920 and 1928 sought to work out in combination policies of research, promotion, subsidization, regulation, and government construction and operation, these policies to be executed by the Shipping Board and the Corporation.[28]

Federal activities in connection with commercial aviation were at first confined largely to research and promotion; but in 1926 certain regulatory authority over aircraft went to the secretary of commerce. Regulation of radio was first assigned to the secre-

[27] See Paul M. Zeis, *American Shipping Policy* (1938), pp. 212-16.
[28] On the promotion and regulation of transportation in general, see S. Rept. 1275, 75 Cong. 1 sess., pp. 349-506; Lyon and Abramson, *Government and Economic Life*, Vol. 2, pp. 746-863.

tary of commerce and labor and then to a temporary radio commission, made permanent in 1929.

Federal regulatory development was to a great extent foreshadowed or paralleled in the states. They extended business regulation from railroads to other utilities, increased the number of business activities subject to regulation, and enlarged regulatory power. Utility regulation was also undertaken by the municipalities; and the number of municipally owned plants steadily increased until 1923.[29] Many of the states passed "blue-sky" laws, designed to prevent the sale of fraudulent securities, and in other laws regulated exchanges.[30]

CHANGES IN ADMINISTRATION

Major policies in the fields of social welfare, agriculture, conservation, and economic control developed in the midst of various and conflicting opinions. The structure of policy now coming into view not only created or signalized new relationships between government and the great pressure groups but also, for this reason and others, substantially restated the problems involved in the realization of democracy and efficiency in government. At this point, attention is called to certain outstanding changes in administration. It was becoming increasingly discretionary, more largely legislative and judicial, and more thoroughly technical. It was also expanding.

Expanding economic control brought additional delegation of legislative powers.

Administration was no longer, even in appearance, "merely the clerical part" of government, and it involved less and less the execution of explicit legislative orders. The practice of delegating legislative power to administrative bodies was extended to addi-

[29] G. Lloyd Wilson, James M. Herring, and Roland B. Entsler, *Public Utility Regulation* (1938), pp. 19, 522-23; Lyon and Abramson, *Government and Economic Life*, Vol. 2, pp. 634-44.

[30] The federal government, generally speaking, left the buying and selling of stocks and bonds unregulated, though the State Department did assume a mild degree of extra-legal supervision over foreign loans, and the Post Office Department sought to prevent the use of the mails for the sending of fraudulent securities.

tional economic areas by enlarging the powers of commissions and increasing their number.[31]

These bodies were alike in that they were set up in such a way as to be substantially independent and were intended to exercise, in addition to executive duties, subordinate legislative functions—investigation, research, planning, publicity, issuance of rules and regulations, and development of policy, subject to the general directions and standards contained in the statutes. Sublegislative powers were also granted to the departments and bureaus and to the president.

Administrative agencies increasingly exercised the judicial function.

Judicial power was also delegated, largely to the commissions but also in lesser measure to departments and bureaus, thus to an extent relieving the courts of an economic regulatory task for which they had demonstrated their inadequacy.

Under the impact of industry a reorganization of the adjudicatory process had become necessary; but certain circumstances precluded any radical re-examination or reconstruction of the judicial system. In this respect, the legal profession and public opinion were both conservative. Nevertheless, from many directions the system came under attack. Sociological jurisprudence, discussed in the preceding chapter, represented one movement. In the states, added impetus was now given to the specialization of courts and the division of general courts into specialized branches. In the federal government, however, the requirements of specialization were met only to a slight extent by the reorganization of the judiciary itself.[32] With respect to economic

[31] Between 1900 and 1929, the federal government established, in addition to the Interstate Commerce Commission, which was acquiring considerable prestige, the Federal Reserve Board, the Federal Trade Commission, the Tariff Commission, the Shipping Board, the Federal Power Commission, and the Federal Radio Commission.

[32] The Supreme Court acquired a certain inflexibility from its constitutional status. Congress did exercise its power to establish inferior courts by setting up specialized tribunals, such as the Court of Claims, the Customs Court, and the Court of Customs and Patent Appeals. On the distinction between constitutional courts and legislative courts, see F. F. Blachly and M. E. Oatman, *Federal Regulatory Action and Control* (1940), pp. 9-12.

adjudication, the device more commonly adopted was to set up a semi-independent administrative agency and provide that its determinations of fact should be conclusive in cases appealed to the regular courts.

Under the principle of separation of powers, there was obviously a limit somewhere to the delegation of legislative and judicial functions. If it proceded too far, the legislative power, assigned by the Constitution to Congress, would be actually exercised by agencies outside of Congress; and if these agencies were controlled by the chief executive, the latter would become in effect a complete legislative authority. The Supreme Court was inclined to approve a considerable measure of delegation when the legislature established for the administrative agency a limiting framework of principles and standards and when the administrative agency was set up, as in the case of the Interstate Commerce Commission, in such a way as to be substantially independent of the executive and to be in intention at least responsible to Congress. Even then the Court insisted that the constitutional rights of individuals affected by administrative decisions should be protected by the judicial or quasi-judicial procedures deemed essential to due process of law.

Administration, now in the ascendancy, was recognized as technical, demanding the merit system.

With the growth of specialization, of specialized administration, and of specialized associations concerned with the quality of public service, the technical side of administration was increasingly recognized.[33]

The presidency of Theodore Roosevelt was marked, not only by extensions of the classified service, but also by the emergence of the modern conception of administration and of the relation of the merit system to administrative efficiency. From then on, less was heard of civil service reform as reform and more of personnel management as a staff function, the primary purpose of

[33] See Fred Wilbur Powell, *Control of Federal Expenditures: A Documentary History, 1775-1894* (1939); Gustavus A. Weber, *Organized Efforts for the Improvement of Methods of Administration in the United States* (1919), pp. 74-83.

which was to promote economical and competent service. At the end of the Hoover administration, 80 per cent of federal employees were included in the classified service.

In state and local governments progress was slower, perhaps because of the greater strength of political machines and the relative weakness of reform leadership, probably also because of certain important differences between federal administration and administration in the states.[34] State administration was still largely decentralized; and the tradition of direct popular control over it persisted. In some important fields of state administration, it was sought to remove administration from politics through the establishment of boards and commissions. In certain fields, professionalism was becoming dominant and thus excluding partisan politics. In the field of elementary and secondary education, moreover, the teaching personnel was already placed on a merit basis through the requirement of special training and of examination.

Administrative activities and costs increased.

Administrative activities and costs increased both in the states and in the federal government, but not for precisely the same reasons and not chiefly at either level of government because of the developments just mentioned.

As in the past, a basic cause of administrative expansion in the states was the growth of population, compelling enlargement of the task of government without necessarily changing its character or adding new activities. Population growth produced, for example, more children to be educated, more inmates in state institutions, more cases in the courts, more roads to be built and maintained, more buildings to be inspected, more sanitary regulation, and more diversity in the agricultural life that government sought to serve. In addition, transfer of work from local units added to the administrative tasks of the state, as did also the central supervision of local activities. In general, the initial expansion did not occur

---

[34] It is possible, too, that the progress of the merit system in the federal government had the effect of retarding progress in the states by increasing there the pressure of the organizational needs of the parties.

on the state level; but activity flowed from private groups and organizations first to the local community and then to the state, taking on at each step new features, a more formal and public aspect, greater energy, and indications of permanent social acceptance.

In addition to population growth, various conditions contributed to state administrative expansion with different force in different states and in the same state at different times. Among them were: the habit of public control and public service acquired from urban necessities; education, science, and invention; extensive and effective private organization of interests, specialties, expertness, research, propaganda, and pressure; humanitarianism, social consciousness, and distributive policies; the rise of public administrative leadership; and the theory of social efficiency and social saving.[35] The composition of the legislature favored log-rolling, discouraged co-ordination of policies, and precluded adequate representation of the general interest;[36] while legislatures were generally willing, under pressure, to accept a principle or an objective without adequate consideration of its eventual administrative or financial implications. Contributions to expansion came also from federal grants-in-aid and other federal policies and administrative activities; an increasing national income, producing more tax revenue and facilitating public borrowing; and a partial shifting of the tax burden from the many to the few. To a large extent, administrative activities were expanding because they were diversifying; and their diversification reflected the diversification of economic and social life and of governmental policies.

Between 1900 and 1929, state governmental costs were rapidly rising, but not at a constant rate and perhaps no more rapidly than during some previous periods. Nevertheless, in the states generally

[35] According to this theory, government as the central organ of social control and social advancement was justified in establishing an activity when it reduced or eliminated private losses and wastes. This theory acted in the expansion of such activities as conservation, construction and maintenance of roads, prevention of disease and accidents, control of crime, etc.

[36] See Carroll H. Wooddy, "The Growth of Governmental Functions," in *Recent Social Trends*, Vol. 2, pp. 1275-76. One activity begot another. Frequently the argument was heard: If that can be done, why can't this be done? If you can spend millions on that, why object to spending a few thousands on this?

expenditure was increasing faster than private income; and though much of this expenditure was desirable and some of it reproductive, the cost of government was growing steadily more burdensome.

This situation was not due entirely to state administrative expansion. Local expenditures were moving upward, but at a slower pace. It was lucky that this was so, because local expenditures amounted to about four times those of the state governments. Highways and education together accounted for about 75 per cent of the increased activity and cost of government in the states between 1915 and 1929.[37]

The net expenditures of the federal government (that is, exclusive of debt retirement and costs of the postal service payable from postal revenue) increased from about 500 million dollars in 1900 to 761 millions in 1915[38] and to 18.5 billion dollars in 1919. In the postwar period, they rapidly declined, but struck a new level at slightly more than 3 billion dollars.[39] In the second half of the twenties, federal expenditures were again increasing.

Expansion of federal activities and expenditures resulted in small part from the conditions that affected the states, but in much larger measure from quite different causes. War, preparation for war, and payment for past wars constituted the big item of expenditure. Only about one-fourth of the federal expenditures in 1930 were devoted to the civil functions. Extension of federal activity into the fields of economic regulation and social welfare was significant from the standpoints of function and power, but did not account for any considerable increase in the total volume of work or in the total expenditure.[40]

[37] The same, pp. 1295 ff.
[38] For analyses of federal expenditure increases, see S. Rept. 1275, 76 Cong. 1 sess., pp. 45-49; Wooddy, Recent Social Trends, Vol. 2, pp. 1274-92, and Growth of the Federal Government—1915-1932 (1934).
[39] S. Rept. 1275, 76 Cong. 1 sess., p. 45.
[40] Studying the new administrative agencies which were established by the federal government between 1915 and 1930, Wooddy estimated "that about 10 per cent of the costs of all civil functions in 1930 were due to these new agencies, and that of the increase in costs from 1915 to 1930 they were responsible for a somewhat larger share, about one-eighth. Clearly these new agencies, while far from negligible, have not been a controlling factor in producing either growth of function or increase in cost." Growth of the Federal Government—1915-1932, p. 547.

THE TAX PROBLEM

It is probable that the proportion of national income spent for governmental activities in the United States, and even in Europe, was no greater and may have been less than the proportion spent for such activities in western Europe during the seventeenth and eighteenth centuries.[41] Nevertheless, American taxpayers were objecting; and the fact that they were objecting raised questions important to the functioning of democracy.

Taxation was not operating as an effective brake on governmental expansion.

In the long run, pressure for activities and appropriations was more effective than pressure against them. As a receiver of governmental service, the taxpayer himself demanded more and better service. Neither roads nor schools could be provided by individual effort. Both made a wide appeal; and expenditure on both could be justified either as unavoidable or as a good investment. Moreover, a number of citizens, ranging from a majority in some states to a small minority in others, because of the indirect levies failed to realize that they were taxpayers at all; but they were more conscious than others of benefits from governmental spending. The fact that individuals were paying or must eventually pay for governmental activity was partially concealed by indirect taxation and by borrowing.

In another sense, the voter had a dual personality: he was a state taxpayer and a federal taxpayer; and it was difficult for him to think in both capacities at the same time. He was more inclined to be preoccupied alternately, during more or less extended periods, with either state spending or national spending, depending on which appeared, for political-party purposes, the more extravagant or scandalous.

From the beginning of our party history, the Outs have almost invariably denounced the party in power for extravagance and demanded economy. In 1916 and 1920, for example, the Republicans condemned "shameless raids on the treasury," while in

---

[41] James W. Martin, discussion on "Problems of Public Finance in the Depression," *American Economic Review* (Suppl.), Vol. 24 (1934), p. 162.

1924, the Democrats objected to "unscientific taxation" and declared that "all taxes" were "unnecessarily high."

As a rule, legislatures disliked to increase taxation, especially just before elections, and to ease the situation provided numerous adjustments to insure a fairer, or at least a politically less hazardous, distribution of the burden among individuals, sections, and classes. Progressive taxes, such as income, corporation, and inheritance levies, introduced more justice into the system, and partly shifted the burden to the wealthier minority. Increasing centralization of assessments and collection tended to eliminate opportunities for evasion. But the need of additional revenue compelled the establishment of new impositions which were in effect regressive, such as sales taxes and the gasoline tax; and, in general, the tendency was to depend more on indirect and less on direct taxation. The general effect of adjustments, improvements, and new taxes may have represented progress from the revenue standpoint, but did not contribute much to the certainty and stability of the taxpayers' outlook.

*The tax system was becoming
more complicated.*

The tax system was becoming about the most complex and intricate field of legislation or of administration; and its difficulties were enhanced by its inherent unpopularity. Taxes were utilized, not only for the raising of revenue, but also for economic, social, and moral purposes. They were levied to assist in regulation, promotion, education, health protection, policing, inspection, and many other activities. To make matters worse, federalism created two great tax systems, legislated and administered separately, largely unco-ordinated, and in part duplicating or conflicting.

Three interacting developments offered encouragement: (1) organization of taxpayers; (2) scientific leadership; and (3) better co-ordination within the legislative mechanism. Organized efforts, usually nonpartisan, were made in most of the states to inform taxpayers what they were paying and how public revenues were spent.[42] Compared with other political and economic problems,

[42] "By far the most significant of recent developments in the field of American taxation is the new temper of the taxpaying public. This new temper scarcely

little analytical and theoretical examination was given to the growth of governmental activities. Most of the illuminating observations on this phenomenon, beginning with those of Henry C. Adams in the previous century, came from students of taxation and public finance; for an extension of the scope of government introduced an element of change, and the problems of a dynamic tax system were different from those of a static system and more difficult.[43] Establishment of a budget system was the central purpose of proposals for improving the operations in fiscal matters of the legislative mechanism.

CENTRALIZATION

What was happening to the practice of local self-government and to the system of federalism?

*In the states centralization
accompanied expansion.*

In his study of government functions, Wooddy estimated that between 1915 and 1929 the net per capita functional expenditures of the states, measured in dollars of constant purchasing power, increased exactly 100 per cent, while those of cities having a population of more than 30,000 increased 35 per cent and other local expenditures 40 per cent.[44] These estimates suggest the relative expansion of administration during this period. They do not throw much light on the extent to which power was centralized. The shift of power was great from the rural units to the state government. If there was any transfer of power between the state and the large cities it was not significant, except locally; and it is probable that the trend over the country, so far as the

---

requires statistical demonstration. Its day to day manifestations are amply recorded in the public press. Among these manifestations may be mentioned the birth of hundreds of new taxpayers' associations, resolutions and activities of farm and trade organizations, the multiplication of tax investigating bodies, both public and private, and the growing volume of reports, studies and recommendations which represent the results of their findings." Clarance Heer, "Trends in Taxation and Public Finance," in *Recent Social Trends*, Vol. 2, p. 1331.

[43] For a recent stimulating discussion of governmental activities by a student of taxation, see Herbert D. Simpson, "The Problem of Expanding Governmental Activities," *American Economic Review* (Suppl.), Vol. 24 (1934), pp. 151-60.

[44] *Recent Social Trends*, Vol. 2, p. 1309.

large cities were concerned, was in the direction of decentralization.[45]

It is probable, though not entirely clear, that the legislative powers of the county were being subjected to further statutory restrictions. In 1930, the county's taxing and appropriating powers were hedged about by many statutory limitations. Its borrowing powers had been restricted by constitutional and statutory provisions for many decades; and a number of states prior to 1900 had introduced central administrative supervision of local indebtedness. This supervision was now adopted by a number of other states. In addition, state administrative supervision of local budgets was established in a few commonwealths; and in three states provision was made for central control of the finances of defaulting local units. There was also a marked tendency to establish state supervision or control of local assessments and local accounting.[46]

State grants-in-aid began, as we have seen, at an early date. The system of state-administered, locally shared taxes appeared before 1900, but was widely adopted and financially important only after 1910. Prior to this time, a large part of state tax revenue was derived from locally administered sources.[47] Afterward, the revenue relationships of the two governmental levels tended to be reversed. As payments from the state grew larger, as administration became more technical, and as the state developed competent administrative leadership, the central agencies assumed a closer supervision and stricter control of local activities.

An entire field of administration was rarely transferred to the state. State administrators usually preferred to work through, or at least with the co-operation of, local boards. With respect to highways, however, the general practice was for the state, first, to give grants-in-aid to the counties, and then to take over the construction and maintenance of a considerable part of the road system. In 1931, North Carolina went the farthest, placing all

[45] It was not, however, an uninterrupted trend. There were swings to and from municipal home rule and county option. See Wilson, Herring, and Entsler, *Public Utility Regulation*, p. 35.

[46] Leonard D. White, *Trends in Public Administration* (1933), pp. 49-68.

[47] Henry J. Bitterman, *State and Federal Grants-in-Aid* (1938), p. 35.

highways within the state under the control of the state highway department, to be built and maintained exclusively by the state.

The plight of the rural community was not unnoticed or unmourned. As soon as the county was "discovered," its inefficiency and political debility were apparent. Several plans were advanced to rehabilitate it as a center of political discussion, as a "nursery of democracy," and as an efficient administrative unit. County home rule and county consolidation were proposed and in some cases provided for by state law; but few counties took advantage of the opportunities thus offered to move again in the direction of local self-government. When the state developed administrative agencies of its own, the retention of local autonomy produced division of authority and responsibility.

National centralization was increasing, partly as a fact, more as a potentiality.

The inadequacy of state economic regulation and the steadily increasing scope of federal regulatory activities, which were partly supplementary to state powers and partly at their expense, did much to create the impression and the fact of centralization.

National centralization is most evident when the federal government is actually crowding the states out of specific fields of activity or when it is increasing its dominance or influence over state legislation or administration. In this period, the activities of the federal government were expanding, but apparently less rapidly than those of the states.

In connection with economic regulation, the effect of Supreme Court decisions, federal statutes, and federal administrative action was to narrow the sphere in which the state could function. But, practically, this sphere had already been narrowed by economic conditions. The tendency was for federal regulatory agencies to co-ordinate their action with that of like agencies in the states; and in some directions Congress sought to strengthen state enforcement through federal regulation of goods and persons in interstate commerce. Moreover, at the end of this period the federal government was by no means exercising its full power over commerce.

With respect to service rather than regulation, national centralization, such as it was, proceeded from much the same conditions as those which accounted for state centralization. The federal government seemed to have abundant financial resources. The states were unequal in ability to pay for services. So, as demands for services became pressing, the federal government extended the system of grants-in-aid. While these were increasing, at least up to about 1925, they constituted a relatively small item in the federal and state budgets; and, before the depression, most of the federal grants were for road construction. The legislating of these grants was made possible by the existence of federal surpluses, and revealed little, if any, intention to increase the power of the federal government. Nor did the grants-in-aid shift activities from the states to the nation. On the contrary, the federal government was stimulating the states to undertake more activities.[48]

The grant-in-aid system tended, however, to put control of certain segments of state administration in the hands of federal agencies; and these instruments of control were among those commonly applied by a superior authority to an inferior one. If they were not used to dominate the state agency, they were in any event influential. Of course, state legislatures could refuse the grants; but refusals were rare.

The immediate pressure for increased use of grants-in-aid came from both federal and state administrators, who were interested in the extension and improvement of services. In many cases, however, more effective pressure was exerted by national private or semi-official organizations, specializing in a particular field of administration. In these organizations, federal and state administrators were both active.[49]

In other ways, the federal government gave assistance to state agencies: it collected and disseminated information, lent expert personnel, and initiated joint and co-operative projects. Federal ad-

[48] "In a sense, the federal-aid system strengthens the states and thereby strengthens but profoundly modifies the federal system. . . . As a matter of fact, the grant-in-aid system operates to reenforce and preserve the states. . . ." V. O. Key, Jr., *The Administration of Federal Grants to States* (1937), p. 375.

"The advocates of the grant-in-aid argue that it combines the administrative advantages of the bureaucratic and the system of local autonomy." Bitterman, *State and Federal Grants-in-Aid*, p. 4.

[49] On official and semi-official associations, see Key, *The Administration of Federal Grants to States*, pp. 178-205.

ministrators also prepared drafts of bills for the state legislatures to consider.

In the discussion of centralization too little attention was ordinarily given to the passing of legislative initiative from the states. In technical matters particularly, state legislation was being increasingly prepared and promoted either by federal agencies or by specialized organizations. The result was a tendency toward uniformity in state policy and law. Indeed, with the regionalizing and nationalizing of problems, uniformity seemed more and more necessary; but it was incompatible with that diversity and experimentalism which were believed to be peculiar advantages of federalism.

As consolidations and intercounty arrangements were proposed to remedy the deficiencies of the county, so interstate compacts were suggested to compensate for the inadequacies of the state. Interstate compacts were tried more frequently than in the past. For certain regional problems they seemed appropriate; for others they were manifestly impracticable. In general, they offered little hope of removing the conditions making for centralization.

During the years prior to the depression, national centralization was increasing less as a fact than as a potentiality. The condition which might make it a fact was the unfathomed reservoir of political power available for use by the national government.

MULTIPLICATION OF AGENCIES

As administration entered the twentieth century, it was becoming more important, more extensive, and more costly; but, with respect to organization, it was following the lines of development that had been laid down in the states before the Civil War. With variations in degree and form, new activities were assigned to new agencies; and, as new fields of activity were entered, the new agencies multiplied. When governmental activity extended beyond the traditional fields, it was more and more concerned with complex, diversified, and specialized objectives and procedures which were pressed upon the legislatures at different times by special groups. The new activities seemed to be separable and they involved an increasing measure of administrative discretion as well as of technical competence. It was natural, therefore, that, when a new activity was adopted, the group that had pressed for it would desire to have it separately established. A considerable proportion of the new agencies continued to be placed under boards and commissions, in part because of influences that had long been in operation— legislative interest in the control of administration, the desire to give legislative form to agencies exercising sublegislative functions, the ideas of trusteeship and representation, as well as the inclination of politicians to increase the number of political positions.[50] Strong, also, were two derivative factors: (1) the special desire of the specialized group to have representation in the administration and development of the new activity; and (2) the effort to remove administration from partisan politics.

It so happened that these various influences and desires were not new; and, as administration developed and agencies multiplied, the impression was created that no changes were taking place in administrative organization, but that legislative neglect, incompetence, or inertia were producing increasing chaos.[51]

Enumerations of the separate administrative agencies were somewhat misleading, since they often included many agencies that had little or no practical importance; but, even so, they were indicative of a condition that required examination. At one date or another between 1910 and 1925, New York State was reported to have 169 departments, bureaus, boards, institutions, commissions and offices;[52] Minnesota, 75;[53] Texas, 85;[54] Pennsylvania,

---

[50] The Massachusetts Commission on Economy and Efficiency found in 1914 that about 50 per cent of all state departments and institutions were controlled by unpaid officials or trustees and about 77 per cent had plural administrative heads. *Report*, November 1914, p. 36.

[51] "The development of the state administrative organization has for a long time past been largely unconscious and consequently haphazard. Endless incongruities and absurdities were the natural result. Where improvements in organization occurred they were usually accidental, partial or sporadic. The present organization of state administration contains little evidence of unified design or systematic planning." John M. Mathews, *Principles: State Administration* (1917), p. 499.

[52] New York State Department of Efficiency and Economy and New York Bureau of Municipal Research, *Government of the State of New York* (1915), p. vii.

[53] Minnesota Efficiency and Economy Commission, *Preliminary Report* (1914), p. 9.

[54] F. M. Stewart, *Officers, Boards and Commissions of Texas*, Legislative Reference Bulletin No. 3 (July 1916).

139;[55] Illinois, over 100; Michigan, 116; Massachusetts, over 200; Utah, 48; Virginia, 95; and Delaware more than 100.[56]

In the federal administrative organization the same trend was discernible. After 1900, two more executive departments were set up; but the total was only ten. A number of separate boards, commissions, and agencies were created during our participation in the World War; but most of these were afterward disbanded. On the other hand, to the Civil Service Commission and the Interstate Commerce Commission, established in the eighties, were added several other plural-headed agencies; and the Veterans' Bureau (now the Veterans' Administration) was created as an independent establishment.

In the states, but more especially in the federal government, the problem of administrative organization appeared to be, not merely a matter of administrative multiplicity, but likewise one of faulty allocation of activities, creating, it was held, overlapping, duplication, conflicts, confusion, inefficiency, and waste.

EXECUTIVE LEADERSHIP

Twice during this relatively short period, a "strong executive" appeared at Washington, achieving an unusual measure of political leadership and challenging the principle of separation of powers. In the states, vigorous and effective executive leadership was almost as common as it was significant.

Reasons for the "strong executive" lay in social, political, and governmental conditions.

From 1900 to 1916, when the popular reaction to "big business" and "bossism" was swelling the tide of democracy to a new flood, the re-conquest of popular rule and the achievement of social justice was a "fight"; and, as in the time of Andrew Jackson, only a "fighting" man could provide the necessary symbolization and, as a practical matter, get the desired results. So governors were found propagandizing their progressive programs, pressing, persuading, and brow-beating legislatures, taking their fights to the

[55] F. G. Crawford, *State Government* (1931), p. 182.
[56] Walter F. Dodd, *State Government* (2d ed., 1928), p. 234.

people, stirring up public opinion, and thus forcing legislatures into compliance.[57]

Opinion in the states looked more and more to the governor for the carrying out of a legislative program. He was expected not only to use his veto power courageously, but also to exercise affirmative leadership, to bring personal and official pressure to bear on the legislators in order that needed laws might be passed.

What a candidate for the legislature might promise his district or his county during a campaign would usually be unknown in other sections of the commonwealth. Of course, when all the elected legislators gathered together in the capitol, they were supposed in the aggregate to represent the state; but it was notorious that they did not, so far as positive results were concerned. The governor, on the other hand, was compelled, at least partially and approximately, to make his views known to the entire state; and, when elected, he had some reason to assert that his policies or at least his general attitude represented what the majority demanded. On the average, governors were superior to legislators in political maturity, experience, and general ability. The executive, moreover, had official resources and weapons that could be employed to bring legislators into line. In addition, he was not in theory or in fact primarily an executive officer.

In the federal government, Congress needed leadership. It could not supply its own. Expansion of governmental functions and of administrative organization was adding to the prestige of the president and extending the range of his discretionary authority and popular contacts. Execution of laws that were at best experimental tended to make the administrator a judge of the adequacy of existing statutes and of the need for new ones. The size and complexity of American society, the obscurity, remoteness, and difficulty of its problems, the inability of most persons to understand and rationally decide them, gave a vast opportunity and power to one who was a focus of national interest, and could at any moment command popular attention. Economic maladjustment nurtured discontent and conflicts which, at least intermittently,

[57] On relations between governors and state legislatures, see Robert Luce, *Legislative Problems* (1935), pp. 220-30.

produced presidents with exceptional public pressure behind them. Policies and policy issues now assumed hundreds of different meanings and relationships. As a result, it was possible for a president to give the appearance of always leading, while constantly adapting himself to the currents of opinion.

One may assume that executive leadership was more representative of the nation as a whole than was the leadership of either house of Congress. It is true that a geographical limitation on presidential nominations persisted after 1900.[58] But while Congress remained predominantly rural in outlook, presidential candidates after 1900, and especially presidents, were predominantly of urban upbringing and presumably of urban outlook. On the whole they were, apparently, better fitted to a technological age; and intellectually their average was high.

Electoral trends, moreover, seemed to favor the choice of presidents who would be political leaders, fairly well attuned to modern conditions and not wholly lacking the administrative viewpoint. The governorship was becoming more than ever a springboard to the presidency; and it was the strong governors—the policy-determining governors—who as a rule won the presidential nomination.[59]

The president's opportunity to become a political leader was described by Woodrow Wilson, some years before he became president, as follows:

The nation as a whole has chosen him, and is conscious that it has no other political spokesman. His is the only national voice in affairs.

---

[58] Of the fifteen candidates of major parties from 1900 to 1936 inclusive, four were from Ohio and six from New York. If Theodore Roosevelt and Coolidge are not considered (both were originally elected as vice-president), Hoover is the only exception since 1856 to the rule that the Republican Party, when it nominates a successful candidate, chooses one from the Middle West. There has been no exception since 1852 to the rule that Democratic presidents come from the most highly industrialized states in the Northeast.

[59] Between the Civil War and 1900, only two men primarily distinguished as governors had been elected—Hayes and Cleveland. (McKinley also had been governor but was better known as a member of Congress.) From the death of McKinley in 1901 to the present time, four presidents have stepped from the governor's office to the presidency—Theodore Roosevelt, Wilson, Coolidge, and Franklin D. Roosevelt. Taft and Hoover were chiefly known as administrators. Of the seven presidents, Harding alone had been a member of Congress.

Let him once win the admiration and confidence of the country, and no other single force can withstand him, no combination of forces will easily overpower him. His position takes the imagination of the country. He is the representative of no constituency, but of the whole people. When he speaks in his true character, he speaks for no special interest. If he rightly interpret the national thought and boldly insist upon it, he is irresistible; and the country never feels the zest of action so much as when its President is of such insight and calibre. Its instinct is for unified action, and it craves a single leader. It is for this reason that it will often prefer to choose a man rather than a party. A President whom it trusts can not only lead it, but form it to his own views.

. . . His office is anything he has the sagacity and force to make it.

.   .   .   .

. . . The President is at liberty, both in law and conscience, to be as big a man as he can. His capacity will set the limit; and if Congress be overborne by him, it will be no fault of the makers of the Constitution—it will be from no lack of constitutional powers on its part, but only because the President has the nation behind him, and Congress has not. He has no means of compelling Congress except through public opinion.

Of course, Wilson added, there were illegitimate means by which the president might influence Congress, but "the reprobation of all good men will always overwhelm such influences with shame and failure."[60]

Government through the "strong executive," attractive to many, frequently recurred but was not yet "normal."

In national affairs, the president as a powerful factor in legislation was by no means an unprecedented phenomenon. Properly included among the influential presidents were Washington, Jefferson, and Lincoln. Andrew Jackson, Tyler, Johnson, Hayes, and Cleveland battled Congress in different ways and with different results. Nevertheless, during much of the time before the Civil War and most of the time from 1865 to 1901, Congress governed the country, as Woodrow Wilson pointed out in his famous dissertation.

The possibilities of presidential leadership were demonstrated by Theodore Roosevelt; and his administration, perhaps more than

[60] *Constitutional Government in the United States* (1911), pp. 68-71.

any in the past, influenced political theory. American political scientists were generally disposed to admire the English system of responsible cabinet government. From this system, separation of powers and checks and balances had been eliminated. Party, parliament, and executive were unified. The members of the executive were also members of Parliament. They were accepted by and responsible to the legislative majority. As a result, it appeared, public opinion was smoothly and expeditiously translated into law; and, at the same time, administration was controlled by the elected representatives of the people. The system in practice departed somewhat from its theory, but it seemed from a distance to work better than our own more artificial "Newtonian" mechanism.

Woodrow Wilson in the eighties thought that the severed portions of power in the American government had finally gravitated together and found unity in the committees of Congress; but in 1900 he had this to say:

It may be, too, that the new leadership of the Executive, inasmuch as it is likely to last, will have a very far-reaching effect upon our whole method of government. It may give the heads of the executive departments a new influence upon the action of Congress. It may bring about, as a consequence, an integration which will substitute statesmanship for government by mass meeting.[61]

Wilson, an admirer of the English system and an enthusiastic exponent of presidential leadership, put his feelings into practice after his inauguration. Taft had recommended that the Cabinet officers be given seats in Congress and permitted to speak from the floor. Wilson decided to speak from the floor himself. The presidential address, personally delivered to Congress, replaced the written message read by a clerk. He had a party majority in both houses; and, through a close working arrangement with the congressional leaders, pushed through a comprehensive and fairly consistent legislative program.

Presidential leadership, however, seemed to call for extraordinary personal energy, emotional heat, or moral elevation, no one of which could be indefinitely sustained. Moreover, presidential domination did not appear to square with the traditions

[61] *Congressional Government*, p. xiii.

of constitutionalism. When Theodore Roosevelt was in office, the Democrats denounced "executive usurpation of legislative and judicial functions";[62] and, when Wilson was in office, the Republicans declared that "under the despot's plea of necessity or superior wisdom, executive usurpation of legislative and judicial function still undermines our institutions."[63] So Theodore Roosevelt was succeeded by Taft, and Wilson was followed by Harding.

THE EFFICIENCY MOVEMENT

While the executive was, or could be, legislatively powerful, he controlled in the states only a small part of administration and in both states and nation a relatively diminishing part. Administration seemed to be disintegrating under the pressure of particular interests. It was complicated by new principles and burdened with new tasks. It had become pre-eminently technical and increasingly expensive. The composition of legislative bodies was not such as to facilitate a comprehensive consideration of the problem of administrative organization. Unable to co-ordinate policy, they could hardly be expected to co-ordinate the agencies that reflected policy.

From various directions came influences emphasizing efficiency through organization.

The interest groups and specialized associations, largely responsible for administrative expansion, had been early and keenly interested in the problem of administrative efficiency. In the fields of education, engineering, public health, public welfare, and crime control, professionalism and expertness had found appropriate applications and in many cases had brought significant improvements to public administration. But the specialists were primarily interested in operations. An adequate approach to the problem of administrative organization demanded that the general or over-all point of view should be co-ordinated and reconciled with the specialized and operating points of view.

In general, the trend of thinking and of public policy was in

[62] Platform of 1904.
[63] Platform of 1920.

the direction of organization in its broader applications—elimination of waste and establishment of law, order, and control. The idea of public planning appeared about 1900 in the form of engineering organization of the layout and growth of cities. From the World War on, the principle of advance planning of public works was discussed by economists and embodied in bills introduced in Congress. The impulsion of social thinking and social action toward diversification and specialization was in part counterbalanced by co-ordinating, integrating, and centralizing tendencies. Increasing complexity of social institutions and problems created needs and desires for simplification of forms and definite location of controls. American participation in the World War furnished an example of what organized social solidarity could accomplish.

The National Municipal League had in the late nineties proposed changes in the organization of municipal government. In 1900 an emergency created by the Galveston flood led to the establishment in that city of the commission plan of municipal government. Its spread to other cities led to the "demolition of the federal analogy, wrecking the idea of checks and balances, and casting on the scrap heap much of the complicated structural accumulation of the nineteenth century."[64] Soon afterward the city-manager or council-manager plan was accepted by the National Municipal League as its "model." By 1929, over 400 cities had adopted this plan and others some modifications of it.[65]

The corporate form of industrial organization seemed to provide a definite concentration of authority and responsibility in the general manager; and in each of the operating departments the location of authority and responsibility appeared equally clear. The efficiency of the corporation seemed to be demonstrated; and, although its position and functions were in few respects analogous to those of a government, the example of corporate organization appealed to those who were seeking something ready-made for a quick and easy reorganization of public administration.

Industry exemplified also the application of technique and ex-

[64] White, *Trends in Public Administration*, p. 212.
[65] The same, pp. 210-16.

pertness to management and operations. The machine itself was a symbol of increased production and economized energy and an example of the results that came from systematic research. Industrial research was applied also to the problem of managing men and materials for greater output in less time and at lower cost.[66]

Students of government were becoming more critical, realistic, and interpretative. The challenge of administration could not long escape them. Goodnow's book on *Politics and Administration*, published in 1900, showed the distinction between the art of policy-determination or legislation and what appeared to be the purely technical task of administration. While this distinction was not an absolute one even then, it became the habit of writers to consider administration simply as the management of men and materials for the accomplishment of tangible results, demanding detached expertness but having little relation to the broader problems of democratic government.

Under the pressure of facts—increasing costs of administration and its apparent inefficiency—privately financed organizations for governmental research appeared. Such organizations rapidly multiplied, independently financed or as adjuncts of universities, taxpayers' associations, chambers of commerce, or associations of government officials. In large and increasing measure, these research bodies, like the universities, put themselves at the service of legislatures and public administrative agencies. From the beginning, legislatures through regular and special committees and commissions had studied problems of administration; and from these investigations certain improvements had resulted. In the second decade of the century, however, special committees or commissions on "retrenchment" or on "economy and efficiency" were set up to survey the whole of administration and to recommend measures for increasing its efficiency and cutting its costs. The proposal for a budget system was usually made and was considered of prior and fundamental importance.

[66] Popular discussion of business efficiency was under way in 1905. Hornel Hart, "Changing Social Attitudes and Interests," in *Recent Social Trends*, Vol. 1, p. 431.

*The movement stressed the role
of the executive.*

The establishment of budget systems represented not only a reorganization of legislative control over expenditures, but also the development of a phase of executive leadership. From the beginning, Congress in making appropriations for the executive departments had acted on requests and proposals originating in the executive agencies and compiled by the secretary of the treasury. The failure of this system either to unify executive fiscal policy or to aid Congress in the formulation of its own policy led to a movement to concentrate responsibility for executive formulation of fiscal policy in the president. The first step was taken in the Sundry Civil Appropriation Act of March 4, 1909. In 1911, President Taft, acting under congressional authorization, appointed a Commission on Economy and Efficiency. One of its conclusions was that executive responsibility in budgetary matters was "essential to obtaining results with economy and efficiency." Congress in 1916 created a Bureau of Efficiency and finally in 1921 established the present budget system, providing for a Budget Bureau located in the Treasury Department but under control of the president. The intention was to make the president responsible for the initiation of a financial program covering both expenditure and revenue.[67]

The movement for a budget system made rapid progress in the states. In 1912, said Leonard D. White: "No American state possessed a budget, in the accepted sense of the word today. . . . In 1929 every American state, except Arkansas, had a budget system in which the influence of the governor was considerable and in most cases controlling."[68]

Along with proposals for a budgetary system, attention was given to the systematization of purchasing and of other activities involved in the fiscal or "business" side of administration. Emphasis on these activities, coupled with the fascination of the corporation analogy, led many students to refer to administration, sometimes

[67] The statements in this paragraph are drawn from an unpublished paper read by Daniel T. Selko at the 1939 meeting of the American Political Science Association; but Mr. Selko is not responsible for the form in which the statements are here made or for any inferences drawn from them.

[68] *Trends in Public Administration*, p. 188.

even to government, as simply a business enterprise; and the conclusion was that, for co-ordinated and responsible direction of such activities, the chief executive should be made the "general manager" or should have a "general manager" directly responsible to the chief executive. To a large extent, this conclusion was accepted by legislatures; and the power of the executive over fiscal policy, fiscal administration, purchasing, and related "business" activities was greatly increased in federal, state, and municipal governments. This development not only enhanced executive leadership in legislation but also gave the executive greater opportunity to control the whole of administration.

When economy and efficiency commissions turned to the task of reorganizing the functional or "line" agencies,[69] the role of the executive, actual and prospective, received even greater emphasis. Two major questions presented themselves: (1) should the executive or the legislature do the reorganizing; and (2) should the executive control the reorganized administration? The efficiency movement was concurrent, and not entirely by accident, with the trend toward the "strong" executive. In the federal government, the constitutional embodiment and traditional theory of administration was that it fell "peculiarly within the province of the executive department" and was subject to the chief executive's "superintendence."[70] At the turn of the century, the federal administrative organization apparently still adhered to the original conception of a few executive departments headed by individuals responsible to the president.

Executives led in the movement but did not usually do the reorganizing.

Congress showed a willingness to delegate within limits the task of reorganization to the chief executive. Except for the Treas-

[69] We are discussing now, not the reorganization of policies and laws, nor the increase or curtailment of administrative activities, nor changes in administrative procedures, but merely what was known as structural reorganization, involving the shifting of activities from one agency to another, the division or merging of agencies, and changes in their relationships to one another and to the chief executive.

[70] Alexander Hamilton in the *Federalist*, Henry Cabot Lodge, ed. (1888), p. 450.

ury Department, the details of organization within the executive departments had been partly left by Congress to executive initiative; and attempts to restrict the president's power to remove executive officers had on the whole failed.[71]

Theodore Roosevelt expressed the opinion that no legislative body could do the job and that the power to reorganize should be delegated to the executive.[72] In 1905, on his own initiative and without congressional direction, he appointed an investigating committee consisting of three assistant secretaries and two bureau chiefs.[73] The Economy and Efficiency Commission of 1911-13 was authorized by Congress and appointed by the president, and consisted in the main of outstanding students of administration who were not federal officials.[74] On the other hand, Congress in 1920 created a Joint Committee on the Reorganization of the Administrative Branch of the government. The establishment of the Bureau of Efficiency in 1913 and the investigatory powers given to the Budget Bureau in 1921 indicated a desire, not adequately fulfilled in practice, to equip the executive branch for continuous organizational studies. President Wilson in 1918 was granted considerable authority to redistribute functions among executive agencies; but the authority was limited to a period of six months after the termination of the war.[75]

In the states, it was frequently the governor, especially when he happened to be a "strong" governor, who took the initiative in urging special investigations. The investigating body, however, was often entirely legislative in composition or was appointed partly by the legislature and partly by the governor.[76] Certain states

[71] Lloyd M. Short, *The Development of National Administrative Organization in the United States* (1923), pp. 35-36, 220, 235, 342, 356.

[72] Annual Message, Dec. 5, 1905.

[73] Weber, *Organized Efforts for the Improvement of Methods of Administration*, pp. 74-83.

[74] Two advisory boards were provided for, one of which was composed of government officials. The same, pp. 84-86.

[75] Short, *The Development of National Administrative Organization*, p. 260.

[76] An important study was made in Illinois under the auspices of a joint legislative committee created in 1913 and reporting in 1915. The actual study, however, was made by a staff of specialists working under the general direction of a professor of political science at the University of Illinois.

also made provision for continuous study by an executive agency in problems of administrative organization.

The movement aimed to establish executive control over a departmentalized administration.

The numerous investigations, studies, and surveys were, with a few exceptions, in agreement on three related conclusions: (1) that all administrative activities, except those of a quasi-legislative or quasi-judicial character, should be brought together in a few departments, the grouping to be, in general, on the basis of functions, considered to be practically identical with major purpose or major objective; (2) that each department should be single-headed; and (3) that each department head should be appointed by and responsible to the chief executive. This scheme obviously contemplated a sweeping extension of executive power over administration; and it is not surprising that it was vigorously advocated by governors and presidents. Theodore Roosevelt proposed to include even the Interstate Commerce Commission in his plan for federal integration.[77]

Most of the scholars who wrote on the problem fell into line. Treatises and textbooks on government and administration agreed generally that all administrative organizations that failed to square with this standardized model were absurdly antiquated and hopelessly inefficient. Two or three dissenting voices were raised among the intellectuals but without any apparent effect. Most of the objections, and these were numerous, came from legislators, politicians, and the specialized organizations interested in particular fields of administration.

[77] His argument was put in a few strong words:
"Economy and sound business policy require that all existing independent bureaus and commissions should be placed under the jurisdiction of appropriate executive departments. It is unwise from every standpoint, and results only in mischief, to have any executive work done save by the purely executive bodies, under the control of the President; and each such executive body should be under the immediate supervision of a Cabinet and Minister." Special Message, Dec. 8, 1908. See also W. F. Dodd, "Proposed Reforms in State Governmental Organization," in *American Political Science Review*, Vol. 4 (1910), p. 250; Leslie Lipson, "Influence of the Governor upon Legislation," in *Annals*, Vol. 195 (1938), p. 73.

Generally, the advantages of a piecemeal, evolutionary process of reorganization were either ignored or dogmatically denied by those who advocated executive integration. Their presumption was that because an organization was old or had not been "consciously planned" it must be wrong.[78]

An effort was made to relate the principle of integrated administration under executive control to the problem of democracy. It was urged that concentration of authority led to a definite locating of responsibility, and enabled the electorate to reward or punish the persons responsible.[79]

Advocates of complete executive power over administration argued also that, with responsibility definitely located in the executive, better executives would be elected. American executives, however, were politicians; and they were not elected as administrators but as legislative leaders. So elected, increased administrative power would not qualify them to exercise it; but it would enhance their power to dominate the legislature and the party, particularly

[78] ". . . All institutions, whatever they may be, should be approached with the presumption that there is, or at any rate once was, a reason for them, appealing at the time of their adoption to the commonsense of the community. Therefore the presumption should be in their favor. An institution, like a man, is to be deemed innocent till proved guilty. Yet a large number of writers approach every institution of government as if it were necessarily bad, and always assume that something better should be substituted." Luce, *Legislative Problems*, p. 695.

"I think, therefore, the example of the British parliamentary system shows that with men, as with animals, a continual conscious adaptation to immediate objects may sometimes, if the conditions are favorable, lead to a fully self-consistent and harmonious system which to the authors is quite unforeseen, and which is not only very different from, but even quite inconsistent with, the theories . . . that they retain continuously throughout the process." Abbott Lawrence Lowell, "An Example from History," in Harvard Tercentenary Publications, *Factors Determining Human Behavior* (1937), pp. 129-30.

[79] "The danger to American democracy lies not in the least in the concentration of administrative power in responsible and accountable hands. It lies in having the power insufficiently concentrated, so that no one can be held responsible to the people for its use. Concentrated power is palpable, visible, responsible, easily reached, quickly held to account. Power scattered through many administrators, many legislators, many men who work behind and through legislators and administrators, is impalpable, is unseen, is irresponsible, can not be reached, can not be held to account. Democracy is in peril wherever the administration of political power is scattered among a variety of men who work in secret, whose very names are unknown to the common people. It is not in peril from any man who derives authority from the people, who exercises it in sight of the people, and who is from time to time compelled to give an account of its exercise to the people." Special Message, Dec. 8, 1908.

when, in the absence of a merit system, executives could manipulate appointments for political purposes. Administrative power would not necessarily be employed for administrative purposes.[80] In general, the advocates of a stereotyped organization rarely faced or sought to solve the dilemma presented by the position of the executive as a legislative leader. Nor was due attention given to the increasing proportion of administrative work that was discretionary or sublegislative.

A conviction that the multiplicity of elective officers was inconsistent with popular control gave rise to the "short ballot" movement. It was expected that the short ballot, by lightening the voter's task, would enable him to exercise more discrimination in marking his ballot, thus encouraging independence and stripping the "machine" of its power to put over hand-picked "slates" composed of party henchmen.

*The results were in general partial
and inconclusive.*

When the reorganization plan was finally formulated, what was done with it? Almost universally, improvements were made in fiscal administration.

With respect to the "line" agencies, the problem of administrative reorganization in the federal government was different in many ways from the problem in the states; but at both levels one difficulty was always present—the pressure of interest groups and specialized organizations. In large measure, the administrative organization merely reflected the situation of policies and of society. Co-ordination and unity were lacking; but the deficiency lay in the

[80] "We are now faced with the question whether American chief executives are to be primarily political or administrative officials. It is anomalous, although not impossible, to entrust administrative authority of the scope now found in many jurisdictions directly to a political executive.

". . . The chief executive is more powerful than ever before, and in control of an organization capable of infinite mischief if abused for partisan or private motives. Hence the necessity for safeguards adequate to the proper control of growing power. Formal legal control of the executive has not kept pace with the growth of power; the informal controls of publicity do not always operate effectively." White, *Trends in Public Administration*, pp. 233, 235. See also his *Introduction to the Study of Public Administration* (1926), p. 203.

structure and movement of policies and in the disunity of social action. In many cases the trouble went back to confused or conflicting philosophies.[81]

In the executive department of the national government, various changes were effected; but no general reorganization took place. On the other hand, there were continued manifestations of a desire on the president's part to control the whole of administration.[82]

Sometimes, in the states, one or two of the general administrative fields were reorganized in much the same spirit as they had been from time to time in the past. In a few instances, as in Illinois, a fairly comprehensive law was passed. Whether, to the extent of its application, any general reorganization plan increased or decreased administrative efficiency was not apparent. It certainly did not stop the rise of governmental costs. Some states, before or during the economy and efficiency movement, had attempted to "freeze" the simplified organization by embedding it in their constitutions, with the result that the constitutional restrictions were evaded; and, as in other states whether "reorganized" or not, administrative agencies continued to multiply.[83]

POLITICAL PARTIES

After 1900 the distinction between the major parties became more blurred; and it appeared that, while they were still serving as electoral vehicles, they were losing their function as parts of the legislative mechanism. Party government was no longer a primary, stable, or decisive factor in the translation of opinion into policy.

---

[81] "Some of today's confusions and inefficiencies in the administration of criminal justice in the United States result from confusions and contradictions in the fundamental concepts on which different parts of the criminal law or its administration are based or on which different practices or methods of administration are based." National Commission on Law Observance and Enforcement, *Report on Prosecution*, No. 4, Apr. 22, 1931, pp. 161-62. See also Sheldon Glueck and Eleanor T. Glueck, *500 Criminal Careers* (1930), pp. 333-34.

[82] President Coolidge, for example, "showed a determination, as far as possible, to make over the personnel in the independent commissions till each should be controlled by a majority whose conception of the commission's functions accorded with his own." George H. Haynes, *The Senate of the United States; Its History and Practice* (1938), Vol. 2, p. 765.

[83] See Luella Gettys, *The Reorganization of State Government in Nebraska* (July 1922), pp. 17-18; Constitution of Massachusetts, Amendments, Art. LXVI.

*Parties were losing
identity.*

With respect to the identity or distinctive character of the party, one may recall the reorientation of the Republican Party under Theodore Roosevelt and, after Roosevelt, its shift toward conservatism under Taft. More illuminating was the variability of the Democratic Party. It nominated Bryan in 1900 and the conservative Judge Parker in 1904; Bryan again in 1908, Wilson in 1912 and 1916, and Cox in 1920; then the conservative John W. Davis in 1924, and after him the presumably "progressive" Alfred E. Smith in 1928.

Over the period the two major parties showed various evidences of philosophical difference; but, by and large, both parties were conservative. Neither was radical. Neither was ever reactionary in the sense of proposing a positive and sweeping reversal of popular trends. The Democrats were less conservative than their opponents with respect to economic and social policies; but they were more conservative with respect to federalism and certain other aspects of political organization. Both parties were middle class, because the country was overwhelmingly middle class in its thinking.

The characteristics of each party were determined for it by a preponderance, rather than by a unanimity, of feeling or opinion within its membership. Its members ranged from Right to Left. In the Republican Party, after Theodore Roosevelt, the greatest concentration of opinion was ordinarily farther to the Right than it was in the Democratic Party. Economically, the country had to all appearances been developing and progressing. Accordingly, a majority of the people were "normally" Republican. The Democratic Party was in the main a vehicle of protest, a means of disciplining the Republicans when the latter became too self-satisfied, arrogant, or corrupt. When such a time came, independent, variable, or discontented voters shifted from the Republican Party and elected Democratic candidates.

In both parties the factors and motives in organization and action were much alike. Both had local and state "machines." Each, within its loose and accommodating ideological framework, was opportunistic in its advocacy of policies. Each, with some respect for consistency, "stood" for the things that seemed likely at the moment to carry a broad appeal to those groups and sections, which, if won over, would produce a majority.

*Conditions were working against
cohesiveness and solidarity.*

Because of technology, specialization, complexity, and the scientific spirit, it was perceived that many public problems were matters of fact rather than of philosophy or sentiment. The professional, the technician, the scientist, the expert, and the intellectual were, at least in their own fields, necessarily independent politically. So were others who were disillusioned by the deficiencies of politicians or were strongly influenced by conceptions of class or group interest. Moreover, groups, sections, and classes cut across one another to such an extent that it was well-nigh impossible for either party to determine a comprehensive and far-reaching program in its platform.

The Solid South remained solid until 1928; and even then the Deep South, except for Texas, went Democratic. The industrialization of the South added to its aristocratic traditionalism an element of Hamiltonian economics. Southern leaders, while calling themselves Democrats, tended to think like conservative Republicans. The West was moved in the main by sectional agrarianism. A purely sectional policy that pleased the West was not likely to please the East. Senators were elected by states and representatives largely by districts. While a state or a district was predominantly of one interest or idea, the candidate who expected to be elected by that constituency was not likely to oppose its particular interest or particular idea.

The direct primary made it possible for a candidate to dissociate himself from party control. He would no doubt "ride on the coattails" of a popular presidential nominee; but he would reserve his freedom of action with regard to those special matters that directly affected the interests of his constituents. His pledges were to them, not to the nation. Able to appeal directly to the people for his nomination, he could on occasion defy the local bosses as well as the national party leaders. Indeed, he might create his own personal organization or "machine." Civil service reform, along with other improvements in administration, were weakening "machine" politics and strengthening personal, as contrasted with party, candidacies.

The system lacked responsiveness and flexibility.

Because of the fundamental identity of the two great parties with substantially the same range of interests and ideals, and because of their acceptance of the same political and economic philosophies, the controversial questions of policy turned on matters of adjustment and correction. Interests conflicted but policy sought to balance and reconcile them, not to protect and foster one interest at the total sacrifice of another. If a fundamental weakness developed in the economic or political structure, the two-party system was ordinarily ill fitted to apply the remedy. It would do so only when unsettled problems accumulated to the proportions of a national scandal or a national emergency. Even then, the system might be unable to act unless it so happened that several favorable factors were working together.

The platform was insufficient to bind the party to a program. On politics, the people were further enlightened by the campaign speeches of the candidates; but, even so, problems were too numerous, too complex, and contained too much political "dynamite" for detailed handling on the hustings. Therefore, on many problems in their entirety and on many aspects of other problems, the candidates retained in effect their independence. During the four-year intervals between presidential elections, numerous unsettled issues accumulated. Although one or two might appear to be paramount or critical, it was rarely clear on which issue an election turned.

Under the circumstances, what the national results of an election would be was more or less incalculable. The parties and the legislative mechanism were subject to post-election reorientations, which were brought about, not only by the election, but also by new situations, the development of personal leaderships, and sometimes by accidents.[84]

No third party produced a realignment; and none was able to establish itself more than momentarily as a major organ of public opinion. In 1912, the Progressive Party polled more votes than the Republicans; but in 1916 progressives and conservatives were again combined under the old name. In the Northwest, particularly in Minnesota and the Dakotas, an extreme progressiveness tinctured with socialism found expression in the Non-Partisan League and the Farmer-Labor Party. In 1924 Senator LaFollette ran for the presidency as an Independent Progressive; and his total popular vote was over 4,800,000, a fair measure of the economic unrest of that time and particularly of the discontent in the agricultural West. The Republicans returned to power, however, and government was again mainly concerned with piecemeal adjustments. In 1928, the appearances of mounting prosperity stilled the clamor of progressivism and almost silenced radicalism. In that year, the Socialists polled only a quarter of a million votes and the Farmers and Workers less than 50,000.

It appeared that the productivity of the economic system had become the supreme determinant of political action. When the economic system seemed to be working well, public opinion was disposed to "let well enough alone" and "keep cool with Coolidge." It reverted to traditionalism, constitutionalism, thrift, speculation, and economic and political stability, and to confidence in the legislative branch as the less affirmative and dynamic part of the policy-determining mechanism. Discontent was never fully

[84] Theodore Roosevelt became president in 1901 by accident. Woodrow Wilson was nominated in 1912 after Champ Clark had received a majority of the votes in the Democratic Convention, and Wilson was elected in that year with a minority of the popular vote. He was re-elected in 1916, partly on the Democrats' legislative record but partly also because, so it was asserted, he had "kept us out of war." The campaign of 1920 was welcomed by Wilson as a "great and solemn referendum" on American adhesion to the League of Nations covenant, which it evidently was not, since the people were then more interested in domestic than in international affairs. Coolidge, who appears to have represented fairly accurately the dominant opinion of his time, also became president the first time by accident. In 1928 the election was decided, apparently, by the prosperity of the country, prohibition, and religion. (Prosperity was to last only a year after the election and prohibition only five years, while the religious issue was wholly irrelevant.)

released; its satisfactions were delayed; and its demands partially frustrated. The country never had a complete political catharsis. The dominance of middle-class sentiment, the prestige of industrialism, the nature of the party system, and the peculiarities of nominating conventions precluded a radical examination of the problem of discontent. They likewise prevented a comprehensive analysis and consistent treatment of conditions and policies in their relation to contemporary discontents and future complications.

From the standpoint of party composition, the legislative mechanism seemed to be working better than it had worked in the past. In 1911-12 a Democratic House faced a Republican Senate and president, and in 1919-20, a Democratic president faced a Republican House and a Republican Senate. During the remainder of the period from 1900 to 1931 the three legislative cylinders seemed to be synchronized. Their harmony, however, was more apparent than real. The division of each party into wings and blocs belied in practice the outward semblances of party unity and party responsibility. During only six years of the thirty—from 1913 to 1918 inclusive—was substantial legislative accomplishment combined with a consistent intra-governmental co-operation.

PRESSURE GOVERNMENT

Leadership came to be increasingly organized and specialized outside the political party system. Private organizations and their leaders influenced policy by propaganda and by pressure. Parties were becoming merely vehicles for persons to ride into office. The elected persons, to the extent that they were controlled by extra-governmental expressions of opinion, were controlled by pressure groups rather than parties.

Pressure groups were taking over the function of registering opinion.

That organized pressures were necessary and inevitable in a democracy was obvious. The influence of many organizations was constructive and resulted in legislation generally believed to be sound. Electoral pressure was in a measure an antidote to the kind of pressure that had previously been covertly and corruptly exerted by the "money power." Lobbying, the spearhead of pressure, was as old as government. In principle, it was a normal, sound, and legitimate means of bringing private opinion to bear on government; and one lobby was in principle no worse than another.

The most effective pressures were dependent, not on propaganda, but on electoral strength. The political power of the American Legion was, apparently, almost entirely due to the belief among members of Congress and state legislatures that the veterans would vote for those who bowed to the Legion's will and against those who did not. The Anti-Saloon League exacted promises from candidates, informed its members of the records of nominees, distinguished between the Drys and the Wets, and actively participated in electoral campaigns for those whom it favored and against those whom it opposed. Furthermore, the League was able to deliver the vote.[85] It had enormous power because its members "voted as they prayed."[86] Similar electoral pressure was used by the American Federation of Labor, the American Farm Bureau Federation, woman suffrage organizations, and municipal good government leagues.

To a great extent, therefore, the process of policy-determination was transferred beyond the legislature and beyond the party system to the pressure-groups. To that extent, the parties and the legislatures no longer even registered a consensus of opinion; they registered the weight of pressures, and unless pressure was felt they failed to register at all. Considerable justification appeared for the idea that the legislature's function was merely to mediate among pressure groups. Unfortunately, mediation was in many cases either impossible or insufficient. Some important interests and

[85] See Peter H. Odegard, *Pressure Politics: The Story of the Anti-Saloon League* (1928).

[86] The influence of its General Counsel Wayne B. Wheeler, was thus summarized without much exaggeration by his biographer:

"Wayne B. Wheeler controlled six Congresses, dictated to two Presidents of the United States, directed legislation in most of the states of the Union, picked the candidates for the more important elective state and federal offices, held the balance of power in both Republican and Democratic parties, distributed more patronage than any dozen other men, supervised a federal bureau from outside without official authority, and was recognized by friend and foe alike as the most masterful and powerful single individual in the United States. Justin Steuart, *Wayne Wheeler: Dry Boss* (1928), p. 11.

ideas were underrepresented or unrepresented by pressure, while others were overrepresented and in some instances misrepresented.

Judged by their effects, propaganda and pressures tended to carry into public policy their own distortions, unbalancing legislation and leaving administration partially unorganized. Propaganda and pressure for political action tended to exploit emotion and to urge speed at the expense of deliberation, while negative propaganda exploited inertia and encouraged inaction.

Moral questions were raised.

From one point of view electoral pressure was a form of bribery. The member of Congress, according to this view, thought only of the salary and perquisites of office. From another point of view, he was merely exemplifying the theory of delegated popular government. He obeyed the commands of his constituents because he was their servant, as he repeatedly assured them. His but to do as he was told—and be re-elected. One difficulty in accepting this view was that the groups which employed electoral pressure were in most, if not all, cases minority groups. In some cases the group that brought pressure was itself asking for a material inducement. It bribed in order to be bribed. Both propaganda and pressure were reflecting on the morals of those who adopted these methods and on the morals, intelligence, and courage of those who were susceptible to them. Both legislatures and the people were being discredited.

There were at all times senators and representatives who could not be moved by pressure or by lobbying. Indeed, in their cases, an attempt to bring such influence might arouse hostility rather than friendliness. The skilled lobbyist either left such men alone or approached them with extreme caution.[87] The direct bribery of legislators had undoubtedly diminished; and the paid lobbyist for business interests, whatever might be his methods, was beginning to be distrusted.[88]

[87] For an example, see *Summary Report of the Federal Trade Commission*, 1934, pp. 272-73.

[88] Luce, *Legislative Assemblies* (1924), p. 399.

On group pressure in the states, see Dayon D. McKean, "A State Legislature

THE LEGISLATIVE MECHANISM

We return again to the legislative mechanism within the structure of government, and will consider its representative character and responsiveness, its internal democracy, its capacity for leadership, its procedural efficiency, its regard for the general interest, and the appropriateness and effectiveness of its product.

Legislatures gained in representation and responsiveness.

The democratizing movement in the early years of the century struck at nominations and at legislatures; and the effect was to make the legislative mechanism generally more responsive. Popular election made United States senators more representative of the opinion of their states and helped to free the state legislatures from "machine" politics. The direct primary, apparently, made both houses of all legislatures more sensitive to changing opinion and pressures. Legislators were becoming less amenable to party discipline, more independent, and more disposed to break apart into sectional blocs or to fly away on individual tangents, more in need of leadership and apparently less able to produce it.

In the states, the initiative, referendum, and recall, and in the nation, the presidential primary, operated ambiguously and did not produce full popular control of state law-making or of national presidential nominations. All of these devices were retained to the extent that they were adopted, for the American people have rarely voted deliberately to abandon any innovation represented to be democratizing.

In the national House of Representatives, as already mentioned, the rules were liberalized and the power of the Speaker was reduced; but the movement stopped far short of restoring effective control to the membership. The House was too large, its membership having increased from 391 to 435. Its average capacity was too low, and its members were too localistic to get things done

---

and Group Pressure," *The Annals*, Vol. 179 (1935), pp. 124-30; Belle Zeller, *Pressure Politics in New York* (1937).

On lobbying in general see Luce, *Legislative Assemblies*, pp. 367-99; S. T. Williamson, "The Lobby on the Job," *New York Times Magazine*, Apr. 17, 1938, pp. 4-16; Edward B. Logan, "Lobbying," in Supplement to *Annals*, Vol. 144 (1929); E. E. Schattschneider, *Politics, Pressures, and the Tariff* (1935).

without leadership or dictation. Woodrow Wilson came into office with a "forward-looking" program, a theory of party responsibility, and a determination as president to exercise party and legislative leadership. He could do so only through an organization and procedure which imposed unity on the Democratic members of Congress. The Democratic platform of 1908 had declared that the House had "ceased to be a deliberative and legislative body, but has come under the absolute domination of the Speaker, who has entire control of its deliberations and powers of legislation"; but in 1916 and 1920 the Republicans were complaining of Democratic "gag rule," "steam-roller" methods in legislation, and "dictatorial" government.

Apart from the question of the division of Congress into two houses, there is reason to question whether either house was set up and organized in such a way as to be really democratic. So far as its territorial basis was concerned, the Senate obviously underrepresented one section and overrepresented the other. On this basis, the House was more fairly constituted; but, when consideration was given to its organization, the power of the committees, "gag rule," seniority, and other matters, its representative character seemed open to serious question. From this point of view, the conference committee, also, was not above criticism. A cloture rule was adopted by the Senate; but filibustering was still possible. This practice was theoretically democratic, since it gave free speech full rein; but its intent and effect were as clearly undemocratic. Senators who filibustered were more often praised than blamed, even though they were patently in the minority and were allegedly frustrating the majority. One reason was that the people admired independence; another was that a majority of the Senate did not always represent a majority of the people.

The House had long since ceased to be a principal forum of discussion. The debates in the Senate usually did little to illuminate problems or guide public opinion. As a matter of fact, the decisive legislative activities were carried on in the offices, the lobbies, and the committee rooms. While the "real work" might be done there, it was not usually done in the public view.

At the turn of the century, Congress contained outstandingly able men; but they were not nationally popular leaders. When

House and Senate were compared with respect to the production of broad-gauge leaders, it seemed that leadership was in inverse proportion to the number of members. The "insurgent" senators were, to an extent, leaders beyond their states. The same can be said, perhaps, of the small group of senators who led in the defeat of the League of Nations Covenant; and the senatorial group which brought about the nomination of Harding in 1920 was strong enough to dominate the government for some time. Always a few senators, because of outstanding ability, independence, or progressivism, enjoyed extensive influence and wide popularity. Likewise, the Speaker of the House and a few of the committee chairmen were known nationally, more perhaps because of position than of superior ability.

Improvement took place with respect to procedural efficiency.

Apart from the question of executive leadership, gains in procedural efficiency were attributable to the practice of delegating legislative powers to administrative agencies; but such practice raised a multitude of questions that were to come to rest eventually on the doorsteps of Congress.

Corollaries of delegation were administrative initiative and advice in the actual work of law-making. The growth of administration, especially of its technical branches, placed an increasing number of experts at the call of Congress. Presidential extensions of the classified service strengthened the principle of merit and gave further assurance that administrative assistance to Congress would be expert and impartial. Then, too, pressures on the national law-makers from the outside were in large measure specialized, technical, intellectual, and even scientific. A bill-drafting service[89] was set up as a congressional adjunct; and a legislative reference service was established in the Library of Congress.

The House Appropriations Committee was enlarged and given exclusive jurisdiction over all appropriation bills. A Budget and Accounting Act was passed. A change was made in the method of voting rivers and harbors appropriations. Three principles were applied to them: (1) lump-sum appropriations; (2) executive dis-

[89] Later called the Office of the Legislative Counsel.

cretion in the allotment of appropriated funds; and (3) utilization of engineering surveys and reports. With reference to the major public buildings in Washington, some progress was made in the direction of adherence to a long-time plan; but, generally speaking, Congress retained its control over individual projects. It appeared that more thorough and intelligent work was being done by special committees and commissions.

The improvements that have been mentioned related in the main to fiscal affairs, and particularly to the supervision of administrative spending. The freedom of debate in the Senate was lauded, on the ground that it permitted criticism of the executive branch; and that body was hailed as the "grand inquest."[90] Legislative control of administration, in the absence of any other effective control, was assuredly necessary. Yet, control of expenditures and of administrative operations did not by any means comprehend the whole or the primary problem of legislation. In some of the most important fields of legislation, expenditure was a derivative or secondary question and rarely a determining consideration.

In fiscal matters, so far as the legislative branch was concerned, the ideal was to unify in one committee the examination of the budget. Measurable progress was made toward the attainment of this ideal; but it was not completely realized. For one thing, as activities expanded and expenditures increased, the Appropriations Committee apportioned much of its detailed work among subcommittees. The budget in practice was a currently adjusted work program rather than an annual review and revision of all governmental policies. The Appropriations Committee was compelled to accept policies already established; and certain essential expenditures demanded by these policies constituted an irreducible minimum below which the committee was practically powerless to go. Moreover, the revenue or Ways and Means Committee remained separate from the budget or Appropriations Committee.

A further obstacle to the co-ordination of fiscal policy was obviously presented by bicameralism. In the federal Congress, this difficulty was to some extent removed by the establishment in 1926 of the Joint Committee on Internal Revenue Taxation. This committee, composed of five members of the House Committee on

[90] Lindsay Rogers, *The American Senate* (1926), p. 206.

Ways and Means and an equal number from the Senate Committee on Finance, was provided with a permanent staff of lawyers, economists, and statisticians, and was authorized to study the federal internal revenue system and recommend measures for its improvement. In both the federal and state governments, the tendency was toward the unification of leadership in fiscal matters and the basing of such leadership on continuous study and expert advice.

At the very time when the fiscal aspects of government received most emphasis, shape was being given to theories that were destined to subordinate the role of public finance as a limitation on governmental functions. One of these theories held that individuals or classes of individuals had "rights" to governmental service and, correlatively, the government had an obligation to render such service. The other theory was that expenditure by the government could be justified if it produced "social saving," or "social profit."

Such regularization of legislation as appeared during this period did not mean that legislative bodies were committing themselves to the general welfare as opposed to the particular welfares of groups and sections. On the contrary, particular welfares were tending to crowd the general welfare out of view. The general welfare was involved in abstractions which seemed to be losing force, such as free enterprise, individualism, liberty, and initiative. It was also involved in the specific interests of the population as consumers; but the consumer interest was, of all, probably the least articulate and the most weakly represented. Another general interest was that of the taxpayer. He made himself felt, but with only temporary and partial effect. Yet, the limits set by taxation seemed to be about the only remaining effective brake on the expansion of governmental activities.

The general interest, in any of its aspects, is not necessarily furthered by the promotion of particular interests, even if this promotion be well proportioned. The general welfare is not a mosaic of special welfares. The conditions created by technological industry were changing the police state into a service state; but it remained to be seen whether government would be guided in the performance of its service functions by haphazard emotional impulses, by group pressures, or by the sounder processes of intellect applied to the idea of the general welfare. For example, conservation policies aimed to protect the public interest in publicly owned resources. It was not possible to formulate and enact at one time a comprehensive policy covering the whole subject; but new implications and new issues appeared as piecemeal legislation was executed; and the whole problem was complicated and its solution retarded by the pressure of private interests for special privileges. Legislative and administrative progress was made; but it was punctuated by the Ballinger-Pinchot controversy in Taft's administration, the Teapot Dome scandal in Harding's, and the deadlock during the Coolidge and Hoover régimes over the method of operating Muscle Shoals.

Up to the World War, the president was almost exclusively the maker of American foreign policy and of American opinion regarding it.[91] After the war, presidents showed more deference to the law-making body, particularly the Senate. The Senate had shown its strength on the League of Nations issue; the public was more interested in international affairs and better informed about them. We were beginning, apparently, to have a public opinion on foreign affairs; but, with respect to European involvements, no reasoned permanent policy reflected national determination and imposed agreement on president and Congress.

Judged by results, legislation cannot
be considered adequate.

Viewing this period with the advantages of hindsight, the shortcomings of the legislative mechanism, judged by its output, are apparent. The economic regulatory legislation of the "Progressive Era" did not resolve conflicts of principle, and, as later events showed, did not insure uninterrupted economic progress. Though the rural vote was in a minority in the country, the representatives of rural areas held a majority in each of the two houses. The result

[91] Theodore Roosevelt's attitude is illustrated by his explanation, after his retirement from presidency, of his Panama Canal policy: "If I had followed traditional conservative methods I should have submitted a dignified state paper of probably two hundred pages to the Congress and the debate would be going on yet, but I took the Canal Zone and let Congress debate, and while the debate goes on the canal does also." Quoted in John H. Latané, *American Foreign Policy* (1927), p. 535.

was a cleavage between rural and urban constituencies and a failure on the part of Congress and the president to agree on basic agricultural legislation.[92]

One cannot say that legislation lagged, more than in the past, behind social need or behind public opinion; but a considerable lag, difficult to justify, was still evident. Congress, like the state legislatures, passed a multitude of statutes; but the larger number dealt with petty matters. In the more difficult cases, legislation issued only after years of agitation, after voluminous reports by legislative committees had gathered dust on the shelves, or after presidents had repeatedly recommended it. The legislative process worked by fits and starts. Most effective in starting it were widespread public discontents, emergencies, publicized scandals,[93] and a presidential leadership backed by progressive opinion.

In spite of procedural improvements, it can hardly be said that Congress regained any substantial measure of public confidence, or, if it did, was able to hold for any length of time what it had regained. Like the state legislatures, it was weighed in the balance and found wanting. In the twentieth century legislative activity had widened in scope and, becoming more complex, had become more difficult as well as more burdensome.[94]

THE CONSTITUTION AND THE COURTS

So far as the substantive economic and social problems were concerned, constitutional amendment had been practically abandoned. Only two amendments dealing with the functions of the federal

[92] The equalization-fee plan was put forth as early as 1922. A bill embodying it was introduced in 1924, again in 1925, and again in 1926. It was passed in 1927 and vetoed; passed again in 1928 and vetoed. The export debenture plan and the domestic allotment plan were proposed in 1926.

[93] It would be interesting, for example, to list the laws and legislative trends that began with some shocking disaster, such as a boiler explosion, schoolhouse or factory fire, steamship sinking, flood, or assassination.

[94] In many respects, changes in the state legislatures paralleled those in Congress. These were, in general: some intellectual and considerable moral improvement of the membership; delegation; standardization; budgetary systematization; and expert assistance. Note should also be taken of the Conference of Commissioners on Uniform State Laws, an official composed of representatives of the several states, which was working out careful drafts of laws that were in many cases accepted by the legislatures. A one-house legislature was recommended by the National Municipal League; and unicameralist amendments were submitted to the people in Oregon, Oklahoma, Ohio, Alabama, New York, Arizona, Massachusetts, and Illinois.

government were ratified between 1900 and 1929—those providing for the income tax and national prohibition—and the prohibition amendment was later to be repealed.

To the judiciary, as well as to the public, the simple pattern imposed by the Constitution was becoming confused. The outlines of the Constitution itself were blurred. Loosely connected with the political structure developed the sprawling and apparently uncoordinated materials of an economic constitution, constantly agitated by social pressures. It can hardly be doubted that constitutional restraints were losing their former clarity and power. One could see, too, that the forces pressing for social and economic legislation had the least patience with constitutional obstacles, while those whose interests lay in the freedom of large industrial enterprises were the most likely to invoke the sanctity of the Constitution and a static construction of the fundamental law.

Holmes and Brandeis exemplified and foreshadowed judicial readjustment.

In intellectual capacity, moral integrity, and legal learning, the average of Supreme Court justices was exceedingly high. Their personal characters, reputation, and conduct were considered irreproachable. But, as already indicated, their task had become one of economic statesmanship and economic expertness. For the democratic and efficient performance of this task, they were handicapped not only by their own economic predilections and by legalism, but also by the adjudicatory process itself.[95] In some cases, the difficulties that appeared in the widening of economic and social law were created by Congress.[96]

The period from 1901 to 1929 was roughly coincident with the service of Justice Oliver Wendell Holmes on the Supreme Bench.

[95] The constitutional labor of the Supreme Court, as Frankfurter says, was "an exercise in statesmanship hemmed in by the restrictions attending the adjudicatory process. Far-reaching political principles arise through the accidents of unrelated and intermittent cases, presenting issues confined by the exigencies of the legal record, depending for elucidation upon the learning and insight of counsel fortuitously selected for a particular case, and imprisoning the judgment, at least in part, within legal habituations and past utterances." Felix Frankfurter, *The Commerce Clause under Marshall, Taney, and Waite* (1937), pp. 21-22.

[96] Dexter Keezer and Stacy May, *The Public Control of Business* (1930), pp. 142-47.

He came to it on December 4, 1902 and resigned on January 12, 1932. His dissenting opinions are an eloquent indication of the economic conflicts of the time and the stresses and strains that economic and social changes imposed on the constitutional structure. Justice Holmes brought to the bench a conception of the law as amenable to the necessities of a changing society; and he was named by Theodore Roosevelt because Roosevelt was satisfied that Holmes had that conception. Louis D. Brandeis, appointed by Woodrow Wilson, exemplified better than Holmes the "social" point of view in contrast with the extreme legalistic one.[97] Between 1907 and 1914 Brandeis had acted as counsel for the people in litigation involving the constitutionality of several state laws fixing maximum or minimum wages. Going beyond the legal precedents and abstractions, he had sought to show by a reference to actual conditions in industry how these laws affected the health, safety, and productivity of the workers. It must be said, however, that during this period Holmes and Brandeis were better known for their dissents than for their dominance of the Court.

*The courts came again
under attack.*

From the standpoint of social legislation, criticisms of the judiciary were most frequent and bitter during the "progressive era" from about 1900 to the World War. Few critics of the courts went so far as to assert that the power to annul federal and state legislation was always used obstructively or unnecessarily. Indeed, an examination of the history of legislative measures disclosed that obstruction and delay occurred as often in the legislative mechanism as in the judiciary. Nor was legislation invariably progressive. The courts at times checked legislative attempts to abridge the civil rights of individuals; and for their obstructive role in this regard they were generally praised. To the progressives, the real threat to individual liberty and security came from economic rather

[97] See Alpheus Thomas Mason, *Brandeis and the Modern State* (1936). Also a distinguished representative of this mode of thinking was Benjamin Cardozo of the New York Court of Appeals, who was appointed to the Supreme Court of the United States by President Hoover in 1932; and in the same group was Felix Frankfurter, who became a Harvard law professor in 1914, and was later to be made a justice of the Supreme Court.

than from political power; but to others a serious danger lay in the spread of governmental interferences, a danger that might be the more insidious when it assumed a humanitarian guise or was entrusted to irresponsible hands.

It was in its recourse to the due process clause that the Supreme Court in the "progressive era" was thought to be most obstructive and met with most public criticism. For many years it had been suspected that the courts were more concerned with the protection of property and profits than of those other interests which were now coming to be thought of as "human rights." The attitude of the Supreme Court, or rather of its majority, to the early social legislation of the states appeared to be quite consistently hostile.

Judicial interpretation of the due process clause assumed that statutes could be declared unconstitutional "upon the basis of a general right of liberty, of a certain degree of freedom from legislative regulation and control."[98] This assumption, combined with the indefiniteness of the commerce clause, had given to the Supreme Court a very great power over the development of economic policies.

The doctrine of the police power offered a way to overcome the obstacles created by the due process clause. Under the police power, regulatory legislation could be justified if shown to have a "reasonable" relation to the protection of the public health, safety, or morals. The general test applied to developing economic and social legislation was "reasonableness." The Court, however, was not in all cases convinced that "reasonableness" had been proved.

Attacks on the Supreme Court were intensified by the decision in *Lochner* v. *New York*[99] in 1905 in which a ten-hour law for bakers was struck down as unconstitutional. While Theodore Roosevelt declared that a changed judicial attitude could be brought about only by the courts themselves, he pointed out that the judges, like any other public officials, should be subjected to public criticism. The Progressive Party in 1912 demanded "such restriction of the power of the courts as shall leave to the people

[98] Ernst Freund, *Standards of American Legislation* (1917), p. 207.
[99] 198 U.S. 45.

the ultimate authority to determine fundamental questions of social welfare and public policy."

To this end it was proposed that

when an Act, passed under the police power of the State, is held unconstitutional under the State Constitution, by the courts, the people, after an ample interval for deliberation, shall have an opportunity to vote on the question whether they desire the act to become law, notwithstanding such decision.

It was also proposed that any decision of a state appellate court, holding a state act in contravention of the federal constitution, should be reviewable by the United States Supreme Court.[100] A number of the members of the Industrial Relations Commission, reporting in 1916, joined in a recommendation "that Congress immediately enact a statute or, if deemed necessary, initiate a constitutional amendment, specifically prohibiting the courts from declaring legislative acts unconstitutional."[101]

For some years after the Lochner decision, the Supreme Court did become more liberal in its treatment of social legislation.[102] One reason for this more receptive attitude was the persistence of progressive opinion and its electoral triumphs. Incidentally, public criticism of the Court doubtless had some effect; and within the Court the attitudes of Holmes and Brandeis were not without influence. In the late twenties, the Court again appeared obstructive. Whatever the reasons may have been for its change of attitude, it was pretty faithfully reflecting the conservative opinion of that time. It was evident that constitutional interpretation, like legislaion, yielded to the impact of conditions and opinion.

Apart from constitutional questions, a widespread feeling existed that the judicial system was not working efficiently or fairly. The Supreme Court of the United States was respected more than the lower federal courts; the latter more than the state courts; and the state appellate tribunals more than the inferior courts. It appeared that there was one justice for the rich and another for the poor. The conviction of Albert B. Fall and Harry Sinclair after

[100] Kirk H. Porter, *National Party Platforms* (1924), p. 337.
[101] *Final Report and Testimony*, S. Doc. 415, 64 Cong. 1 sess., p. 61.
[102] Freund, *Standards of American Legislation*, pp. 211-12; Charles Warren, *The Supreme Court in United States History* (1923), Vol. 3, p. 473.

long-drawn-out litigation following the Tea-Pot Dome scandal hardly sufficed to restore public confidence. Criticism of the Sacco-Vanzetti and Mooney trials was not confined to radical agitators. The persistence of lynching in the South presented only one of many evidences of disrespect for the law and for the courts. Numerous studies and investigations were made of judicial administration; and movements to reorganize the judiciary and to expedite judicial procedure gained headway.

POSSIBILITIES OF CONTROLLED OPINION

Reminders appeared both in war and peace that governmental power might be employed to suppress speech, shackle thought, and control opinion. During the war and the years following it, America had an illuminating lesson in the psychological and moral effects of active militarism.[103] Through its Committee on Public Information, the federal government during the war conducted elaborate propaganda that, combined with the official suppression of counter-propaganda, produced for a time an amazing solidarity of opinion. Under the Espionage Act and other statutes, punishment was visited on those guilty or alleged to be guilty of expressions at variance with official opinion or intended to obstruct the prosecution of war or "persuade to disloyalty." A Censorship Board was established; and, though it did not censor domestic mail or the press, the Board as well as agents of the Department of Justice and the Post Office Department called attention to "seditious" material. Much of this material, in some cases of a quite inoffensive nature, was barred from the mails or made the basis of prosecutions.

Other interferences in this period with intellectual freedom had still less justification but were partially explained by the war, by religious fundamentalism, and by fear of communism. Most of these had to do with public education. The anti-evolution laws enacted in some of the states indicated that the idea of scientific freedom and freedom of speech did not yet extend to all textbooks and teachers. Quite as notorious was "Big Bill" Thompson's crusade for the establishment in Chicago schools of his personal

[103] Lucille B. Milner and Groff Conklin, "Wartime Censorship in the United States," *Harper's Magazine*, Vol. 180 (1940), pp. 187-95.

prejudice against England. "Teachers' oath" laws appeared in a number of states. In many cases, teachers were disciplined or dismissed because they were, or were suspected of being, Communists. Perhaps even more serious were attempts by politicians to dominate state institutions of higher education. Pressure came usually from the governor, the legislature, or the board of trustees. Sometimes, governmental control did not openly assert itself, but proceeded from the fact that the university depended for its support chiefly on state appropriations. Consequently, presidents and faculties, to a more or less serious extent, tacitly accepted censorship.

The American Civil Liberties Union (until 1920 the National Civil Liberties Bureau) was organized in 1917 to defend the rights of free speech, free press, and free assembly. It took cognizance of apparent violations of the civil rights and provided legal or financial aid to persons prosecuted for exercising such rights. The American Association of University Professors, organized in 1913, had among its numerous committees one on academic freedom and tenure.

Ordinarily, the courts were relied upon to protect civil rights in justiciable cases; and, in this respect, the Supreme Court maintained a notable peacetime record. Unfortunately, many serious attacks on liberty were not of such a nature as to permit judicial protection; and, more unfortunately, it appeared that the courts themselves, especially the lower courts, might under certain circumstances be unduly influenced by current popular feeling.

Efforts were made in the states to regulate lobbying by law. The regulatory acts usually required registration and depended for their effect chiefly on publicity. Apparently the laws were not generally enforced.[104]

Through other channels, government was developing means by which opinion might be influenced. Public administrators were active in private and semi-official associations. Governmental research and the publications and reports of government offices presented information that carried authority. The Department of Agriculture's far-flung organization was already capable of molding farmers' opinions.

[104] Logan, Supplement to *Annals*, Vol. 144 (1929), pp. 65-76.

PART II

THE LATEST TIME OF TEST

During the years from 1787 to 1929, a small country became a vast and powerful nation. Economically, its main interest shifted from agriculture to industry; socially, from rural life to urbanism. Substantial individual and community self-sufficiency were replaced by technical specialization and by complex interrelationships and interdependencies. The territorial frontier disappeared and with it that type of extensive and exploitative development which had stimulated the imagination, bred confidence, and preserved the appearance, as well as measurably the fact, of equal opportunities. Increasing productivity remained the prerequisite of economic progress; but productivity, as well as the distribution of the products of industry, came to be more dependent on intensive development through invention, research, organization, and management, and less on the bounties of nature and the operation of a free market.

In this process of transition, abuses and injustices had crept in and private economic power had tended to concentrate. The practical insufficiency of individualism and localism, the discontent and demands of the industrial wage earners and the farmers, combined with the general needs of a more complex society, expanded the functions of government and tended to centralize its power. In the meantime, social change seemed to be constantly accelerating, producing intricate, complex, and acute problems, and creating maladjustments and tensions of equal urgency.

Democratizing movements had met almost invariably with partial frustration; but eventually they had made government more responsive to public opinion, particularly to group opinions. The process of opinion formation, however, revealed serious shortcomings, owing to the inadequacy of individuals and to the multiplicity, specialization, and partiality of leaderships. Among the concepts and symbols that operated to give order to public thinking, the traditional persisted with little evidence of discrimination, rationalizing and fortifying the natural inertia of preoccupied human beings and compromising or blocking the fulfillment of new ideas.

For social progress and the general welfare, public problems required integrated and intelligent treatment, and opinion demanded integrated, objective, honest, and free leadership. Intellectualism and science seemed to offer the essentials of the needed leadership; but the application of intellectual and scientific leadership to social problems was belated and limited.

Government, rather than private organization, was increasingly looked to for solutions, and faith in governmental power grew; but the legislative mechanism, where primary responsibility resided, did not offer much assurance of efficient performance. The mechanism was not unified and made effective by the political party. Neither the democratizing urge nor the movement for efficiency had made any changes that promised adequate improvement in the timeliness and quality of legislation. Two major tendencies appeared: one, to delegate legislative power to the growing bureaucracy; and the other, to depend for legislative, as well as administrative, functioning on executive leadership.

American government had evolved and was still evolving within a fairly stable framework of ideas and of law. The legal foundation was the Constitution; the ideological foundation was individual liberty. Liberty, translated into political terms, meant democracy. Democracy had achieved a working identification with the Constitution; and, whether correctly or not, it was felt that one supported the other. Constitutionalism, however, was a stabilizing element in political evolution, while democracy had been a dynamic influence. Conditions and trends indicated the possibility of danger either to the Constitution or to democracy, or to both. The goal of security was replacing that of liberty, while the ideal of democracy was losing emotional appeal. Government *for* the people was becoming more attractive than government *of* or *by* the people; but the concept of social justice and the practice of economic control were driving government on to do more for the people with less assurance of giving them satisfaction.

On the eve of the depression, the outlines of the many-sided problem of realizing democracy and "making it work" were perceptible though at points obscure. The depression, with its political concomitants, served both to clarify and to complicate the problem. A 12-year period, from 1929 to 1941, though its ultimate significance may now be partially hidden, supplies materials for the remainder of the study.

We call this "the latest time of test." Of course, democracy has been continually tested; but at times the test has been especially exacting and consciously critical, as during the Revolution, the establishment of the Constitution, and the Civil War. The issues at present seem comparable. We have not necessarily come to the end of a road or even to a sharp turning-point. Underlying factors and political phenomena in our time are not on the whole remarkable because of their novelty. For most of them the past provides parallels. Yet, little doubt can exist that the present is epochal and critical, judged by the acceleration of trends, the magnification of problems, and the intensification of strain. If and when we have successfully met this latest test, the experience acquired will contribute, as equally painful experience has contributed in the past, to the stable evolution of efficient democracy.

This part of the book contains eight chapters. The first, Chapter VI, reviews the social and economic policies of the depression years. Chapter VII includes a discussion of the expanding bureaucracy and its relation to the problem of political power. Chapter VIII deals with centralizing trends. Chapter IX takes up again the question of congressional adequacy and the related fact of presidential domination. In Chapter X we examine the workings of the kind of national government that we now have. The question of governmental management of public opinion is dealt with in Chapter XI. Chapter XII, with considerable reference to the past, discusses the position of the Constitution in relation to the question of governmental stability. Finally, in Chapter XIII, we point out those aspects of the present international crisis that appear to have permanent significance in the realization of democracy, efficiency, and stability.

CHAPTER VI

DEPRESSION POLICIES, SOCIAL AND ECONOMIC

So far as domestic affairs are concerned, this latest time of test is given its distinctive economic and political identity by the beginning, in October 1929, of what came to be known as the great depression. Psychological confusion, political overturn, and other circumstances produced an unprecedented surge of national policy-making. In this chapter, we shall be particularly concerned with the policies aimed at social justice and economic control.

PSYCHOLOGICAL CONFUSION

The apparent reversal in 1929 of what had seemed to be pre-destined progress produced many of the manifestations of opinion that had characterized the popular reaction to previous depressions; but these manifestations were now more striking and their political effect more sweeping because the economic system, the country, and the government had changed and grown and because popular and group expectations of government had increased.

Public opinion was confused,
unsettled, and disunited.

Industrial leadership appeared to be discredited; and in the spring of 1933 it was said that the "rulers of the exchange of mankind's goods" had "admitted their failure" and "abdicated."[1] The private organization of society was still unintegrated. To the scientists and intellectuals, particularly, conditions stimulated curiosity and opened fresh avenues of inquiry. It became clearer than ever that popular leadership was necessary.

One of the early effects of the depression was to arouse the social conscience and to fortify the feeling of humanitarianism and the concept of social justice. Increasingly, individuals and organizations,

[1] First Inaugural, *Public Papers and Addresses of Franklin D. Roosevelt*, Vol. 2, pp. 11-12.

many of which had hitherto been deemed conservative, proclaimed their intellectual dissatisfaction and moral indignation over the fact that depression had been permitted to occur and over the suffering that it had brought.[2] The political implications of these feelings were epitomized by Felix Frankfurter, later to be an associate justice of the Supreme Court, as follows:

To realize that there is a new economic order and to realize it passionately, not platonically, is the central equipment for modern statesmanship. Only thus shall we be able to understand the new problems and devise ways, however tentative and halting, for dealing with new problems. We cannot carry on upon the old maxims. . . . The governing issue of our time is whether we are capable of so organizing production and distribution as to avert these terrible ups and downs in business, with their disastrous moral and economic consequences.[3]

The depression made material interests more strongly, crudely, and critically political; and the net effect may have been to expand rather than contract the area of selfishness. Huey P. Long, promising the poor a redistribution of wealth, became governor of Louisiana in 1928 and United States Senator in 1930; and was already boss-dictator of his state. Charles E. Coughlin, Detroit priest, utilizing the propaganda possibilities of the radio, was denouncing bankers and politicians and winning a formidable popular following. In California, Dr. Townsend evolved his panacea for old-age dependency and the economic ills of the country. Other panaceas new and old, of many types, clamored for a hearing.

It may never be possible to determine whether there was incipient in the populace any real and widespread revolutionary spirit, or even any extensive desire for radical change either of social or political organization or of public policy. Sporadic manifestations of violence occurred.[4] The radical and "lunatic" fringes became more vocal and probably wider. But such phenomena had characterized other depressions. It may well be that, in this case, had national

---

[2] On such expressions see Charles A. Beard and Mary R. Beard, *America in Midpassage* (1939), pp. 66-67, 98-111, 515.

[3] "What We Confront in American Life," *Survey Graphic*, Vol. 22 (1933), p. 134.

[4] The milk strikes and resistance to farm mortgage foreclosures in 1933 and the subsequent "sit-down" strikes suggest what might result from long-continued economic distress or from a class feeling of injustice.

policies been extremely conservative and political leadership unsympathetic, a revolutionary spirit might have grown to dangerous
proportions. Popular protest expressed itself in Republican defeats
in the congressional election of 1930 and the presidential election of
1932.

POLITICAL OVERTURN, 1932

When Herbert Hoover was inaugurated in 1929 he had appeared
to many as a president ideally qualified for the task of government
in the technological era. Though he believed in the principle of
executive leadership, he could not render it effective. His legislative
majority was split; and in the Senate actual control was in the hands
of the Democrats and the Republican "Progressives," these two
groups acting at times as a virtual coalition. After the elections of
1930, the Republicans and Democrats were practically deadlocked
in the Senate and the Democrats had a small majority in the House.
Under these circumstances, especially as the depression deepened,
Mr. Hoover's position as president became extremely difficult; and,
as a political leader aiming at party victory in 1932, his task proved
to be an impossible one.

As the election of 1932 grew near, the two-party system functioned in a fairly orthodox manner. No third party appeared. The
Democratic platform declared for "a drastic change in economic
governmental policies"; but its specific proposals were pretty much
in accordance with recent legislative trends. The first proposal was
for "an immediate and drastic reduction of governmental expenditures by abolishing useless commissions and offices, consolidating
departments and bureaus, and eliminating extravagance; to accomplish a saving of not less than 25 per cent in the cost of Federal
Government. . . ."[5] The platform declared for a "sound currency,"
and "the removal of Government from all fields of private enterprise except where necessary to develop public works and natural
resources in the common interest"; and the party "solemnly" promised to maintain "the national credit by a federal budget annually
balanced on the basis of accurate executive estimates within revenues,
raised by a system of taxation levied on the principle of ability to

[5] Leroy D. Brandon and South Trimble (compilers), *Platforms of the Two
Great Political Parties 1932 and 1936* (1936), pp. 335-39.

pay." The document closed with the old party slogan: "Equal rights to all; special privileges to none."

Nor did the Democratic candidate in his campaign speeches suggest anything essentially novel or departing in principle from traditional progressivism. He endorsed the party platform. At the start, he pledged himself to "a new deal" for the American people and declared that "forgotten" men and women were looking to the Democratic Party for "more equitable opportunity to share in the distribution of national wealth"; he advocated reforestation of marginal and unused land, and "planned use of the land"; he mentioned that the cause of the railroad problem, as of other problems, was "the entire absence of any national planning"; he subscribed to "the philosophy of social justice through social action"; and he said that he would seek "to restore the purchasing power of the American people."[6] The election of 1932, resulting in a popular plurality of about 7 millions for Franklin D. Roosevelt, offered but slight indication of increasing radicalism.[7]

RELIEF AND SOCIAL SECURITY

Before the new administration took office, the number of unemployed had increased to around 13 millions.

In spite of its social reorientation and the expansion of its activities, government in 1929 had been adjusted to the normal workings of the economic system and based on the expectations of a high level of national income. Depressions had occurred before; but their political effect had been in a measure cushioned or counteracted by extra-governmental conditions. Direct relief of individuals, purely for purposes of relief, had never been accepted as a national responsibility. At this time, relief was first given locally through existing private organizations, financed by charitable contributions, with some assistance from local and state funds. Local and philanthropic expenditure rapidly mounted.

State appropriations for relief increased; and to obtain funds resort was had to bond issues. From 1929 to 1932 state and local expenditures and indebtedness grew only a little more rapidly than

---

[6] *Public Papers and Addresses*, Vol. 1, pp. 647-865.

[7] The "radical" parties (Socialist, Workers, Farmer-Labor, Socialist-Labor, and Communist) polled 344,183 votes in 1928 and 1,028,357 in 1932.

during the preceding decade; but outlays for relief enormously increased. The credit of state and local governments was limited; and the situation gave renewed impetus to the economy and efficiency movement described in the preceding chapter. Quite generally, state and local governments achieved substantial reductions by cutting salaries and in some cases curtailing activities other than relief. These governments, however, were under strong pressure to preserve or restore whatever objects of expenditure came under attack, with the natural result that pressure was brought to bear on the federal government by private groups and by state and municipal officials to assume a substantial share of the relief burden.

Relief of the unemployed became a major and continuing national responsibility.

Whether or not any government could remove the basic causes of unemployment, it was obvious that state governments could not do it. The most they could do was to reduce certain kinds of unemployment and to mitigate its effects.[8]

In Mr. Hoover's administration, policies primarily for relief did not appear until 1932. Even then they were confined to ordering the transfer to the Red Cross of wheat and cotton owned by the Grain and Cotton Stabilization Corporations, and granting authority to the Reconstruction Finance Corporation to make temporary loans to the states for relief purposes.

During Mr. Roosevelt's first and second terms, a large amount of unemployment persisted. When the new president was inaugurated, the bottom of the depression had been reached and unemployment had slightly declined; but the number on relief was increasing, due in the main to the exhaustion of the private savings of marginal families. The stigma formerly attached to dependency appeared no longer applicable to the literally unnumbered host of depression victims. Social workers, who had long viewed unemployment as a social rather than an individual problem, now put the blame on society and declared that the jobless had a "right" to public support.

[8] The states had been regulating private employment exchanges and had set up public offices for labor placement. In January 1931, Wisconsin enacted the first American unemployment compensation law.

Whether in the form of grants-in-aid to the states or directly administered by the national government (through the Civilian Conservation Corps, general work relief, or public works projects), federal assumption of the relief function was probably the most far-reaching centralizing step that had yet been taken in times of peace. Protracted unemployment created another definable pressure group; and centralization of relief gave this group a peculiarly direct relationship with government. This relationship, as well as the circumstances attendant on the administration of relief, placed additional emphasis on humanitarianism and on the concept of social justice and affected, as we shall note later, the workings of the party system and of the legislative mechanism and the power of the president. Relief, moreover, introduced many new and extremely complicating elements into the structure of policy and the task of government.

The devising of work projects and the fitting of work to the aptitudes of the unemployed led the federal government to direct, and in large measure to initiate and promote, activities extending through the whole range of governmental service, federal, state, and local, and intruding at some points into the field of private enterprise. Those activities included, for example, municipal sanitary work, adult education, recreation, simple manufacturing, research, theatrical productions, and painting of murals in public buildings. As soon as relief policy passed beyond the stage of financial assistance to the states, it quickly lost unity and clarity and became confused with economic recovery, agricultural adjustment, character building, labor policy, and social uplift—indeed with practically every civil activity. In general, unemployment and relief added enormously to the complexity of public problems and of public policies both in the federal government and in the states.

*The national government undertook
to guarantee "social security."*

In June 1934 the President informed Congress that at its next session the federal government might well initiate the task of providing security "against the hazards and vicissitudes of life." "Fear and worry," he said, "based on unknown danger contribute to social unrest and economic demoralization. If, as our Constitution tells us, our Federal Government was established among other things 'to promote the general welfare,' it is our plain duty to provide for that security upon which welfare depends."[9]

Following the report of the Committee on Economic Security, appointed by the President, Congress passed the Social Security Act of 1935. This act, also centralizing in effect, created a federal-state system of unemployment compensation, provided grants-in-aid to the states for payment of old-age pensions, set up a system of old-age insurance wholly federal, and contained provisions relating to aid for dependent children and the blind, maternal and child welfare services, extension of public health activities, and vocational rehabilitation. No such law could immediately supplant relief activities; but it was expected as it came into operation to reduce the relief load and in future depressions largely to obviate the necessity for emergency relief measures.

LABOR LEGISLATION

At the beginning of the depression, industrial wage earners (exclusive of "white-collar" workers and hired farm laborers) constituted the largest group in the population having substantially the same occupational status and similar, if not the same, economic interests. The bulk of organized labor was in the American Federation of Labor and the railroad brotherhoods. The Federation was organized largely on the craft basis; its outlook had become predominantly middle class; and, while acting as a pressure group, it refrained from any attempt to form a labor party or to throw its political strength to one or the other of the major parties.

The labor movement now proceeded some distance through the stage of organization and conflict.

Industrial wage earners, to the extent that they were organized, had generally in principle and to a large extent in practice ceased

[9] Message to Congress, June 8, 1934, *Public Papers and Addresses*, Vol. 3, p. 291. "The millions of today want, and have a right to, the same security their forefathers sought, the assurance that with health and the willingness to work they will find a place for themselves in the social and economic system of the time." Address by President Roosevelt, Aug. 15, 1938, as printed in the *New York Times*, Aug. 16, 1938.

to act as individuals. Those identified with the organized labor movement had, in their opinion, proved the effectiveness of private organization when it was perfected and left free by public authority to measure its strength against that of employers. They were winning freedom from public interference, though they had not yet attained completeness of organization. Labor, then, in its effort to advance its own interests, had reached a stage midway between private and governmental control. Labor organization and collective bargaining had become first principles in the creed of all who professed to be "liberals" and "socially minded."

Labor organization and labor action against either the employers or the government demanded solidarity and discipline which in turn called for powerful leadership. The power implicit in labor leadership was not merely labor or industrial; it was also political.

Probably no other association of comparable size or influence was constitutionally so democratic or actually so much the creature of personal leadership. The workingman was of all citizens least adequately equipped to act in public affairs as an individual, but his organized leadership was in many respects the most unsatisfactory from the standpoint of a broad and rational consideration of the national welfare. To be sure, a certain amount of labor leadership was provided by the intellectuals, social scientists, social workers, and middle-class organizations; but these, as already pointed out, were by no means integrated in their thinking.

The principle of conflict also presented certain problems that need to be kept in mind. A kind of bargaining that depended ultimately on force or a kind of governmental intervention that was determined by group voting power did not reasonably insure that either public interest or economics would be taken into account. Since the conception of "industrial democracy" which had been held by Louis D. Brandeis and others was not practically worked out, the alternative course created a power able to deal on fairly even terms with that of large-scale industry; but the two powers in conflict necessitated an umpire.

Organized labor, dividing, suffered internal conflict. On one side was the American Federation of Labor; on the other, the Committee for Industrial Organization, later the Congress of Industrial

Organizations. Both of the rival organizations, but more especially the latter, endeavored with considerable success to extend the area of labor organization not only among skilled workers, but also among the unskilled, unemployed, hired farm laborers, "white-collar" workers, professional employees, and persons in the public service. Both of the major organizations, but more particularly the CIO, used the strike weapon frequently and aggressively, the more radical unions resorting for a time to the "sit-down" technique. Finally, both organizations were active and effective pressure groups, substantially aligning their members with the party in power. The CIO became more than a pressure group. It actively participated in partisan and semi-partisan organization and in the financing of the Democratic campaign in 1936.

Government now defined "fair labor practices," encouraged and protected unionization, and established wage and hour standards.

If government was to intervene further in industrial relations, much could be said for an integrated, balanced, or co-ordinated intervention, one that would take due account of the fact that capital and labor were not operating in separate economic or social compartments, that both were inextricably entangled in the same problem, that both represented concentrations of power, and that labor's claims on the social conscience could be satisfied in the long run only by increasing the efficiency and productiveness of industry. Integration of governmental policy toward capital and labor was contemplated in the National Industrial Recovery Act;[10] but, after that experiment had run its course, public policy veered back to the traditional separateness of industrial management and industrial relations, a separateness that had been exemplified, if not fixed, when the Department of Labor was established.

To the determination of public policy toward labor came a variety of facts, feelings, and ideas. Among these were moral and ethical judgments regarding what constitutes fairness in human relations; ideas of social justice—the "living" or "decent" wage, right to leisure, better distribution of wealth and income; emphasis on

[10] Discussed on pp. 252-53.

"human" as distinguished from "property" rights; developing conceptions of new "natural" rights belonging to industrial workers— the "right to work," "right to a job," and the assimilation of the idea of employment with the idea of property; and an amorphous feeling that these "rights" of labor took precedence over statutory and constitutional prescriptions. Other contributions came from the "do-nothing" attitude of industry, the general antagonism of corporations to unionism, and revelations of methods used by corporations to combat organized labor;[11] the democratic progressive tradition which indicated a broad middle ground between *laissez faire* and regimentation, an area where public policy was not yet fully or conclusively developed; hostility to big business, the conception of it as "entrenched greed," and the purpose to break concentrated economic power. Exaggeration of the wealth and profits of industrialists and of the wage-paying capacity of industry joined with underestimation of the delicacy of the economic mechanism. Industrial workers were still largely unorganized, particularly in the mass-production industries. It was hoped that strikes might be reduced and industrial peace furthered. Finally, labor policy was affected by the theory of purchasing power, derived from the importance of the wage-earning class as consumers, by a preoccupation with nominal standards and money wages, by governmental commitments to price-raising, and, in the beginning, by certain proposed methods of reducing unemployment, as by "spreading work."

[11] "England has powerful labor unions but nothing like the Wagner act. Why not? Because the great body of England's employers did not think it was proper for them to try to destroy labor unions by discharging active members, spying on them, or otherwise hurting employees who joined organizations. . . .

. . . .

"The story of labor legislation under the New Deal is merely a continuation of the story begun many years ago. The working people of the country turned to the government for protection when they failed to find it in industry. . . .

. . . .

"The reasons for the failure [of NRA] were many, but an important one was the inability of industrial leaders to think in terms of their industries as a whole or the country as a whole. This fault becomes apparent in the controversy over the right of employees to organize. Employers feared that labor unions would encroach upon management rights, and so they tried to prevent organization or to control organization. . . ." Excerpts from address by William M. Leiserson, as printed in the *New York Times*, Dec. 6, 1939.

The core of labor policy is to be found in the National Labor Relations Act, approved July 5, 1935,[12] and the Fair Labor Standards Act, approved June 25, 1938.

The National Labor Relations Act (1) asserts the right of employees to organize, join unions of their own choosing, and bargain collectively; and (2) declares certain practices to be unfair labor practices on the part of employers. The act prescribes that representatives selected by a majority of the employees shall be the representatives of all.

For the administration of the law, a National Labor Relations Board is established.

Prior to 1933, the federal government had made no effort to regulate the minimum rate of wages in private employment, where interstate commerce was involved.[13] President Roosevelt in April 1933 telegraphed the governors of 13 industrial states, urging that these states follow the example of New York.[14] Subsequently, Congress passed a number of laws in which labor standards were established or provision made for their establishment. The final basic enactment is the Fair Labor Standards Act of 1938,[15] which fixes statutory minima, alterable on the upward side by administrative determinations for particular industries.

In connection with or in addition to the developments just mentioned, the labor movement during the depression years advanced well into its third stage, that of administrative recognition and participation. Not only did labor as a group figure almost solidly in the makeup of the majority party strength, but also an unprecedented recognition was given to labor leadership in presidential

[12] The doctrine embodied in the National Labor Relations Act was foreshadowed by the activities of the War Labor Board during the World War, by the report of President Wilson's Second Industrial Conference published in 1920, by the Railway Labor Act of 1926, by the Norris-LaGuardia Act passed during Mr. Hoover's administration, as well as by Section 7a of the National Industrial Recovery Act and the various labor relations boards established during the administration of that act.

[13] Leverett S. Lyon, Myron W. Watkins, and Victor Abramson, *Government and Economic Life*, Vol. 1 (1939), p. 471.

[14] *Public Papers and Addresses*, Vol. 2, p. 133.

[15] For a fuller discussion of labor relations policies, see Lyon, Watkins, and Abramson, *Government and Economic Life*, Vol. 1, pp. 363-490.

counsels and to the friends of labor in the actual work of administration.

AGRICULTURAL ADJUSTMENT

The depressed condition of agriculture, even before the general economic collapse in 1929, had been such as to lead farmers to look to the national government for measures of immediate relief. The agricultural state of mind, particularly in the West, had its roots in the frontier tradition and in pioneering habits, and tillers of the soil were proverbially individualistic and supposedly provincial; but the farming population was being drawn by the telephone, rural free delivery, the automobile, the radio, and education into the main and increasingly uniform stream of American life. Agricultural thinking, conservative in many matters, had always been economically and politically radical in times of distress; and its political emphasis from 1921 on was shifting from the concept of liberty to that of security, from individualism to organized action, and from self-reliance to the acceptance of centralized governmental aid. Reduced to simplest terms, the primary interest of the agricultural group was in prices. With respect to this key aim, farmers had been unable to get results satisfactory to themselves by direct organized private effort. Feeling that an invasion of their individual liberty was less serious than economic distress, they were in general ready to acquiesce in an unprecedented extension of government control.

The farmers as an occupational group had been losing in relative size. They appeared to be organized but actually were not. The Farm Bureau Federation and the Grange did not include even a substantial minority of the farm population and this minority was not a cross-section of the whole. The farmers appeared to possess no more class solidarity, perhaps even less, than during previous periods of agricultural unrest.

Yet, as in the past, the farmers were politically powerful; and, now, the agricultural policies previously adopted[16] were continued

[16] Prior to 1933, assistance to agriculture had taken various forms: educational and demonstration work carried on by the federally aided land-grant colleges and county agents; regulation particularly concerned with commodities and transactions; tariff concessions; reclamation; combating of animal diseases and plant pests; furnishing of market information; banking and monetary changes; pro-

with some modifications and to them were added a variety of others, more sweeping and more positive, constituting unprecedented assertions of national governmental power and equally unprecedented qualifications of agricultural individualism.

The immediate and more specific purpose was relief. A longer-range objective was to equalize the farmers' economic position with that of other portions of the population by raising agricultural income; the ultimate aim, perhaps, was to rearrange the entire economic structure of the country, relocating its productive forces, apportioning land and labor so as to create the maximum and optimum of national well-being, "a balanced abundance."[17]

In the Agricultural Adjustment Act of 1933, the federal government attempted to restore the material well-being of farmers as a whole to the level of the most favorable previous peacetime period, introducing a broad plan of controlling production. Governmental policy thus passed from advisory guidance to over-all planning and implemented activity for the purpose of determining the direction and magnitude of agricultural enterprise.

The Agricultural Adjustment Act of 1933, declared unconstitutional in part by the Supreme Court, was followed by the Soil Conservation and Domestic Allotment Act of 1936, providing likewise for benefit payments, but giving more emphasis to conservation of the soil and employing less compulsion.[18]

---

vision of credit; construction of roads; railroad regulation; rural free delivery; promotion of agricultural co-operatives; and government acquisition of crop surpluses.

Measures taken during the Hoover administration included: creation of the Federal Farm Board, designed to encourage co-operation among farmers and to stabilize the market for agricultural products; provision of additional capital for the federal land banks; and drought relief. Mr. Hoover took his stand against agricultural export subsidies, crop control and price-fixing, and inflation. See William Starr Myers and Walter H. Newton, *The Hoover Administration* (1936). On agricultural policies in general during this period, see Lyon and Abramson, *Government and Economic Life*, Vol. 2 (1940), pp. 893-947.

[17] *Annual Report of the Secretary of Agriculture*, 1935, p. 1.

[18] In various other laws and administrative measures, provision was made for storage and insurance of crop surpluses; reduction of interest on farm mortgages, extension of credit to farmers; drought relief, flood control, conservation of water supply in drought areas; land-use planning, government purchase and retirement of sub-marginal lands, resettlement and rehabilitation of stranded farm populations, assistance to tenants in acquiring farm ownership; diversion of farm products from one use to another and research in new uses for such products;

The "new means to rescue agriculture" were at their inception declared by the President to be experimental;[19] but he stated later that the Agricultural Adjustment Administration was never intended to be "either a mere emergency operation or a static agency."[20]

Aside from whatever political motivation and economic effects these farm policies may have had, together with the farm credit policies later referred to, their social implications were obvious. The purpose was to redistribute income and opportunity; the procedure, to do by an exercise of governmental power what Theodore Roosevelt had said could be done only by publicity; and the effect, to place the national government in substantially a new relationship to the rural population. Broad social purposes and paternalistic implications were especially apparent in the Tennessee Valley experiment and in the establishment of the Rural Electrification Administration.[21]

SOCIAL POLICIES IN GENERAL

The public works program starting in June 1933 was designed to both supply relief and promote recovery. In connection with public works construction, as with relief administration and agricultural adjustment, objectives and effects ranged through the fields of social welfare and conservation. At the same time, efforts were made to stimulate private building, especially in the field of housing. Here, again, the objectives were both economic and social. On the social side, the idea was to provide decent homes for the "ill housed," to eliminate slums and blighted areas, and to distribute national wealth and income more justly.

---

promotion of agricultural exports through reciprocal tariff agreements, subsidizing of certain exports, negotiations looking to barter arrangements with certain foreign nations, use of surplus products for relief purposes; promotion of rural electrification, and, in the Tennessee Valley, intensive regional rural improvement.

[19] "If a fair administrative trial of it is made and it does not produce the hoped-for results I shall be the first to acknowledge it and advise you." Message to Congress, Mar. 16, 1933, *Public Papers and Addresses*, Vol. 2, p. 74.

[20] The same, Vol. 4, pp. 432-33.

[21] Remarks of President Roosevelt at Press Conference, the same, Vol. 3, pp. 466-67; Message to Congress, Jan. 15, 1940, *Washington Star*, Jan. 15, 1940; *Public Papers and Addresses*, Vol. 4, pp. 172-73.

In the field of health, the activities of the United States Public Health Service were expanded. Relief administration brought the federal government into contact with local physicians; and in certain areas a system resembling "socialized medicine" was extemporized. The Civilian Conservation Corps tended to lose its character as a purely relief agency. Promotion and regulation of recreation, as governmental policies, became more important.

The preceding references do not constitute a complete statement of relief, social welfare, agricultural, labor, or related policies, nor has the discussion indicated the bewildering number of laws and executive orders in which the policies were set forth. Throughout the depression period, these policies were characterized on the whole by expansion, "liberalization," proliferation, refinement of detail, and increasing cost. In various respects, policy changed from time to time. No principles limiting governmental action in these fields have been established. The rising and spreading structure of policy represents a rapid and almost revolutionary change in the relations of government, especially of the national government, to individual citizens, marking an almost unreserved abandonment of even the slowly expanding limits, previously recognized, to what government can do for individuals, localities, and groups.

In accordance with the ideal of social justice and responding in varying degree to emergency needs, practical necessity, group pressures, and considerations of political expediency, government was enlarging, centralizing, and complicating its task. With respect to matters that had rested traditionally in the sphere of individual liberty or local self-government, the people were accepting national service and control in the expectation of relief, a better living, or a more equitable share of wealth and income.

Basic to the general welfare, however, was the restoration of conditions favorable to industrial production. Without such conditions, any redistribution of income through taxation, borrowing, spending, and inflation would be temporary and largely illusory and might, indeed, prevent the creation of income. We come, therefore, to those aspects of the enlarging task of government that can be more definitely classified as economic-control policies. It should be understood, however, that the social policies just discussed involved, directly or indirectly, a considerable measure of economic control; while the policies to which attention will be called in the remainder of this chapter were in large part motivated by humanitarian or distributive aims.

PRE-"NEW DEAL" ECONOMIC PHILOSOPHY AND POLICIES

In order to indicate more clearly the significance of the new or expanded policies, it may be helpful to summarize the general attitude toward public economic policy that was largely determining when the political overturn occurred in 1932.

American democracy had experienced two sorts of crises: wars and cyclical depressions. American political and economic wisdom, as expressed through the governmental mechanism, had not succeeded in preventing either type of recurring catastrophe. While theories of industrial freedom, private initiative, individualism, *laissez faire*, and economic automatism were still widely held and deeply felt, they were by no means in complete accord with the truth of the situation. In various ways, as we have seen, private agreements, combinations, concentrations, and controls had been established; and in a measure they had substituted the deliberate policies of a relatively few financiers and industrialists for the free operations of a competitive market. Government, too, had stepped in, first to eliminate the abuses of competition and later, within certain segments, particularly transportation and the public utilities, to regulate industrial policies and industrial administration. Moreover, up to the World War, government had sought, with administratively inadequate means and without substantial practical effect, to destroy monopolies and to eliminate those private controls that interfered with free competition.

By and large, the popular attitude toward governmental economic controls depended largely on the economic situation. When the country was generally prosperous, little demand was made for public action; but, when economic depression came, it was accompanied by popular protests that could not safely be ignored by politicians. Thus, government had come to bear in the popular mind a primary responsibility for the economic condition of the country.

With respect to his philosophy, Mr. Hoover appears to have been a compound of Hamilton, Jefferson, John Quincy Adams, Cleveland, and Theodore Roosevelt, a compound tinctured with engineering and strongly infused with social and technological thinking. His philosophy was in accord with Anglo-Saxon traditions of statecraft and with the evolutionary adaptive process that American government had experienced.

The "American system," declared Mr. Hoover, "is founded on the conception that only through ordered liberty, through freedom to the individual, and equal opportunity to the individual will his initiative and enterprise be summoned to spur the march of progress." In "self-government by the people outside of government" was to be found the solution of many complex problems, not in "the extension of government into our economic and social life."[22] He felt that recovery would come, as it had come in the past, through the working of economic forces. He told Congress that depression could "not be cured by legislative action or executive pronouncement." Some people were confident, he said, "that by some legerdemain we can legislate ourselves out of a world-wide depression"; but, in his mind, such views were "as accurate as is the belief we can exorcise a Caribbean hurricane by statutory law."[23]

Nevertheless, the federal government during Mr. Hoover's administration developed within the frame of his philosophy a substantial economic program,[24] though it did not go as far in all direc-

[22] As specific examples of policies destructive of the American system, Mr. Hoover cited increase of public expenditures "by yielding to sectional and group raids on the public treasury," inflation of the currency, putting the government into the personal banking business, reduction of the tariff from a protective to a "competitive" basis, entrance of the government into the power business, government employment of all surplus labor on public works, and party control of the Supreme Court.

[23] William S. Myers (ed.), *The State Papers and Other Public Writings of Herbert Hoover* (1938), Vol. 1, pp. 429-30, 578.

[24] Without attempting a complete statement of executive actions and legislative accomplishments, the following may be mentioned, in addition to the social and agricultural policies referred to earlier in the chapter: increase of appropriations for federal public works and efforts to stimulate state, municipal, and private construction activity; starting of work on the Boulder Dam; establishment of the Federal Stabilization Board to co-ordinate public works programs; the initiation of an international moratorium on intergovernmental debts; establishment of the Reconstruction Finance Corporation; enactment of a banking law (the Glass-Steagall Act of 1932); the granting of authority to the Reconstruction

tions as he would have liked, and in some cases congressional enactments did not follow promptly his recommendations.[25]

The repairs and additions to the structure of economic control undertaken by the Roosevelt administration fall under the following heads: money and banking, general industrial organization and production, electric power, transportation, public spending, and taxation. Our purpose, it should be kept in mind, is not to describe these policies in detail, or to appraise their economic justification and effects. It is rather to show their scope and novel features, and how they were altering the task of government and the relationship of government to the people.

A mere listing of these policies may easily create a misleading impression. Whether their purpose was recovery or reform, it is not to be assumed that they were in all cases economically justified, or that they did not in some cases actually retard recovery. The program, if such it may be called, was initiated at a time when the recurrence of bank failures and the development of panic conditions in February 1933 spread and intensified popular fears and feelings of insecurity. Action on a wide front, if not economically necessary, appeared psychologically and politically desirable. The general structure of policy, as well as the pressures and motivations that help to account for it, will be referred to in succeeding pages. At

---

Finance Corporation to make loans for reproductive public works up to $1,500,000,000; creation of a system of Federal Home Loan Banks; amendment of the national bankruptcy law; waterway development; reorganization of the Federal Power Commission; and investigation of the stock exchanges. If it is assumed that these items were economic assets, one should probably place on the liability side the enactment of the tariff act.

[25] Presidential proposals along economic lines which were rejected or not fully accepted by Congress or, for other reasons, were not given complete effect included: world economic stabilization; a balanced budget; modification or investigation of the antitrust laws; construction of the St. Lawrence seaway; petroleum conservation; lease of Muscle Shoals; regulation by the Power Commission of interstate distribution of electricity; consolidation of railroads; banking reform; reallocation of activities relating to the merchant marine; and reorganization of the Radio Commission. It appears also that attention was given by the President to regulation of stock exchanges. On the other hand, the President took his stand against various proposals, including: agricultural export subsidies, crop control, and price-fixing; suspension of the antitrust laws and establishment of something similar to what was later known as the National Recovery Administration; a managed currency; inflation, making the Reconstruction Finance Corporation a general loan agency; and spending on useless or unreproductive public works.

this point, the purpose is merely to show what the different parts of the structure were coming to be.

"DRIVING THE MONEY-CHANGERS FROM THE TEMPLE"

From the beginning of American history, money and banking had occupied a strategic position in economic affairs, had been viewed by the populace as symbols of oppressive economic power, as keys to prosperity, and as instruments for the redistribution of wealth; and they had become central issues in some of our most memorable political conflicts. These strategic factors in the distributive system, viewed as barometers of social justice, had likewise served as tests and gauges of the sensitivity and strength of political democracy.

Concentrated private control of the industrial system, a matter of increasing concern after the Civil War, became after 1900 more and more a function of private finance. From this point of view alone, control of banking appeared to offer a means of controlling the entire productive and distributive system. Just before Mr. Roosevelt's inauguration, congressional investigations had given fresh and ample publicity to the manipulatory and "predatory" aspects of "Wall Street."

Under a wartime act, which was held to be still in effect, the President issued a proclamation on March 6 declaring a national bank holiday and vesting the Secretary of the Treasury with extensive powers of banking control. An emergency banking act was passed three days later, granting the President further powers to control foreign exchange transactions, gold and currency movements, and banking transactions in general. Later in the year, a law was enacted establishing a federal system of insurance of bank deposits.

For the supplying of credit to private enterprise, as well as to other public agencies, the Reconstruction Finance Corporation established in 1932 was retained. The various farm-credit agencies, already in existence, were consolidated and their organization and operations extended; moratorium and other legislation was enacted; the Home Owners' Loan Corporation and the Federal Housing

Administration were created; and the Export-Import Bank was established. Incidental to its investment banking function, the federal government, particularly through the Reconstruction Finance Corporation, assumed virtual managerial functions over certain of the private debtor corporations.

The significance of these and other similar policies in the present study lies in their indication of the acceptance, by the federal government, of five substantial roles: (1) as investment banker; (2) as general underwriter of financial losses; (3) as engineer of recovery; (4) as Good Samaritan to individuals in financial distress; and (5) as organizer and manager of economic enterprises.

Money had long been viewed as a prime instrumentality for political control of economic conditions. "Cheap" money issues had seemed to provide an easy way to raise prices, reduce the burden of debt, and stimulate industrial activity. Mr. Hoover, following the policy that had been determined by the elections of 1896 and 1900, had rigidly adhered to the gold standard. It was now departed from: President Roosevelt indicated his purpose to raise prices through changes in the gold value of the dollar.[26]

The various procedures and devices adopted to adjust the value of the dollar to the assumed economic needs of the country represented in this field a power of control far more extensive than any similar authority that had previously been exercised in the United States. In the President's view, the government possessed effective price controls, which should be used, like the levers of a machine, for different purposes of adjustment as needs arose.[27]

Following certain regulatory efforts, both state and federal, Congress now enacted laws dealing with trade in securities, with the stock exchanges, and with investment trusts and investment advisers, designed on the one hand to protect investors and on the other to curb speculation and correct abuses. Through this legislation, especially the Securities Exchange Act of 1934, the federal gov-

[26] For a systematic discussion of monetary policies during this period, see Lyon, Watkins, and Abramson, *Government and Economic Life,* Vol. 1, pp. 152-98.

[27] Statement to press conference, Feb. 18, 1938, as printed in *New York Times,* Feb. 19, 1938.

ernment took on additional managerial activities, assuming considerable control over corporate financing and over the forms of special economic organizations.[28]

ACTION AIMED AT GENERAL INDUSTRIAL ORGANIZATION AND PRODUCTION

The banking and monetary policies just mentioned were based on a theory that certain over-all governmental controls and stimulants could be beneficially applied to economic life; but these devices did not deal directly with the general process or the general organization of production. These latter were subject at the time to the antitrust acts, designed to enforce competition, and to these and other acts regulative of business practices. In the states, the movement against concentrated economic control had in recent years been most conspicuously directed against the chain stores and aimed at the preservation of the "independent" small retailers. The principal governmental weapon used had been taxation.

These various general measures are of interest from four important angles. First, they had a bearing, which was not always properly emphasized, on the efficiency of the economic mechanism, its capacity to produce, to sustain economic progress, and thus to supply the first requisites for meeting the economic expectations of the people. Second, these measures aimed at a more equitable distribution of wealth and income and a more democratic, as well as more efficient, distribution of private economic power. Third, they influenced or might influence the economic organization of society, defining, bringing together, or dispersing the several great groups that were acting, on the one hand, economically, and on the other, politically. Fourth, these measures indicated a general, comprehensive relationship between government and economic life and therefore the assumption by government of a peculiarly difficult task.

In 1933, so far as domestic affairs were concerned, the conditions of economic progress were present; but, to realize progress (assum-

---

[28] For a summary statement of governmental activities involved in regulation of the stock exchanges, see *Investigation of Executive Agencies of the Government,* S. Rept. 1275, 75 Cong. 1 sess., pp. 757-58. For a discussion of governmental policy relating to speculation, see Charles O. Hardy, "Recent Developments in the Theory of Speculation," *American Economic Review* (Suppl.), Vol. 27 (1937), pp. 272-73.

ing a favorable world situation) it was necessary for all classes and groups to "pull together" on a sound basis and toward a common objective. Industrialism had in truth created "economic principalities," in which the lives of thousands of individuals were more vitally affected by the decisions of a corporation than by the policies of the government. It was evident, however, to the industrialists themselves that their power was not as concentrated and as wieldy as was popularly supposed. Financiers and industrialists were, like the lawyers and judges, charged with a lack of social conscience; but a definite and far-reaching social responsibility in the private enterprise system could not be realized without reorganization.

Industrial leaders, aroused by the depression, proposed plans by which industry might set up its own leadership and make a united effort, with the aid of government, to restore production and employment. Trade associations seemed to provide means of liaison between industry and government. These had been useful in the conferences that had accompanied wartime controls; and, partly as a result of this experience, trade associations had rapidly developed. During the years between the First World War and the depression, they had represented industry in the trade-practice conferences held by the Federal Trade Commission; but the practical effect of these conferences and of the codes that issued from them was limited by the antitrust laws. On the whole, the Commission's experiment with "industrial self-government" had been inconclusive.[29]

In May 1933, President Roosevelt asked Congress to provide "the machinery necessary for a great cooperative movement throughout all industry in order to obtain wide reemployment, to shorten the working week, to pay a decent wage for the shorter week and to prevent unfair competition and disastrous over-production." He explained that employers could not do this "singly or even in organized groups, because such action increases costs and thus permits cut-throat underselling by selfish competitors un-

[29] In 1916 Woodrow Wilson said to a group of business men: "It is hard to describe the functions of that commission [Federal Trade Commission]; all I can say is that it has transformed the government of the United States from being an antagonist of business into being a friend of business." Quoted in E. Pendleton Herring, "Politics, Personalities, and the Federal Trade Commission," *American Political Science Review*, Vol. 28 (1934), p. 1018.

willing to join in such a public-spirited endeavor." He added that "one of the great restrictions upon such cooperative efforts up to this time has been our anti-trust laws"; and he proposed that private industries should be permitted, "with the authority and under the guidance of government," to "make agreements and codes insuring fair competition."[30] When he signed the National Industrial Recovery Act a month later, he said that history would probably record the act "as the most important and far-reaching legislation ever enacted by the American Congress. It represents a supreme effort to stabilize for all time the many factors which make for the prosperity of the Nation, and the preservation of American standards."[31]

Specifically, the act aimed at once to raise wage rates, create employment by spreading work without reducing pay, and put a bottom under prices. It combined the ideas of reducing technological unemployment, strengthening labor organization, preventing predatory or unfair competition, establishing economic planning, inaugurating self-government in industry, and providing integrated public supervision of the economic system.[32]

Whatever the economic, constitutional, administrative, or other shortcomings of the law may have been—and these were evidently many and serious—it was based on a conception of the interdependence of the various groups and factors in economic life and of the need for an integrated political treatment of the economic problem. It admitted, too, the lack of integrated leadership and control in industry; and it undertook in a measure, not only to reform business practices, but also to provide an improved economic organization.[33] The act was represented to be only a single important feature of a comprehensive program that was creating "a new order."[34]

When in May 1935 the Supreme Court declared the act unconstitutional, no attempt was made to revive it in its original comprehensiveness; but much the same principles with respect to prices

---

[30] *Public Papers and Addresses,* Vol. 2, p. 202.

[31] The same, p. 246.

[32] On the National Industrial Recovery Act, see Lyon and Abramson, *Government and Economic Life,* Vol. 2, pp. 1035-61, and the references thereto appended.

[33] "We undertook by lawful, constitutional processes to reorganize a disintegrating system of production and exchange." *Public Papers and Addresses,* Vol. 3, p. 130.

[34] The same, Vol. 4, p. 15.

and labor were applied to the bituminous coal industry. The principle of price-fixing was likewise embodied in the Robinson-Patman and Miller-Tydings Acts, as well as in resale price-maintenance and loss-leader laws passed in various states; and the labor provisions of the National Industrial Recovery Act were re-enacted in different forms.

General economic effects came from other less specific or less direct features of governmental action. It was the total effect of a large and rapidly changing structure of policy, along with the verbal attacks of administration spokesmen on business, that was represented to be destructive of "confidence" and thus detrimental to productive enterprise. Agricultural and labor policies, while social in objective, were primarily economic in long-run effect. The National Labor Relations Act bore directly on the problem of industrial organization and administration. It appeared on occasion during this period that the balance of power between employers and employees was more than redressed, that organized labor was exercising certain powers of industrial management without assuming commensurate responsibility, and was determining such matters as prices and output without regard to the desires or interests of consumers, sometimes in contradiction to governmental policies, and in some instances contrary to the interests of wage earners themselves.

The recession of 1937, followed by Democratic reverses in the congressional elections of 1938, brought indications of a change in the attitude of government toward private industrial leadership; and, at about the same time, government policy seemed to be swinging from the theory of controlled economic organization back to the principle of competition. In his message to Congress of April 29, 1938, the President outlined this reorientation and incidentally his revised politico-economic philosophy. He declared that "among us today a concentration of private power without equal in history is growing," and asserted that "the power of a few to menace the economic life of the nation must be diffused among the many or be transferred to the public and its democratically responsible government. . . . The enforcement of free competition is the least regulation business can expect." He remarked further: "A realistic system of business regulation has to reach more than consciously immoral acts. The community is interested in economic results. It must be protected from economic as well as moral wrongs. We must find practical controls over blind economic forces as well as over blindly selfish men."

To meet the situation, the President recommended "a thorough study of the concentration of economic power in American industry and the effect of that concentration upon the decline of competition."[35] To conduct the proposed study, Congress established the Temporary National Economic Committee; and in the meantime, the Department of Justice proceeded with a fresh program of enforcement of the antitrust laws, a program fashioned in the spirit of the President's message, embodying an industry-by-industry approach to the monopoly problem, seeking not merely punitive and moral but also economic results.[36]

SPENDING

Another type of general economic control, perhaps even more difficult in practical operation and more complicating in effect, was involved in the so-called spending policy.

Implicit in budgetary principles and in their rapid and widespread adoption after the turn of the century were the following assumptions: that revenues and expenditures must be kept in balance; that deficits were an evidence of bad government; that thrift was a virtue in public as well as in private affairs; that public debt was on much the same footing as private debt, having limits beyond which it was unwise to go; and that reduction of the public debt testified to sound policy and good government. These assumptions were apparently still dominant in all sections of opinion when the depression came.

While Mr. Hoover stood for a balanced budget, recovery and relief measures involved increased federal outlays; expenditures rose and revenues fell; deficits occurred; and the national debt grew.[37] After his inauguration, President Roosevelt promptly pointed out to Congress the "profound effect" of the accumulated deficit on the national economy. Recovery, he declared, depended on the credit of the national government.[38] He asked and was

---

[35] *New York Times*, Apr. 30, 1938.

[36] See Thurman W. Arnold, *The Bottlenecks of Business* (1940).

[37] For figures of expenditure, revenues, and debt, see Brookings Institution, *The Recovery Problem in the United States* (1937), pp. 664-72; S. Rept. 1275, 75 Cong. 1 sess., pp. 45-53.

[38] "Too often in recent history liberal governments have been wrecked on

granted discretionary authority to revise veterans' allowances and to reduce the compensation of federal officers and employees. When this action was taken, the "general" or "ordinary" expenditures of the federal government were brought within the revenues. The whole budget, however, was far from balanced.

In subsequent years, with generally increasing expenditures, constantly recurring deficits, and mounting debt, less was heard of budget-balancing as an economic or fiscal policy, and more was said to justify expenditure and to minimize the importance of the debt. In certain fields, abnormal expenditure appeared unavoidable; in others it was politically advantageous; and in still others it was a result of policies that were believed to be desirable. A considerable part of the so-called recovery and relief expenditures, however, was justified by a general theory of spending or "pump-priming" for recovery; and these outlays, as well as others in large amounts, were supported by the argument that they raised purchasing power and thus contributed to recovery.

Advance planning of public works and their expansion in times of depression had been under discussion for more than a decade.[39] Though an increasing percentage of federal expenditures was going to public works between 1920 and 1932, the situation of the building industry in 1933, combined with the need of unemployment relief and the apparent need of recovery stimulants, seemed to justify an extraordinary emergency expenditure on public works. At the same time, an effort was made to stimulate private building, especially in the field of housing. Housing policy differed, however, from general public works policy in that housing was traditionally a private and on the whole a highly decentralized enterprise, an enterprise that in the main had been publicly promoted and regulated only through municipal zoning and building regulations.[40]

---

rocks of loose fiscal policy. . . . We must move with a direct and resolute purpose now. . . . Such economies which can be made will, it is true, affect some of our citizens; but the failure to make them will affect all of our citizens. The very stability of our government itself is concerned and when that is concerned the benefits of some must be subordinated to the needs of all." *Public Papers and Addresses*, Vol. 2, pp. 49-51.

[39] See Harold G. Moulton, "Demobilization and Unemployment," in Frederick A. Cleveland and Joseph Schafer, *Democracy in Reconstruction* (1919), pp. 293-304.

[40] The federal government had temporarily promoted housing during the First World War through the United States Housing Corporation.

Passing through a stage when fresh additions to the public debt were rather comprehensively defended as "investments," deficit-spending came in due time to be considered in influential quarters not only a desirable economic instrument but also a permanent one. To the extent that this view represented economic theorizing and not merely rationalization, it developed largely as a result of the recession of 1937, which came at a time when expenditure had fallen off and the budget was more nearly in balance than it had been for some years. Overlooking other factors that had been operating, some economists, and apparently the President also, assumed that the improvement of the government's financial position was somehow a cause of the business reaction.

Thus, from various directions came influences tending to a breakdown of the budgetary principle and leading to the employment by government of an instrument of economic control that was generally admitted to require for its safe and effective handling the utmost wisdom and courage. Eventually, the very magnitude of the nation's expenditures destroyed the usefulness of the instrument. As an economist pointed out:

The policy of expanding and contracting expenditures for public works in relation to the successive phases of the business cycle, widely accepted in this country not so very long ago, has been thrown into the discard as both spending and debt have mounted to such levels that the variations about it have ceased to be nearly so important as the level itself.[41]

TAXATION

The burden of federal taxation substantially increased. The need for additional revenue led in some cases to the raising of existing rates, but more frequently to the tapping of new sources. In the search for additional revenue, the federal government, as well as the states, showed a marked preference for indirect over direct taxation. In the meantime, attention turned to the question of tax immunity, hitherto enjoyed by the securities and salaries of one governmental level from taxation by the other. Increased holdings by the federal government of property in the states also became a matter of concern.

Tax policy would have been difficult enough if its only purpose had been the raising of revenue for a stabilized government. But

[41] Leo Wolman, "Labor Policies and the Volume of Employment," in *Academy of Political Science Proceedings*, Vol. 18 (1939), p. 72.

taxation was employed as a social instrumentality and for economic purposes. Social aims in taxation produced unexpected economic effects; and taxation for strictly economic purposes produced unanticipated results. Furthermore, government was not stabilized: it was rapidly expanding.

During this entire period, the tax system as a whole was becoming not only more burdensome (though still insufficient to meet expenditures), but also more complicated and confusing, less clear in its economic and social effects, more questionable in its political aspects, and, as we shall point out more fully later on, less compatible with federalism and less efficacious as a means through which democratic control might be brought to bear on the expansion of governmental activities.

We have thus noted certain types of general economic control. We shall now turn to two specific fields, electric power and transportation, for additional illustrations of what was happening to the governmental task.

ELECTRIC POWER REGULATION

Electric power is graphically linked with technological progress and, before the depression, had become one of the principal stakes in the controversies over conservation and economic concentration.

Prior to 1933 utility enterprises, constituting local monopolies, had been subjected to both municipal and state regulation, chiefly with respect to rates. A number of municipalities tried public ownership and operation. These attempts at monopoly regulation and price-fixing had not been signally successful.[42] In 1914 large local corporations and management companies dominated the utilities industry; but by 1924 holding companies had become a prominent feature of the economic landscape. Between 1907 and 1933 a number of states passed laws designed to regulate utility holding companies. The federal government had taken steps to safeguard the water resources of the public domains; it was constructing

[42] "The only method of government price control which has been extensively developed in this country is, as a matter of fact, the public utility type. To my mind the results have been extremely sad. . . ." (Edward S. Mason, "Methods of Developing a Proper Control of Big Business," in *Academy of Political Science Proceedings*, Vol. 18 (1939), p. 46.) "Public utility regulations of many states have turned out to be a means of sanctifying privileges, rather than of protecting the public." (Adolf A. Berle, *The Berle Memorandum*, reprinted from the *Capitol Daily* of Aug. 20-23, 1938, p. 19.) On utility regulation in general, see Lyon and Abramson, *Government and Economic Life*, Vol. 2, pp. 616-745.

power-producing dams; and it had developed Muscle Shoals as a war measure.

President Roosevelt in 1934 appointed a National Power Policy Committee; and, in submitting one of its reports to Congress on March 12, 1935, he pronounced his famous "death sentence" on those utility holding companies that could not "justify themselves as necessary for the functioning of the operating utility companies."[43]

The Public Utility Act of 1935 gave to the Securities and Exchange Commission extensive regulatory powers over interstate holding company systems controlling gas and electric utilities. The act also directed the Commission, "as soon as practicable after January 1, 1938," to carry out a reorganization of these systems so that each might be economically integrated within a single area. It was provided that the Commission should approve the appointment of receivers for interstate utility holding companies going into receivership and, if the Commission consented, might itself serve as receiver.

The act represented an assumption by the federal government at once of regulatory power, managerial supervision, and reorganizing authority over a highly important industry. The purpose of the act was evidently partly to eliminate abuses, partly to protect investors and consumers, and partly to increase the power of state commissions to fix intra-state rates. Its objective was not to restore competition, but to make monopoly manageable.

The Tennessee Valley Authority Act of 1933 originated from a broader and bolder conception. While it stemmed from the Muscle Shoals project, it transcended, in the President's words, "mere power development; it enters the wide fields of flood control, soil erosion, afforestation, elimination from agricultural use of marginal lands, and distribution and diversification of industry. In short, this power development of war days leads logically to national planning for a complete watershed involving many states and the future lives and welfare of millions." And he concluded with this forecast: "If we are successful here we can march on, step by step, in a like development of other great natural territorial units within our borders."[44] Under the act, the federal government undertook

[43] Public Papers and Addresses, Vol. 4, pp. 98-101.
[44] The same, Vol. 2, pp. 122-23.

in this region the production and distribution of electric power. In this connection, the Tennessee Valley undertaking was also envisaged as a form of regulation—"yardstick" regulation—and as a means of reducing monopoly prices by government competition.

The Rural Electrification Administration was established to aid in bringing cheap electricity to farm homes, and the Electric Home and Farm Authority to finance purchases of electric appliances. Municipal electric plants were included among the projects to which the federal government gave financial aid; and largely as a result of this aid municipally owned plants considerably increased in number.

Electric power development tied in with other federal policies dealing with navigation, flood-control, forestry, soil erosion, wild-life preservation, and military preparedness. Thus, policies relating to recovery, relief, power, business regulation, transportation, conservation, agriculture, and national defense were all interrelated.

TRANSPORTATION POLICY

After the beginning of systematic national railroad regulation in 1887, governmental authority in this connection had been extended and tightened, becoming increasingly mandatory, until, in the Transportation Act of 1920, the federal government assumed what has been aptly termed managerial supervision over the railroad system.[45]

The railroads were hard hit by the depression; and many were saved from receiverships by loans from the Reconstruction Finance Corporation. Some relief was also afforded by rate adjustments. On May 4, 1933, the President asked for emergency railroad legislation, stating that he was not yet ready to submit "a comprehensive plan for permanent legislation."[46] The Emergency Transportation Act of 1933 was in part amendatory of the 1920 act; but it announced the broader and more affirmative purpose of eliminating unnecessary duplications and wastes, promoting financial reorganization of the carriers, and in general improving transportation in all its forms.

[45] Lyon and Abramson, *Government and Economic Life*, Vol. 2, pp. 764-65. On transportation policies in general during this period, see the same, pp. 778-863.
[46] *Public Papers and Addresses*, Vol. 2, pp. 153-54.

The Coordinator appointed under this act proposed a comprehensive program,[47] one result of which was the passage of the Motor Carrier Act of 1935, which established federal managerial supervision over motor carriers similar to that which was being exercised over the railroads.

The ideal was evidently, as the Coordinator pointed out, a transportation, rather than merely a railroad, policy. With respect to the railroad system alone, governmental policy was discordant enough, paralyzed by conflicts both of theory and of interest. With respect to the transportation system, however, these conflicts were more extensive and more inveterate.

Government had constructed, and was still constructing, maintaining, and policing, a vast highway system that in part duplicated the railroad transportation system and in part competed with it. The highway promotion policy of the government reflected conflicts of interest and of economic theory and, unlike railroad policy, revealed the difficulty of establishing co-ordination of policies under federalism. During the depression, federal aid for highway construction increased, and was justified under the spending theory.

For more than a hundred years, too, government had been endeavoring, separately from its land transportation policies, to promote and regulate water transportation. Inland waterways, heavily subsidized by the government, were in competition with the railroads and were defended at times for that very reason. During the depression, the plight of the railroads did not prevent the federal government from making additional and unusual outlays for river improvements and giving serious consideration to plans for expensive canal construction.[48]

Regulation of shipping had been undertaken, but separately from the regulation of railroads. Promotion of a merchant marine had, as we have seen, various and often confused objectives, none of which appeared to have been satisfactorily achieved.

From 1915 to 1926, development of aviation was aided by the federal government; and after 1926 it was both promoted and

---

[47] *Report of the Federal Coordinator of Transportation*, 1934, H. Doc. 89, 74 Cong. 1 sess., p. 14.

[48] Proposed canal systems included the Great Lakes-St. Lawrence waterway development, the Florida ship canal, and the Lake Erie-Ohio River canal.

regulated. For the study of aviation problems, the President appointed a special commission in 1934. Transmitting its report to Congress in January 1935, the President remarked that it was becoming "more and more apparent that the Government of the United States should bring about a consolidation of its methods of supervision over all forms of transportation"; and he suggested that Congress take into consideration "the necessity for the development of interrelated planning of our national transportation."[49]

Nevertheless, the growing structure of transportation policy was characterized in general by segmentary expansion with little progress toward integration or removal of contradictions. Certain steps toward administrative unification will be referred to in the following chapter.

GENERAL NATURE AND SIGNIFICANCE OF ECONOMIC POLICIES

In some measure, domestic governmental policies adopted from 1933 to 1940 were extensions or adaptations of policies already accepted, or represent the adoption of proposals and the application of ideas that had at one time or another come to the surface. But in many cases the new policies constitute a marked departure from the ideas that had previously dominated American thinking and had appeared to be essential elements of the American way of life. Policies in this latter category may be illustrated by the virtual acceptance of an unbalanced budget and of a steadily increasing public debt, the assumption by the government of the investment-banking function, and the controls involved in the agricultural adjustment program.

New Deal policies in general were quite commonly interpreted by their advocates as not designed to substitute for capitalism a socialistic or communistic system, but, rather, as intended to preserve the traditional economic system in its broad outlines and essential operations, the effort being to exploit or explore more extensively, thoroughly, and fruitfully than American government ever had in the past the middle ground between *laissez faire* and complete economic collectivism. But this interpretation, assuming that it is the correct one, neither removes any difficulties nor decides the ultimate outcome.

[49] *Public Papers and Addresses,* Vol. 4, pp. 68-69.

Had American government during the depression premised its action either on absolute *laissez faire* or on absolute socialism, its task would have been fairly simple; for the acceptance of either doctrine more or less predetermines a consistent trend of policy. But occupation of the middle ground, necessarily a shifting ground, presents government with innumerable doubtful and debatable choices, involving the balancing of advantages against disadvantages and giving rise inevitably to compromises, inconsistencies, and conflicts. When these choices are made in an atmosphere of distress and tension, it is inevitable that not only the policy-determining process but also the policies themselves should bear an emergency appearance and should be experimental at the very time when experimentation is most dangerous.

Though Mr. Hoover and Mr. Roosevelt both compared the depression to war, it proved much more difficult in a depression crisis to draw the line between the ordinary and the extraordinary. Preoccupation with ends led to a relative neglect of means. The experience of this period revealed, more clearly than ever before, the difficulty of producing a single policy with a single clear objective and with limited predictable effects. Action seemed to be taken sometimes merely for the sake of action; and the idea of change as a social characteristic appears to have been made one of the guiding principles of legislation.

Those who determined policy seemed to possess undue confidence in the virtue and potency of government, so long as government was controlled by the socially minded. The "social-mindedness" or "liberalism" of government was generally expressed in terms of power and material things. But concentrated economic power came under intelligent and comprehensive examination only after the structure of policy had been erected. The President introduced a spiritual note in his first inaugural,[50] which was occasionally repeated thereafter; but in the practical formulation and presentation of policies it appears that the dominant conception of "the more abundant life" was pre-eminently materialistic. Material benefits were accorded to the farmers, organized labor, the unemployed, the veterans, the old people, the silver-mine owners, and others.

[50] The same, Vol. 2, p. 12.

Something was done directly for the middle-class investors and depositors. Policy in general was directed to particular interests rather than to the general welfare.

Aside from political aims, most of these policies have both social and economic purposes. The result often is that no certain approach is made to either the social or economic goal. A clear distinction between social and economic legislation has never been consistently observed, and probably cannot be; but, when social legislation is given an extraordinary emphasis and is accompanied by conditions unfavorable to objective economic thinking, it is inevitable that dubious economic justifications should be advanced for desirable social ideals.

Government attempts to exercise control over the economic system at various key points; and this control has advanced far beyond the mere prohibition of abuses. Regulation now extends into fields where it has not previously been tried; and in some areas, as well as over the system as a whole, management by government is supplanting regulation. Governmental regulative and managerial policies seem to be cumulative. It appears to be almost a natural law that a power once assumed should be retained and should steadily gather new accretions of authority. With each assumption of responsibility, government seems to be making further experimentation and additional controls almost inevitable, because of the political obstacles to the making of correct choices, the difficulty of providing beforehand for all contingencies, the fact that partial measures of control always leave open possibilities of evasion, and the obscure relationships and infinite criss-crossings of economic causes and economic effects.

Joined with confidence in the potency of governmental authority, public policy has been marked with evidences of a waning faith in individual initiative and private enterprise, and with an absence of any deeply felt concern for the traditional economic freedoms or for local self-government and clear-cut federalism. The direct and immediate effect, on the whole, is to invade or further to restrict areas of individual choice, of private initiative and control, individual responsibility, and local authority. The social ideals in view are equality and security rather than freedom; the political purposes, realization and concentration of power.

CHAPTER VII

BUREAUCRACY AND PUBLIC POWER

Stimulated by the policies just reviewed, administrative activities rapidly multiplied, assuming in some cases novel forms, and proceeding in some directions beyond what had formerly been viewed as the reasonable scope of government.[1] At the same time activities that had previously been only partially developed and conducted on a modest or experimental scale came to be prosecuted more extensively and intensively. New policies required from Congress, already overburdened and now pressed for speedy action, an unprecedented delegation of legislative authority to executive and administrative agencies. These developments sharpened issues involved in administrative power and administrative responsibility.

GROWTH OF BUREAUCRACY[2]

Neither the size of the bureaucracy nor the rate of its growth is indicated by figures of total expenditure. Administrative expenditure in 1936, for example, accounted for only about 17 per cent of total federal expenditures.[3] The size and recent expansion of the federal bureaucracy appear most clearly in personnel statistics. The number of federal employees was about 583,000 in 1932. During the early months of the Roosevelt administration, a reduction was accomplished; but in succeeding years the personnel increased, and in 1939 it exceeded 920,000, passing the peak of employment during the First World War.[4]

More than 40 per cent of this increase of personnel was accounted

[1] See Arthur G. Coons, "The Functions of Government in the Literature of Economics," *Annals,* Vol. 206 (1939), pp. 17-22.

[2] The term "bureaucracy" is used here in no invidious sense. It is meant to describe an organized collectivity of administrative officials who possess an extensive range of duties and powers.

[3] See *Investigation of Executive Agencies of the Government,* S. Rept. 1275, 75 Cong. 1 sess., pp. 49-53.

[4] *Annual Report of the United States Civil Service Commission for the Fiscal Year Ended June 30, 1933,* p. 8; *Annual Report . . . June 30, 1939,* p. 157.

for by five great agencies: the Treasury, War, Post Office, and Navy Departments, and the Veterans' Administration. Of the already established civil agencies, the Department of Agriculture experienced the most remarkable expansion. Its 27,000 employees in 1933 had multiplied to 108,000 in 1939. Excluding the military establishment and the Post Office Department, about one-fourth of the remaining federal personnel was in the Department of Agriculture. Relatively large increases, however, were represented by new agencies, such as the Public Works Administration, the Home Owners' Loan Corporation, the Social Security Board, the Tennessee Valley Authority, the Works Progress Administration and, in the aggregate, by many other new establishments.

Estimates of state and local governmental employees vary somewhat. The number in 1939 was probably more than 2,500,000. The best estimates available covering the depression period indicate that between 1929 and 1937, state personnel increased at about the same rate as that of the federal government, municipal employees slightly declined in number, while those engaged in public education or working for the counties, townships, and other minor units were about 10 per cent more in 1937 than in 1929.[5] Total governmental employment, according to the same estimates, increased 17.5 per cent during that period. Again using the same figures, public employees in 1937 constituted 11.6 per cent of all public and private employees.

The independent establishments in the executive branch of the federal government had tended to multiply before 1933. At the beginning of the Roosevelt administration, there were, in addition to the ten departments, 24 independent agencies having separate staffs. On June 30, 1939, the number of such agencies had increased to 49.[6] The total number of administrative agencies having their

[5] U.S. Bureau of Foreign and Domestic Commerce, *Income in the United States 1929-1937* (November 1938), p. 36; Edward R. Gray and William R. Divine, "One in Every Nine Works for the Government: A Review of Public Payrolls," *National Municipal Review*, Vol. 28 (1939), pp. 204 ff.; National Civil Service Reform League, *Proceedings of the Fifty-Seventh Annual Meeting*, Dec. 15, 1939, p. 11.

[6] *Annual Report of the United States Civil Service Commission for the Fiscal Year Ended June 30, 1939*; Lewis Meriam and Lawrence F. Schmeckebier, *Reorganization of the National Government* (1939), pp. 240-61. Agencies that were

own staffs, including the Office of the President, was 60. Numerous unstaffed boards, committees, and commissions, ex officio and otherwise, were in existence. Some of these exercised co-ordinating and advisory functions; several, like the National Munitions Control Board, had powers of some importance.

Apparently, much the same influences that had tended to multiply administrative agencies in the states were at work in the federal government; and these influences were aggravated by the pressures incidental to depression conditions. When federal agencies, including the unstaffed ones, were considered, the impression created was one of diversity and complexity, as well as multiplicity. The federal government, like the states, appeared to have adopted the maxim: "When in doubt, create a board." Most of the independent establishments were boards or commissions. Yet, on June 30, 1939, the ten executive departments accounted for 81.3 per cent of the federal administrative personnel; and the largest two independent establishments—the Veterans' Administration and the Works Progress Administration—were single-headed.

ADMINISTRATIVE POWER

During a century or more of our history, students and observers of American government had looked upon administration as, in the main, merely routine execution of the law; and the chief executive himself, though admitted to be, at least nominally, the head of the administration, was recognized only grudgingly to be a part of it.

Wide discretionary and policy-determining authority, amounting in fact to law-making, had for centuries been exercised by the courts; but the judiciary was conceived to be a separate branch of government; and it did show distinctive characteristics with respect to organization, procedure, impartiality, professional integrity, control, effectiveness, and adaptability.

During the eighties of the last century, the form and essential characteristics of modern administration began to appear in the national government. Increasing legislative activity, the shortcom-

---

renamed after Mar. 4, 1933 or represent an enlargement or consolidation of preexisting agencies are counted as pre-existing agencies.

ings of legislative bodies and of the traditionally constituted courts, and the nature of the new social and economic responsibilities of government were making imperative, on the one hand, more extensive delegations of discretionary authority to administrative agencies outside the traditional judicial organization and, on the other, the development of administrative initiative and guidance in the legislative process. As time passed, powers already delegated were reinforced and given greater scope, while new and various types of discretionary authority were granted to administrative agencies both old and new. Thus, policy-determination, whether expressed in formal rules and regulations, in decisions, or in some other manner, was becoming an administrative function of the first importance.

The many and various separable powers that were coming to be exercised by administrative officials were not all alike. Some were derived from constitutional provisions; others from statutory. With respect to purpose, these powers were political, military, social, or economic; or they might be otherwise classified. Some had little or a remote relation to individual rights and obligations; in the case of others, this relation was direct and substantial. Powers were formally expressed in different forms and procedures.

The question of power is at the heart of the problem of government. Power, obviously, is not exactly measurable by the number of constitutional or statutory grants of authority, public expenditure, the size of the governmental personnel, the number and relationship of administrative agencies, their activities and volume of work, or the total or net effect on private activities and freedom, although each of these may bear a more or less close relation to the importance of the power-complex. It is well known that neither size nor energy is an accurate indication of power.[7] Because of its generally

[7] Perhaps the most helpful method of studying governmental power would be through the case method, that is, an analysis of it at various points of impact. If various typical laboring men, farmers, small businessmen, and corporations were selected, it would be possible to determine concretely how social units are actually affected by governmental action. Some light is thrown on the subject by the number of reports made to federal agencies by individuals and corporations. A majority of these are administrative, that is, made incidentally to the performance of some administrative function. During the year ended June 30, 1938, the number of administrative returns was 97.5 million. About one-third of these, however, were

imponderable and incalculable nature, administrative power is peculiarly liable to misrepresentation by way of either exaggeration or under-estimation. The interesting thing is not the existence of governmental power: theoretically and potentially, government is omnipotent. The crucial question has to do with the possibilities inherent in the exercise of power and its points of impact.

Powers, apparently vast and vital, may be administratively inexercisable, as seemed to be the case with the National Recovery Administration; or an effort to execute contradictory or inconsistent policies may result in a practical neutralization or disappearance of power, as may be the case to some extent with respect to the regulation of transportation. Conceivably, an administrative situation may be such as to produce extensive deadlocks. Autocratic government is not necessarily powerful government. As conditions precedent to the realization of administrative power, the grants of power that are contained in policies must be so organized as to be harmonious and mutually self-supporting and the administrative instrumentalities to which the grants are made must be similarly organized.

Depression policies widened
administrative authority.

In the field of economic regulation, when narrowly viewed as the special province of the "independent" boards and commissions, discretionary authority was being widened to cover additional areas of economic life, applied to additional private activities, and broad-

---

applications for governmental favors or privileges. More than a third were connected with taxation. A smaller though still sizable number were involved in governmental regulation of private enterprises. (*Report of the Central Statistical Board on Returns Made by the Public to the Federal Government*, Dec. 31, 1938, H. Doc. 27, 76 Cong. 1 sess.) It is stated that in 1927 the Curtis Publishing Co. was required to file 14 reports in the United States at a cost of $850; but in 1937 it filed 44,610 at a cost of $21,100. Tax Policy League, *Tax Relations among Governmental Units* (1938), p. 4.

"No matter how efficient a corporation may be within itself, the factors today outside of its control are of greater importance in determining the profitmaking possibilities than ever before. The acts of government both in our own country and abroad today have a very great bearing on the economic situation and in turn affect in no small measure the profits of an organization such as your corporation." From Report of Lewis H. Brown, president of Johns-Manville Corporation, quoted in *New York Times*, Mar. 3, 1939.

ened from regulation of rates and services to managerial supervision and industrial reorganization. The goals toward which administrative discretion was to work were made in some cases comprehensively and basically affirmative, consistent with the assumed general responsibility of government for the economic welfare of the country.[8]

Regulation, in its narrow sense, however, comprised only a part, and perhaps not the larger or the more significant part, of federal administrative power in the economic sphere. Various instrumentalities were at the President's or administrators' disposal to control or stimulate the economic system.[9] Power, largely discretionary and of a sweeping and novel character, was wielded by the President and his subordinates under the spending and lending policies. So wide was the discretion exercised under these policies that they were practically what administration made them.

To be sure, administrative discretion was in some instances narrowly limited by statute law; but congressional law-making itself

[8] For a succinct statement of the discretion assigned to the "independent" commissions, see Wilson K. Doyle, *Independent Commissions in the Federal Government* (1939), pp. 6-13.

"That these powers [of the Interstate Commerce Commission] involve such broad discretion that their exercise will seriously affect, if not define, the essential character and direction of the nation's policy toward these important economic enterprises, must be conceded. In vesting the commission with these powers Congress has, it is true, provided certain guides or limitations such as, just and reasonable, compatible with the public interest, or reasonably necessary or appropriate. But such vague terms obviously constitute no more than purely formal limitations upon the commission's powers of decision. The other commissions within this group have not been given the same extensive range of powers. But such powers as have been given to them similarly involve a significant control over public policy." The same, pp. 7-8.

[9] Examples were: the President's control of the gold content of the dollar, his power to cause the issue of paper money, his discretionary authority over American commerce under the Neutrality Act, and his power to reorganize administrative agencies; the Secretary of the Treasury's operation of the 2 billion dollar stabilization fund; the powers of the Federal Reserve Board over banking and credit; stimulation of banks and industrial enterprises by the Reconstruction Finance Corporation; the authority of the President and Secretary of State to lower tariff rates through reciprocal trade agreements; execution of the antitrust laws by the Department of Justice; the fixing of wages and hours and the conciliation of industrial disputes by the Department of Labor; the development and "yardstick" policies of the Tennessee Valley Authority; and the incalculable influence exerted by governmental publicity and by presidential and other executive pronouncements.

was in a measure within the power of the administrators. Owing to their expert knowledge and experience and, in some cases, to their affiliation with or leadership of pressure groups, their opinions and recommendations carried great weight with congressional committees and in many instances were decisive. In short, national legislation invoked governmental power and determined the general direction of its exercise, but the bureaucracy to an extent originated it, exclusively applied it, and within broad limits expanded or contracted its application and effect.

Growth of bureaucratic power did not necessarily restrict individual liberty.

In the direct and immediate intention or effect of policy, so far as it developed, one could not find any sweeping, direct, and immediate challenge to private liberty, except perhaps to the liberty of the corporation. The Anglo-Saxon conception of liberty is ordered liberty, liberty under law, the liberty of one individual assured by the restriction of another's. In this modern age, for example, individual freedom in the use of the highways has been extraordinarily restricted and regulated, compared with the freedoms that existed in the horse-and-buggy era. The reasons for the change are well known; and it is recognized to be protective, not only of life and property, but also of freedom itself.

Frequently, public regulation shifted restrictions on individual freedom from private possessors of power to other individuals or to the government. The National Labor Relations Act, for example, curtailed the freedom of private employers through a shift of power to labor unions and the government; but the individual worker may have neither directly lost nor directly gained much freedom. He had already lost or was losing to large-scale industry his freedom of contract. Similarly, the farmers' individualism and independence were no longer what they were in the days of the self-sufficient pioneer. These qualities had been restricted in scope by co-operative enterprises, tenantry, agricultural technology, taxation, debt, the complexities of modern economic life, and other conditions. Farmers, like industrial wage earners, now chose to exchange some of these restrictions and some of their remaining individualism and freedom for the hope of economic improvement, equality, and security. Conceivably, they might gain by the exchange certain free choices that they did not possess before.

While no great significance seems to lie in the direct and immediate impact of recent policies on individual liberty in economic affairs, the utmost significance may attach to indirect and long-run effects. These are likely to come, it would seem, less from regulation in specific areas and from tangible restrictions than from the cumulative and unanticipated effects of general controls and of social welfare policies, not only on the economic system, but also on the integrity and intelligence of government, on the ideals and morals of electoral groups, and finally on the strength of the democratic principle, which formerly drew its sustenance from the idea of liberty.

ADMINISTRATIVE RESPONSIBILITY

Extension of governmental regulations and restrictions and the transfer of power from private to public hands has been supported on the theory that government is controlled by the people, who remain collectively free, their government serving as trustee of their liberties. If administrative agencies are to determine policies that are related significantly to basic group interests and to the general welfare and that deal with controversial questions on which opinion fluctuates, popular government requires that the bureaucracy shall be responsible and responsive to the preponderant public or group opinion.[10]

The Constitution was framed at a time when governmental power was feared. The framers of the Constitution were conscious of the disposition of men to abuse and usurp authority. This fear and this acknowledgment of original sin contributed strongly to the kind of governmental organization that was established. For a hundred years, the question of the control of governmental power appeared to be settled, owing in the main, probably, to the economic and social conditions of the developing nation, the restricted sphere

---

[10] For an amplified statement of this view, see Herman Finer, "Administrative Responsibility in Democratic Government," *Public Administration Review*, Vol. 1 (1941), pp. 335-50.

of government, the relative freedom and equality of opportunity—expanding opportunity—enjoyed by individuals, the comparatively large role played by the states, the wide and frequent election of public officers, and the decentralization of state administration, permitting direct popular control of administrative officials in the local units.

As bureaucracy became larger and more costly, the need increased not only for democratic safeguards but also for co-ordinative devices, professional standards, and scientific personnel administration. The problem became therefore one of reconciling honesty, efficiency, stability, and self-regulation with responsibility and responsiveness.

Responsibility is not assured by localism,
group control, or boards.

Genuine local self-government may be an efficacious means of reconciling public authority with individual liberty; but this means cannot be employed to any significant extent in an age of economic unity and interdependence on a regional and national scale, when imperative needs exist for expert, uniform, and centralized action.

Informally and in part extralegally, public or group opinion is brought to bear directly on administrative agencies. Administration, like legislation, is subjected to pressures, lobbying, and propaganda.[11] In the federal government as well as in the states, various departments and bureaus are considered to be representative of and in a measure responsible to a special clientele. Each has its definite constituency.[12] In semi-public and private associations, administrative officials are brought into contact with organized group opinion.

Recognition that the success of administration depends on the understanding, consent, and co-operation of those administered has led to the establishment of additional procedures. Before an administrative decision is made, hearings are frequently held. Sometimes

[11] See E. Pendleton Herring, *Public Administration and the Public Interest* (1936); Donald C. Blaisdell, *Economic Power and Political Pressures*, Temporary National Economic Committee Monograph No. 26 (1941), pp. 70-73.

[12] For example, in the federal government, the Departments of Agriculture and Labor. "We are first and last the investors' advocate." Address by W. O. Douglas, chairman of Securities and Exchange Commission, *New York Times*, May 21, 1938.

the group is permitted to draw up the rules that are to govern it. In some cases the private group becomes a quasi-public administrative agency. In the field of agriculture as well as labor certain national policies are executed only after a vote has been taken of the persons concerned.

These devices appear to have serious defects. They constantly emphasize and enforce responsibility to special groups rather than to the whole people or to the majority. They mold administrative policies in the form of particular interests rather than the general welfare. They accentuate and tend to perpetuate disunity both in administrative organization and in the structure of policy; and they thus make it more difficult to create in the administration a force capable of counteracting the particularism and localism of Congress. Finally, these devices encourage, not only bureaucratic leadership, but also bureaucratic management of public opinion.

The board or commission setup, particularly in the states, has been employed to keep administration out of politics, to protect professional standards, and for other purposes; and whatever may be the merits or demerits of the board, it seems to be a necessary stop-gap in certain states and in certain areas of administration until the legislature and executive are improved and the tone of party politics raised. Because of the plural make-up of the board, it may and often does possess a representative character and a deliberative capacity. When the board is made by law specifically representative of specialized or of interest groups, such groups are even more likely to have a voice in the determination of administrative policies. Moreover, as substitutes for such boards or in addition to them, many advisory bodies have been set up, so constituted as to represent different areas of interest, knowledge, and expertness.

In the federal government as well as in the states, when the legislative and judicial functions transferred to the bureaucracy involve regulation of economic enterprises, they have been as a rule assigned to "independent" boards and commissions. In legal theory, these bodies are independent of the executive and are considered to be arms of the legislature and theoretically under its control. They are made "independent" by plural membership, long and overlapping terms, provision in most cases for representation of the minority party, and freedom from removal by the president except for specified causes.[13] The Supreme Court decisions that uphold the exceptional status of these bodies and permit them to exercise wide discretionary authority are based on the theory that they are not executive agencies, and are not constitutionally or properly subject to executive control.[14]

Apart from legal theory, plausible reasons are advanced for the independence of these bodies. It is argued, for example, that the economic questions assigned to them require a gradual, continuous, stable, and nonpartisan development of policy, difficult or impossible to obtain from executive departments under shifting political heads or from politically controlled boards. Independence is also held to be conducive to impartiality, considered essential in the adjudication of controversies.

Nevertheless, these bodies, in addition to their judicial and peculiarly sublegislative functions, perform administrative tasks, including delegated legislation, not essentially different from those assigned to the executive departments and to the chief executive. The whole field of economic control and of economic policy-determination is not and apparently cannot be allocated to independent boards and commissions. Only a part of the control complex is in their possession.

The regulatory board is a special creation for a specific purpose. It is established to fulfill certain important objectives of government in the economic sphere. In this sphere, conditions change, sometimes rapidly, and with these changes come upheavals of opinion and of political overturns. "One is brought to the conclusion," says Herring, "that for the present the control of business remains too controversial and too vital a political issue to be relegated successfully to a commission independent of close control by the policy-formulating agencies of the government. Administrators cannot assume the responsibilities of statesmen without incurring likewise the tribulations of politicians."[15]

[13] A single-headed agency might also be made "independent" of the executive. An example of such agency in the federal government was the General Accounting Office.

[14] *Rathbun* v. *U.S.*, 295 U.S. 602 (1934).

[15] Herring, "Politics, Personalities, and the Federal Trade Commission," *American Political Science Review*, Vol. 29 (1935), p. 35. See also Herring, *Public Administration and the Public Interest*.

The board, then, by no means solves the problem of responsibility; and, to the extent that the board is independent, it obviously complicates the process of administrative co-ordination.

The political party is not trusted to enforce responsibility.

The political party is an instrument of popular control. In its impact on administration, and in the name of democracy, the party system had applied to appointive officials, high and low, the principle of rotation in office ("To the victor belongs the spoils"), inaugurating a system by which administrative responsibility of a sort was crudely, wastefully, and often corruptly enforced. After some years came the civil service reform movement, based largely on a conception of administration as a ministerial function, demanding mere obedience to and execution of the law. The movement was motivated in the main by disgust with corrupt party politics. Later, the motivation changed; and emphasis shifted to administrative efficiency, the need for qualified public employees, and the supposedly nonpolitical character of most administrative work. As time passed and administration grew in importance, expertness in this branch of government was urged as a panacea for almost all political ills. The merit system became a touchstone of public and private virtue, and recently it has made considerable progress in state and local governments.[16]

A permanent civil servant may be intelligently sensitive to popular feeling without being chosen by and under the orders of a politician. Yet, it is a familiar fact that a vast bureaucracy, more or less in proportion to its irresponsibility, develops a set of peculiar characteristics: rigidity, unimaginativeness, fondness for red tape, hostility to innovation, greed for power, and contempt for the outsider, to say nothing of tendencies toward internal intrigue and cliquism. Politicians, representing the party or the pressure group, can provide a partial antidote when given a measure of power over the bureaucrat.

In recent years, moreover, penetrating and realistic studies of political processes have contributed to a better understanding of

[16] It was reported at the beginning of 1939 that the system had been adopted by 14 states, 674 cities, 169 counties, and 5 special districts. G. Lyle Belsley, "The Advance of the Merit System," *State Government*, Vol. 12 (1939), pp. 7 ff.

parties and politicians and somewhat to their rehabilitation in the esteem of scholars;[17] and the question has been raised whether the total exclusion of the political party from administration may not weaken or alter the party system in certain of its essential or desirable aspects.[18]

*An inclusive merit system does not
solve the problem.*

No one questions the correctness in principle of the merit system. The doubt is regarding the bounds of its application. The process of administrative policy-determination involves many experts; and among them are some who make a special effort to impose their own ideas of policy on government. Their task is essentially political; and it can be suspected that many of them are or ought to be politically minded. In any event, the handling of facts is not an entirely impersonal procedure; it is conditioned by personal attitude, class-consciousness, social philosophy, and conception of interest. If administrative policy is to be democratic, it would seem that this class of experts should reflect the preponderant popular attitude, consciousness, philosophy, or conception. No intelligent political executive would wish to be advised exclusively by persons out of tune with his political objectives; nor can a political executive be held responsible unless he has power to appoint and dismiss his employees.[19]

*Professionalism likewise
has shortcomings.*

Various professions now play a large part in administration; for example, the law, medicine, education, social work, and engineer-

[17] Reference here is to the studies of Gosnell, Herring, Lasswell, Merriam, Salter, and others.

[18] "Civil service reform must be considered along with the reform of politicians in policy-determining positions. . . . Bringing needed talent into the public service does not necessitate a frontal attack on the politicians. . . .

". . . It may be that centrally controlled and disciplined parties will prove the only means of holding an able and powerful bureaucracy to account. . . ." Herring, *The Politics of Democracy* (1940), pp. 365-67.

[19] See Kenneth C. Cole, "The 'Merit System' Again," *American Political Science Review*, Vol. 31 (1937), pp. 695-98. Compare Charles Edward Merriam and Louise Overacker, *Primary Elections* (1938), p. 285; Herring, *The Politics of Democracy*, p. 30.

ing. The qualifications and standards enforced by a profession are valuable contributions to administration. Helpful stimulation and restraint come also from the opinion of the professional group acting on the administrative official. But if the latter is responsible only or primarily to his professional group, his responsibility is not political and it is not democratic, for professions, such as those mentioned above, are in a measure interest-groups, tending to become self-governing and partially self-perpetuating and intentionally insulated from politics.

It has been urged by many that general administration, apart from the several recognized professions that engage in it, should be recognized and treated as a profession. If what we have just said about professionalism is true, the professionalizing of administration as administration would seem to take us farther than ever from a solution of the problem of responsibility. In administrative policy-determining positions the need is for responsiveness as well as detachment, for breadth as well as specialization, for flexibility as well as standardization.

CONTROL BY CONGRESS, PRESIDENT, AND THE COURTS

We turn now to certain more tangible and clear-cut means of enforcing administrative responsibility through the governmental organization. Congress and president are presumably responsible directly to the people. The modern bureaucracy cannot be made directly responsible; but, theoretically, it will be to all intents and purposes democratized if it is controlled by either Congress or the president. Judicial control, however, must also be considered.

Congress does not and cannot enforce
administrative responsibility.

It is asserted by some that the federal regulatory boards and commissions are or ought to be controlled by Congress. In a measure, of course, they have been so controlled, through senatorial confirmation of appointments, granting or withholding of appropriations, occasional investigations, congressional debates, statutory review of powers, and pressure by individual members of Congress. Every one of these legislative controls has been or may be applied, generally speaking, to the ordinary executive agencies and, within limits, to the president himself. Undoubtedly, these controls create a measure of responsibility to Congress; but it is generally recognized that Congress, being as it is and functioning as it does, the controls are insufficient to produce complete, continuous, effective, and immediate responsibility. Congressional action is slow and fitful. It is not suited to the active and intelligent direction of an administrative agency.[20] Congress is divided within itself; and the Senate often disagrees with the House.[21] At times, Congress has been dominated by the president or even, perhaps, by the regulatory board itself and the pressure group that supports it. There is, moreover, some reason to doubt that Congress itself is ideally constituted to be responsible to preponderant opinion. In any event, Congress does not possess or cannot exercise the one essential instrument of control: power to appoint and remove.[22]

Presidential control of administration is
actual, extensive, and increasing.

While independence of the executive is in theory an attribute of the regulatory commissions, such independence has varied according to the commission, the time, the circumstances, and the particular

---

[20] "A scrutiny of the *Congressional Record* and of the hearings before the Appropriations Committee reveals little appreciation of the problems of the [Federal Trade] Commission as an administrative agency. When congressmen discuss its affairs, their interest is obviously dictated by the situation in their own locality." Herring, "Politics, Personalities, and the Federal Trade Commission," Pt. 1, *American Political Science Review,* Vol. 28 (1934), p. 1022. See also Robert Luce, *Legislative Procedures* (1922), pp. 174-75, and *American Political Science Review,* Vol. 29 (1935), p. 295; John Preston Comer, *Legislative Functions of National Administrative Authorities* (1927), pp. 185-97.

[21] ". . . It is not uncommon for the [Federal Trade] Commission to be under fire in the Senate for exercising its powers too gingerly and in the House for daring to use them at all." Quoted from a former commissioner, Abram Myers, in Herring, *American Political Science Review,* Vol. 28 (1934), p. 1021.

[22] It has been abundantly demonstrated that the policies of a commission may be vigorous or lax, radical or conservative, progressive or reactionary, depending on the type of men who are appointed to it. A classic example is the change in the Federal Trade Commission brought about by the appointment of William E. Humphrey. More recently, in the case of the National Labor Relations Board, it appeared to many that the objections generally made to the policies of the Board might have been removed had its dominant members been changed; and in 1940 they were changed. In the states it has not been an uncommon practice for a legislature to obtain political control of an independent board by abolishing it and setting up a new one.

question of policy. The power of appointment offers opportunity for control; and, however secure in their tenure the members of regulatory boards may be, they can be gradually brought into adjustment with the politically dominant public opinion. Even the Supreme Court has revealed in the long run its responsiveness to political currents. The executive has had other means of influencing and at time dominating regulatory policy. That portion of economic control assigned to him, to executive departments, and to certain other agencies is indisputably under his authority. As will later be pointed out, presidential authority was in practice very greatly increased during the depression years over that part of the bureaucracy which was supposed to be substantially independent.

The judiciary cannot supply the kind
and degree of control required.

Because of the extensive discretionary authority that they exercise and because the exercise of this authority involves or may involve individual rights, administrative authorities are and should be in some respects subject to control by the courts. The development of regulatory boards and commissions in the federal government has been marked in general by restriction of judicial control; and this restriction has been justified, not only by the incapacity of the courts for economic regulatory work, but also by the judicial procedure and supposed independence of the administrative regulatory bodies. Though the Supreme Court may from time to time be politically reconstituted and politically influenced, responsibility of an administrative agency to the court is not primarily a political responsibility or a means of establishing democratic control over the bureaucracy. Judicial control over administration is democratizing, however, to the extent that it prevents arbitrary administration, keeps the bureaucracy within the limits of its assigned discretion, and protects the constitutional rights that are essential to democracy against both the legislature and the administration. The democratic aspect of judicial control is important but negative.

During the depression years, the movement against what was termed "administrative absolutism" gained strength. One of its phases was a demand for increased judicial control over regulatory agencies. Another was a proposal that administrative rule-making be subjected to certain general restrictive and unifying procedures.[23]

ADMINISTRATIVE ORGANIZATION

Various conditions were again focusing attention on the question of administrative organization. Among such conditions were the rapid piling-up of policies, with ends and means insufficiently coordinated; continual deficits and growing debt, creating demands for economy; expansion of the bureaucracy and multiplication of agencies, and increasing bureaucratic authority, pointing to the need of both efficiency and responsibility. The administrative situation, along with pre-depression trends and other depression developments, fixed attention on the position, possibilities, and power of the presidency.

Administrative economic controls showed
lack of integration.

In the administration of Theodore Roosevelt, the question of integration was becoming clear. Economic control was at that time either latent or active in taxation (including the tariff), spending, monetary control, supervision of banking, regulation of railroads, enforcement of the antitrust laws, conservation, promotion of agriculture, and protection of labor, as well as in governmental publicity and presidential pronouncements. Some of these controls were not organized separately as controls. As a whole, they were not integrated; but with the exception of the Interstate Commerce Commission, the administrative agencies concerned with control were directly responsible to the president. At that time, an opportunity may have existed and the possibility was perceived of integrating in the Department of Commerce and Labor the emerging functions of economic regulation. Subsequently, and especially during the depression period, new and old categories of governmental power over economic life underwent remarkable development.

---

[23] For a discussion of these proposals, see Frederick F. Blachly and Miriam E. Oatman, *Federal Regulatory Action and Control* (1940), pp. 4-5, 183-230; Doyle, *Independent Commissions in the Federal Government*, pp. 70-87; Robert R. R. Brooks, *Unions of Their Own Choosing* (1939), pp. 226-27.

It may be assumed that these governmental checks and stimulants are capable of affecting beneficially the productive and distributive processes. On this assumption, it is desirable that they should so operate as to bring about the maximum expected results. If private enterprise is to be controlled because it lacks the organization, capacity, and will to control itself in the public interest, it is essential that government should embody the type of organization, the statesmanship, and the decisiveness that private enterprise lacks. Government must produce desirable results, not merely go through motions.

It is not difficult, however, to find among federal governmental controls suggestions of confusion, misunderstanding, conflict, unanticipated results, and partial paralysis.

On June 30, 1939, at least 13 federal administrative agencies were functioning in the field of transportation with, presumably, some direct economic effect.[24] With three exceptions, all had substantial policy-determining powers.[25] In addition, the transportation system was affected by labor and agricultural policies, by the price of coal, and by military requirements, credit control, and taxation. Other fields of administration—for example, agriculture, labor, and foreign trade—when tested by the ultimate net effect of controls, could be shown to lack co-ordination. In many cases, moreover, the primary objective of control is not economic but social; and in some instances it is neither economic nor social but political. Social and political purposes not only set limits to economic policies but produce incidental economic repercussions.

It is true that many apparent administrative conflicts are traceable to statutory prescriptions rather than to administrative discretion; but even these conflicts are not irrelevent to the problem of administrative organization. Congress in recent years has shown itself less and less capable of initiating economic legislation. The

[24] Agriculture Department (Bureau of Public Roads), Civil Aeronautics Authority, Federal Emergency Administration of Public Works, Interstate Commerce Commission, Maritime Commission, Maritime Labor Board, National Advisory Committee for Aeronautics, National Labor Relations Board, National Mediation Board, Panama Canal, Railroad Retirement Board, Reconstruction Finance Corporation, and Works Progress Administration.

[25] The exceptions are the Panama Canal, the Railroad Retirement Board, and the National Advisory Committee for Aeronautics.

preliminary research, the recommendations, the supporting information and reasoning, and even the drafting have to come, at
least as government is now constituted, from the administration.
A favorable response of Congress depends upon a number of
factors, chief among which is the strength of the outside pressures
exerted on behalf of the proposed legislation. In this respect, a
small segmentary or specialized control agency is likely to be at a
disadvantage, particularly if its work is regulatory rather than
promotional, more particularly if it deals with antagonistic interest
groups that neutralize each other, and still more particularly if it
has no political head.[26]

*The depression gave impetus to the administrative
reorganization movement in the states.*

Additional comprehensive state and local surveys were made;
specific fields of administration were separately and intensively
studied; scattered agencies were consolidated; in general, progress
was made toward integration of activities; many states improved
their systems of financial control; and, generally speaking, governors obtained greater power to direct and control administration.
The council-manager plan made gains in the cities; and, though
it was adopted by few counties, a number of legislatures passed
laws permitting its adoption. The demand for reduction of governmental expenditure continued to be the main driving force behind
the reorganization movement. A secondary objective was efficiency,
which involved economy but not necessarily reduction of expenditure. The idea of a "planned" cut-and-dried reorganization and the
conception of a departmentalized, hierarchical administration, integrated under executive control, retained for many politicians and
students much of its former fascination.

The actual results of reorganizations were still difficult to evalu-
ate; but, with respect to the study of administrative organization,
a noteworthy feature of the depression years was a continued reaction against dogmatism, along with a partial rehabilitation of the

[26] Perhaps a lesson could be drawn from the failures of the Interstate Commerce
Commission to obtain congressional action on its recommendations. With the Commission's experience that of the Department of Agriculture might be contrasted.

inductive method and growing skepticism of reorganization as a panacea.[27]

At Washington, the chief issues involved integration and executive control of both process and result.

In his message to Congress of December 3, 1929, and December 8, 1931, Mr. Hoover mentioned the need of a general administrative reorganization. In the second message, he made, in addition, two specific recommendations: (1) that the Shipping Board "should be made a regulatory body acting also in advisory capacity on loans and policies, in keeping with its original conception" and that its executive functions should be transferred to the Department of Commerce; and (2) that all construction activities of the federal government should be consolidated into an independent establishment known as the "Public Works Administration."[28] In a special message of February 17, 1932, the President pointed out that the possibility of a comprehensive reorganization by congressional action was remote and proposed that authority be delegated to the executive to carry out a gradual and systematic reorganization "predicated on a sound and definite theory of government."[29]

[27] See A. E. Buck, *The Reorganization of State Governments in the United States* (1938); William Henry Edwards, *The Position of the Governor in Recent Administrative Reorganizations in the States* (1937), *A Factual Summary of State Administrative Reorganizations* (reprinted from *The Southwestern Social Science Quarterly*, Vol. 19 (1938)), and "Has State Reorganization Succeeded?" *State Government*, Vol. 11 (1938), pp. 183 ff.; Charles S. Hyneman, "Administrative Reorganization: An Adventure into Science and Theology," *The Journal of Politics*, Vol. 1 (1939), pp. 62-75; Kirk H. Porter, *State Administration* (1938); A. C. Millspaugh, *Public Welfare Organization* (1935), pp. 437-67, 519-23, and "Democracy and Administration," in J. M. Mathews and James Hart (eds.), *Essays in Political Science in Honor of Westel Woodbury Willoughby* (1937), pp. 64-74.

[28] William S. Myers (ed.), *The State Papers and Other Public Writings of Herbert Hoover* (1934), Vol. 2, p. 54.

[29] The same, pp. 114-15. By an act approved June 30, 1932, Congress gave the executive continuing authority to transfer executive activities and executive agencies by executive order, setting a 60-day time-limit for such orders to become effective and prohibiting the abolition of any statutory activities. The authority did not extend to the elimination of any executive department. The President submitted a number of reorganization orders on Dec. 9, 1932. In the meantime, a Democratic president and a Democratic Congress had been elected; and a resolution disapproving the Hoover proposals was adopted by Congress in January 1933. See Meriam and Schmeckebier, *Reorganization of the National Government*, pp. 187-96.

Authority to reorganize was granted to President Hoover in 1932. It was modified on March 3, 1933; but President Roosevelt, when he took office, possessed extensive powers to regroup, consolidate, transfer, or abolish executive agencies and functions. Congress did not retain a veto over the president's reorganization orders; but the authority granted to him was to expire in two years.[30] Under this authority a considerable amount of reorganization was effected by executive order.[31] Under the same or other authority, the President made changes in emergency agencies and created new agencies.[32]

With respect to integration in the field of transportation, the President, in his message to Congress on June 7, 1935, saw "no reason why the responsibility for the regulation of intercoastal, coastwise and inland waterways should not be vested in the Interstate Commerce Commission," which, he hoped, would "ultimately become a Federal Transportation Commission with comprehensive powers."[33] Nevertheless, the Merchant Marine Act of 1936 created a separate United States Maritime Commission; and this body was given expanded authority by the Merchant Marine Act of 1938.

Nevertheless, a growing feeling in Congress that expenditures could be reduced through reorganization led to the passage of a Senate resolution early in 1936 to create a special investigating committee. In April, a similar committee of the House was established. The Brookings Institution was employed, first by the Senate committee and later by both groups, to make detailed studies aimed primarily at reduction of expenditures. In the meantime, the President appointed his own Committee on Administrative Management.[34]

The President's program, which seems to have been identical with his committee's, aimed primarily at efficiency, not at reduction of expenditure. So far as concerned administrative structure, efficiency was to be obtained through the integration of all executive

[30] The same, pp. 198-200.
[31] For the details, see the same, pp. 200-12.
[32] The same, pp. 212-14.
[33] *Public Papers and Addresses*, Vol. 4, p. 240.
[34] The same, pp. 216-24. The Brookings Institution report was published as Senate Report 1275, 75 Cong. 1 sess. For the report of the President's Committee, see President's Committee on Administrative Management, *Report with Special Studies* (1937).

and policy-determining activities of the administration in twelve departments responsible to and under the control of the President. His power was also to embrace certain functions of financial control, exercised by the independent General Accounting Office, and of personnel administration, exercised by the Civil Service Commission. The regulatory boards and commissions were to be placed in appropriate executive departments, where, presumed to remain independent, they were to act only as administrative courts. The details of the reorganization were to be entrusted to executive discretion.[35]

With regard to the President's plan, the "one grand purpose," according to his committee, was "to make democracy work," "to make our Government an up-to-date, efficient, and effective instrument for carrying out the will of the Nation." Observing that the President is "the one and only national officer representative of the entire Nation," the Committee declared that "as an instrument for carrying out the judgment and will of the people of a nation the American Executive occupies an enviable position among the executives of the states of the world, combining as it does the elements of popular control and the means for vigorous action and leadership— uniting stability and flexibility." Hence the President, equipped with "modern types of management," would enable American democracy to face, without failing, "one of the most troubled periods in all the troubled history of mankind."[36]

The President's Committee recognized the three capacities of the chief executive: (1) as "political leader—leader of a party, leader of the Congress, leader of a people," (2) as ceremonial head and symbol, and (3) as executive and administrator. Purely executive work and administrative policy-determination were to be centered in him, assuming that, in this way, executive and routine administrative work would be made efficient, and policy-determination co-ordinated and responsible.

This means of obtaining efficiency and preserving democracy did

[35] *Public Papers and Addresses*, Vol. 5, pp. 668-81; President's Committee on Administrative Management, *Report with Special Studies*, pp. 36-38. For criticisms of the proposal, see S. Rept. 1275, 75 Cong. 1 sess., pp. 785-811, and Blachly and Oatman, *Federal Regulatory Action and Control*, pp. 143-68.

[36] President's Committee on Administrative Management, *Report with Special Studies*, pp. 1-3.

not, apparently, appeal strongly to Congress or to the country. On the contrary, organized propaganda, pointing at the proposed additions to presidential power, raised the cry of "dictatorship." No reorganization law was passed.

In April 1939, a less ambitious proposal for authority to reorganize was enacted into law.

Some progress was made toward integration, and presidential control of administration markedly increased.

Under the congressional authorization of April 1939, the President made numerous changes, including the creation of three new agencies: the Federal Loan Agency, the Federal Security Agency, and the Federal Works Agency. These ranked in size and importance with some of the executive departments. This latest reorganization was substantially integrative;[37] but it did not affect the General Accounting Office, the Civil Service Commission, or the regulatory boards and commissions.[38]

These latter were, as we have already pointed out, subject, partially or indirectly, to presidential control; and certain chief executives in the past are known to have influenced or attempted to influence the policies of these "independent" bodies. What happened during Franklin D. Roosevelt's first administration is well told in the following quotation:

When President Franklin D. Roosevelt embarked upon his plans for national recovery, he gathered into his hands every strand of authority that might lead toward his objectives. At the level of the presidential office, a greater degree of integration was introduced into the federal administrative organization than has ever been witnessed in peace-time experience. And the reach of the President did not falter before the independent commissions. . . . The tasks of the Federal Trade Commission, the Tariff Commission, or the Interstate Commerce Commission could not be separated from the rehabilitation of trade and industry. Yet how could these establishments participate in a national recovery program and still remain independent administrative agencies? . . . The judicial

---

[37] Integration was carried further when the head of the Federal Loan Agency was appointed Secretary of Commerce.

[38] For details, see Schmeckebier, "Organization of the Executive Branch of the National Government of the United States: Changes between July 16, 1938, and April 25, 1939," *American Political Science Review*, Vol. 33 (1939), pp. 450-55.

calm of the Interstate Commerce Commission was left undisturbed, but the most able and aggressive commissioner was created federal coordinator of transportation. The Tariff Commission was reduced to a harmless position through the passage of the reciprocal tariff act. The Radio Commission was abolished outright and a New Deal commission took its place. The President secured the resignation of Hoover's chairman of the Power Commission and added two appointees of his own. Only in the case of the Federal Trade Commission did he meet opposition; and when William E. Humphrey demurred, the President demanded his withdrawal in no uncertain terms. . . .[39]

At this time or later the National Recovery Administration was established with a single administrator;[40] the Board of Governors of the Federal Reserve System was reorganized in the direction of political control;[41] administration of the Fair Labor Standards Act was assigned to a single-headed division in the Department of Labor; price-fixing in the bituminous coal industry, first entrusted to a board, was later delegated to a single-headed division in the Department of the Interior; a new United States Maritime Commission was established with the terms of its members limited to six years; the Social Security Board was made a subordinate unit in the single-headed Federal Security Agency; the President refrained from appointing a board for the Federal Alcohol Administration, though one was provided by statute; and he summarily removed the chairman of the Tennessee Valley Authority.[42]

By January 1939, President Roosevelt had appointed all the

[39] Herring, *American Political Science Review*, Vol. 29 (1935), pp. 32-33. See also George H. Haynes, *The Senate of the United States; Its History and Practice*, Vol. 2 (1938), p. 831.

[40] Replaced by a board in September 1934.

[41] "While still nominally independent, it is safe to say that at no period since the Reserve System was established, except during and immediately after the war, has it had so little real independence as it has had since 1935. Some of its most important monetary powers have been vested in the Secretary of the Treasury. Moreover, the summary way in which terms of existing members were cut off by law in 1935 serves as a warning that the Board in fact, though not in form, holds office at the pleasure of the party in power." Leverett S. Lyon, Myron W. Watkins, and Victor Abramson, *Government and Economic Life*, Vol. 1 (1939), p. 189.

[42] The intention of Congress seems to have been to make the Authority an independent agency. The law creating it provided that any member might be removed from office at any time by a concurrent resolution by the Senate and House of Representatives. The President was also authorized to remove for a violation of section 6 relating to the merit system; and the Acting Attorney General held that he had general power of removal. 48 Stat. L. 58, 60, 63.

members of the Board of Governors of the Federal Reserve System, the Federal Deposit Insurance Corporation, the Securities and Exchange Commission, the National Labor Relations Board, the Federal Communications Commission, the United States Maritime Commission, Civil Aeronautics Authority, and the Maritime Labor Board; and a majority of the members of the Interstate Commerce Commission, the Federal Trade Commission, the United States Tariff Commission, and the Federal Power Commission.

The traditional form of independent-board setup had been modified in the Civil Aeronautics Authority, which was originally composed of two boards and an administrator, each with substantially no power over or responsibility to the other. The intention was to separate promotional from regulatory activities and administrative from quasi-legislative and quasi-judicial. In 1940, however, the President, acting under discretionary authority to reorganize granted by Congress, abolished the Air Safety Board, and transferred the other board and the administrator to the Department of Commerce. The Board, according to the President's assurances, was to remain independent in the performance of its quasi-judicial duties.[43]

President Roosevelt was under no illusions that political power could or should be neutral in the presence of politico-economic conflict. He declared in January 1936 that his party in the preceding months had "built up new instruments of public power. In the hands of a people's government this power is wholesome and proper. But in the hands of political puppets of an economic autocracy such power would provide shackles for the liberties of the people."[44]

Whatever may be the correct or final plan of solution, the problem of administrative organization appears to be organic rather than structural, involving questions not so much of size and assigned activities as of power, responsibility, and effect. Apparently, the fundamental need is to infuse into this living body of administration principles of balanced growth and of self-control, reconciling stability with flexibility. It seems quite possible that the federal

[43] The House of Representatives voted to reject this reorganization but the Senate upheld it by a vote of 46 to 34. *New York Times*, May 15, 1940.

[44] *Public Papers and Addresses*, Vol. 5, p. 16.

bureaucracy has already grown to such size and possesses such large and variegated power that the need cannot be met solely by internal changes.[45] Evidently, the functioning of public administration in the economic sphere should have been made complementary and supplementary to the functioning of the economic system itself. It appears, therefore, that in order to organize and conduct effective administration in this sphere, political science, as well as political leadership and public pressures, need in some way to be co-ordinated with and perhaps directed by economic research and industrial experience.

More or less by a process of elimination the President became the hope or the fear of those who were concerned with the problems of democracy or of effectiveness in administration. It becomes necessary, then, to examine the appropriateness of the presidency as an instrumentality for attaining these fundamental objectives. The critical problem in administration is the problem of discretionary authority, subordinate policy-determination, or sublegislation. The question of the role of the presidency in this sphere involves considerations closely related to or identical with those that are involved in his role as leader of Congress. The two roles will therefore be discussed together in a later chapter.

[45] "Participants in every large undertaking carried on by a hierarchy of power tend, if left to the natural course, to routineering, to absorption in the immediate task, and to indifference in respect of larger objectives." Charles A. Beard, in Preface to M. L. Wilson, *Democracy Has Roots* (1939), p. 11.

CHAPTER VIII

CENTRALIZATION

By 1900 it was fairly clear that, if the larger economic and social problems required governmental solutions, those solutions were beyond the effective reach of the states. In the meantime, new perceptions of conditions and tendencies and new conceptions of the public interest and of social justice increased the number, range, and complexity of the problems that were conceived to be governmental responsibilities. The depression of the thirties emphasized the national spread of economic problems. At the same time, as an emergency, it shifted the burden of action to the level of government that had superior financial resources and could act quickly.

Centralization has three aspects, the political, the legislative, and the administrative. The Constitution had established both legislative and administrative federalism. In both, as well as in the broader political sphere, profound changes have been taking place and these changes are for the most part in the direction of centralization.

POLITICAL AND LEGISLATIVE CENTRALIZATION

For a time the depression brought to the national government that unity of support which comes in crises. The sweeping victory of the Democratic Party in 1932 and 1936 produced an approach to political unanimity in all governments, and this situation was favorable to national subordination of the states, to uniformity of policy among the states, and to the co-ordination of federal and state legislation. Historically, the Democratic Party was the party of individualism, localism, and states' rights, while the Republican Party traditionally stood for nationalism and central authority; but depression problems during Mr. Roosevelt's first term were pressing with tremendous urgency; national action, when not the only way of meeting them, appeared to be the quickest and easiest; and ideas of economic interest, accentuated by the depression, were stronger than traditions or constitutional and political theories.

At first, judicial decisions partially blocked federal expansion in the economic sphere, notably in the case of the National Industrial Recovery and Agricultural Adjustment Acts; but later the attitude of the Supreme Court became highly favorable to broad applications of the commerce clause and less disposed to interpose the restrictions on social and economic legislation that had formerly been read into the due process clause and other provisions of the Constitution.

President Roosevelt, more perhaps than any preceding chief executive, cultivated close relations with the governors of the states and at times seemed to view himself as properly their leader. This association and leadership were almost exclusively concerned with matters of policy.[1]

Probably more effective as national determinants of state legislation were the federal aid laws. These have been rightly represented as a middle course between the traditional federalism based on a division of functions, powers, financing, and administration at one extreme and absolute centralization at the other.[2] But the apparent effect, nevertheless, was to shift the determination of policies to the federal government and to lessen initiative, responsibility, diversity, and experimentation among the states. The constitutional status of the spending power subjected this development to almost no judicial review; and, outside the courts, the intrusion of this legislative and administrative transformation into the federal system had at no time been referred to tested principles.

In some fields, legislative federalism reasserted itself. The repeal of the eighteenth amendment returned liquor control in large part to the states.[3] National legislation and national administrative

---

[1] "It is a major purpose of my Administration to strengthen the bonds between State and Federal executive authorities, to the great common ends to which we are all devoted." *Public Papers and Addresses of Franklin D. Roosevelt*, Vol. 2, pp. 103-04, 133, 304; Vol. 3, p. 499; Vol. 4, pp. 25-26.

[2] Jane Perry Clark, *The Rise of a New Federalism* (1938), pp. 295-96.

[3] "It is one of the paradoxes of American politics that we have destroyed the possibility of centralization in the field of liquor control at the same time that we have been attempting to achieve greater centralization in a number of activities hitherto believed to be completely in the field of state authority." Dayton E. Heckman, "Contemporary State Statute for Liquor Control," *American Political Science Review*, Vol. 28 (1934), p. 628.

activities in a number of instances, as in crime control, promoted, supported, or implemented the exercise of state powers.

Independently of federal leadership or control, the movement for uniform state laws made progress.[4] Uniformity, brought about by co-operation among state authorities, was to an extent a substitute for and preventative of centralization. State co-operation was also applied to certain regional situations, and to certain interstate problems calling for reciprocal aid.[5]

INTERSTATE CONFLICTS

Although any solution of the larger economic problems was beyond the reach of the states, state and local economic policies retained great significance. State economic policies fell into two classes: (1) regulation, analogous to, and in part correlated with, that undertaken by the federal government; and (2) regulative, protective, and promotive measures which placed burdens on interstate commerce and were largely and obviously inconsistent with the economic good of the nation.[6]

When it is recalled that one of the primary purposes of the Con-

[4] See W. Brooke Graves, *Uniform State Action* (1934) and files of *State Government*; Rodney L. Mott, "Uniform Legislation in the United States," *Annals*, Vol. 207 (1940), pp. 79-92.

[5] For example, apprehension of fugitives from justice, parole supervision, relief of persons moving from one state to another. See Garland C. Routt, "Interstate Compacts and Administrative Cooperation," in *Annals*, Vol. 207 (1940), pp. 93-102; Hubert R. Gallagher, "Work of the Commissions on Interstate Cooperation," the same, pp. 103-10; National Resources Committee, *Regional Factors in National Planning and Development* (1935), pp. 34-70.

[6] F. Eugene Melder, "Trade Barriers between States," *Annals*, Vol. 207 (1940), pp. 54-61. "It may be news to many lovers of the breakfast egg that in some states the definition of a fresh egg is one that is laid within the confines of the State." (Luther A. Houston, "Tariff War among States," *New York Times*, Dec. 3, 1939.) On the general subject, see testimony of Frank Bane, *Investigation of Concentration of Economic Power*, Hearings before the Temporary National Economic Committee, 75 Cong., Pt. 29, pp. 15738-56; J. H. Rogers, *Capitalism in Crisis* (1938), pp. 135-53. For specific references to statutes, see Works Progress Administration, *A Digest of State Laws Relating to the Problem of Interstate Trade Barriers for States Whose Legislatures Convene in 1940* (1940).

State and local promotional schemes included the following: (1) preferences to state residents in the granting of public contracts; (2) granting of encouragement to new industries, through tax exemptions, gifts of land, labor-relations policies, etc.; (3) state and municipal advertising of local products, attractions, and commercial, industrial, or residential advantages. Bureau of Agricultural Economics, *Barriers to Internal Trade in Farm Products* (1939).

stitution was to eliminate commercial restrictions and conflicts among the states and that American history had been marked by convincing evidences of growing national unity, the reappearance of interstate jealousies, competition, and conflicts was a matter that could not be easily explained. General underlying causes might be the following: (1) increasing need for legitimate exercise of the states' police power to protect property, health, morals, and safety; (2) increasing need for the application of the police power to interstate commerce; (3) pressing need of revenue; (4) political and psychological sensitiveness and tension; (5) the depression, contributing to tension and inducing state governments to undertake the promotion of the economic interests of their people within the areas left to them by federal policies; (6) the example and effect of autarchy in world affairs;[7] (7) the example set by federal policies, departing from orthodox economics and imposing regulations and restrictions in the interest of groups and sections; (8) the power of interest groups within the state to obtain from the legislature piecemeal forms of protection and promotion; and (9) lack of broad economic knowledge and of concern with the general welfare on the part of both state legislatures and state electorates.

A reaction against interstate trade restrictions made its appearance in 1938. The counter-movement, however, did not hold out much promise that interstate trade barriers could be eliminated or permanently prevented without federal legislation, much less that other forms of interstate conflict and competition would disappear; nor did it appear to be going to the roots of the situation.[8]

[7] Melder, "The World Situation and State Trade Barriers," *State Government*, Vol. 12 (1939), pp. 68 ff.

[8] States and sections continued to appropriate money for publicity; cities and even counties set up "booster bureaus," supplementing chamber-of-commerce and other private propaganda. The Granite State had a "Commission for the Promotion of the Wealth and Income of the People of New Hampshire." (*New York Times*, Dec. 4, 1939.) The governor of Connecticut declared: "We set about deliberately to create those conditions that we thought and hoped would encourage business and private industry to create more jobs." (*New York Times*, Nov. 17, 1939.) It was reported in the press that New Jersey, like Connecticut, was winning industries from New York and other states by a "carefully planned promotion and advertising campaign based on the absence of any state income tax, corporate or personal; on friendly relations between capital and labor, and other appeals to companies dissatisfied with their present location or seeking expansion and decentralization of production." (*New York Times*, Feb. 18, 1940.) Pennsylvania like-

Interstate economic competition made its appearance in the national legislative and administrative processes with reference, for example, to labor standards and freight rates. Some of the most serious conflicts appeared in the field of taxation. Not only were taxes used specifically and deliberately as economic weapons by both the nation and the states, but duplication of taxes, inequality of taxable resources, differences in the aggregate burden, and the general complexity of the tax system were in effect discriminating, harmful both to federal-state and interstate relations, and detrimental both to legislation and administration.[9]

ADMINISTRATIVE CENTRALIZATION

In recent years discretionary authority has grown more rapidly in federal than in state administration; and, as we have just noted, a significant phase of federal administrative authority is its increasing operation on state legislation and administration. In other words, the power referred to in the preceding chapter was tending to become a nationally centralized bureaucratic power. Federalism at least in theory brought the exercise of public authority closer to popular supervision and adapted governmental policy to diverse feelings and interests. One of the merits of federalism was that it scattered both the perversions and the errors of government. "It limits the scope of the damage which can result from mistaken action by those high in office."[10] Nevertheless, the problems that arose from administrative power were coming to be identified more and more with the national bureaucracy.

An altered fiscal situation of the federal government and the states suggested at least a relative change of activity. Federal expenditures in 1929 amounted to little more than one-fourth of total governmental expenditures; but in 1936 they were one-half.[11]

wise advertised its "friendliness" to business. In the meantime, alarm spread in New York State over the reported exodus of its industries (*New York Times*, Feb. 6, 14, 20, 1940), while southern governors conferred on a program "to assure this section of its rightful place in the economic and cultural advancement of the United States" (*New York Times*, Jan. 21, 1940).

[9] James W. Martin, "Tax Competition between States," *Annals*, Vol. 207 (1940), pp. 62-69.

[10] Nicholas Roosevelt, *A New Birth of Freedom* (1938), pp. 110-11.

[11] National Industrial Conference Board, *Cost of Government in the United States* (1938), p. 8.

A similar shift occurred in the public debt; the federal government accounted in 1929 for about one-half of the total and in 1938 for almost two-thirds.[12]

The chief factor in national administrative centralization was federal financial aid to the states. Prior to the depression, federal grants-in-aid were used primarily to stimulate the states to undertake or expand some activity. During the depression, emphasis shifted from stimulation to support. Increasing employment of this device was justified by the alleged inadequacy of state tax resources and credit, by inequalities among the states with respect to wealth and income, and by the need of uniformity in legislation and administration.

Expansion of federal aid was accompanied by an extension of the scope of federal supervision and control over state administration. It may be true that the power to withhold or suspend federal grants was rarely used to force compliance from a state agency;[13] but little doubt can be entertained that, through the instrumentality of federal aid, national officials by various means imposed their plans and methods on state administration.

In this process, the states were not necessarily losing activities. On the contrary, the result may well have been an increase of state activities. If state personnel was increasing up to 1938 at about the same rate as federal personnel, it would seem to indicate that state personnel was becoming weighted on the operational side while federal power was represented more largely by policy-determination and direction and by money to spend on operations. In short, the states seemed to be gradually becoming operating units under national control.

Many types of federal-state co-operation and of federal leadership or control in state administration, not always or necessarily connected with federal aid, had long been in operation, arising from the overlapping of federal and state activities. In connection with such arrangements and in other aspects of administration, a comprehensive interweaving and intricate interplay of state and

[12] National Industrial Conference Board, *Economic Record*, Vol. 1 (1939), p. 184.
[13] V. O. Key, Jr., *The Administration of Federal Grants to States* (1937), p. 156.

federal activities developed, characterized partly by co-operation and partly by conflict.

Taxation contributed to the centralizing trend. Students of the subject had long been considering and some had suggested a substantial centralization of tax administration in the federal government, its revenue collections to be shared with the states.[14]

The relationship of the federal government with municipalities is an interesting phase of national centralization, as well as of separatism or disintegration within the highly urbanized states.

Equally significant were the extending and vitalizing of federal contacts with individual citizens. Previously these contacts had been increasing and had been drawing closer to the mainsprings of individual interest and welfare. But now millions of individuals, through relief, public works, social security, and agricultural adjustment, became partially or wholly dependent on the federal government for their support. In some states, the bulk of the population had more to do with the nation than with their states. The psychological effects cannot be calculated; but among them must have been a considerable and probably permanent enhancement of the prestige of the nation, a relatively sharp focusing of popular interest and expectation on the government at Washington, and a relative, if not an absolute, decline of popular confidence in the states.

Centralizing trends could, of course, be weighed against their off-sets and against certain countertendencies. Those who were fearful might draw some comfort from the thought that in this country an emergency has usually been featured by centralization. Some might take encouragement from the decentralization of federal administration itself. Yet the percentage of federal civil employees located at the capital was rising. It was 9.0 per cent in 1916, 11.6 per cent in 1933, and 13.4 per cent in 1939.[15]

It was possible to see in the Tennessee Valley Authority a device that, while perhaps "encroaching" on the states, would avoid the

[14] Clarence Heer, "Relations between Federal, State, and Local Finances," in *American Economic Review* (Suppl.), Vol. 26 (1936), p. 178.
[15] Computed from figures in *Annual Report of the United States Civil Service Commission*, 1933, p. 8; 1939, p. 157.

worse evils of centralized bureaucracy. A similar conclusion might be reached with regard to federal governmental corporations in general; but it should be pointed out that adoption of the corporate form by a national governmental agency, even if it be chartered by a state, did not divest the agency of its essential national and governmental character.[16]

On the whole, it appeared in 1940 that the traditional concept of federalism as a constitutionally established and judicially enforced balance or division of powers no longer corresponded to the reality; and no longer did the doctrine of states' rights figure appreciably in the philosophy of public men.

Within the states generally, except for state-municipal relations, it appeared that the centralizing tendency continued. The general movement was indicated by increased state grants-in-aid and shared taxes; expansion of state supervision and control over locally administered services, as well as over local appropriations, debts, and taxation; further decadence of the township; school consolidation; establishment of additional state police systems; entrance of state governments into the field of relief; integration of public welfare work; extension of state control over highway administration; and an apparently more rapid increase of state than of local public personnel.

The rural counties continued to discharge a variety of duties; but their work tended more and more to be merely operational. The forms of local government were being preserved by means of complex fiscal and administrative arrangements; but the spirit of local self-government appeared to be no longer compatible with the conditions of the age. The rural county was becoming, not only in legal theory, but also actually, a district, in many cases an unsuitable one, for the operations of state administrative agencies. Organizations and individuals viewed with apprehension the passing of local self-government, still thought to be the "bulwark" or "nursery" of democracy; and they proposed methods of preserving the county by making it a more efficient and economical unit. Chief

[16] Ruth G. Weintraub, *Government Corporations and State Law* (1939), p. 166. See also John Thurston, *Government Proprietary Corporations in the English-Speaking Countries* (1937), p. 10.

among these methods were consolidation of counties and the integration and departmentalization of county administration in accordance with the council-manager plan that was being widely adopted in the cities.

A universal application of either method to the counties met with both practical and theoretical difficulties. In general, further state centralization, so far as rural areas were concerned, appeared both inevitable and desirable.[17]

With respect to the municipalities, however, the movement seems to have been, on the whole, toward decentralization.

[17] As the author has said in another place, centralizing movements and motives were generally traceable "to concrete facts—financial and human inadequacies in the face of social needs and popular demands. . . . 'Centralization' has a sinister sound; but the centralizing movement, if such it should be called, actually originated below though it may have been promoted above. It represents an unavoidable and reluctant effort to deal with conditions rather than theories. On its upper and broader levels, popular government has been working crudely— groping half blindly—toward the twin goals of equalized service and equitable taxation." *Local Democracy and Crime Control* (1936), p. 47.

CHAPTER IX

CONGRESSIONAL WEAKNESS AND PRESIDENTIAL DOMINATION

The discussion of bureaucracy in Chapter VII revealed that the growth and apparent disorganization of administration emphasized the question of executive power. In fact, this question had been central during the entire course of the reorganization movement. In the federal administration, the movement has brought a measure of integration and a larger measure of presidential control. In view of the exercise by the bureaucracy of policy-determining authority, presidential control raises the question of the appropriateness of the presidency for the exercise of legislative power. The same question is raised by the relationship of the executive to Congress. We shall examine in this chapter the situation of Congress and it will be seen how that situation, along with other factors, produced presidential domination of the law-making branch.

Though separation of powers and checks and balances had been generally held to be the central characteristics of the American governmental mechanism, essential to stability and liberty, the practice in war emergencies and the pre-depression trend in times of peace were to shift legislative power to the chief executive. The explanation of the wartime practice was simple: speed and coordination of policy and action were imperative; national danger and a pre-eminent national purpose inhibited public controversy and public criticism of the government; concentration of leadership and direction was vital; and temporary dictatorship appeared inescapable.

To the peacetime trend, the contributing factors had already become fairly clear. Foremost among them were the size, duality, general inefficiency, and unrepresentative features of legislative bodies, their lack of internal cohesion, and their incapacity for external leadership. Then, the "battle" against political corruption, economic power, and "entrenched privilege" dramatized personal leadership and carried over to peacetime politics the symbolism of war emergencies. In the meantime, rapidity of social change, greater complexity and urgency of public problems, and absence of co-ordination or integration of pressures had the effect of strengthening leadership where leadership was visible, single-minded, and purposive. The growth of administration and increasing delegation of legislative power to it somewhat relieved the legislature but transferred a larger measure of legislative initiative and responsibility to administrative agencies and to the executive himself. Possibilities of control were inherent in patronage.

The executive was aided by his position as representative of the whole state or the whole nation and as head of the party, a position that was particularly strong in a presidential or gubernatorial election year when the strength of the party lay in its solidarity and when the success of a legislative or congressional candidate might depend on the consistency of his support of the executive. Another contribution came from the superior personal capacities of executives compared with legislators, or, at least, the illusion of superiority. Finally, in all peoples, Americans not excepted, the desire for personal leadership and the need of it was contributing a fundamental, strong, and constant influence toward concentration of power.

In the case of the president, the factors favorable to executive power in general were multiplied tenfold by special circumstances: centralization of activities, of power, and of public interest in the national government; the president's control of foreign relations; his command of the army and navy; and the unique advantages of his office for propaganda purposes. Woodrow Wilson as scholar had written, and as president had demonstrated, that the office possessed an immeasurable potential influence. The expansion of government and the increase of its power, together with the perfection of communication facilities, especially the radio, not only widened the president's opportunity but enabled him at any time of his own choosing to speak directly and intimately with the people. Conditions and trends had been at work for many years making it possible for an active and shrewd president to manipulate problems and policies in such a way as to develop and retain leadership; for, next to the economic state of the nation, the policies advocated by the president were most important in making or breaking his influence.

During his first two administrations, President Franklin D. Roosevelt had at all times a Democratic majority in both houses of Congress and until 1939 the majority was overwhelming. His third term began with a substantial Democratic majority in each house. His position as national party leader was never seriously disputed; but, from his standpoint, the success of the party depended on his domination of the Democratic majority in Congress. A congressional revolt against his legislative leadership would have meant personal and party failure. No general revolt occurred.

CONGRESSIONAL REPRESENTATION

Representation in state legislatures and in Congress has shown defects from two points of view—from that of public and group opinions, the public interest, or the general welfare, and from that of population. Representatives are apportioned among relatively small territorial units, generally one to each unit. Elections occur at regular periods and issues accumulate. Because of the multiplicity of issues and their complexity and because of the overlapping of opinions regarding them, the elected legislator represents no clear body of opinion. On some questions he represents a majority; on others, a minority. Too often, his primary responsiveness is to the local bosses and other persons of influence who nominate him, not to those who elect him. In addition, the legislative districts are not equal in population. Because of constitutional provisions, failure to reapportion, and rural-urban jealousies, rural districts are generally overrepresented in state legislatures.[1]

[1] "Although in twenty-one states the urban population is now in a majority, in only eleven of them can that majority control the legislature." David O. Walter, "Reapportionment and Urban Representation," *Annals*, Vol. 195 (1938), pp. 13-14.

The Senate is particularly unrepresentative,
on the basis of population.

A majority of the population in 1930 was in the 16 states of the industrial Northeast—the region north of the Potomac and Ohio Rivers and east of the Mississippi—but these states were represented by only one-third of the members of the Senate. In contrast, an area consisting of 26 states—the states of the South and of the prairie and Rocky Mountain regions—had 52 of the 96 senators, though it contained only 35.7 per cent of the population. New York State had 12,588,066 inhabitants. Twelve states[2] in the prairie and mountain regions had 8,334,445, about three-fourths as many. The population of 12½ millions had two votes in the Senate; the population of 8⅓ millions had 24 votes. The rural and farming areas of the country were grossly over-represented; and this over-representation gave them control of the upper chamber.

The House of Representatives also is inaccurately
representative of population.

Apportionments within the states are faulty.[3] Between apportionments, population increases or decreases in the congressional districts; and the districts in the aggregate are so arranged as to weight the influence of the ruralites.[4] Malrepresentation in legislative bodies has resulted in a corresponding malrepresentation in the party organizations and conventions;[5] and the Electoral System, through which the president is chosen, is also weighted in favor of the rural states.[6]

[2] N.Dak., S.Dak., Nebr., Kans., Mont., Idaho, Wyo., Colo., N.Mex., Ariz., Utah, and Nev.

[3] See Laurence F. Schmeckebier, *Congressional Apportionment* (1941), pp. 127-92.

[4] According to one estimate, 51.8 per cent of the representatives were from districts predominantly rural; according to another, 61.6 per cent. Arthur N. Holcombe, "Present-Day Characteristics of American Political Parties," in Edward B. Logan (ed.), *The American Political Scene* (1936), pp. 34-35.

[5] Walter, "Reapportionment and Urban Representation," *Annals,* Vol. 195 (1938), p. 15.

[6] Because of the constitutional provision that the number of electors in each state shall be equal to the number of representatives apportioned to the state plus the two senators. Naturally, figures indicating representation of population do not tell the whole story. Within an electoral unit predominantly rural, the party

*Neither House nor Senate has appeared responsive
to conditions and trends.*

Public problems in the technological era are dynamic. Problems
and opinion are both changing—problems more rapidly than opinion. When public opinion changes, a change of opinion in the
legislative body is obviously requisite to representation. A change
of legislative opinion, however, is not enough. The legislature
must also adapt itself to changes in problems; for opinion must
be translated into effective policy.

The long-run change in American life has been from a rural
agricultural régime to a régime of technological industry and
urbanism. What is assumed to be a short-run change—that which
confronted the congresses elected in 1930 and afterwards until
1940—was signalized by the depression. The basic problems posed
by this change were economic, having their roots in technological
industry and branching out into all the complexities of a great,
interdependent, urban society. In the presence of these changes, was
Congress changing or capable of change? Was Congress dynamic?

So far as party membership is concerned, the election of 1930
transferred control of the House to the Democrats by a slight
margin. The Senate was about evenly divided. In the next three
elections, those of 1932, 1934, and 1936, both House and Senate
become more lopsidedly Democratic.[7]

The change in the party complexion of Congress was a decided
one; but party votes were rare on early New Deal legislation. The
change in party membership evidently did not reflect accurately
the change, if there was one, with respect to representation. Both
parties continued, as in preceding years, to have their right and

---

situation may be such as to cause the elected legislator to lean toward interests
other than agricultural. On the other hand, in a predominantly urban district, the
farm vote may be decisive.
   [7] The Democratic membership is shown below:

	House	Senate
73 Cong., 1933-34 (as of Dec. 21, 1933)	313	60
74 Cong., 1935-36 (as of Mar. 21, 1935)	319	69
75 Cong., 1937-38 (as of Dec. 20, 1936)	333	75

The figures are from the Congressional Directories corrected to the dates shown
above.

left wings, their conservatives, and their progressives. A substantial part of the Democratic majority did not reflect a radical trend of opinion. Nor did it represent any desire to make drastic adaptations of policy to new conditions.

Another method of inquiring how much adaptation really occurred is to examine changes in the personal composition of the two houses. The percentage of members with no previous consecutive service in the houses to which they were respectively elected is shown below:

	Senate[8]	House[9]
71 Cong., 1929-30 (as of May 1, 1929) 10.4		14.5
72 Cong., 1931-32 (as of Nov. 27, 1931)......16.7		18.2
73 Cong., 1933-34 (as of Dec. 21, 1933)......20.8		37.3
74 Cong., 1935-36 (as of Mar. 21, 1935)......13.6		23.2
75 Cong., 1937-38 (as of Dec. 20, 1936)......14.6		20.7
76 Cong., 1939-40 (as of Dec. 20, 1938)......13.6		24.6

It will be noted that when control of Congress passed to the Democrats in 1931, the actual change in membership was not substantially greater than it had been in 1929 when Hoover became president. The substantial change occurred in the election of 1932. In the Seventy-third Congress (1933-34), more than one-fifth of the senators and almost three-eighths of the representatives were "new."

So far as personalities are concerned, these percentages suggest the degree of adaptability possessed by the two houses. They only suggest; for the new members included both Democrats and Republicans and some of the changes were brought about by political or personal occurrences of no significance.[10] Moreover, the re-election of an "old" member might indicate change, to the extent

[8] For the Senate, in considering those with no previous consecutive service, only those are counted who were elected at the last preceding election or subsequently appointed.

[9] Included in the figures for the House are those who had no previous experience there and those who had served one previous nonconsecutive term. A few members had had previous nonconsecutive service of more than one term. If these were included, the percentages would be slightly higher, but not sufficiently so to affect the conclusions.

[10] No significance, for example, would attach to a new member when he succeeded an incumbent who was not a candidate for renomination and re-election. See Paul DeWitt Hasbrouck, *Party Government in the House of Representatives* (1927), p. 181.

that he changed his opinions in order to win re-election. No doubt this was the situation in many cases in 1932 and afterward. Nevertheless, the percentages indicate in some measure the readiness of the electorate to change and the capacity of the party and legislative systems to register the electoral disposition.

The accompanying table shows for each of five great regions and for the Seventy-second and Seventy-third Congresses (1931-32 and 1933-34) the total number of apportioned representatives, the number of "new" members, and the ratio of "new" members to the total apportionment.

COMPOSITION OF SEVENTY-SECOND AND SEVENTY-THIRD CONGRESSES

Region	Total Represen- tatives	New Members in Seventy-Second Congress		New Members in Seventy-Third Congress	
		Number	*Per Cent*	Number	*Per Cent*
Industrial Northeast[a]..	225	44	*19.5*	81	*36.0*
South[b]...............	133	26	*19.6*	32	*24.0*
Prairie states[c].........	34	5	*14.8*	14	*41.2*
Mountain states[d]......	14	1	*7.1*	10	*71.4*
Pacific Coast[e].........	29	3	*10.3*	16	*55.6*

[a] All states north of the Potomac and Ohio Rivers and east of the Mississippi, including W. Va.

[b] All states south of the Potomac and Ohio Rivers, except W. Va., and east of the Mississippi, including Ark., Tex., Mo., and Okla.

[c] Minn., Iowa, N. Dak., S. Dak., Nebr., and Kans.

[d] Mont., Wyo., Colo., Utah, Nev., N. Mex., Ariz., and Idaho.

[e] Wash., Oreg., Calif.

It appears from this table that the percentage of "new" members elected in 1930 was greatest in the industrial Northeast and in the South; and the percentages for the two regions were almost exactly the same. The full reaction of the voters was registered in the election of 1932; and the percentages show striking changes. The South shifted less than one-fourth of its members; but the representatives elected in the mountain states were more than two-thirds "new" and those from the Pacific Coast more than half, while more than 40 per cent of the prairie representatives were "new" and 36 per cent of those from the industrial Northeast.

The South has been practically unchangeable with respect to party allegiance. Except for occasional Republican victories along its borders and its more general rejection of the Democratic presidential candidate in 1928, the South has remained Democratic. Its political contests are fought in the primaries; its vote is inhibited by the Negro question; it is rural in outlook as well as in fact; and its attitude is conservative. Operating within this ideological straitjacket, a large number of its voters have a relatively poor opportunity to express intelligent or independent choices in elections.

Studies of Congress prior to the depression, as well as studies of state legislatures, indicated that rural constituencies are more stable, less changeable, and, apparently, less adaptable to changing national conditions than urban constituencies.[11] It seems reasonable to infer that in the process of democratically adapting public policy to shifting economic conditions, the weighting of representation in favor of the rural population has made for lag and distortion of policy.

It would seem that possibly half of the congressional districts in the United States are what may be called "stand-pat" districts. In these districts a majority of the voters are pretty thoroughly committed to the incumbent representative, if he chooses to run for re-election, and are almost absolutely committed to one or the other party. Generally speaking, the Democratic stand-pat districts are in the South; the Republican in the Northeast and the West, most frequently in the rural areas. In such districts, political discussion tends to be stagnant and political issues localized. The representatives from such districts may accurately represent the decisive opinions and attitudes of their constituents; but these opinions and attitudes are quite different from those of the districts where election results are determined by an alert independent vote. In other words, stand-pat constituencies do not themselves represent the nation. To be sure, something can be said for these districts. They

[11] Hasbrouck, *Party Government in the House of Representatives;* Stuart A. Rice, *Farmers and Workers in American Politics* (1924); Walter, *Annals,* Vol. 195 (1938), pp. 11-20.

The sweeping turnover in the West in 1932 suggests merely that if farmers suffer long enough and become sufficiently conscious of their particular interests they are likely to revolt. The agricultural depression, however, had begun more than ten years before, and as late as 1930 the political turnover in the prairie states was less than in the industrial Northeast.

insure that no national landslide will quite wipe out minority representation; and they make it likely that the majority representation will include men who can on occasion be more or less independent of party discipline and executive domination.

The figures just presented take on added meaning when compared with the following, which show for each region the number and percentage of representatives in the Seventy-third Congress who had served from six to seventeen consecutive terms.

	Total Representatives	Members of Long Service	
		Number	Percentage of Total
Industrial Northeast	225	51	22.7
South	133	43	32.3
Prairie states	34	5	14.7
Mountain states	14	1	7.1
Pacific Coast	29	2	6.9

The South, as would be expected, had a larger percentage of "old" members than any other region. The industrial Northeast was next; while the West, in its sweeping revolt against the Republican Party, replaced with "new" members a number of Republican representatives who had seen long service.

Congressional leadership was not well adapted to the requirements of a changed situation.

With the figures above in mind we can now turn to the question of leadership. Owing to the size of the House and its generally lower caliber, the individual member counts for less, control through organization and leadership counts for more, and the actual process of law-making takes place largely in the committees, where the committee chairmen usually exercise great influence.[12] The chairmen are appointed from the members of the majority party on the basis of seniority. Thus, they are in most cases men who have had previous and often long experience in the House. The nominal, and for most practical purposes, the real leadership consists of the Speaker, the majority members of the Rules Com-

[12] "Rarely does a measure become law against the advice of a committee, and rarely does the majority of a committee report against the advice of its chairman." Robert Luce, *Legislative Procedure* (1935), pp. 122, 653.

mittee, and the chairmen of the more important standing committees.[13] To show the distribution of these leaders by states we shall
compare the Seventy-first Congress (1929-30), Republican-controlled, with the Seventy-third Congress (1933-34), Democratic-
controlled. The distribution appears below:

	House Leaders in Seventy-First Congress[14]	House Leaders in Seventy-Third Congress[15]
Industrial Northeast	21	9
South	0	22
Prairie states	7	0
Mountain states	2	1
Pacific Coast	2	0

The leadership of the House in the Republican-controlled
Seventy-first Congress was predominantly from the industrial
Northeast. Leadership in the Democratic-controlled Seventy-third
Congress was predominantly from the South. These leaders came
in general from the "safe," "stand-pat," or "rock-ribbed" districts.
With respect to residence, both groups of leaders tended to be small-
town or rural. The Republican group was more urban and more
metropolitan than the Democratic; but the great majority of the
Republican leaders were resident in small towns and represented
rural districts. More than two-thirds of the Democratic leaders
were from places of less than 50,000 and more than half from towns
of less than 10,000. Superficially viewed, the House leadership in
either Congress would seem to have left much to be desired. Both
groups, of course, included men of ability; but it is inconceivable
that either group represented the pick of the country's talent in
1928 or in 1932.

The Democratic leadership appears the more incongruous; for
the South is not only in many respects the section least representa-

[13] Agriculture, Appropriations, Banking and Currency, Civil Service, Education,
Flood Control, Foreign Affairs, Immigration and Naturalization, Insular Affairs,
Interstate and Foreign Commerce, Irrigation and Reclamation, Judiciary, Labor,
Merchant Marine and Fisheries (later Merchant Marine, Radio, and Fisheries),
Military Affairs, Mines and Mining, Naval Affairs, Patents, Post Offices and Post
Roads, Public Lands, Rivers and Harbors, Roads, Ways and Means, and World
War Veterans' Legislation.
[14] As of Jan. 9, 1931.
[15] As of Dec. 21, 1933.

tive of the dominant factors in American life, but it is also the section that receives almost no stimulation from inter-party political competition; that has the highest percentage of non-voters in elections, the least adequate public schools, the highest rate of illiteracy, the lowest per capita expenditures on public libraries, the fewest library borrowers,[16] and relatively the fewest outstanding universities and technical institutions; that has been subjected over many years to a draining away of its talent to other regions; and that until recently has lagged, probably more than any other region, in the solution of its own state and local problems.

The leaders of the House, it should be kept in mind, are not responsible to the whole nation,[17] nor are they responsible even to the House membership. They do not resign when repudiated. The fact is that a mechanism designed both to accelerate and obstruct legislation placed in substantial control of the House, at a time when both democracy and efficiency were peculiarly important, a group that was essentially unrepresentative and presumably ill adapted to a pressing legislative task.

The Senate contains abler and, from the national viewpoint, more representative men.[18] Its smaller size gives opportunity for persons of exceptional capacity to make themselves felt regardless of seniority. The Senate is more flexible and adjustable. Nevertheless, because of its extremely unrepresentative character, it appears to be more amenable to sectional influences than the House and at times less disposed to maintain its independence of the executive.[19]

[16] Howard W. Odum and Harry Estill Moore, *American Regionalism* (1938), pp. 176, 534.

[17] For example, prior to the election of 1938, it was charged that John J. O'Connor, chairman of the Rules Committee of the House, had prevented passage of the wages and hours bill. Here was a proposal of first importance and of national interest; but the question of the rightness or wrongness of O'Connor's position was decided, not by the nation, but by a single district in New York City.

[18] On the distribution of Senate committee chairmen in the early New Deal period, see George H. Haynes, *The Senate of the United States; Its History and practice* (1938), Vol. 2, pp. 1060-61.

[19] It has been suggested that the so-called public opinion polls will make legislative bodies more responsive. Such polls, when carefully organized and directed and based on approved statistical methods, have demonstrated their accuracy as means of forecasting election results and are now frequently used between elections to ascertain by sampling the reactions of the people to a variety of specific questions. In the case of most questions of public policy, however, the best the polls can do is

The twentieth amendment has served to make the legislative mechanism more promptly operative.

On March 2, 1932 a constitutional amendment to eliminate the short or "lame-duck" session of Congress was proposed, and on February 6, 1933 it was ratified. Up to that time the president had remained in office after the November election until March 4, even though his party may have been defeated. Worse than that, the new legislators, unless called into special session, did not meet until about thirteen months after the election; while the old Congress, no longer representative of public opinion, began its second regular session about one month after the election. Always reflecting an out-dated public opinion and frequently repudiated by the people, this Congress was in no position to determine national policies and usually did little beyond passing the annual appropriation bills. The twentieth amendment fixed the date of the presidential inauguration on January 20, and the beginning of the senators' and representatives' term on January 3. The change was in the direction of more responsive government.

LEGISLATIVE EFFICIENCY

What has just been said indicates that neither house of Congress was constituted in such a way as to be reasonably representative or adaptable. Maladjustment in the legislative mechanism persisted; and in this fact lay one reason for presidential domination. A stronger reason lay in the belief that only through executive domination could the immediately necessary legislative efficiency be attained.

The preliminaries of policy-determination are to be found in four areas: (1) the legislature, strictly speaking, (2) the executive, (3) the bureaucracy, and (4) private individuals and groups. Of these, the legislature had appeared in the past the least responsive to the conditions that call for intelligent and effective action.

---

to indicate very roughly what the general inclination of the public is or is likely to be. The polls already exercise considerable influence over legislators, but it may be questioned whether this influence in the more important fields of legislature results in a genuinely beneficial responsiveness. See Lindsay Rogers, "Do the Gallup Polls Measure Opinion?" *Harper's Magazine*, Vol. 183 (1941), pp. 623-32.

Changes had taken place in legislative organization and procedure; but they were not considerable when viewed in the light of administrative and social changes. Indeed, the principal manifestations of legislative improvement had taken the form of a transference of policy-making and to a considerable extent of policy-determination from the constitutionally established legislative bodies to the people, to the executive, and to administrative agencies.

Recent congressional organization and procedure
give no added assurance of efficiency.

During the depression Congress showed little improvement with respect to organization and procedure. Evidently, the democratizing alterations instituted before the First World War did not increase the ability of Congress to "get things done" with its own resources.

Some students of government had already advanced the idea that legislation should be regarded as a distinct profession demanding special talents and experience;[20] and it is generally believed that legislators become qualified by experience. This belief seems to be the only sensible argument for the seniority rule. Certainly, in a large assembly such as the House of Representatives, experience of a kind is necessary for effective functioning. It has already been noted, however, that, when in 1933 the burden of legislation was heaviest, the proportion of new members was unusually large. Because of this fact, as well as the size of the House, leadership was required; and this leadership, so far as it was congressional, passed, as we have seen, to experienced members, a majority of whom were from the South and from rural districts. Naturally, they were in general elderly men.

Many investigations, inquiries, and studies by congressional committees[21] were undertaken in a more or less objective spirit and with a real desire to obtain the relevant facts and to draw sound conclusions from them. In some instances, owing to the committee's power to compel the production of information, facts were assembled that could not have been brought to light in any other

[20] For example, E. W. Crecraft, *Government and Business* (1928), pp. 208-09.
[21] For a summary treatment of congressional investigative work during the New Deal period, see M. Nelson McGeary, *The Developments of Congressional Investigative Power* (1940).

way. Committee hearings, when held, offered a measure of protection to the public and opportunity for the presentation of evidence. In some cases, too, the committee practically handed over the organization and direction of its research work to trained students.[22]

Nevertheless, the conditions that limit the freedom of decision of individual senators and representatives and of Congress as a whole limit the freedom of committees. Politics, local and sectional demands, and group pressures, to say nothing of executive and administrative influences, bind the committee members in varying degrees to certain points of view, certain general policies, and not infrequently to specific pieces of legislation. The committees reflect the individual shortcomings of the members, particularly those of the committee chairmen. They are not elected to conduct research and they have other legislative duties. They lack time as well as training.

The system of standing committees, even when supplemented by special committees, is ill adapted to an integrated or co-ordinated study of public problems or to an examination of particular problems on a priority basis. The committees themselves are separate, for the most part unco-ordinated, frequently jealous of one another. Their studies are haphazard, rarely related to one another, and some important problems are not taken up at all because of political or other reasons.[23] Neither house has had a standing committee on industry or economics. Each has a labor committee; but one recent investigation in the labor field was referred to a special committee, while another was handled by the judiciary committee.

[22] For example, when the Senate and House special committees on the reorganization of the executive branch employed the Brookings Institution to make the detailed studies. Increased use was made of the questionnaire method by congressional committees; for example, in the investigation of labor conditions in the American Merchant Marine and of the National Labor Relations Board, by the Senate sub-committee studying profit-sharing, and by the Temporary National Economic Committee.

[23] "It has begun to be perceived that the existing legislative machinery of most countries does not sufficiently provide for the study of economic and social problems in a directly practical spirit by those on whom the duty falls of passing into law measures dealing with them, because legislatures incessantly occupied with party strife and with the supervision of the Executive in its daily work of administration have not the time, even if a sufficient number of their members have the capacity, for such investigation." James Bryce, *Modern Democracies* (1921), Vol. 2, p. 412.

Constitutionalism and judicial review had created legislative difficulties peculiar to the American system. After passing during the early depression years much unconstitutional legislation, Congress was later quite successful in bringing its acts into accord with the Supreme Court's judgment. This gain was accomplished by fuller and clearer statements of legislative intent and by a change in the attitude of the Court, perhaps also by more deliberation in the enactment of laws. On the whole, however, it does not appear that Congress has recently made much progress in the standardization of legislation or its simplification through formulas.[24]

Delegation of legislative power to administrative agencies insures that within certain fields detailed legislation which would be done worse or not at all by Congress itself will be done reasonably well. Though control of the administrative agencies is still conceived to be a function of Congress, a body so constituted is incapable of continuous and effective control, and no further steps have been taken to bring the committee system of Congress into coordination with the executive departments.

Much of the members' time and thought continue to be diverted to matters that are largely irrelevant to their immediate or more important duties.[25] Congress still acts as a municipal legislature for the District of Columbia. Local and special legislation still claims a part of the members' time.

*Centralization and experimentation did
not lighten the task of Congress.*

In some directions, legislative centralization probably contributes to efficiency, since, in certain cases, the whole of a problem may be more easily dealt with than a part; and, from the viewpoint of the

[24] See Ernst Freund, *Standards of American Legislation* (1917), p. 249; V. O. Key, Jr., *The Administration of Federal Grants to States* (1937), pp. 319-40.

[25] What we may call the extraneous work of a legislator includes the circulating of letters (even Christmas cards) to constituents, sending franked copies of speeches printed in the *Congressional Record* but not always delivered in Congress, mailing of other franked matter, running of errands, entertaining constituents in Washington, reading home papers, getting jobs for political friends, protecting job holders, and obtaining appropriations for their districts or states. In the case of many legislators these demands were so numerous and pressing as to leave little time for the study of pending bills. Joseph P. Chamberlain, *Legislative Processes: National and State* (1936), pp. 39-50; Luce, *Legislative Problems* (1935), p. 684.

personal capacity of its members, Congress is better equipped than the state legislatures. On the other hand, Congress in the past followed the states rather than led them. To a large extent, they did the experimenting; and the national law-makers profited from their findings and mistakes; but federal legislation based on state experience is necessarily tardy and seems inappropriate at a time of crisis.

Whether because of legislative lag or other reasons, national problems had multiplied, becoming more complex and confused, as well as more urgent; and in many cases no clear solutions were advanced either by public opinion or by the students. If speedy action were to be taken, experimentation on a national scale was in a measure unavoidable; but it imposed on Congress the necessity of watching with extraordinary care the results of its experiments and of promptly modifying or abandoning them as need arose. It did not appear that Congress was capable of the necessary vigilance, carefulness, and promptitude.

Some improvement has appeared
in the state legislatures.

Legislative improvement, apparent in the states, may have been due in part to the assumption by the federal government of a larger portion of the legislative load and financial burden and in part to the influence exercised over state legislatures by federal grants-in-aid and by federal administrative agencies. Pressure in the states for balanced budgets was another primary factor. Still another was the growing practice of delegating policy-determining powers to state administrative agencies and municipalities. Other contributions were made through the closer contact of universities and research institutions with the legislatures, and through such organizations as the Council of State Governments, the American Legislators' Association, and the Interstate Legislative Reference Bureau.

In Nebraska, a one-house legislature was adopted by popular vote in 1934. The members are relatively few in number and are elected from single-member districts on nonpartisan ballots. Constitutional amendments providing for unicameralism were proposed in a number of other states.[26] Beginning with Kansas, a number of states established legislative councils designed to conduct research work on public problems and prepare programs for the law-making bodies.

THE BUREAUCRACY IN RELATION TO CONGRESS

Within the framework of government, it is the administration, not the legislature, that has a fairly permanent staff of experts and students, that commands sources of information, that is in direct contact with social and economic conditions, and that can know how public policies are actually working. To a large extent and as a matter of routine the administrative agencies act within their respective fields as policy-making bodies, frequently at the request or under the instructions of Congress. The exercise of sublegislative power by administrative agencies tends to increase the dependence of Congress on these agencies with respect to the appraisal of the general principles that control administration.

Administrative assistance in legislation helped,
but revealed shortcomings and dangers.

With respect to many technical or otherwise nonpolitical matters, the benefits of administrative assistance to Congress can scarcely be exaggerated. On political subjects and on matters affecting the organization and power of the administration itself, the results are more problematical. In effect, congressional dependence on the bureaucracy in this connection means a further increase of administrative power; and this power is one over Congress itself. Such dependence may be dangerous, in proportion to the irresponsibility of the bureaucracy, its lack of co-ordination and consistency, and its ability and disposition to exert pressure as an interest group.

Are government employees to form
a pressure group?

As administrative power increased, the extra-governmental groups representing interests and specialties had established direct

---

[26] Alvin W. Johnson, *The Unicameral Legislature* (1938), and "Unicameralism Marks Time," *State Government*, Vol. 12 (1939).

relationships with administrative agencies. Whether or not this relationship was legally recognized in the agency's setup, public or group representation came to be an important feature of administrative operations. Administrative agencies were to an extent isolated centers of power. They were able to traffic in particular pressures and to use their clienteles, as well as their patronage and discretionary authority, to bring influence to bear on Congress, probably also on the president. How much lobbying was done or pressure engineered by administrative agencies, it is impossible to say; but evidently it was not wholly eliminated by law.

Government employees were organized in large numbers; and in most cases their organizations were affiliated with the American Federation of Labor or the Congress of Industrial Organizations. Could such organizations strike? Or could they, without striking, bring pressure on Congress and the president? It seemed to be an established principle in the federal government that public employees would not be permitted to strike. Isolated strikes did occur among municipal employees.[27] Pressure and lobbying by public school teachers in the states and municipalities were frequent and seemed to be quite effective.[28]

The problem became more complicated when relief workers organized and brought pressure to bear on government. The political campaigns of 1936 and 1938 brought to light instances both of political activity by relief workers and the use of administrative powers to intimidate persons on relief. The act making relief appropriations for the fiscal year 1939-40 contained provisions designed in general to take relief "out of politics" and to prevent the formation of a permanent pressure-group supported by the government and using its electoral power to control government. In 1939, however, strikes occurred in a number of places by relief workers to force restoration of the "prevailing wage."

With regard to government workers, a principle had been established and with difficulty was being maintained. The principle

[27] See Lyman S. Moore, "Municipal Government and Labor Disputes," *American Political Science Review*, Vol. 31 (1937), p. 1123.
[28] See *New York Times*, Jan. 27, 1940, Mar. 27, 31, 1940. Henry Parkman, Jr., "Lobbies and Pressure Groups: A Legislator's Point of View," *Annals*, Vol. 195 (1938), p. 101.

eliminated strikes, coercion, and intimidation. It did not rule out organization and organized or unorganized pressure. Even the limited principle met with considerable humanitarian and "liberal" criticism. Would it survive the growth of bureaucracy and of electoral power within it?[29]

GROUP PRESSURES

The pressure groups had by now taken over extra-constitutionally a part of the traditional parliamentary functions: study of public problems, crystallization and registration of opinion, development of leadership, carrying on of debate, and supervision of the bureaucracy. Policies shaped by group pressures and directed at group interests were not peculiar to the depression years; but now the interaction of government and private groups appeared to become more intimate, more sensitive, more extensive, and less restrained by fiscal principles, tradition, and morality. Certain indications of this trend have already been noted: the distributive nature of social objectives; applications of specific policies to agriculture, labor, the veterans, the unemployed, the aged, and various economic segments; the apparent impotence of a general interest, such as that of taxpayers, to resist special pressures and control spending; and the increasingly close relationship between administrative agencies and their respective constituencies.

The forms of pressure underwent apparently no significant changes during the depression. The same might be said, perhaps, of the aggregate weight or strength of pressure; but its total or net effect seems to have increased. The pressure of agricultural groups appeared consistently almost irresistible. Labor pressure was exerted with unusual alertness and activity but its effect was diminished by schism and became markedly less during the later years. New sources of pressure appeared in the unemployed and the aged and to these also government was noticeably sensitive. Direct pressure on government from "big business" probably decreased both in amount and effect; but considerable effort was made by "big business" to defend itself indirectly through propaganda. The im-

---

[29] In September 1941, the State, County, and Municipal Workers of America, a CIO union, inserted into its constitution a section authorizing the national executive board to establish rules and regulations governing strike procedures.

pression is that the influence of specialized, professional, and intellectual groups, of taxpayers and consumers, and of the middle classes generally may have gained in variety of objectives and in activity but lost in tangible accomplishment. The power of the veterans, however, was decisively demonstrated. The stimulation of group pressures by governmental leaders appears to have attained unusual proportions. Additional stress was laid on the relation of organization to the success of propaganda and pressure; and one is struck by the number of organizations formed in this period purely for the purpose of influencing government, with little real participation on the part of their members and with only a nominal associational unity.[30]

*Group pressures produced legislative action, as
well as disintegration and confusion.*

Due partly to the radio and partly to a greater sensitivity on the part of the public and the government, pressure in large volume was generated with unprecedented speed. Technology, introducing instantaneous nation-wide communication, had quickened the tempo of pressure, along with that of industrial and social change. Incidentally, government, becoming extraordinarily responsive to pressures, seems to have become also more quickly incited to action or to inaction. Practically a new concept took form, that of "timing" in relation to political leadership and opinion formation. Public opinion was seen to have its moments of maximum receptivity, its moments of preoccupation, its "fatigue-points," and its normal ebbs and flows. Frequently, the substance of a public address or governmental action appeared less important than its "timing."

In general, the strongest and most active organizations were pressing for particularistic benefits. To be sure, they brought to the legislator a measure of the specialized assistance that he needed; but the different specializations pressed upon him were not always impartial and were rarely integrated with one another.

In many cases, legislators are really desirous of representing

---

[30] For examples of pressure organizations of a largely fictitious character, see *Ratification of Constitutional Amendments by Popular Vote,* Hearings before the Senate Committee on the Judiciary, 75 Cong. 3 sess., pp. 32-33, 77-78.

what they conceive to be the general interest, not merely the particular interest that appears to be predominant in their states or districts. Almost universally, however, the general interest is conceived to be attained either through a balancing or adjusting of particular interests as expressed in pressures or through an indiscriminate and somewhat conscienceless satisfaction of all articulate group demands.

No automatic integration of particular interests or of particular group demands can be accomplished locally. The important problems of policy are state, regional, national, and international. If local opinion is to constitute a reasoned conception of the general welfare or even an intelligent consensus of particular opinions, this integrated local opinion must be inculcated into the locality from some source that is broadly educated, objective, even scientific. This type of leadership is not generated by a party system that rests on a mosaic of localisms and it is rarely typified by a legislative candidate. Nor is it from any other quarter exerting a continuous influence sufficient to determine a preponderant local demand. The legislator, therefore, becomes a delegate rather than a leader; and as a delegate he is obedient to pressures that are in the main unco-ordinated.

When these local delegates come together in a mass at Washington, it is expected that the alchemy of their association will produce a balancing and adjustment of unco-ordinated and often conflicting pressures; but these pressures are, for the most part, local to the legislators, especially to the representatives, who are elected every two years.[31] They are not sensitive to national pressures except as these come to them on non-localized problems, such as the Supreme Court proposal, or in the form of pressure from the president.

In practice, the mingling of local delegates at Washington fails to mediate rationally among pressures.[32] "Adjustment" generally

[31] An important consequence of the single-member district to the legislative process is the opportunity thereby given to the partisans of particular projects of law to campaign in each district, bringing pressure to bear on the local representative to get him to pledge himself, publicly or privately, to favor their bill. Chamberlain, *Legislative Processes: National and State*, p. 31.

[32] "Our representative legislative bodies have demonstrated their inadequacy for synthesizing group conflict into a unified conception of the public interest." E. Pendleton Herring, *Public Administration and the Public Interest* (1936), pp. 6-7.

takes the form of attempting to satisfy all groups that are active and articulate, ignoring those that are inactive and inarticulate, though these latter may constitute a majority of the people. The impact of minority pressures on Congress produces in that body "trades" and "log-rolling."[33] It appears that, in the absence of an integrating leadership, the representation of localities will be preponderantly representative of the material interests of minority groups and will probably be progressively less representative of the public interest or the general welfare.

Progress toward harmonizing of groups was doubtful or inconsiderable.

Conflicts and divergencies in pressures on Congress would have been mitigated and the intensity of pressure sensibly diminished had two or more pressure groups achieved reconciliation of their purposes or had each group come to understand more fully and sympathetically the needs of other groups.

In the exercise of pressure, agricultural and labor groups were frequently in agreement but usually acted independently. Attempts were made to induce farm and labor organizations to present a united front against what was conceived to be a common enemy. Frequently, the proposed alliance involved a sort of inter-group log-rolling. As a rule, however, neither group was consistently active in the other's behalf. The two groups did not achieve like-mindedness or a real community of interests. On the part of agriculture, the more general sentiment was one of hostility.

The depression, as well as governmental policies and propaganda and the attitude in general of business leaders, appears to have encouraged class conflict, at least after the initial period of co-operation and until the recession of 1937.[34] Widespread unemployment emphasized inequalities of wealth and income. A militant program on

---

[33] "Log-rolling is a term of opprobrium. . . . Log-rolling is, however, in fact, the most characteristic legislative process." Arthur F. Bentley, *The Process of Government* (1935), p. 370.

[34] "But the impression was clear in the investigator's mind at the end of the field work in 1935 that the line between working class and business class, though vague and blurred still, is more apparent than it was ten years before." Robert S. Lynd and Helen Merrell Lynd, *Middletown in Transition* (1937), p. 451.

the part of labor proved measurably successful so far as labor's immediate aims were concerned. The "sit-down" strikes, the impression that they were blessed with the sympathy of government, and the assertion of new "rights" of labor, seemed to be widening the cleavage between management and wage earners. Though collective bargaining is viewed by some as a means of integration, the labor policies of government, especially the administration of the National Labor Relations Act, apparently contributed to the solidarity of capital as well as labor by consolidating opposition between the two.

With the recession of 1937, however, and the introduction of the President's Supreme Court bill, "big business" became less isolated and class alignment less clear-cut. The intra-class conflict between the American Federation of Labor and the Congress of Industrial Organizations also tended to blur class lines. In 1939, it appeared that class conflict, while latent, was no more clearly asserting itself than during previous periods of American history.

Some encouraging evidence appeared that private industrial and financial leaders were in larger measure recognizing and accepting their social responsibilities;[35] though their opportunity to demonstrate "social-mindedness" was to some extent curtailed by public policy. For example, relief of the unemployed, frequently declared to be a proper charge against industry, was taken over by the government, and the Social Security Act and the National Labor Relations Act brought within the area of legal compulsion certain important aspects of social responsibility. Increased taxation, enlarging the benevolent sphere of government, restricted that of private business.

The social responsibility of an industrial executive is too frequently interpreted by the proponents of social justice as a responsibility exclusively to his employees. He is also trustee for the stockholders, who are numerous in the case of the big corporations; and most stockholders are not rich. He has a responsibility to the consumers—these are still more numerous—and to the public generally. These different groups often make variant demands and entertain conflicting conceptions of their immediate needs. Moreover, the

[35] Temporary National Economic Committee, *Final Report and Recommendations*, S. Doc. 35, 77 Cong. 1 sess., p. 9.

possibilities of corporate unselfishness in one direction or another are limited by competitive conditions.

Assumption of social responsibility is in practice more than a matter of morals or emotion. It is primarily intellectual, largely concerned with organizational and operating efficiency and with the determination of price policies in the public interest, with due regard for the interests of the groups most directly concerned—the stockholders and the wage earners.[36]

Economic statesmanship, if it is to become a social force, must appear, not only in industry, but also in the other and electorally more powerful pressure group. Little evidence appeared that in the agricultural and labor groups the broad economic elements of the general welfare were much better understood or, if understood, were more influential than they had been before the depression.

*General or integrative pressures
remained relatively weak.*

Particularistic and disintegrating pressures might be counteracted by those of a general nature and integrative effect.

Middle-class citizens have certain common attitudes and feelings and a comparatively direct identification with the general welfare; but they have shown practically no disposition to act together and press forward as an organized pressure group and little tendency to subscribe to a definite program.

Lawyers remain in a position of great and peculiar influence, both in industry and government, contributing to political leadership, intimately linked with the judicial branch, and constantly acting as a liaison between citizens and the government. It can hardly be said, however, that, during this period, the legal organizations produced any significant unanimity of opinion on public policies among their members; and lawyers were suspected perhaps more than ever before of feeling a vested interest in the status quo. The National Lawyers Guild, however, represented a reaction from the conservatism of the American Bar Association and, sympathetic toward a radical labor movement, appeared to reflect a tendency toward

[36] On the general subject, see Edwin G. Nourse and Horace B. Drury, *Industrial Price Policies and Economic Progress* (1938).

"social action" as well as a fundamental division among lawyers.

A somewhat similar movement appeared in the medical profession. The American Medical Association remained the principal national professional organization of the physicians.[37] "Socialized medicine" served as the gauge of battle in this professional field; and counter-movements arose against the individualistic philosophy of the Association.

The engineering profession is divided into a score or more of specialties. Engineering organizations are related to and affiliated with trade and industrial associations. Engineers are largely represented in organizations devoted to research in the physical sciences. A substantial proportion are government employees; and they are dominant or highly influential in certain fields of public administration. To many factors may be traced evidences of a certain reorientation of the engineers' outlook; and contributions of engineers to economics and political science may have been influential in certain quarters; but the effect was scarcely to integrate pressures.

Additional attempts were made to organize on the basis of the consumer interest; and some were able to see a new or growing "consumer movement." Nevertheless, though the consumers possess ultimate economic power as well as ultimate political power, as a pressure group they are still relatively weak, mainly, perhaps, because they are not a group; they are everybody. Generally speaking stockholders and policy holders, like consumers, did not recognize their common economic attribute as a vital or paramount interest.

The general policy of deficit-spending, together with the concealment of increased taxation through indirect levies, had the effect of encouraging pressure by the groups that desired expenditure, while failing to encourage a counteracting pressure from the taxpayers.[38]

[37] See Harold F. Gosnell and Margaret J. Schmidt, "Professional Associations," *Annals*, Vol. 179 (1935), pp. 25-33.

[38] A survey by the Institute of Public Opinion in June 1939 indicated that one-quarter of the adult voters did not think they were taxpayers. Most of the persons who were not conscious of paying taxes were in the lower income level. In general, Democrats were less conscious of taxes than Republicans and persons living in small towns were more conscious than those living in cities or on farms. "Voters who look upon themselves as taxpayers are for President Roosevelt by a small majority, whereas those who say they pay no taxes approve overwhelmingly of him as President." *New York Times*, June 21, 1939.

At all times there were congressional advocates of economy and a balanced budget; but, lacking presidential leadership and support, they could not muster enough strength in Congress or in the country to re-establish the clear-cut policy put forth by the Democratic Party in 1932 and by the President in March 1933.

The results were: a confession that Congress was unable to determine financial policy without presidential initiative, the creation of vested interests in spending that were certain to maintain if not increase their pressure on Congress, and the putting of Congress progressively at a greater disadvantage in relation to the president.

PRESIDENTIAL DOMINATION

In his first inaugural address, President Roosevelt outlined the basic elements and revealed the philosophy and aims that were to determine his position with respect to policy determination. He asserted that "this nation asks for action, and action now." "We must move," he said, "as a trained and loyal army," for without "common discipline . . . no leadership becomes effective." He assumed "unhesitatingly the leadership of this great army of our people dedicated to a disciplined attack upon our common problems." The people, he declared, had "registered a mandate that they want direct, vigorous action. They have asked for discipline and direction under leadership. They have made me the present instrument of their wishes." In the following more specific terms, he forecast the possibility of a temporary dictatorship:

It is to be hoped that the normal balance of executive and legislative authority may be wholly adequate to meet the unprecedented task before us. But it may be that an unprecedented demand and need for undelayed action may call for temporary departure from that normal balance of public procedure.

I am prepared under my constitutional duty to recommend the measures that a stricken Nation in the midst of a stricken world may require. These measures, or such other measures as the Congress may build out of its experience and wisdom, I shall seek, within my constitutional authority, to bring to speedy adoption.

But in the event that the Congress shall fail to take one of these two courses, and in the event that the National emergency is still critical, I shall not evade the clear course of duty that will then confront me. I shall ask the Congress for the one remaining instrument to meet the crisis—broad executive power to wage a war against the emergency, as great as the power that would be given to me if we were in fact invaded by a foreign foe.[39]

In his second "fireside chat" on May 7, 1933, the President reviewed some of the policies that had been adopted and powers that had been conferred upon him, and sought to allay any fears that might have been aroused regarding the constitutionality of the procedure.[40] Nevertheless, his message to Congress of January 3, 1934, closed with these words:

A final personal word. I know that each of you will appreciate that I am speaking no mere politeness when I assure you how much I value the fine relationship that we have shared during these months of hard and incessant work. Out of these friendly contacts we are, fortunately, building a strong and permanent tie between the legislative and executive branches of the Government. The letter of the Constitution wisely declared a separation, but the impulse of common purpose declares a union. In this spirit we join once more in serving the American people.[41]

The "generous and intelligent support" that Congress gave during the early years consisted largely in an unquestioning acceptance of the President's ideas and the enactment with little debate or amendment of bills drafted by the President's advisers and endorsed by him. Executive drafting of bills may have been carried no farther than in certain previous administrations,[42] but the circumstances of their enactment pointed to something exceptional. No other president had so thoroughly monopolized legislative initiative or so completely and for so long a time dominated the legislative process.

Theodore Roosevelt, Woodrow Wilson, and Franklin D. Roosevelt have been the three modern "strong" presidents. Judged by the degree of subordination to which the other branches of government were reduced, by the variety and effectiveness of the weapons used, and by actual achievement, Wilson was stronger than the first Roosevelt, and the second Roosevelt was stronger than Wilson, though Franklin D. Roosevelt's domination fell far short of dictatorship, even a temporary one, in the Hitlerian sense of the word.

Joined with the various factors mentioned at the beginning of this chapter, conditions in 1933 were especially favorable to a

[39] *Public Papers and Addresses*, Vol. 2, pp. 12-16.
[40] The same, p. 161.
[41] The same, Vol. 3, p. 14. See comments in Luce, *Legislative Problems*, p. 218.
[42] Luce, *Legislative Problems*, pp. 203-04.

marked reassertion of presidential leadership. Public opinion was distressed. A real emergency existed. A substantial program of legislation was demanded and needed. Many, including apparently the President, believed that revolution threatened, unless the program were speedily enacted. Owing to the nature of the program, and the weaknesses of Congress, laws could not be enacted with the necessary promptitude without an exceptional exertion of executive leadership.[43]

The state of public opinion and of the party system served to give the President a blanket mandate. The Democratic Party had been the minority party, a party of protest, composed of incongruous elements, and out of office for twelve years. It was brought into power mainly by a vote, not for Roosevelt or the Democrats, but against Hoover and the Republicans. The task of Roosevelt as party leader was to give his party a constructive and progressive record and provide for its success in succeeding elections. This partisan political task was inseparable from the legislative task. Both imposed an exceptional burden of leadership on the President. In view of his overwhelming triumph in 1936 and indications of his popularity afterward, it would not have been surprising had he considered his political judgment superior to that of his critics, had he believed that his will should be the arbiter of party policy and national legislation (the two were, for the most part, identical), and had he in the end come to consider himself the one man indispensable to party success, as well as to democratic and efficient government.

Linked with this matter of "grand strategy" was another consideration that went to the foundations of policy, as well as of democratic theory. The progressivism developed in the "New Deal" aimed at a redistribution of national income in favor of underprivileged groups. Specifically, it provided subsidies or other pecuniary advantages to certain sections of the population, notably the farmers, the industrial wage earners, and the unemployed. Such provision was dictated by humanitarianism and conceptions of social

[43] "Nor should we overlook the natural affinity of democracies always for executive power. Unwieldy, more or less aware of their own incompetence, they turn inevitably to simple solutions—and executive power is such a solution. There have been, moreover, epochs when the simple solution seemed the only solution, the only alternative to social disintegration. . . ." Edward S. Corwin, *The President: Office and Powers* (1940), p. 134.

justice, as well as by party strategy. Incidentally, the President was granted discretionary authority to allot lump-sum appropriations aggregating many billions of dollars and the rapid growth of administration supplied him steadily with substantial resources in patronage.[44]

Conditions and policies, therefore, gave an extraordinary opportunity for the winning of popularity to a leadership that assumed responsibility, took credit, controlled the purse, held the spotlight, and, whether intentionally or not, exploited the particular material interests, envies, and fears of individuals and groups, including members of Congress. Thus, consciously or unconsciously manipulating economic and social tensions and bending policies and public funds to the purposes of power, a president could, conceivably, perpetuate himself in office with constant aggrandizement of power.

[44] "[There are] illegitimate means by which the President may influence the action of Congress. He may bargain with members, not only with regard to appointments, but also with regard to legislative measures. He may use his local patronage to assist members to get or retain their seats. He may interpose his powerful influence, in one covert way or another, in contests for places in the Senate. . . .

". . . Such things are not only deeply immoral, but they are destructive of the fundamental understandings of constitutional government and, therefore, of constitutional government itself. They are sure, moreover, in a country of free public opinion, to bring their own punishment, to destroy both the fame and the power of the man who dares to practise them.

". . . The reprobation of all good men will always overwhelm such influences with shame and failure. . . ." Woodrow Wilson, *Constitutional Government in the United States* (1911), pp. 71-72.

"The conclusion seems inescapable that the power of the President to guide legislation rested in considerable measure upon his wide discretionary authority over the distribution of funds and jobs; but the relative weight to be given this factor must remain a matter for individual judgment." Herring, "Second Session of the Seventy-Third Congress, Jan. 3, 1934, to June 18, 1934," *American Political Science Review*, Vol. 28 (1934), p. 864.

"The necessity of using patronage to unify policy is the most fundamental weakness of our civil service. After the Executive has yielded patronage, his whole legislative program begins to disintegrate. His only remedy is to embark on more spending and more patronage." Elliott, *The Need for Constitutional Reform*, p. 200.

It is not intended to imply that all members of Congress were or could be controlled by patronage. Patronage was a two-edged instrument. In some cases, through senatorial confirmation, the instrument could be wielded by Congress against the President. Note the controversy between the President and Senators Glass and Byrd over certain judicial appointments. *New York Times*, Feb. 8, 9, 10, 19, 21, 1939; also Kenneth C. Cole, "The Role of the Senate in the Confirmation of Judicial Nominations," *American Political Science Review*, Vol. 28 (1934), pp. 875-94; Luce, *Legislative Problems*, pp. 117-30.

CHAPTER X

"MAKING DEMOCRACY WORK"

It was pointed out in a previous chapter that the plan to place all administrative policy-determination in the President's control was supported on the theory that it would "make democracy work." The same theory was used to justify the President's domination of Congress and his attempt to make the Supreme Court "co-operate." Measured by activity and quantitative results, government was undoubtedly *working*. But was it democratic government that was working? And, if so, was it working in such a manner as to give reasonable assurance of qualitative as well as quantitative results? As we have seen, sufficient control and sufficient guidance did not come from Congress. Did they come from the party system or from the scientists and intellectuals? Or, finally, from the President?

INDICATIONS OF CHANGE IN THE PARTY SYSTEM

Though no essential alteration occurred in the outlines of the party system, certain influences and tendencies were observable. In what direction were they moving? Toward or away from governmental efficiency? Toward or away from democracy?

Class characteristics were, at least temporarily, more conspicuous.

If democratic government is to be party government, and if the latter is to be achieved through the two-party system, several conditions appear to be necessary. The first is general agreement on the essentials of democracy, particularly majority rule, involving on the part of the majority tolerance of opposition. Democracy rests on the assumption that conflicts will be settled by discussion and vote, and that those outvoted will accept the majority decision and co-operate in the task of making it effective. If the majority is intolerant of opposition and by one means or another suppresses free criticism, a step will have been taken toward controlled elections and a one-party system.

Some have confused the free enterprise system with democracy, just as others have confused social with political democracy. While neither economic freedom nor social justice *is* democratic government, both have a vital relation to the achievement of a democratic, as well as an efficient, government. Economic freedom produces inequality in the distribution of private economic power. So it has been argued that when the free enterprise system operates within the structure of democracy, a conflict is inevitable between the few who possess economic power and the many who possess political power. We are further warned that when conflict threatens the very existence of a powerful class or aims at a wholesale transfer of power from one class to another, there can be no settlement by discussion and majority decision. A situation similar to this was once presented by the southern slave-holding interest; and it resulted in civil war.

Except for the irreconcilable conflict over slavery, which was a sectional as well as a class struggle, no fundamental opposition incapable of resolution or compromise has thus far developed in American politics. It has been almost axiomatic in our political life that no party or candidate should set section against section or class against class. This rule has not always been observed; but that it still operated was shown by the composite nature of party membership.

During the depression years, the Democratic strategy was not essentially different from that of the Federalists in 1789, the Democrats at the beginning of their long ante-bellum dominance, or the Republicans in 1861. The idea was to create and hold an electoral majority by satisfying a combination of groups, notably the farm, labor, relief, and lower middle-class groups. This strategy, which proved remarkably successful, involved a strong attack on "big business" and an incidental alienation of the upper middle classes. In consequence of this strategy, political campaigning, public policies, and governmental propaganda put extraordinary emphasis on separate group and class interests.

So far as "big business men" and industrial wage earners were concerned, the resulting political cleavage was quite distinct. In general, however, group politics did not take the form of durable partisan attachments; and the ordinary criteria of economic interest, such as income or wealth, were by no means exclusively divisive or decisive.[1] Moreover, the durability and solidarity of labor's political affiliation were made questionable by the internal division of organized labor and by the fact that organized labor as a whole could not guarantee under all circumstances the victory of one party or the defeat of another. Persons on relief were, apparently, durably attached to the Democratic Party; and the Negroes evidently transferred their allegiance from the party that had freed them in the past to the one that favored them in the present. The farmers of the North and West, who had shifted in large numbers to the Democratic Party in 1932, were returning to the opposition in 1938 and 1940.

The middle classes were never united or as a whole durably attached. The balance of electoral power lay with them. Because of their characteristics and mentality, they are, more than any other portion of the population, concerned with the general welfare. On them, therefore, rests especially the duty of checking the political exploitation by either party of class and group interests. This is in essence the task of integration.[2]

Yet, as we have seen, the conditions that qualify the middle classes for this role preclude their effective exercise of it. They have no clear-cut, deeply felt, distinctive interest. Highly organized into specialized and professional groups, they have left their general political interests and consequently their voting power unorganized and largely inarticulate.

The attachment of the "Solid South" to the Democratic Party remained as dependable as ever during the depression; but, outside of the South, sectionalism seemed to be decreasing in American

---

[1] See, for example, Institute of Public Opinion Survey, *New York Times*, Mar.3, 1940; and W. F. Ogburn and L. C. Coombs, "The Economic Factor in the Roosevelt Elections," in *American Political Science Review*, Vol. 34 (1940), pp. 719-27.

[2] On the political function of the middle classes, see Arthur N. Holcombe, *The New Party Politics* (1933), and "Present-Day Characteristics of American Political Parties," in Edward B. Logan (ed.), *The American Political Scene* (1936), pp. 1-52; Alfred M. Bingham, *Insurgent America* (1935); Gilbert Seldes, *Your Money and Your Life* (1938), pp. 335-36.

politics. Such a decrease might result from a more widespread regard for the general welfare or, what would seem more likely, from issues cutting across sectional interests and from a country-wide distribution of benefits.

Emphasis on production or on distribution served
again to distinguish party philosophies.

From the beginning of American constitutional government, a difference in emphasis on the production or on the distribution of national wealth has been reflected at critical times in party philosophies. On one side has been an idea that government should promote industrial production and expansion by certain protective and stimulative measures applied to the system at the top, the distribution of the benefits being largely left to the natural workings of the system. On the other side has been a feeling that direct measures, if any were called for, should be applied to distribution at the bottom of the system as a matter of justice to the less prosperous masses, the top of the system being of interest chiefly from the standpoint of policing and ethical supervision. In 1940, this difference in emphasis had again become clear; but neither of the two presidential candidates denied the need of the other's approach. Distributive politics are obviously unworkable without industrial productivity, while industrial stimulation is socially unjust and politically impracticable unless the income produced is distributed with some measure of equity.

This difference in economic emphasis is related to a difference in the attitude toward power and in the conception of democracy. On the one side, political power is distrusted and economic liberty stressed; on the other, private economic power is attacked and a strong government serving the masses is held to exemplify democracy. In past campaigns, democracy, dictatorship, and power had been subjects of charges and counter-charges; and they figured exceptionally in the 1940 campaign. One may dismiss the phenomenon as a feature of campaign tactics or assume that it sprang from a real danger; but it should be noted in any event that it has been invariably related both to economic philosophy and to a real or assumed class struggle.

*Party principles in general were undergoing
restatement and losing strength.*

An assumption of the two-party system is that within the frame-work of fundamental agreement, each of the two parties will maintain at its core a distinctive constitutional philosophy, point of view, or set of general principles. When the implications of "New Deal" policies came to be appreciated, they appeared to be opposed in many respects to the principles that had been held by Jefferson, Jackson, Cleveland, and Wilson. These policies departed especially from the ideas of strict constitutional construction, individual free-dom, states' rights, and minimized national government, doctrines which became during the depression years more Republican than Democratic. It is not clear, however, that the Republican Party has permanently adopted these principles or that they retain for Repub-lican leadership the meaning that they formerly had for the Democratic. In any event, it would seem that these four principles are no longer securely fixed in the core of either party; and one might go so far as to say that they are vanishing altogether from American politics. The same may be said of the principle of separa-tion of powers. Moreover, the party contests of the depression period seem to indicate that no feature of the mechanism of political democracy is any longer a major party rallying-cry.

*Unprincipled at its core, the system showed potentials
of and a trend toward national bossism.*

Generally speaking, the "machines" are really unprincipled. The "boss" gives his followers tangible inducements. Such inducements, whether or not intended as such, are inherent in national policies; specifically in relief, agricultural subsidies, payments to the aged, and higher wages and shorter hours for labor. Recent legislation has provided not merely increased patronage, but also, to millions out-side of government, subsidies, jobs, contracts, pensions, miscel-laneous favors, friendliness, and charity—the stuff out of which bosses are made.

No national boss has arisen in the past, largely for three reasons. First, federalism and local self-government have left to the states and localities control, not only of the nomination and election machinery, but also of the major part of the spoils of office. Second, in the national government, Congress, maintaining its potential power, has intermittently asserted its supremacy and has participated in the control of federal patronage. Third, the conception of the president as a national leader and the tradition of the presidency as an office of vast and high-minded responsibility, operating in the full light of publicity, has established for the presidency a moral standard incompatible with the cruder arts of bossism. It is a commonplace, however, that any president can, through the party organization, bring about his own renomination; and it was fully demonstrated in 1940 that organization, with a favorable or complacent public opinion, permits a popular president to obtain renomination even for a third term.

The possibility of national bossism appeared to be acutely presented by national administration of relief. For the purpose of eliminating the political activities that had become increasingly apparent, the so-called Hatch Act was passed in July 1939.[3] This legislation was thought by many observers to be the most far-reaching reform of its kind since the Civil Service Act of 1883. It was viewed in some quarters as the most effective, if not the only, positive curb placed by Congress during the depression on presidential power.[4] Its application was made more sweeping when in

[3] The law of 1939 applied only to actions connected with the election of the president, vice-president, and members of Congress. Otherwise its scope was sweeping. It extended to all officers and employees in all federal administrative agencies, except the president and vice-president, persons whose compensation was paid from the appropriation for the office of the president, heads and assistant heads of departments, and officers appointed by the president with the advice and consent of the Senate "who determine policies to be pursued by the United States in its relations with foreign powers or in the nation-wide administration of Federal laws." The acts declared unlawful were: intimidation or coercion of voters; use of official authority to interfere with or affect the election or nomination of candidates for national offices; promises for political purposes of employment, position, work, compensation, or other benefit; threats for political purposes to deprive any person of any such benefit; soliciting or receiving campaign funds; the furnishing or receiving for political purposes of a list of names of those receiving relief or other benefits from federal funds; and the use of any money appropriated for relief or public works projects for the purpose of interfering with an individual's right to vote.

For the President's interpretation of the act, see his Message to Congress, Aug. 2, 1939.

[4] For discussions of the possible effects of the act, see Charles T. Lucey, "Did the President Sign Away 1940?" *Saturday Evening Post*, Jan. 27, 1940, pp. 27ff.;

1940 its provisions were extended to all state employees paid wholly or partly from federal funds.

While such laws may eliminate some of the grosser manifestations of "machine" politics, they cannot, even if scrupulously enforced, remove relief or other federal benefits from "politics." All policies are in "politics"; and, if felt to be beneficial and skillfully propagandized, they carry their own influence to the voters. The tangible or material inducements that have been frequently mentioned in this study contribute to the strength of the president as a potential boss as well as a leader, especially when an impression is abroad that it is he who is the sympathetic and generous dispenser of bounties. To an extent such an impression may be well founded; for, when the allotment of funds is delegated to him, he has the opportunity to give or deny, to help his friends and penalize his enemies—essentially the same opportunity on a loftier plane that the old-time boss enjoyed. It appears that federal benefits are effective "vote-getters," and the more direct, personal, and needed the benefits are, the greater is their political effect.[5]

The depression weakened conservatism and made the conservative party the minority party.

One of the theories supporting the two-party system is that one party will be conservative and the other radical or progressive. In America each major party has had elements of the Right and elements of the Left; and in neither party has one set of elements consistently predominated. Both parties have moved steadily forward. Yet, since the Civil War, the Republican Party as a rule has been properly termed conservative; and it was clearly so during the depression.

The conservative party naturally enlists a large measure of support from those classes that are most interested in stability and in the maintenance of the status quo; and this party logically emphasizes the promotion of industrial production. Regardless of

Henry N. Dorris, "Hatch Bill Poses New-Type Politics," *New York Times*, July 30, 1939.
[5] George Gallup, "Federal Benefits Held Vote-Getters," *New York Times*, May 20, 1936.

the merit of this viewpoint, an important stabilizing function has been performed by the sustained strength and periodical triumph of conservatism. Up to the depression, conservative government was the rule; radical government, the exception. Conservatism came to be associated with prosperity and in general with "sound" governmental and economic conditions; and American conservatism was progressive enough so that it "kept the jump" on its opponents, or, to change the metaphor, "stole their shirts." Because of the discrediting political effect of the latest depression, the party tactics of the New Deal, and the wide coverage of its policies, the conservative party was loosed from its traditional moorings, thrown into confusion, and reduced to the role of seemingly unimportant and not always consistent fault-finding. Much of the new-found strength of the Democratic Party came from new voters and in considerable measure from groups that were growing in numbers and self-consciousness. It appears, therefore, that the Republican Party is no longer the "normally" majority party. For a parallel to the present situation, one would have to go back to the beginnings and compare the Jeffersonian Republicans with the Federalists or the Jacksonian Democrats with the Whigs.

The party system resisted
realignment.

For responsiveness and effectiveness, parties should change to meet new conditions, problems, and opinions. The change may be brought about by a shift of classes or groups, giving to each of the parties a clearer philosophy and to the holders of the dominant philosophy in each party a more secure control.

Since the Civil War, each party leadership in Congress has ranged from ultra-conservative to radical; frequently a president has been opposed by members of his own party; and at times presidents quite naturally have attempted to eliminate such trouble-makers. Presidential efforts in this connection have not always been successful; and the chances of failure with a resulting diminution of the president's own prestige probably explains why chief executives have in the past interfered so rarely in the nomination of senators and representatives.

In such an undertaking the president comes up against certain traditions and constitutional theories. Dictation of nominations in his party, other than the nomination for the vice-presidency, is likely to make the president look like a boss. Separation of powers and checks and balances imply that members of Congress should be independent of the executive, not unquestioningly and unvaryingly obedient to him. Finally, federalism, "states' rights," and "home rule" are involved. Constitutionally, the senators are set up as representatives of the states and, while the members of the lower house are conceived to be more directly responsible to the people, custom has made them in general delegates from districts. Any "outside interference" with the local choice of local officials is likely to be resented; and this likelihood extends to the choice of senators and representatives.

When, during the depression years, the latest, most thorough, and most open presidential "purge" was undertaken, the President evidently believed that by setting up candidates who would give him "100 per cent support" and by giving them his support in the primaries, he could obtain a more serviceable Congress and as head of his party enforce that discipline which the direct primary system had appreciably undermined. At the same time, by eliminating from the Democratic membership of Congress, as from the executive branch, all who were not "New Dealers," he could measurably advance a realignment of parties and make the operations of the party system a real contest between two basically different schools of thought.[6]

Little progress was made toward eliminating conservative Democrats from Congress. On the contrary, impelled by the business recession and influenced probably by the attempted "purge," the independent middle-class vote was moving toward conservatism. As a result of the primaries and the general election of 1938, Congress retained its quota of conservative Democrats and acquired more Republicans.

After the election of 1938, the President held no less strongly to the theory of party alignment, but seemed more interested in

[6] On this subject, see President Roosevelt's article in *Collier's*, Sept. 27, 1941.

allaying conflict within his party.[7] Others, more conservative than he, had agreed with him on the shortcomings of the party system.[8] Between 1936 and 1940, the major parties did seem to be representing more sharply defined differences of thought. On the whole, however, the slight realignment that occurred followed the pattern of group interests; and the Democratic but conservative Solid South was a formidable obstacle. In 1940, though circumstances must have exerted strong pressure on the minds of conservative Democrats, very few of them openly deserted Mr. Roosevelt.

In the notable cases of realignment in the past, a new party had at first embraced and propagated the ideas that were too extreme for the old leaderships. During the depression years, no new party developed any considerable strength. Much of the discussion of this form of realignment centered around the idea of a national farmer-labor party. Labor organization was supposed to possess the leadership and discipline necessary for cohesive party composition. But labor was itself divided; and the farmers were more so. In any event, neither group had anything to gain by joining a third party, since the party in power was giving them as much as they could reasonably expect from the standpoint of group interest.

Growing electoral independence induced responsiveness; but to what?

Another assumption of party government is that independent voters will be numerous enough to impose on the parties a sense of responsibility and keep them actively bidding for support. A survey in January 1940 indicated that 19 per cent of the voters called themselves independents and that neither party could claim even the nominal allegiance of anything like a majority of the electorate. It appears that more than 11 million voters were unconcerned with party labels.[9] But what is the real meaning of independent voting?

It is probably true that politicians are now more sensitive and bid more actively for support; but the elasticity thus shown is

[7] Address at the Jackson Day Dinner, Jan. 7, 1939.
[8] Nicholas Murray Butler, Address of Sept. 5, 1937, *New York Times*, Sept. 6, 1937.
[9] Institute of Public Opinion Analysis in *New York Times*, Jan. 14, 1940.

not an elasticity of the party as a whole; and the additional responsiveness is to particularistic pressures, not to an independent vote primarily concerned with the general welfare.[10]

*Problems, parties, elections, and government
accented personal presidential power.*

A further assumption of party government is that elections decide in general terms those controversial questions of policy that involve principles. Public problems have now become so complex and change so rapid that it is even less possible than in the past for a presidential or congressional election to decide clear-cut issues and to impose on the victorious party a definite responsibility for carrying out a legislative program. Only the suggestions of such a program emerged in 1932, and some of the principles then clearly stated were abandoned before 1936. In the latter year the results of the election were interpreted by the President to constitute a general mandate for legislation of a highly controversial character which had not been advocated during the campaign. The contest in 1940 was equally inconclusive.

Thus, it appears that a presidential election now means, more than ever, a vague and debatable indication of popular feeling, subject to different interpretations and affording the president as dominant leader a wide latitude for the initiation and manipulation of policies. Elections therefore turn largely on personalities, and, among personalities, those of the presidential candidates are of overshadowing influence. Elections are becoming votes of confidence in the leader. They resemble plebiscites, but not yet controlled plebiscites in which the leader decides the result beforehand.

*The party system does not
unify government.*

A final assumption is that the party in power is capable of making government function as a co-ordinated mechanism, while the minor-

[10] "Observers have not failed to note that, in the midst of attacks on New Deal spending, more than fifty successful Republican candidates for the House lent encouragement to the flock of Dr. Townsend. It did not escape them either that, under the leadership of Senator Lodge, the winning Republican ticket in Massachusetts issued some promissory notes on the Treasury, and that Mr. Lodge has since raised the ante to the old folks at home." Arthur Krock, "In the Nation," *New York Times*, Dec. 22, 1938.

ity party, also unified, is a responsible critic of the administration, thus preparing and proving its preparedness to take power.

At times in the past and particularly in recent years the executive and legislative branches have functioned in many respects as a co-ordinated mechanism. The direct primary system of nomination, however, combined with state and district representation in Congress and complicated by group pressures, has made party discipline and party unity much more difficult either in or outside the government. So far as the majority party is concerned, party government, if it operates, does so only to a slight extent under its own power. The energizing force comes largely from the president. It is infused from above, not generated and sustained in the body of the party. Moreover, presidential domination of a localized party organization and of a localized and normally discordant Congress puts a president under tremendous strain while largely side-tracking the deliberative function of Congress and its development of leadership.

With respect to the minority party, Congress is the sole theater of its national governmental activities. In general, party lines were not drawn in Congress on early New Deal measures. After the elections of 1938, the minority in the House of Representatives attained considerable cohesiveness and established a fairly consistent record; but it did not produce national political leadership. Nor was it produced by the minority in the Senate. In the American system, the candidate for president, before and after his defeat, is considered the leader of the minority party; but at no time during recent years and rarely before has he been a member of Congress bearing responsibility. No defeated candidate during the last hundred years has been a real and effective leader of the congressional minority.

The general conclusion that may be reached from the considerations and developments just mentioned is that, despite changes, some for the better, little if any progress seems to have been recently made toward a clearer differentiation of parties, toward the moral and intellectual integrity of either party, or in general toward making the party system a more serviceable instrument for the achievement of governmental responsiveness and efficiency. In some respects, the system seems to have settled in a new mold which, while inducing rigidity, tends to remove checks on governmental expansion and on distributive policies and to ignore the problems of industrial productivity and stable social progress.

THE DEMOCRACY OF PERSONALIZED PRESIDENTIAL LEADERSHIP

The party system, as well as the government itself, is such as to encourage the development and exercise of personal presidential power.[11] The previous discussion has indicated that the president is not an agent of his party, and that elections do not decide specific policies or, except in a vague way, general principles. The people choose for president a person whose candidacy is more or less an accident or willed by himself; and his election clothes him with a mandate derived from general confidence in him or protest against his opponent. Nevertheless, despite the limited popular control involved in his selection, it is still possible that through him the people may be represented and obtain restrained and intelligent leadership. If so, the shortcomings of the system can be looked upon either as more apparent than real, or as inherent in democracy itself.

The president's representative character and periodical responsibility are increasingly open to question.

The idea that the executive, better than the legislature, represents the whole people was accepted in the early years of the Republic;[12] and subsequent experience has proved the idea to be well founded both in the states and in the nation, in spite of the fact that the executive is a partisan, sometimes merely a factional, and not infrequently a minority, representative.

We showed in the preceding chapter that congressional leadership is predominantly sectional and that, during the depression, such leadership was not only essentially unrepresentative but was,

[11] "[As]matters stand today, presidential power is dangerously *personalized*, and this in two senses: first, that the leadership which it affords is dependent altogether on the accident of personality, against which our haphazard method of selecting Presidents offers no guarantee; and, second, that there is no governmental body that can be relied upon to give the President independent advice and whom he is nevertheless bound to consult. . . ." Edward S. Corwin, *The President: Office and Powers* (1940), p. 316.

[12] W. S. Carpenter, *Democracy and Representation* (1925), pp. 61-63; W. E. Binkley, *The Powers of the President* (1937), pp. 106-07.

on its face, ill adapted to conditions and problems. The workings of the party system, however, have practically restricted the choice of presidents to the industrial and urban Northeast, in the main to New York and Ohio. In a sense, the restriction is undemocratic; but, in another sense, it gives to the presidency at least a superficial adaptation to modern conditions and problems. It has been felt that the president is in a better position than Congress to consider the general welfare and to resist group pressures.[13] He is; but he is a politician, not a sage. As a politician, his intuitions might suffice, if policies were exclusively matters of public opinion; but governmental policy has become so vast and intricate that public opinion also is baffled by it. In the main, it demands of government a general attitude, a general purpose, and certain general results. Opinion creates, rather than eases, the task of public policy-determination. It makes few of the perplexing choices. These are left to political leadership.

Every president has had to choose at times between standing for the general welfare while opposing special groups or yielding to these groups at the expense of the general welfare. Moral and just choices, however, are becoming more and more difficult to make, since it becomes constantly farther beyond human capacity to deal at one time and in one policy with all social problems. They have to be attacked piecemeal; and each piecemeal attack helps or hurts some pressure group. Conditions and trends, therefore, have been making it tempting for a president to manipulate particular welfares.

That presidential action, like congressional, can be paralyzed by conflicting pressures is illustrated in the recent history of railroad legislation. Efforts were made through special committees to work out plans for the rehabilitation of the roads, but with little result. Management and labor did not agree.[14] No comprehensive permanent railroad legislation was enacted.

[13] William H. Hessler, *Our Ineffective State* (1937), p. 26. A pointed example is found in veterans' legislation. The House of Representatives was most quickly and most thoroughly obedient to veterans' pressure; the Senate, less so; and the President least of all. George H. Haynes, *The Senate of the United States; Its History and Practice* (1938), Vol. 2, pp. 1089-93.

[14] President Roosevelt's letter to representatives of management and labor, Mar. 6, 1936, *Public Papers and Addresses*, Vol. 5, pp. 109-11.

As pressure groups develop and assert power over government, the tendency is for them to demand a group-minded president, with a disposition to make promises to groups as such, to offer them material inducements, and to abandon those restraints that are inherent, not only in constitutional morality, but also in just and solvent government and in conscientious leadership. Thus, a president tends, in domestic affairs, to maintain a nominal independence and the appearance of organic unity of leadership by seizing and holding the initiative, while assuming in fact the leadership of different and divergent, but powerful, pressure groups.[15]

As the power of the executive grows, his representative function, such as it is, becomes less genuine. As public opinion loses integration and clarity, as the president's power to control opinion increases, he tends in domestic affairs to become on the one hand more irresponsible, so far as the general welfare is concerned, and, on the other, more handicapped by his own human limitations, more afflicted by the absence of principle, and more subject to the pressures and conflicts that have largely destroyed congressional leadership.

Nevertheless, the results of a personal presidential domination are alleged to be democratizing.

Many believe, as did Woodrow Wilson and others since the turn of the century, that the executive has become in America the effective, central, and superior institution in the legislative process. It is well known that the "strong" presidents are the very ones that the masses have contemporaneously applauded and that history in general has been inclined to vindicate.

Unlike Jacksonian Democracy and the later Populism, the social program of the New Deal was almost bereft of any proposals for democratizing the structure or machinery of government; but nevertheless a democratizing effect would come, it was argued, from the improvement of citizenship brought by an expected higher standard of living, from the restoration of the people's faith in representative government, from the development of the pressure-possibilities of

---

[15] Compare Donald C. Blaisdell, *Economic Power and Political Pressures*, Temporary National Economic Committee Monograph No. 26 (1941), pp. 68, 70.

the benefited groups, and from the imposition of leadership upon them.

The curbing of private economic power seemed to be justified also, not only on grounds of social and economic desirability, but also on the basis of its contribution to political democracy. Movements in American history for social justice, democracy, and purity in politics had been closely and logically associated with fear of monopoly and distrust of concentrated wealth. To Jefferson and later thinkers, commerce, industry, and urbanism were inimical to that self-sufficient individualism which kept alive the spirit of liberty. Left to its evolutionary tendencies economic life seemed to be breeding private industrial dictatorships and class war, either of which, it was agreed, was incompatible with democratic government.

It was argued further that economic power and great wealth had been created largely through special privileges granted by government, and that these privileges, as well as immunity from public regulation, had been won through an oligarchic manipulation of the party system and corrupt control of government. Finally, it was charged that the possessors of economic power were "Fascist-minded," that they were not in fact devoted to a genuine democracy, that they had thus far tolerated free discussion and social legislation only because these aspects of popular government had not interfered with their own power and privileges, that their demands for individualism and liberty were selfish and reactionary, and that their devotion to the Constitution was confined to its least democratic features. From this reasoning it appeared that to restrict the economic and political power of this group was to advance democracy.

THE EFFICIENCY OF PRESIDENTIAL DOMINATION

Partly under the influence of early depression conditions and partly in continuation of previous trends, the assumed efficiency of presidential leadership came to be closely associated with "planning."

Legislation had been in the main a piecemeal process, a concession to popular grievances, a product of pressures and compromises, embodying a growing accumulation of policies and administrative functions and powers that were to a large extent unintegrated and unco-ordinated. Law-making had lacked foresight; it had not kept abreast of the times; in some fields policies were of doubtful wisdom, while in others no policies had been determined in spite of pressing need.

The waste involved in this process had been most concretely manifested with respect to physical matters, public works, and natural resources. These were subject to engineering treatment, to precise, noncontroversial expert handling, expressible in blueprints, maps, and definite long-range programs. The need, the organizations, and the techniques of city planning had been established before the depression; and progress had been made in the application of the principle of engineering planning to highways, other internal improvements, public buildings, and land use. The establishment of the independent commissions, particularly the Tariff Commission and the Federal Trade Commission, and of the budget system illustrated other aspects of the same movement: a substitution of specialization for political opportunism and the development of balanced policy on the basis of information. The research movement, the spread of the scientific spirit, and the development of scientific activities not only contributed to the ideal of planning but were basic to its realization.

The essence of the concept of public planning, then, is the application of the best available intelligence to policy-making. It proposes a measurable elimination of lag, friction, and waste, by setting up "specific technical, workable ways of doing things set in priority schedules of time and spatial relationships."[16] In short, it aims to make policy determination efficient.

Executive leadership, as exemplified by Theodore Roosevelt and Woodrow Wilson, had meant that the president received facts and opinions from others, distilled them into the essence of policy, and compelled or persuaded Congress to crystallize the product into law. The "strong" executive made himself a clearinghouse of opinions and a focus of pressures.

[16] Howard W. Odum and Harry Estill Moore, *American Regionalism* (1938), p. 255. (Author's italics omitted.)

As secretary of commerce, Mr. Hoover had made extensive and successful use of conferences with business leaders and representatives of business and specialized organizations to achieve standardization of products and other desirable objectives. As president he appeared to envisage a mobilization under presidential leadership of the intellectual resources of individuals, organizations, and institutions outside government for the purpose of (1) co-ordinating and integrating opinions and pressures in policy-making, (2) maintaining private initiative, and (3) getting results without enlarging governmental powers.[17]

From the onset of the depression, there was much discussion of social planning and economic planning, not merely the planning of cities and of public works, but an organized, comprehensive, and orderly formulation of policies.

In President Roosevelt's mind, planning had, apparently, two principal features: (1) the programming of governmental action with respect to natural resources and public works, and (2) the creation of a broad structure of policy, each part co-ordinated with the rest, and all designed to realize the social and economic objectives of the administration.

Perhaps the most important features of the national planning movement under Mr. Roosevelt were its shift of attention from private co-operation, emphasized during the Hoover administration, to the organization of research and the co-ordination of research within the framework of government, the attempt to subject governmental research to centralized leadership and a measure of centralized supervision, and the idea that policy-planning is properly an executive and administrative function. The latter view was consistent with the idea of legislative leadership and of administrative integration under executive control.

Experience with "planning"
revealed its difficulties.

The government attempted to organize planning; but probably the most characteristic feature of policy-making, so far as most of the major acts were concerned, was the absence of internal organiza-

[17] *State Papers and Other Public Writings,* Vol. 2, p. 410.

tion, lack of research techniques, and identification with political and personal influences.[18]

The emerging and more difficult problems involved in government planning were, in general, the problems of social science; but, when social scientists are called to participate in government planning, they are compelled to function within an environment that is determined primarily by the president and secondarily by Congress. This environment is political.

The problem comes to focus at the point of contact between planned policy-making and policy determination. While the latter must be political, it is essential that the political authorities shall be guided by factual studies and scientific thinking, particularly essential when the voters seem disposed to confide full powers in leaders or a leader. Such guidance implies a political leadership genuinely committed to the scientific spirit and method and strong enough to convince the electorate that a scientific approach to the general welfare is preferable to the ordinary political processes.

Planning has been given another meaning—broad and detailed governmental control of the economic system. In this sense, it involves a fairly complete substitution of governmental programs for private industrial and agricultural policies and for the determinations of private organization, competition, and economic "laws." The programs thus substituted are administratively formulated and are mandatory on the people, not advisory to the people's representatives. It is in this sense that the terms "economic planning," "social planning," and "a planned society," have been most commonly used. Objections have been based, not alone on the object lesson presented by European totalitarianism, but also on the logic of planned economic control. The workability of such a plan, it is argued, depends on its stability in certain respects and in other respects on its amenability to prompt change in response to changing economic conditions. It cannot safely be exposed to party controversies and group pressures, and consequently its execution as well as its revision must be accompanied by a suppression of public criticism and of opposition parties and groups.

[18] In the informal, but important, "planning" nucleus, known first as the "Brain Trust," and later as the "New Dealers" or the "bright young men," specialized knowledge did not seem to be emphasized.

Probably the most familiar and clearest example of an approach to economic planning in our government is presented by the agricultural policies. Another type of planning is already in a sense or in a measure established, taking the form of governmental intervention at strategic or key points; but, as one student points out, "This interventionism has followed changing political expediencies; its aim has been *political* equilibrium in the democratic society rather than the shaping of the economic process according to a predetermined pattern."[19] Moreover, the development of public economic policy in this country does not demonstrate that the strategic points have always been wisely selected or intelligently manned.

Is the presidency capable of integrating and "planning" policy?

The conception of executive leadership in legislation envisages the president as the final reviewing and integrating authority in the planning process. He becomes the bottleneck through which the plans, adjudged to be scientifically sound and presumably related to one another, are passed on to Congress. Thus, his leadership or domination of Congress, based on popularity and political skill, would be strongly reinforced, under this conception of planning organization, by his command of intellectual resources and intellectual authority.

The questions involved in this development are related to some that were raised in a previous chapter during the discussion of responsibility and efficiency in administrative policy determination. One proposed method of obtaining democracy and effectiveness in that connection is by integrating administration under presidential control. That method would promise the desired results if the president were himself responsible and efficient. If he were democratically controlled and competent to develop and co-ordinate policy-determination, he would theoretically be competent for one or both of these roles—legislative domination or sublegislative control. The two roles do not require the same machinery, or the

[19] Gerhard Cohn, "Is Economic Planning Compatible with Democracy?" in Max Ascoli and Fritz Lehmann (eds.), *Political and Economic Democracy* (1937), p. 27. "Sound planning is not based on control of everything, but of certain strategic points in a working system." Charles E. Merriam, "Planning Agencies in America," *American Political Science Review*, Vol. 29 (1935), p. 208.

same sort of integration. We shall examine first the appropriateness of the presidency with respect to general policy-determination.

The president tends, as we have said, to be more and more subject to group pressures and more and more group-minded. He can guide and integrate the pressures and resolve conflicts in his own mind, if he himself possesses authoritative knowledge and judgment, or if he is willing to put himself in the hands of others who possess these requisites. But the president is not elected as an intellectual authority; and as a politician he cannot hold aloof from any source of judgment that has voting power.

The president, moreover, serves in seven differing capacities: (1) as chief of state; (2) as executive or chief administrator in the narrow sense; (3) as controller of administrative policy-determination; (4) as leader of Congress; (5) as initiator and largely as determiner of foreign policies; (6) as commander-in-chief of the army and navy; and (7) as head of his political party. In all these capacities his work is now more burdensome than in earlier years.

With respect to the planning of administrative policies alone, it appears likewise that presidential control has serious limitations. In a great bureaucracy where administrative policy-determination is extensive, important, complex, and controversial, the capacity of the executive to enforce responsibility on his subordinates is subject to limitations both official and personal. Only a part of the president's time can be devoted to administrative control. If he could give all of it to this task, it would still be impossible for his mind to encompass the whole area and to plumb the depths of the problem of policy.[20]

In recent years the chief executive has seemed at times to be not

[20] "Of course, the advocates of the President's plan strongly urge the claims of administrative *unity* and *efficiency*. But are the two things necessarily synonymous in the case of so vast an organization as the national government? It seems to me clearly not; but rather that efficient administration must in such a case always depend to an important extent upon the expert knowledge and pride in his job of the largely independent bureaucrat. In other words, administration in the sense of the daily task of carrying out the laws and performing the public services for which they provide is a *pluralistic*, not a *monistic* universe; and to imagine the President as a sort of boss of the works under whose all-seeing eye everything takes place, is merely to imagine something that does not exist and never will." Corwin, "The President as Administrative Chief," *The Journal of Politics*, Vol. 1 (1939), p. 44.

so much controlling, or even leading, as presiding over a somewhat heterogeneous council, not unlike Congress itself. It appears that, when bureaucracy becomes large enough, it tends in more or less important sectors to be independent and irresponsible, whatever its nominal control may be. The Cabinet, directly responsible to the president, is no longer adequate to give representative and efficient counsel. The departments, as well as the bureaucracy in general, represent to a large extent various particularisms and focuses of pressures. Moreover, because of its size, its elements of permanence, and the independence or semi-independence of certain of its parts, the bureaucracy tends to show within itself variations and conflicts of opinion, ranging from the extreme Right to the extreme Left. Conflicts are not alone within the membership of boards and commissions: they occur also among the politically controlled departments and agencies.

Presidents, even when the bureaucracy was smaller and less unwieldy, gathered around themselves personally selected groups of advisers. These groups represented the president's personal conception of his needs, rather than the current pattern of public opinion. With an increase both of the bureaucracy and of presidential power, the danger has become real that presidential councils may be controlled by persons who know how to play "palace politics," keeping themselves near to the throne by the arts of friendship rather than statesmanship, making little pretense of any direct responsibility to the public, and not only advising but also manipulating presidential power.

Executive domination, especially in the early years of the depression period, produced speedy congressional action on a number of important bills;[21] but it was not convincingly demonstrated that presidential power or the emphasis on planning actually produced a planned body of public politics.

[21] The banking bill of 1933 was introduced, reported out of committees without amendment, and passed by both houses in one day. The day after the President delivered his economy message, a bill to carry out his recommendations was reported out by a select committee appointed to consider it. One analysis showed that during the first months of the New Deal, "the time of passage of eleven of the President's outstanding measures through the House shows an average period of only three and two-thirds hours debate on each measure." Binkley, *The Powers of the President*, p. 269.

As time passed, less was said about planning. In 1939 problems of foreign relations and defense were becoming critical. They cast additional doubt upon the soundness of any planning confined to domestic policies. In the campaign of 1936 "planning" was made something of an issue and was attacked as undemocratic. In 1940, little attention was given to its meaning or method.

Those who support and those who question the ability of Congress to stand on its own feet can cite sound or unsound action taken at presidential dictation and sound or unsound action taken by Congress when asserting its initiative and independence. For even the extraordinary power of President Roosevelt over Congress has not been complete and continuous. Had Congress been left to its own devices, it is quite likely that legislation from 1933 on would have been different and it would almost certainly have been less in volume and scope. Whether the quality of legislation on the whole would have been better and its effect more beneficial may be questioned. On certain matters, speed was clearly necessary; and, apparently, speed could be obtained only through presidential domination.

While Congress never formally abdicated its constitutional powers and retained technical responsibility for all laws, presidential dictation of policy and domination of the law-making processes did not increase public respect for Congress. Nor was it increased by the delegation of sweeping powers to the executive and the administrative agencies. Nor did the methods used by the President to influence individual members of Congress tend to rehabilitate that body in public esteem. It seemed that the forces that were shifting the legislative center of gravity were working toward a permanent location of legislative initiative and power in the executive. That any president will be capable of democratically and efficiently exercising that power, under the existing constitutional system, is open to serious question.

CHAPTER XI

MANAGED OPINION

Public policies, governmental centralization, bureaucratic expansion, and presidential domination emphasize the relationship between political power and public opinion. How these two forces interact determines whether government is essentially popular or essentially dictatorial. In a democracy, as in other systems, we expect governmental leadership and assume that it will influence opinion; but, when a balance is struck, government must be in reality the servant, not the master. Since public opinion became an important feature of government, dictatorial management of opinion in other countries has generally been accompanied by an extreme concentration of political power in a small group or in one man. In 1787 and even after the Civil War a legislative dictatorship in this country might have been conceivable; but it is so no longer. The trends reviewed in preceding chapters indicate that as legislatures are now constituted, governmental influence over opinion will be increasingly executive influence.

While we are now dealing with a problem that precludes concrete analysis and definite conclusions, we can ask two questions. First, is American government, now more thoroughly concentrated in the president, gaining a larger opportunity to manage public opinion and thus in essence to reduce popular control? Second, are the elements and processes of opinion formation, outside of government, growing in strength and effectiveness, thus presenting to private forces a correspondingly larger opportunity to control official power?

GOVERNMENTAL INFLUENCE

The government's modern role in the management of opinion emphasizes the following: presidential propaganda, federal administrative propaganda, governmental control of private media of publicity, the inherent effect of a vast bureaucracy, interference with educational institutions, and restriction of freedom of speech.

*Presidential propaganda increased
in quantity and power.*

Governmental influence in the depression years was predominantly executive and administrative; and, to the large extent that it was national, its tone was struck, its plane fixed, and its strategy determined by the President. This development need not be interpreted as a calculated expression of a personal will to power. In the past, annual reports, occasional presidential addresses, congressional legislation, debates, and investigations, and the periodical election campaigns might have appeared sufficient to synchronize government with public opinion; but, before the depression, these established procedures had been supplemented by other means of informing and persuading the public. Various circumstances of the depression years tended to make government an extraordinary source of "news" and also to emphasize as never before the administrative need of explaining policies and "educating" the public.

During the depression years, President Roosevelt employed the various media, methods, and devices of publicity perhaps more than any previous president. History may credit him with being the shrewdest and boldest political tactician that had, up to his time, occupied the office. The New Deal represented an unprecedented distribution of material inducements among the more numerous groups and sections of voters; and there can be no doubt of the tremendous political influence that accompanied the distribution. Whether deliberately planned or not, the tendency and in most cases the effect of each allotment and project was to sustain and increase the popularity and influence of the President.

So largely was the President credited with policy determination and so influential were his pronouncements that his attitude and words strongly affected that aspect of public psychology known as "business confidence." Presidential influence not merely played on the surface of politics or economics. It was capable of determining, not only *what* people thought, but, among the more impressionable, *how* they thought.

Aside from the distinctive policies that were advocated or exploited, much of the attitude revealed in presidential propaganda was orthodox. It was similar at various points to the ideas of popular presidential leadership developed by Jackson, Theodore Roosevelt, and Woodrow Wilson and, since 1900, by the "strong executives" generally; but significant differences appeared. Along with the courage, realism, and social sympathy of the presidential appeals, one detects random expressions and recurring undertones that suggest a conception of the relationship between president and people different in many respects from any that had previously been publicly expressed.[1]

Administrative propaganda, largely controlled by the President, grew in volume, range, variety, and implications.

Federal administrative publicity was greater in volume than presidential and more varied and specialized in content; and it was in larger measure related to administrative operations and based on research.

Much informational and explanatory publicity was purposely or incidentally propaganda. Another part, that which issued directly from the political officials of the bureaucracy, was as clearly calculated to influence political opinion as was the President's own publicity; and, except for occasional discordant voices and speeches "out of turn," the administration in its political utterances took its cue from the President.

In 1939, of the more than 900,000 federal employees, 86.6 per cent were in the "field services," that is, scattered over the United States, with a relatively small number stationed in foreign countries. A field force of this magnitude if in direct contact with the electorate, as much of it was, may become an extremely potent means of forming opinion. How many federal employees function positively, actively, and influentially as part of a political or factional "machine," it is impossible to say. The new employees, whether they were or were not in the classified civil service, became in general promoters of administration policies. When, for example, the philosophy of social work became the policy of the President and when social workers were employed to carry out that policy, it was inevitable that they should promote opinion favorable to the President.

[1] *Public Papers and Addresses*, Vol. 2, pp. 14-16, 65; Vol. 5, pp. 8-18, 235; Message to Congress, Apr. 14, 1938.

The Department of Agriculture was in a peculiarly favorable position to influence the political views of the farmers. The department could perform its administrative tasks only by a close contact with individual farmers; and this could be accomplished only by a comprehensive organization. Such an organization, given appeal and prestige by the material benefits that it dispensed, could be used to mobilize the farm population for pressure purposes, and might be virtually transformed into a political machine.

It is a commonplace that bureaus work for their own perpetuation and expansion. This natural impulse to propagandize in their own behalf is all the greater among bureaus that are created in the spirit of social regeneration and are looked upon as revolutionary and "on trial"; and their propaganda is all the more effective when leaders are competent, when material inducements are dispensed, when the self-interest of a private pressure group is exploited, and when the bureaus' clientele has to be "educated" to facilitate administrative operations.

Apart from administrative operations, private groups are brought into contact with federal bureaus. Most of the professional associations include government officials. Public officials figure as members and officers of other types of association, including some of the pressure organizations. Devices to make administration responsible to the people provide opportunity for administrators to influence as well as be influenced. Public commissions and conferences bring public officials and private leaders together. In some cases, government bureaus stimulate the organization of citizens' associations.

Federal publications, as a recent writer says,

probably exceed in number and variety those of any other government or of any commercial publisher. In size they range from pamphlets to ponderous volumes, and in content they vary from articles with a popular appeal to technical treatises of value mostly to the trained scientist. Taken as a whole, they constitute a great library covering almost every field of human knowledge and endeavor.[2]

---

[2] Laurence F. Schmeckebier, *Government Publications and Their Use* (rev. ed. 1939), p. 1. On government publicity in general see also *Investigation of Executive Agencies of the Government*, S. Rept. 1275, 75 Cong. 1 sess., pp. 523-53; James L. McCamy, *Government Publicity* (1939); Laurence Sullivan, "Government by Mimeograph," *The Atlantic Monthly*, Vol. 161 (1938), pp. 306-15;

The printed publications are supplemented by mimeographed material and, of course, by ordinary correspondence. Publicity has also been obtained through press releases, the commercial publication of books written by government officials, magazine articles, letters to newspapers, exhibits, demonstration projects, moving-picture films, stage productions, forums and adult education classes, and radio programs.[3] One should include, too, the "inspired" books and articles, written or ostensibly written by outsiders from material supplied by insiders, and the films and newsreels prepared with the assistance of federal agencies.[4]

No doubt the bulk of federal publicity was needed for popular enlightenment. Federal bureaus were constantly publishing information which could be used against as well as for the party in power. The President himself sponsored studies of a scientific character. In general, government publicity probably had the effect of developing greater public interest in public questions. Indeed, there were those who, from this point of view, felt that the government should do much more publicity work than it did.[5]

On the other hand, a considerable part of administrative publicity could fairly be interpreted as partisan, factional, or personal. To the extent that they were engaged deliberately in such propaganda, federal agencies were doing at the taxpayers' expense what the political party was supposed to do out of its own campaign fund. To the extent that this propaganda strengthened the party in power, the latter obtained an undue and improper advantage over the opposition.[6]

Schmeckebier, *The Statistical Work of the National Government* (1925); E. Pendleton Herring, "Official Publicity under the New Deal," and Elisha Hanson, "Official Propaganda and the New Deal," *The Annals*, Vol. 179 (1935), pp. 167-86; W. Brooke Graves, "Public Reporting in the American States," *Public Opinion Quarterly*, Vol. 2 (1938), pp. 211-28; T. Swann Harding, "Informational Techniques of the Department of Agriculture," *Public Opinion Quarterly*, Vol. 1 (1937), pp. 83-96; Charles A. Beard and Mary R. Beard, *America in Midpassage* (1939), pp. 595-616.

[3] The federal theater project and the adult education classes sponsored by the Works Progress Administration were terminated in 1939.

[4] See Beard, *America in Midpassage*, pp. 596-601.

[5] National Advisory Committee on Education, *Federal Relations to Education* (1931), Pt. 1, p. 76.

[6] Herring, *The Annals*, Vol. 179 (1935), p. 174.

Mainly for purposes of economy, attempts had been made by Congress to control administrative publicity by law,[7] but without conspicuous success. Bureaucratic propaganda was to an extent self controlled by its own lack of integration; and, in the measure that governmental propaganda returns eventually in the form of pressures, unintegrated propaganda contributes to the disintegration of policy.[8]

It was proposed to integrate in the President control over the "informational" services;[9] and a step in this direction was taken when Congress in 1941 authorized annual appropriations for the United States Information Service and defined its duties, thus to

[7] Employment of "publicity experts" is forbidden by the act of Oct. 22, 1913 (38 Stat. 208, 212), unless funds are "specifically appropriated for that purpose."

The House Committee on Appropriations, reporting in January 1938 on the Independent Offices Appropriation Bill for 1939, said:

"The Committee views with disfavor the tendency to expend disproportionate sums for the printing of publications, often on high-priced paper and under expensive covers, or the preparation of press releases, magazine articles, broadcasts, motion pictures, etc., the primary purpose of which is to build up a public demand for the services of the agency issuing the publicity. There has been some improvement in this respect, but the committee believes a substantial reduction of outlay in this quarter can be effected by many of the agencies without diminution of service." (H. Rept. 1662, 75 Cong. 3 sess., p. 3.)

The Treasury and Post Office Departments Appropriation Act for the fiscal year ending June 30, 1940, prohibited the executive departments and independent establishments from sending through the mails postage free any informational material, with certain exceptions, unless in response to a request. 53 Stat. 654, 683.

[8] "The present isolated, atomized organization of federal publicity offices has been remarkably ineffective in combating the hostility to government as a stereotype. It has spent its energies in promoting the programs of segments, often of segments within the same subject of operations. . . ." McCamy, *Government Publicity*, p. 245.

[9] "If the Bureau of the Budget is to be developed into a serviceable tool for administrative management to aid the President in the exercise of over-all control, it needs greater resources and better techniques. . . .

. . . .

"A division of information should be established to serve as a central clearing house for the correlation and co-ordination of the administrative policies of the several departments in the operation of their own informational services, and to perform related duties. The United States Information Service might well be transferred to this division. . . ." President's Committee on Administrative Management, *Report with Special Studies* (1937), pp. 17-19.

For an argument against centralization of government relations with the press, see Arthur Krock, "Press vs. Government—A Warning," *Public Opinion Quarterly*, Vol. 1 (1937), pp. 45-49.

On co-ordination of federal publicity, see *Public Opinion Quarterly*, Vol. 1 (1937), pp. 87-94.

some extent facilitating presidential control of administrative propaganda.

Many means of controlling private media of publicity
have become available to the government.

Government is not only conducting propaganda and counter-propaganda and is, in other ways, engaged in the direct management of opinion; but also it is now in a better position to influence or control private media of publicity.

Criticisms of the press and denunciation of conservatives by the President and his subordinates were in the nature of a verbal preventive or protective war. Destroy confidence in a source and you destroy the influence of propaganda emanating from it. It is possible to reward or punish the press, or portions of it, by alterations in the mail rates; and it has been alleged at various times that the low rates at which newspapers and magazines are carried in the mails amount to a subsidy.[10]

The Post Office Department, incidental to its administration of the postal service, is called upon to exclude from the mails certain classes of communications. In most cases, the action taken by the department is clearly in the public interest. Occasionally, however, a publication may have been denied the use of the mails because of a single article or a picture or series of pictures which were allegedly obscene or scurrilous, or because of supposedly subversive views.[11]

The National Labor Relations Board is engaged in a task that brings governmental power to bear at critical points on the structure and processes of opinion. It strengthens labor pressure on employers and weakens employer pressure on labor, going so far as to prevent anti-union propaganda on the part of employers. Opportunities for the control of private publicity are enjoyed by the Federal Trade Commission, incidental to the general administration of its business regulatory functions, in particular its enforcement of legislation applying to advertising. The secretary of

[10] *New York Times,* Jan. 8, 9, 1938.

[11] For various charges of attempted intimidation of the press by administrative agencies, see report of address by Elisha Hanson, general counsel of the American Newspaper Publishers' Association, *New York Times,* May 20, 1939.

labor under the immigration law possesses an extraordinary power "to restrict personal liberty and freedom of individual action of human beings."[12] Income tax returns have been used for other than fiscal purposes.[13]

The Federal Communications Commission, charged with the regulation of radio, has power to classify stations, prescribe the nature of the service to be given, assign frequencies, determine the location of classes of stations or individual stations, regulate the apparatus to be used, make regulations necessary to prevent interference, establish areas or zones to be served by any station, and make rules applicable to broadcasting, records, programs, etc. The Commission grants and revokes licenses to stations. The federal laws prohibiting monopolies and restraint of trade have been made applicable to the manufacture and sale of radio apparatus; and, in case a licensee is found guilty in a court of violating such laws, the court may revoke the license, as well as impose the other penalties provided by law. The Commission's specific powers are, in the main, technical. It may, according to the law, exercise these powers "as public interest, convenience, or necessity requires." The law forbids the Commission to exercise any power of censorship and prohibits any regulation that interferes with the right of free speech; but it also provides that no person shall utter by means of radio communication any obscene, indecent, or profane language. The Commission has made the content of programs one of its criteria for the renewal of a license.

The Commission, obviously, is vested with discretionary authority that may easily be abused. It has been publicly charged that partisan control of the licensing authority, combined with the fact that licenses are granted for short periods, produces, in effect, a partial administration monopoly of the air, since the radio companies, it is alleged, cannot run the risk of offending that power on which their lives depend. It is a rule of the Commission that rival party candidates should be given equal opportunities to use the microphone. Nevertheless, the President, as president, is favored.

[12] *Annual Report of the Secretary of Labor, Fiscal Year ended June 30, 1939,* pp. 213-14.

[13] *Federal Register,* Vol. 4, p. 2025; Vol. 5, pp. 194, 4444.

A vast modern bureaucracy may inherently and
unconsciously control opinion.

For the purpose of policy-making, as well as for the administration of policies, experts, scientists, and intellectuals have multiplied in the federal service. While this mobilization of brains may leave much to be desired, nevertheless the intellectual resources of the national bureaucracy have increased, and in various directions its prestige is enhanced. Enhanced prestige may have in some sections of opinion a real though undefinable influence.

Moreover, a bureaucracy redirects and to an extent suppresses the opinions of its employees. Individuals, when they become employees, are affected not only by legal curbs on their political activity, but also by the mere fact that they hold public jobs. The tendency is in part to silence and neutralize them; in part, to turn them into protagonists of the government's policies. As the government's personnel increases and as opportunities in public employment widen, it does not seem far-fetched to believe that this sort of governmental influence may contribute to the formation of quite definite political attitudes, especially among young people and more especially among those in training for the public service. Already the belief is widely held that "radicals" of a certain type should not be employed by government. If such "radicals" are excluded from government employment, as to an extent they are, or if a radical government should exclude "reactionaries," would a sensible person aspiring to the public service be likely to express either "radical" or "reactionary" opinions? How extensive this indirect and largely unconscious intimidation is cannot be estimated; but it may be considerable and may be expected to increase with the growth of a centralized national bureaucracy. One safeguard against it lies in the scattering of governmental power; but federalism and local self-government are becoming relatively weaker, and necessarily so.

Further potentialities of government-controlled
higher education appeared.

College and university students during the depression years were almost equally divided between the publicly and the privately controlled institutions; and the total educational and general expenditures of the two classes of institutions were about the same. They differed, however, with respect to the sources of their receipts. The public institutions derived about 69 per cent of their support from public funds and about 16 per cent from student fees, while the private institutions received 37 per cent of their income from endowment and from gifts and grants and about 50 per cent from student fees.

During the depression, it was charged that government, while liberally subsidizing its own institutions, was jeopardizing the sources of support of the private universities and colleges (1) through taxation, which would have the effect of reducing gifts and grants, and (2) through inflationary policies, which would depreciate the purchasing power of fixed income from endowments.

If, as some suggested, these institutions were to depend relatively more on gifts and grants and relatively less on general endowment funds, the tendency might be to specialize the private institutions according to the interests of particular donors. On the other hand, if student fees were to be further increased, it would seem that the private institutions would lose students and become more than ever restricted to serving the sons and daughters of the rich.[14]

The public institutions are exposed to an undefined measure of governmental control, while the private institutions, so long as they depend on private support, are substantially independent of such control. It is difficult to say that either class of institutions is more devoted to academic freedom than the other. To the extent that dependence or subservience exists, it would tend to be political

[14] A comparison of enrollments in 1933-34 and 1935-36 does not show much relative change. Of the resident enrollment in all institutions, the privately controlled had 49.8 in 1933-34 and 49.2 in 1935-36. In all institutions except teachers' colleges and normal schools, the privately controlled had 56.4 in 1933-34 and 55.2 in 1935-36. On the other hand, excluding teachers' colleges and normal schools, the percentage attending privately controlled institutions declined from 64.3 in 1921-22 to 55.2 in 1935-36. "The shift to the publicly controlled institutions is thus seen to be rapid." U.S. Office of Education, *Biennial Survey of Education*, 1932-34, Bulletin 1935, No. 2, p. 34; *Abridged Statistics of Higher Education*, 1935-36, Bulletin 1937, No. 2, pp. 12-13. See Report of Office of Education, in *Annual Report of the Secretary of the Interior, 1939*, pp. 72-73.

See also Harold G. Moulton, and others, *Capital Expansion, Employment, and Economic Stability* (1940), pp. 96-104.

in the case of the public institutions and economic in the case of the private. In both classes, special conditions or relationships might influence attitudes.

In this period governors again attempted to control the boards of state educational institutions, and, through the boards, the presidents and faculties. Mississippi, Louisiana, and Wisconsin furnished publicized instances of such interference. The federal government, too, because of the financial aid and administrative supervision that it gave to the land-grant colleges, was in a position to control to some extent research and teaching. Military training in colleges and universities offered a possible further means of governmental educational control. Moreover, during the depression, "for the first time in the history of public education in the United States, the Federal Government advanced funds directly to individual schools, or as wages to individuals for engaging in educational work."[15] The extension of adult education, discussion classes, and forums during the depression, to the extent that these were either educational or propagandistic, represented an enlarged opportunity for basic control by the federal government.[16]

Governmental restrictions on freedom of opinion have been in the main potential or indirect.

The growing power of the federal government and its increasingly close relation to the processes of opinion-formation created a

[15] U.S. Office of Education, *Federal Aid for Education 1935-36 and 1936-37*, p. 11.

[16] Certain "assumptions" on which the "philosophy" of adult education was said to be based included the following: "Educational opportunities for adults constitute a necessary protective device for a democratic form of government. . . . It is a public responsibility to provide educational opportunities for the study and revision of thought relative to social-economic problems that are occassioned by changing conditions in like situation. . . ." U.S. Office of Education, *Adult Education*, Bulletin 1937, No. 2, pp. 6-11.

Stanley High, "America Talks It Over," *Reader's Digest*, April 1938, pp. 73-75. "Suppose we could transport our forums to Germany, to Italy, to Russia, what would happen to them? The answer seems clear. They would be suppressed as dangerous propaganda. Dangerous propaganda for democracy from the point of view of the non-democratic state. Then good propaganda from our own point of view? Obviously." Mary L. Ely, *Why Forums?* (1937), p. 213.

"Soap boxes are too cheap in New York to justify the cost of maintaining forums. We stopped forced feeding and the program just died of inanition." Col. B. B. Somerwell, quoted in *New York Times*, May 9, 1939.

substantially new situation with reference to the civil liberties. Government had not deliberately adopted any definite policy of suppression or infringement. The more serious threat was coming insidiously through the extension of the regulatory and service functions and the multiplication of contacts with individuals, through the sharpening of group conflicts, and through the control of government by particular viewpoints. Private groups have been quite willing to suppress opinions disagreeable to themselves; and government has now become so large that its branches and agencies are analogous to pressure groups, competing and maneuvering with each other and the private groups for leadership, influence, aggrandizement, profit, and power.[17]

As the scope and objectives of administration widen, its requirements penetrate at different points into the area of opinion. These administrative invasions are incidental to broader policy objectives; and, in many cases, their aim is to protect the public against private misrepresentation, in the absence of any other means of protection, or to protect certain groups, assumed to be otherwise defenseless, against intimidation by the economically powerful. In some instances, the infringements illustrate the advance of governmental paternalism and in others merely excessive administrative zeal; but, in general, it appears that the tendency is to treat the idea of free opinion as subordinate or secondary to social justice and economic control.

Many of the discretionary powers of the bureaucracy can be used for purposes of intimidation. Punishment or the threat of punishment has been used to swing individuals and groups into line. In the case of individuals, punishment by government officials may be nothing more than a "snub"; in the case of a group or a section it may be a withdrawal of actual or prospective benefits; in the case of corporations or of the capitalist class, it may be taxation or regulation.

---

[17] "In this country the coercion of pressure groups on men and institutions, not excepting the pressure on and by government itself, threaten impartial investigation and uncolored statements of results. Institutions, and, what is worse, individuals, feel the menacing pressure of governmental potentialities even worse than acts, overhanging them in areas in which such constraint has never gone before." From address by Owen D. Young, quoted in *New York Times*, May 8, 1940.

In the totalitarian countries, government propaganda and the various regulatory and intimidatory devices of the bureaucracy would lack effectiveness were it not for the repression and terrorism engineered by the special political police. America has had no such institution and its ordinary police are markedly decentralized. Several departments of the federal government, however, have developed special investigational agencies. Of these, the Federal Bureau of Investigation comes nearest to being a national police force.[18] It is possible also to strike indirectly at opinion through the prosecuting function. According to the press, the American Civil Liberties Union in April 1940 had found a dozen recent federal and state prosecutions that provided basis for an accusation that criminal statutes were being used for "ulterior political purposes."[19]

That the federal government in recent years has deliberately inflicted discriminatorily punitive measures is not proved. It has been felt, however, that "big business" as a whole and certain corporations and individuals had been selected as special objects of vindictiveness. The existence of the feeling may have been sufficient to produce an effect.

In the federal government, the threat, if there was one, to freedom of opinion was still largely potential. In general, the Constitution and the Supreme Court were, as in the past, effective restraints on governmental action infringing the civil liberties; but, as in the past, occasional instances showed that judicial power could be used with questionable effect on individual rights. With respect to the executive branch, intolerance, such as it was, was directed against conservatism and private economic power, in favor of the less articulate classes with whose demands the administration sympathized. The idea also seemed to be gaining strength that the corporation as such had no right to use its funds, collected from the public, for the expression of opinion, though it was apparently considered legitimate for an individual or a governmental authority to use funds similarly collected for the same purpose.[20]

[18] Arthur C. Millspaugh, *Crime Control by the National Government* (1937).
[19] *New York Times*, Apr. 7, 1940.
[20] Corporations had been prohibited from contributing to campaign funds.
"Even where a utility speaks and spends directly and openly against Government ownership it raises the question to what extent a publicly granted monopoly

With respect to overt attacks on freedom of opinion, Congress, more than the executive, laid itself open to criticism. The Committee on Un-American Activities illustrated the possibilities of abuse inherent in legislative investigation. The investigating committee is equipped, if it be so minded, to intimidate as well as enlighten public opinion, for it is armed with power to subpoena information and punish for contempt, able to dispense with judicial impartiality and rules of evidence, act as prosecutor rather than judge, exercise practically unlimited inquisitorial powers, and command publicity.[21]

In state and local government, events revealed some disturbing likenesses between the techniques of American bosses and European dictators. In two notorious instances during the depression period, a boss attempted to suppress freedom of opinion.[22]

POSSIBLE CHANGES IN PUBLIC OPINION

It is evident that enlarging opportunities exist for governmental management of public opinion. Such opportunities are available to state and local governments, Congress, federal administrative agencies, and, in greatest measure, the president. These opportunities have not been fully employed; and their employment is not always conscious and deliberate; but that the opportunities exist, and are increasing, places on government, particularly on the president, the duty of exercising leadership and power in a heightened spirit of

---

may properly use funds collected from the public to perpetuate itself through control of public opinion." *Utility Corporations*, S. Doc. 92, 70 Cong. 1 sess., Pt. 71A, p. 4.

"In effect the National Association of Manufacturers is a vehicle for spending corporate funds to influence the opinion of the public in its selection of candidates for office. It may be questioned whether such use of the resources of corporate enterprise does not contravene the well-established public policy forbidding corporations to make contributions in connection with political elections." From recess report of Senate Civil Liberties Committee, *New York Times*, Aug. 15, 1939. The second "Hatch Act," passed in 1940, prohibited any campaign contribution in excess of $5,000.

[21] With respect to new legislation, certain limited legal controls over the sources of propaganda and pressure have been clearly justifiable. For example, by an act of June 8, 1938, all agents of foreign principals engaged in publicity work in this country are required to register with the Department of State. The intention and effect of the act are evidently to bring into the open previously anonymous sources of foreign propaganda.

[22] The reference is to Huey Long and Mayor Hague.

restraint. To citizens generally is presented the need for a more vigilant, subtle, and penetrating supervision of public activities.

We shall turn now to the elements and processes of opinion-formation outside of government, asking whether these have been growing in strength and effectiveness, thus presenting to private forces a correspondingly larger opportunity to counteract official influence and control governmental power.

Were fundamental attitudes changing?

It is too early to draw significant conclusions relative to recent changes in popular attitudes. What the Lynds said of Middletown[23] may be more or less applicable to the entire country, namely, that "basically the texture of culture had not changed."[24] The Lynds' latest study, however, was made in 1935.[25] It may be that during the next five years the changes that were earlier "disguised by the thick blubber of custom" broke to the surface and produced more palpable effects. It would not be conceivable, however, that the attitudes of those adults who suffered relatively little from the depression would be greatly changed. The significant and lasting effects were doubtless imprinted on the mental and emotional make-up of children and youth, the unemployed, migrants, and others who in various ways were caught in the toils of abnormality and maladjustment.

The concentration of responsibility in the national government, the giving of confidence to it, and the reality of the impact of depression policies on the lives of individuals created during the early years and perhaps permanently a greater popular interest in public affairs. This stirring of political thought was in part attributable to national governmental leadership; and it was believed to be one of the real gains of the time.

The depression brought also an increased supply and use of information. In the function of supply, both the radio and the movies

[23] Muncie, Ind.

[24] Robert S. Lynd and Helen Merrell Lynd, *Middletown in Transition* (1937), pp. 489-90.

[25] It might also be pointed out, though not in disparagement of the Lynds' excellent study, that it was made from the sociological viewpoint and apparently without an adequate testing of the relation of economic and social attitudes to the working of the economic system.

were utilized. Statistics of newspaper, magazine, and library circulation indicate that during the depths of the depression the American people, or some of them, did considerably more reading than before 1929. While much of the increased reading was of fiction, "serious" books were also in greater demand.[26] Popular interest in history and economics apparently rose above any high mark previously set. It is impossible to say, however, that this development was matched by increasing popular ability and determination to discriminate between the sound and the fallacious. In general, these years were not marked by any convincing demonstration of enlarged political capacity on the part of the American people.

The depression itself, along with the policies and activities of government, undoubtedly contributed to habits of thinking that tended further to break down the characteristics traditionally associated with individualism. Long before, these characteristics were becoming less appropriate to the conditions of modern life. Individual liberty as an emotionally active concept appears now to have lost much more ground to the idea of security publicly rather than individually guaranteed. Americans, at least from 1932 to 1937, seemed more willing than ever before in peacetime to accept discipline under a persuasive leadership. This change was most evident and possibly of greatest political significance among the farmers and in the rural sections, from which, in the main, had come the democratizing movements of the past.

If the feeling and appropriateness of individualism have been declining we should hope for a working compromise between the extreme of individual self-sufficiency or independence on the one hand and the extreme of passive following or regimentation on the other. An approach to such a compromise would be indicated by an intensification of the spirit of co-operation and an elaboration of its techniques. The fact of social and economic interdependence is probably now more generally admitted; but the fact is so complex that its acceptance can hardly become to any appreciable extent an individual motivation. In all likelihood, individuals in the mass, recognizing the fact of interdependence and the need of co-operation, are

[26] See Lynd, *Middletown in Transition*, pp. 252-60.

the more disposed to leave to government the responsibility for dealing with the fact and meeting the need.

Although new and influential associations and movements appeared and a few novel associational objectives were actively propagandized, the pattern of social organization in its larger aspects remained essentially unaltered. Certain organized groups grew in numbers and strength. The trend toward association on a national basis persisted; but no marked progress seems to have been made through private initiative toward the integration of specialized organization. One may hazard a guess that the specialized associations were becoming less important compared with the growing influence of the organized interest-groups and of the government. The net effect of other developments was apparently to deprive private association of much of the meaning that de Tocqueville and others have attributed to it.[27] Notwithstanding tonics administered by the federal government, local face-to-face discussion showed no reassuring signs of revival.

One may take note, however, of certain developments in the field of recreation and entertainment. These, in pioneer days, had been neighborhood enterprises, spontaneous, personal, individualistic, and co-operative; but, later, technology and large-scale organization introduced mechanization and mass-production methods into leisure-time pursuits and certain forms of cultural expression. The movies, the radio, the automobile, chain-newspapers, and syndication were more or less similar in that they represented commercialization, standardization, and uniformity, along with a degree of technical dependence and passivity on the part of the consumer or user.

The depression years seem to have been marked, however, by wider popular interest and active participation in recreation, in musical and theatrical production, and possibly in writing. Individualistic games were more extensively played, not merely witnessed. The multiplication of local orchestras, of civic theaters, and neighborhood playhouses might also indicate a return to individual

[27] Among such developments were the radio, increased dependence on gifts and grants for financing, and a possible loss of fluidity and adaptability due to the institutionalizing or institutional affiliation of associations.

participation, spontaneity, initiative, and private non-commercial co-operativeness. Perhaps to some extent these movements, like recourse to the movies and the radio, represented escapism and a diversion of time and interest from social and political problems. Perhaps they signified a decline of materialism—the exploration of a new and more worthy way of life. How far they can be construed as favorable to popular government is problematical; the paths of art or of recreation and of democracy are not always parallel.

Of considerable political significance was a movement in literature and art featured by social realism and "social evangelism." This tendency "was more widespread among the young and rising —and frequently jobless—intellectuals than among the older and better established."[28] According to Allen, "the new mood was most widespread in New York"; but the Beards point out as significant "the wide distribution of skills and powers throughout the country."[29] Social sympathy, tinctured with political radicalism, was also strongly evident in poetry.

Whether or not this literary movement was merely a sign of emotional release, whether it accentuated or blurred class cleavages, whether or not it indicated a growing spirit of revolt, it possibly bore in its political aspects some such relation to the demands for social justice that "muck-raking" at the turn of the century had borne to governmental reform. The case for social justice had now passed from the abstract to the concrete, from the area of easily recognizable needs to the outer fringes of social neglect. The extension and intensification of social realism, unless merely a phase of artistry or a by-product of a transitory governmental leadership, meant that distributive policies, with their political and economic implications, had not yet approached any definable limits.

The depression years appeared to bring additional recognition of the value of youth. The "accent on youth" was carried from social life, fashion, and industry into college administration and politics. Akin to this tendency was an inclination to apply to the ponderosities of education and government the method of trial-

[28] Frederick Lewis Allen, "Since Yesterday: The Social Climate of the Nineteen-Thirties," *Harper's Magazine*, Vol. 180 (1940), pp. 177-85. See also Beard, *America in Midpassage*, pp. 623-727.

[29] *America in Midpassage*, pp. 663-64.

and-error rather than the customs formed out of accumulated experience.

In the formation and assertion of character, as well as in the associational life of the country, women were important from the standpoint of numbers, positive activity, and influence. In the direct face-to-face promotion of social welfare programs and ideals they seemed to be more uncompromising, more persistent, more genuinely enthusiastic, and, on the whole, more effective than men.[30] It was said that Americans had become "soft"; and this change was attributed by some to feminine influence. This influence was unquestionably great, and its content was more emotional than that of men. It is quite likely that the public influence of women tended to emphasize social justice rather than economic enterprise, security rather than liberty.

Before the depression the shift from individualism had been accompanied by a release of minds from socially imposed restraints. In general, the appeals of morality and of tradition were, apparently, continuing to lose force. Religiously and perhaps racially, Americans might be becoming more tolerant; but increasing tolerance did not seem to include economic theory and political philosophy.[31]

Some signs appeared of a religious reawakening. Attacks on religious institutions abroad and indications of religious intolerance at home provoked defensive reactions and some assertions of clerical leadership.[32]

Yet, it is not at all clear that the depression itself or the depression policies of the government gave any larger place in American culture to "social values more noble than mere monetary profit." A constant and dominant role was played by money as a symbol of justice, as a subject and instrument of public policy, as an object of group pressure, and as politicians' bait. If anything, the nobler values—"the joy of achievement," "the thrill of creative effort,"

---

[30] On women as leaders, see Ordway Tead, *The Art of Leadership* (1934), pp. 86-94. On women's organizations, see Bessie L. Pierce, "The Political Pattern of Some Women's Organizations," *Annals*, Vol. 179 (1935), pp. 50-58. On the campaign of the National League of Women Voters against patronage, see *Public Opinion Quarterly*, Vol. 1 (1937), pp. 119-23.

[31] Lynd, *Middletown in Transition*, p. 426.

[32] For example, see *New York Times*, Jan. 28, 1938.

"the joy and moral stimulation of work," "honesty," "honor," "sacredness of obligations," "faithful protection," and "unselfish performance"[33]—were subordinated to the idea of a primarily materialistic redistribution.

Public leadership, especially that of an attractive and popular "strong executive," produces a wide, an apparently deep, and possibly a durable impression on the minds of people, particularly of the young. When a president has served three terms, the persons who come to voting age have been under his influence and in a measure educated by him continuously since the age of nine. They may have slight recollection of or experience with any other equally compelling political example. Under such circumstances, it is the part of those who are concerned with fundamental trends to ask with regard to this pre-eminent influence whether its effect is to enhance the dignity of the presidential office, elevate the plane of public discussion, inculcate intellectual honesty, and contribute to a deeper faith in democratic institutions. Does it distract attention from the substance of policies to the tactics by which they are "put over"? Does it imply and encourage popular acquiescence rather than popular initiative? Does it set a dubious example to private propagandists as well as to future presidents? Does it clarify or obscure the fact that democratic government is a co-operative enterprise—an intricate and far-reaching one—not a man, and that it is established on principles and operated by forces that are far more important than any single personality?

The feeling for freedom of opinion appeared from some angles to be weakening.

The years of domestic crises were marked by increased private organization and activity aimed at combating intolerance and protecting the civil liberties. Nevertheless, political manipulation of persons on relief, along with the popular support won by the intolerances of Mayor Hague, Huey Long, and Father Coughlin, showed that, among large numbers, the habit of freedom might yield to material inducements, to demagogic appeals, or to political

[33] The phrases are quoted from President Roosevelt's first inaugural address. *Public Papers and Addresses*, Vol. 2, p. 12.

strategy. Civil liberty was prized most by those groups whose demands were unsatisfied and who were striving to make their opinions socially and politically dominant. The demand for liberty of opinion was closely bound to group interest. The problem of civil liberties almost always arose incidentally. Thus, it was intertwined with the labor conflict, religion, sex, morality, child welfare, peace, order, and convenience. Viewing unrestrained private propaganda as a danger to freedom of speech, some proposed government censorship[34] or counter-propaganda by government, thus leaping from the frying pan into the fire.

The guarantees of free thought and free speech—not merely the legal guarantees but also those rooted in the public mind—were divested of their former simplicity. Considerable evidence appeared in support of Grenville Clark's observation that

. . . large elements of the population have lost what I may call the "feel" for civil liberty that so preeminently characterized the Revolutionary generation. It is a far cry from the time that Edmund Burke said of the Americans of 1775 that "they snuff the approach of tyranny in every tainted breeze."[35]

Private scientific leadership advanced; but its possibilities were not yet sufficiently realized.

Research was both demanded and encouraged by conditions during the depression. Economic breakdown, widespread and persistent unemployment, agricultural maladjustment, critical pressures upon

[34] Max Lerner proposed federal regulation of anti-social propaganda by a board "wise in the way of words, tolerant of their latitude, but so tenacious of the ethics of the thinking craft that they could recognize the spurious and dishonest." In the last resort, the board could ban "material that is poisonous and spurious." *Ideas Are Weapons* (1939), pp. 23-24.

"As against the dangers of a supine public under the control of propagandists and commercial advertisers, at least one suggestion may be offered. This is a proposal for the development of a great national bureau of publicity. Through the growth of a judiciously handled intelligence and entertainment organization directed by the state (to include federal broadcasting, syndicated films, and other services), a great deal might be done, it would seem, to arouse the public to freer, more enlightened activity. The aim of such a bureau would be the collection of information on all socially important subjects and its dissemination to the public by means of the various scientific and artistic devices of the day. . . ." Marie Swabey, *Theory of the Democratic State* (1937), pp. 130-31.

[35] From address before American Newspaper Publishers' Association, *New York Times*, April 28, 1938.

government, the governmentalizing of social problems, unbalanced budgets, the expansion and centralization of public activities and powers, the obscuring of liberty—these emphasized the baffling complexity of the "unseen reality," while the propagandizing of panaceas by individuals and groups and the quick acceptance of novel ideas by government and groups presented to social scientists an unusual and serious challenge.

Except in the tax-supported agencies, research, as in the past, was dependent for its financial support on private endowments, gifts, and bequests. Apart from endowments, grants from foundations continued to be the most important means of financing private research. The aggregate capital resources of the foundations did not appear to be decreasing and their total assets were possibly about equal to the endowments of all privately controlled universities and colleges. After 1934, foundation grants appeared to be on the increase; and a larger proportion of such grants was going to the support of research in economics, government, and public administration.[36] In foundation grants, as in university teaching, the shift of interest to public administration was an outstanding development; and in this field foundation grants were an important aid in the establishment and operation of a number of private associations and agencies.

Gains appeared in the application of the scientific method and spirit to public problems. Scientists, physical, natural, and social, were revealing fresh evidence of a feeling that they were in part responsible for increasing social complexity and that scientific discovery and technological invention might be employed to destroy the civilization that science had created and, along with it, the scientific spirit itself.[37] Contemporary attacks on democracy were also seen as attacks on science; and scientists bestirred themselves in the defense of intellectual freedom, of political democracy, of intelligence in politics, and of the scientific faith.[38] To the extent that

[36] Raymond Rich Associates, *American Foundations and Their Fields* (1939); Harold Coe Coffman, *American Foundations* (1936).

[37] In 1937, the American Association for the Advancement of Science began a series of five conferences on "Science and Society." See H. G. Moulton, "Science and Society," *Science*, Vol. 87 (1938), pp. 173-79.

[38] For public expressions of these views by scientists, see *Science News Letter*, July 3, 1937, p. 3; May 7, 1938, p. 298, Aug. 20, p. 117, Sept. 17, p. 181, Dec.

this bestirring is socially influential, it may mean a partial return to social leadership of some of the intelligence formerly diverted to material advancement.

In the sector of administration, as well as in the broader fields of government and economics, certain analyses and interpretations were symptomatic of a spread of scientific imagination in the social sciences and of a gathering revolt against fixed patterns, cut-and-dried "plans," preconceived principles, unproved theories, orthodoxy, and classicism. Political science found fresh materials for analysis and interpretation in farflung areas.

Direct contacts increased between public authorities and students of public problems. At all levels of government, surveys and special studies were made by presumably impartial scholars and experts.[39] The universities were setting up bureaus or institutes of government or public affairs, sometimes specially endowed.[40] In the state and municipal governments but most notably in the federal government, university professors and members of research institutions were increasingly called upon to fill official positions. Private institutions and agencies co-operated with government departments and bureaus in the financing and prosecution of special studies. Steps were taken to make public-private intellectual co-operation organized and continuous.

Was the promise of mass-education to be fulfilled?

From what has just been said one can hardly draw the conclusion that education won its "race with catastrophe," that the method and spirit of science were yet in greatest possible measure controlling and meliorating the processes of democracy. Social change and the confusions and tensions resulting from it seemed to be developing more rapidly than scientific reinforcement. There is little reason to believe that the immediate economic and political leadership of the

---

24, p. 406, Dec. 31, p. 419; Jan. 7, 1939, p. 4, Jan. 14, p. 23, Feb. 18, p. 99, Sept. 30, p. 214, Dec. 16, p. 389, Dec. 23, p. 406, Dec. 30, p. 419; Jan. 20, 1940, p. 42, Apr. 27, p. 261. See also Swabey, *Theory of the Democratic State.*

[39] Scientists in general were now pretty well distributed over the entire country. The geographical center of the scientific population was near Columbus and Cincinnati. *Science News Letter*, Aug. 12, 1939, p. 105.

[40] As at Princeton, Virginia, Pennsylvania, North Carolina, and California.

pressure groups was becoming less subjective or more receptive to scientific direction or that the mental habits of the people were rapidly changing. Intellect was not yet, nor did it appear to be becoming, the main driving force in social behavior. It still seemed to be true of man, as it was amply demonstrated in Germany if not in America, that "mere rationalism leaves him unsatisfied."[41]

More or less restricted in the beginning to the "three R's," the function of the schools had expanded to include the physical and mental health of the child, his home activities, manual training and domestic science, vocational education, agriculture, the arts, play and sports, safety, and in a few instances automobile driving. More and more the education of children had come to be looked upon as an easy route to almost any desirable social goal; and little by little legislatures had loaded the schools with various special tasks and ceremonies. The pressure groups had their own conceptions of what kind of "social order" should be taught.

To the lay observer, tangible progress in certain directions seemed to be under way, continuing trends that had begun before the depression. Regimentation was slowly breaking down. Efforts were made to give children individual treatment. More opportunity was being accorded to the exceptional child, as well as to the retarded and handicapped. The schools seemed to be appreciating the national need for leaders. Curricula gave greater time to the social studies. The teaching of American history and "civics" emphasized the development of democracy and the actual workings of government.

Adult education, conducted by the Works Progress Administration, as well as by state and municipal agencies, appears to have reduced illiteracy and accomplished vocational readjustments.[42] Generally commended was the work of the Civilian Conservation Corps. The young men in this body, besides accomplishing useful public works, submitted to an unusual and probably beneficial educational experience.[43]

Those who guide the higher learning were experiencing on their plane much the same questioning and stirrings of conscience that

[41] Irving Babbitt, *Democracy and Leadership* (1924), p. 68.
[42] U. S. Office of Education, *Adult Education*, Bulletin 1937, No. 2.
[43] The same, pp. 28-35.

roused the lesser educators to words and action. The purpose and content of higher education were widely discussed. Somewhat radical experiments have been undertaken. It is evident, on the whole, that the colleges and universities are endeavoring to give their students, including those in the professional schools, a broader cultural background and are attempting, like the elementary and secondary schools, to perform a selective function, with an eye on the need for intellectual leadership. Much more attention is given to the social studies, particularly economics and political science, and, in the latter, public administration is increasingly stressed.[44] In these branches, students have been showing unprecedented interest.

Special questions were presented with reference to the small private college. Apart from its financial plight, which was serious, it was meeting, not only the competition of the universities, but also in some sections that of the publicly controlled junior colleges. In general, the small college was becoming a "feeder" to the university,[45] gaining in freshmen but losing in upperclassmen, thereby possibly growing weaker in "college spirit" and alumni loyalty. Small colleges, particularly in the West, had been predominantly denominational, and, stamped with special religious and moral standards, had possessed a peculiar independence and had emphasized non-specialized types of public service.

What was happening to education during the depression years, so far as it affects the minds and characters of individuals, will bear fruit in the future. Was this vast effort to produce, any more than in the past, stable, discriminating citizens and sound, honest, politically effective leaders? Was education setting up adequate defenses against undesirable management of opinion?

*The volume and techniques of private propaganda
were evident, its effects problematical.*

Propaganda probably increased in volume during the depression, a natural result of the tensions of the time and of the larger role

[44] Charles S. Ascher, "Expand Teaching of Public Service," *New York Times*, Feb. 6, 1938. The most conspicuous indication was the founding, through a gift by L. N. Littauer, of the Harvard Graduate School of Public Administration.
[45] U. S. Office of Education, *Abridged Statistics of Higher Education, 1935-36*, Bulletin 1937, No. 2, p. 15.

played by government. Partly because of the developed interest in social psychology, partly because of the extensive use of propaganda by authoritarian governments, and partly because of the radio, the power and potentialities of propaganda were generally appreciated.

But the dangers in propaganda may be and probably have been exaggerated. Much of it is futile. Some defeats itself. A part is cancelled by counter-propaganda. The best of it fails when it attempts too much. It has been demonstrated in numerous instances that the objectives of a private organization can be gained without stooping to misleading publicity or to illegitimate or undue pressure. Some opinions deepen and spread, until finally they win universal and unquestioned acceptance; but others fail to gather momentum under constant pressure and propaganda. Prohibition seemed to be a trend, and it achieved in a constitutional amendment the same triumph as woman suffrage; but, unlike woman suffrage, it met reversal. One difference is that once woman suffrage is won the pressure necessary to maintain it is intrinsic in it. Pressure is not intrinsic in prohibition. It might be if all wets were disfranchised, or if everybody suddenly lost his liking for liquor.

Political influence is produced not merely by calculated communication but also by the complicated conditions of society. The sources of a person's attitude or of his opinion are frequently undiscoverable. Often they are unknown to him. Influence may proceed only indirectly or incidentally from a person or group and it may be unintended, accidental, or even unconscious. An event or a condition may exercise tremendous influence of its own weight.

Some of the devices identified with objectionable propaganda are probably necessary if political discussion is to be carried on at all and reach the multitude. Some of these devices are harmless, and others, not so innocent, have little effect on opinion.

With reference to the objective effects of propaganda, it is not so much the total quantity or average quality that is of greatest practical concern as it is the result obtained when, at any given time, a balance is struck. If an imbalance exists, it is not exclusively an imbalance among sources. The most serious imbalance is probably among ideas. During recent years good government has not seemed to depend so much on an alert public opinion as on the alertness of competing group opinions and on their freedom of access to essential channels of communication.

Private media of publicity have vast
political significance.

The American newspaper continues to be primarily a news-gathering and news-disseminating agency;[46] but in its editorial columns and sometimes through the suppression, presentation, or coloring of news it endeavors to influence political opinion. Even when faithfully reproducing speeches and reporting events it is a carrier of propaganda. From 1926 to 1937 newspaper circulation substantially gained, despite increasing competition from the talkies, the radio, and magazines. Much was said of the waning influence of editorial opinion on the voters. The fact is that editorials had long before ceased to exercise much political influence.[47] During the depression an increasingly important role was played by the columnists. In general, the importance of the newspaper in opinion-formation appeared to come chiefly from that which it transmitted rather than from what it originated. As a transmitting agency, the daily press has been steadily improving.

Among media of propaganda, the radio has now captured a unique and resourceful position. So important is the new method of political appeal that a "radio voice" is included among the desirable, if not essential, qualifications of a presidential candidate. The radio appears to be more centralizing and nationalizing in its operations and effects than the press; and more than other media it emphasizes and encourages personal leadership. It appears that the decline in local face-to-face discussion may be compensated for to some extent by the mass-contacts established through the radio; and the possibilities in this connection are enhanced through successive presentations of controversial views, radio debates, and radio "forums."

The motion picture, like the radio, aims primarily at entertainment; but it may carry propaganda.[48] The conflict in the movies

---

[46] On the relation of the press to political influence, see O. W. Reigel, "Propaganda and the Press," *The Annals*, Vol. 179 (1935), pp. 201-10.

[47] Alexis de Tocqueville, *Democracy in America* (rev. ed., 1900), pp. 187-88. James Bryce, *American Commonwealth* (new ed., 1921), Vol. 2, p. 277.

[48] See Beard, *America in Midpassage*, pp. 581-616.

between the artistic and entertainment function on the one hand and their use as a medium of propaganda on the other was becoming more evident during the depression years and apparently was not being resolved.

Was the existing private control of media of publicity desirable?

At this point, we state another question that we are not able conclusively to answer. Nevertheless, it raises issues that are directly pertinent to our problem of maintaining a fully and honestly informed public and preserving to private forces adequate opportunity to counteract governmental management of opinion. It is obviously necessary that neither governmental nor private propaganda should be eliminated. Both should continue in the proportions required by democratic and efficient government. Protagonists of governmental propaganda asserted, however, that the media of propaganda, as well as its sources, were controlled by a few holders of industrial and financial power, that their purposes were ranged against those of a government representing the masses, and that this monopolistic private control was essentially selfish, in effect deceptive, and even anti-democratic.

Newspapers, most magazines, the radio, the motion-picture industry, and book-publishing (in large part) are privately owned, commercial, profit-making enterprises.

The tendency toward local newspaper monopolies continued,[49] requiring for their establishment, especially in the cities, a substantial investment of capital. The business of non-local newsgathering is more nearly monopolized than is the newspaper publishing business. The important news-gathering agencies, such as the Associated Press, the United Press, and the International News Service, are few in number. These are, however, service associations controlled, at least nominally, by the member-newspapers. As a class, newspaper owners probably tend to think along the same lines as "big business." Many newspaper publishers are independent of outside economic influence; but, naturally, they are not independent of personal, social, and institutional biases.

[49] Alfred McClung Lee, "Recent Developments in the Daily Newspaper Industry," Public Opinion Quarterly, Vol. 2 (1938), pp. 126-33.

The moving-picture business is largely controlled, so far as production is concerned, by a few corporations. In spite of the common assumption that the class-feeling or economic attitudes of the producers or the demands of the international market cause the discouragement or suppression of films dealing with certain subjects, the evidence is not altogether clear.[50]

Radio, unlike the other two media, is in a measure a natural monopoly; and broadcasting facilities must, from their very nature, be owned by a relatively few individuals or corporations or by the government. Because of the restricted ownership of broadcasting stations, the question is pertinent whether freedom of speech can be preserved on the air and political censorship avoided.[51] Difficulties are introduced by the fact that radio time is necessarily limited and certain forms of censorship over programs have to be imposed. The radio has probably stimulated rather than reduced newspaper circulation; and the broadcasting of speeches serves as a useful corrective of bias and inaccuracy in the press; but it was stated in the spring of 1940 that newspapers possessed a proprietary interest in one-third of all licensed radio stations.[52] Thus, the possibilities of reciprocal control through press-radio competition were apparently diminishing.

In spite of a partially monopolistic private control and of a probable general sympathy with "big business," these media are not necessarily able to manage opinion or suppress freedom of opinion; and they are not necessarily disposed to use such power as they possess selfishly, anti-socially, or undemocratically. Whether competitive or monopolistic, they are to a large extent controlled by their subscribers or audiences. A measure of control is coming from professionalization and professional standards. Correctives are supplied by books and magazines. Public meetings, forums, discussion groups, and adult education classes, especially when conducted under private auspices, are useful means of counteracting dishonest, biased, or misleading publicity.

[50] For a discussion apparently based on this assumption, see Beard, *America in Midpassage*, pp. 585-616. Compare Arthur L. Mayer, "Who Wants Good Movies?" *The Nation*, April 20, 1940, pp. 511-12.
[51] See "Propaganda on the Air," in *Propaganda Analysis*, Vol. 1, No. 9 (June 1938), pp. 1-4.
[52] *New York Times*, April 25, 1940.

Even if no such checks were operating, it still would not follow that the identification of press, radio, and movies with "big business" presented a serious danger to democracy. Private industrial and financial power, such as it is, is still unintegrated and largely competitive.

The depression and the individual losses and exposures that accompanied it left the industrial leaders and the financiers, especially the latter, temporarily isolated in popular disrepute. Partly due to this fact, partly because they were made scapegoats and subject to an almost unremitting political barrage, partly because their material interests seemed jeopardized by governmental policies, and partly because of the added power and favored position of organized labor, class-feeling and solidarity among business leaders tended to intensify.

Nevertheless, even among the relatively small number of the wealthiest and economically most powerful, it is difficult to believe that the dominating characteristic is an unmitigated Bourbonism. The Bourbons, it should be recalled, had everything to lose and nothing to gain from revolution. So far as power is concerned, most American business leaders have, apparently, little either to lose or to gain from a shift of economic control; for they can shift with it, provided the political system remains democratic. On the other hand, if they are to face the prospect of a proletarian revolution or a proletarian dictatorship, there can be little doubt of their position. They are unable to see any possibility of reconciling their conception of democracy with communism. In the end, it is possible that attitudes of business leaders will be determined, not so much by what they possess or want to retain, as on the kind of approach that it made to a close politico-economic relationship, if such a relationship develops.

In the newspaper business, group interest, as well as devotion to liberty in the abstract, places editors and publishers among the most active champions of freedom of opinion and, so far at least as their own enterprises are concerned, among the most determined opponents of political interference. Yet, the evidences, especially in the daily press, of a considerable psychological unity, if not class feeling, relative to governmental and party policies, does present a problem.

For, during the depression, it was political power that was acting indirectly as the most effective check on the private owners of publicity media. A national government antagonistic to big business had effective methods of influencing public opinion, regardless of newspaper opposition. To such an extent did the President himself make the front-page and the headlines that he was able successfully to play the reporters against the owners and editors. But what would happen if and when the holders of economic power gained control of government? Would the public then enjoy as fair a presentation of opinion?

The discussion in this chapter does not end with a definite and comprehensive conclusion. We have been dealing with a balance of forces and on each side are complex, intangible, and variable elements. The strength and behavior of the forces may be quite different when a change occurs in the economic situation of the country, its political complexion, or its critical problems. Already, in fact, the world crisis has put the question of managed opinion in a new light. The most that can be said, perhaps, is that those entrusted with political power have a larger opportunity than in the past to manage opinion. The forces depended upon to control political power do not appear to have experienced an equally rapid course of strengthening. Government's opportunity, too, is capable of concentrated exploitation.

If this opportunity should be fully exploited, would public opinion any longer be really free, and would our public authorities, despite electoral formalities, be genuinely responsible to the people?

CHAPTER XII

THE CONSTITUTION AND STABILITY

The latest time of test brought extraordinary public emphasis on an alleged pressing need of breaking with the past. President Roosevelt remarked that March 4, 1933 "represented the death of one era and the birth of another."[1] The idea of a peaceful revolution of some sort was evidently accepted by the country's political leadership and met with no general condemnation from public opinion.

More than a century and a half before, the democratic movement, then one of protest and attack, had necessarily asserted the right of revolution. The framers of the Constitution, however, were more concerned with stability. Yet, as far-seeing statesmen, they anticipated change. They knew that new conditions would press upon the structure that they were erecting; but they expected it measurably to resist pressure and restrain impetuous action. Because it was calculated in large measure to satisfy the requirements of efficient republican government, as they appeared at that time, the Constitution, supported by the idea of constitutionalism and protected by the Supreme Court, was to serve as the central stabilizing element in the structure and mechanism of American government.

STATICS AND DYNAMICS

America of all countries became apparently the most dynamic; and its political history unfolded during a peculiarly dynamic age. The prime characteristic of American life was incessant, fundamental, and vital change. For a century our history was dominated by national expansion and individual pioneering; destruction was carried on concurrently with construction; population was rapidly increasing while families and individuals were continually on the move; agriculture spread over the land; and industry transformed social and economic life.

From the start the American people were tinctured with radi-

[1] Address on Mar. 4, 1937.

calism and, judging by the things that condition human behavior, ought to have been the most thoroughly radical or mercurial of all peoples.[2] They had no trace of that social passivity, economic, familial, or tribal fixity, and political neutrality that for centuries maintained stability in the Orient. Americans were never deferential like the British masses, nor docile like the German. America never developed or soon eliminated certain elements that made for stability in the government of England—the Crown, the state church, the hereditary nobility, and the official class. The new republic, especially as it spread over the West, had before its eyes relatively few physical reminders of a past that was institutionally and sentimentally bound to the present and the future, that invoked veneration, and impelled preservation.

Nevertheless, Americans had brought with them to the New World and succeeding generations retained a substantial and essential part of English character and history. They possessed, for one thing, a fundamental respect for law; and they showed much of the Anglo-Saxon genius for political organization, a genius that has generally expressed itself, not in a sudden or brilliant extemporization of institutions, but in gradual and apparently unsystematic evolution achieved by piecemeal changes and due regard for precedents. Thus, it is not altogether paradoxical that the American people should have accepted constitutionalism, the essence of which is restraint imposed by the authority of a law that has exceptional elements of permanence. Moreover, national expansion, progress, and power seemed to confirm the practical wisdom of this choice; and, as time passed, the idea of popular government came to be associated in America with constitutionalism.

The Constitution gathered moral sanctions.

From Washington's administration until well into the twentieth century constitutionalism was one of the transcendent ideas in Amer-

[2] ". . . [The] English kings had planted the seeds of the Revolution when, in their zeal to get America colonized, they had granted such political and religious privileges as tempted the radicals and dissenters of the time to migrate to America. Only historical research could reveal the fact that from the year 1620 the English government had been systematically stocking the colonies with dissenters and retaining in England the conformers." Claude H. Van Tyne, *The American Revolution, 1776-1783* (1905), pp. 3-4.

ican political history. To most Americans the Constitution became to such a degree institutionalized and traditionalized that it was simply taken for granted. It became a symbol; and no small part of its utility lay in this aspect of it. Its symbolism was derived, in the main, from association—partly accidental and largely unconscious—with such ideas and facts as national unity, expansion, and power, material prosperity and progress, and democracy.

In addition to or associated with constitutionalism, America, like every other society, retained and developed extra-legal stabilizers. They may be variously named—folkways, manners, morals, habits, customs, traditions, faiths, ideals, symbols, stereotypes. During the period when they are building up their power to control the thought, speech, and actions of individuals, they represent a precipitation of social experience, a crystallization of collective reasonableness, a relatively fixed consensus of opinion regarding what is necessary and proper.[3]

Law, broadly conceived, represents a crystallization of morals, a formal embodiment of the experience—the moral sense—of the community. The fundamental law is not primarily concerned with the ends of government, except as these are stated, without legal sanctions, in the Preamble. The Constitution is primarily concerned with means. Morality has essentially the same concern. Both subordinate the momentary desires of the individual to general procedures that social experience has proved to be necessary for the accomplishment of permanently satisfactory ends.

Thus, the authority of the Constitution came to rest on an habituation that was acquired by some but inherited by many. It was a tradition, in the best sense of that word; and, from the nature of the case, it could be nothing else. The ultimate sanctions of the Constitution are moral; its support is in the hearts and minds of the people.

[3] Some of the familiar features of the "living" Constitution of America were stated by Freund about twenty years ago, as follows: "Absence of militarism, absence of official caste, decentralized administration, popularized education, great vocational mobility, absence of sharp sectional or denominational antagonism, a very pronounced consciousness of national achievement and promise—these are the things that impress American institutions with their distinctive character, and there is neither any possibility nor any need of giving all of them constitutional formulation." Ernst Freund, *Standards of American Legislation* (1917), p. 183.

The Constitution, serving primarily as restraint,
was expected to be adaptable.

The idea that the Constitution is a flexible instrument to be progressively adapted to changing conditions has been generally accepted; and a signal merit of the original document was its capacity in important respects for adaptation to the developing needs of a dynamic society.

We have demanded from the Constitution both elasticity and rigidity, both a dynamic and a static quality. We have needed and expected two sorts of adaptation: the Constitution to the nation and the nation to the Constitution. It has been our boast that the fundamental law could be stretched, not broken; but the fact is that because of unavoidable circumstance we have had, in that law and in the social conditions that support and modify it, an extremely delicate balancing of forces, one making for release, the other for restraint. The Constitution has had to yield to the pressure of conditions and of popular demands in order to maintain its utility and even its existence; but, were it to yield too easily or too quickly, it would destroy itself by destroying its prestige and undermining the morality that supports it.

Our constitutional system, therefore, embodies a fundamental dualism, a dualism that is inherent in individual personality and in society itself, but peculiarly apparent in the personality of Americans and in American society. On the one hand, the system accepts change, and, on the other, resists it. It yields and it restrains. Should it cease to do one or the other, it would lose its traditional American character.

The adaptive function passed
largely to the judiciary.

When the formal amending process was made difficult and slow, the practical task of adaptation by interpretation was largely shifted to the courts, which also enforced the restraints of the Constitution. The prestige of the Constitution and the strength of constitutionalism, as it had developed in America, depended ultimately on the attitude of the people toward the Supreme Court. To the extent that morality found expression in law, the courts in dispensing justice became the makers and guardians of morals. To this fact, as well as to the solemn decisiveness and ceremonial aspects of judicial procedure, may be attributed the respect in which the courts had long and generally been held. This respect had been naturally accorded in greatest measure to the Supreme Court; and, except for rare and minor lapses, its members and the court as a whole had earned respect.

APPEARANCES OF WEAKENING CONSTITUTIONAL AUTHORITY

Substantially new social and economic conditions had made their appearance or attained magnitude after the Civil War: large-scale industry, urbanism, immigration from southern European countries, industrial conflicts, inequalities of wealth and income, and class and group divisions in the population. To such conditions, in their modern aspects, the letter of the Constitution was a stranger, and a considerable proportion of the population came to lack Anglo-Saxon traditions as well as the American historical background. When the pioneering period was over, the American people gradually awoke to the fact that they were living in a radically changed environment that presented disturbing challenges to old ways of thinking and acting.

Under the impact of the new environment, the constitutional frame of government has steadily dwindled in importance compared with the actual government. Ideas of the proper sphere of government have altered. Much of America's political machinery has been established and is functioning outside the formal constitutional structure. Except to lawyers and other students, the powers, functions, problems, and trends of government appear to have little relation to any specific constitutional provisions.

The development by the judges of a great body of constitutional law, representing in important controversial areas the Constitution itself, has tended in general to strip the instrument of clear meaning to the masses. With respect to the economic functions and policies of government in particular, what the Constitution is in the marginal area of social movement and controversy can only be determined by lawyers and often only by the courts after protracted litigation. The economic functions of the national government have grown out of constitutional provisions that are brief, general, and of disputed meaning; and in many cases it has seemed that a decision one way or the other might be equally logical. In such cases, constitutional law appears to be not a fundamental thing known to and accepted by the people, but rather a result of litigatory accidents and the bent of the judicial mind. Moreover, the judges not infrequently have disagreed or changed their minds.

Nor do the specific provisions of the Constitution cover now so large a part of what are considered fundamental "rights" and "obligations." In recent years we have heard of certain "principles" or "rights," or a "higher law," outside the realm of formal law, to which, we are told, government must or should conform. Much has been said, for example, of the "rights" of labor and of children, of the "duties" of government, that "no American shall starve," that the budget must be balanced, or that capitalism is a part of the "American system."

In popular discussion, the Constitution has tended to become a catchword interchangeable with abstract terms, such as power, democracy, justice, human rights, individualism, liberty, privilege, progress, reaction, liberalism, conservatism. These terms have had different meanings to different men; and they are highly charged with emotion. Consequently, the Constitution itself has become to many—probably to a majority of the people—an abstraction with hazy outlines and variant meanings and with little or no practical significance, except as an expedient for the defense of vested interests.

The entrance of psychology into political science and wider recognition of the strength of underlying dynamic social forces have tended further to obscure the outlines of the Constitution.[4] Thus, it was possible for Felix Frankfurter, as a professor of constitutional law, to write that "the Constitution of the United States is not a printed finality but a dynamic process,"[5] and that it "is most significantly not a document but a stream of history."[6]

The sociological school of jurisprudence, stressing the fluidity of

[4] See Charles E. Merriam, *The Written Constitution and the Unwritten Attitude* (1931), pp. 11-12.
[5] *Mr. Justice Holmes and the Supreme Court* (1938), pp. 75-76.
[6] *The Commerce Clause and the Constitution* (1937), p. 2.

law, including constitutional law, came close to joining those who would subordinate the courts to political power and exclude both legalism and conservatism from constitutional evolution. If legalism is defined as a disposition to interpret the law, as some do the Scriptures, according to the letter rather than the spirit, its objectionable features are easily recognizable. On the other hand, social need is a matter of opinion and this opinion is finally expressed in a democracy through the political, not the judicial, process. Moreover, as we have said, the conscience of the judge is primarily a legal conscience. His prime qualification is or should be judicial temperament, impartiality, intellectual independence, and determination to administer the law without fear or favor. While the judges are in part legislators and as a matter of fact decide political questions, they do so by the judicial rather than the legislative process, with legalistic reasoning and in a measure of isolation from popular pressures.

Nevertheless, as these pressures became stronger, they put greater strain on the judicial assumptions and on the principle of judicial independence; and it was inevitable, when popular thinking and political action had become more realistic, that the Supreme Court should be viewed as a group of men rather than as a mysterious and sacrosanct institution.

Concurrent with and in part related to national prohibition but having manifold causes, crime appeared in the twenties and early thirties to be reaching the proportions of a menace to all law and to the prestige of government itself. In the past, criminal gangs and alliances between criminals and "machine" politicians were fairly common in the large cities; but now rival racketeering enterprises waged private wars against one another, and extended their operations beyond bootlegging, gambling, and prostitution into the sphere of legitimate industry, in some instances dominating labor organizations, terrorizing businessmen, and levying tribute upon them.

Many believed that they were observing in this country as in the world at large a general moral deterioration. As we have noted previously, the tendency of thinking and of writing after 1900, indeed the tendency of the scientific attitude, was one of skepticism, leading to a general disposition to question traditional standards and values. The tendency increased during the twenties and was apparently accelerated by the depression. The scientific spirit, while encouraging skepticism and demanding intellectual freedom, proposed to set up a new morality in the form of intellectual honesty. This morality, if it could have obtained a hold on the populace, would have had an enormous political effect, in that it would have subjected the forces both of change and of stabilization to the control of something more than transitory ideas and expedients. Unfortunately, the scientific spirit and intellectual honesty did not establish their sway over politics.[7] Feeling insecurity, people were no doubt seeking stable and durable foundations for thought and conduct; but, in the political sphere, because of their economic insecurity, they looked to government for relief and protection and were hardly likely in their mood to attach importance to the niceties of constitutional limitations.

Despite the spread and intensification of antiquarian interest, the traditions and precedents inherited from the past were losing their vital hold on the present and were failing, under the challenge of change and complexity, to give continuity to political thinking. As we have seen, certain fundamentals were fading from the party system. The ideas of federalism, of minimized government, and of balanced budgets were either broken down or seriously shaken. The Democratic Party repealed its ancient two-thirds rule. Public life took on unorthodox behavior. Military conscription was introduced in peacetime. International law disintegrated. The tradition against a third term was, at least temporarily, discarded. The magnifying of personal presidential leadership tended to ignore the doctrine of separation of powers and the maxim of government by law. The memorable figures of the past—Washington, Jefferson, Jackson, and Lincoln—were frequently referred to, but apparently in the main to prove almost any case, not for the purpose of showing what they actually stood for or of testing the contemporary validity of their philosophies. We were cutting ourselves adrift from historical anchorages.

From the last decade of the nineteenth century, the environment

[7] See J. Donald Adams, "The Collapse of Conscience," *Atlantic Monthly*, Vol. 161 (1938), p. 3.

had been in process of stabilization with respect to many factors, for example, territorial expansion, population growth, ethnic change, and urbanism. We are still, nevertheless, in process of psychological transition; and apparently we have not yet had time either to create new stabilizing philosophies or to relate and adjust the old to new conditions.

THE "MORALS OF DEMOCRACY"

The theme of President Roosevelt's Jackson Day address on January 8, 1938, was that he, like Jefferson, Jackson, Lincoln, Theodore Roosevelt, and Woodrow Wilson before him, was "working with all his might and main to restore and to uphold the integrity of the morals of democracy." In this speech, however, no reference was made to the Constitution. The "basic morals of democracy," he said, rested on "respect for the right of self-government and faith in majority rule." In his view, those who were violating the morals of democracy were the small minority of economically powerful. On the other hand, his administration was seeking "to serve the needs, and to make effective the will, of the overwhelming majority of our citizens and . . . to curb only abuses of power and privilege by small minorities."[8]

This exposition of the "morals" of democracy seemed to overlook the fact that morality does not consist in doing what we like but rather in subjecting our desires to restraint. Morally viewed, constitutional democracy is an exercise in collective self-mastery.[9] In such a government, the majority has a moral right to make its will effective. But the majority is often made up of fairly distinct minorities. The fact that these minorities are separately satisfied

---

[8] On the practical need of new social values, and new individual goals, see T. V. Smith, *The Promise of American Politics* (1936), pp. 29-47. For Mr. Hoover's conception of moral integrity in government, see his address printed in *New York Times*, Oct. 27, 1937. For another Republican attack on the public morals of the Democratic administration, see Mr. Dewey's speech printed in *New York Times*, Mar. 28, 1940.

[9] "Self-government is not a mere form of institutions, to be had when desired, if only proper pains be taken. It is a form of character. It follows upon the long discipline which gives a people self-possession, self-mastery, the habit of order and peace and common counsel, and a reverence for law which will not fail when they themselves become the makers of law: the steadiness and self-control of political maturity. And these things cannot be had without long discipline." Woodrow Wilson, *Constitutional Government in the United States* (1911), p. 52.

with what the government is doing and that they form an over-powering political combination does not mean that the morals of democracy are being maintained and strengthened. It is felt by many that the results are exactly to the contrary.

Furthermore, in a constitutional democracy the minority as such has moral claims. These were presented by Chief Justice Hughes when he said: "For we protect the fundamental rights of minorities not only in the interests of individuals and minorities but to save democratic government from destroying itself by the excesses of its own power."[10]

The morals of democracy also have roots in economic necessity. During the depression years, whether or not democracy was really "working," the national government, standing for social justice and economic control, was supported by those groups that had most to gain from democracy. The kind of democracy that they emphasized —government directly and immediately *for* the people—no longer appeared in a mood to brook constitutional objections or constitutional delay. But constitutional delay, if applied to distributive demands, may be a means of maintaining the system of increasing production on which an expanding program of social justice depends. Unless such increasing production is reasonably assured, the moral basis for transferring economic power from private to public hands becomes much less clear.

ECONOMIC CONFLICT AND CONSTITUTIONAL STRAIN

In periods of rapid change and acute strain, the rigidity of the Constitution has always been its most apparent aspect. In this country, during the period of exploitation and development, the psychology of adventurous progress was in the ascendancy; but, as a practical matter, the bonds of the Constitution were held lightly under such conditions; and, so long as they did not restrict exploitation and development, were illusorily associated with economic

[10] Address before joint session of Congress, Mar. 4, 1939, *New York Times,* Mar. 5, 1939.

"If democratic institutions are to survive, it will not be simply by maintaining majority rule and by swift adaptation to the demands of the moment, but by the dominance of a sense of justice which will not long survive if judicial processes do not conserve it." Address before the American Law Institute, May 16, 1940, *New York Times,* May 17, 1940.

progress and social justice. In the older sections, individuals who had succeeded in the quest for property and economic power tended to be satisfied with the conditions under which they had won success. They, and the sections that they dominated, tended to grow politically conservative, advocates of the kind of constitutionalism that protected their interests; and they were disposed to use their economic power to make the Constitution mean what they felt it should mean. On the other hand, the strugglers and the less privileged, when confronted by a system that seemed to close the door to individual initiative, adopted as their goal economic rather than political security, change rather than stability, an unobstructed democracy rather than an economic individualism protected by a rigid constitutionalism.

Outside the legal profession, the Constitution during the depression period was apparently held in deepest reverence and was most frequently invoked by those who felt themselves adversely affected by public economic control. This identification of the Constitution with the vested interests and privileges of a minority, largely discredited by the depression and put politically on the defensive, was not likely to enhance the respect of the majority for the fundamental law. When appropriated by particular economic interests, the Constitution was flung into the arena of class and party conflict and the advocates of constitutional restraint, however sincere they might be, were inevitably suspected of ulterior motives.

Moreover, at a time when the groups controlling government were aiming at a redistribution of economic power and income, the Supreme Court became, like the Constitution, the last refuge of those whose interests lay in the preservation of the *status quo*. At such a time, the Court was subject to popular criticism and its position necessarily became delicate and might become precarious. In the course of this study, we have noted other periods in which this situation arose—in the Jacksonian era, after the Dred Scott and income-tax decisions, and at the beginning of social legislation in the states. For law was not only the embodiment of morals; it was also the "specific language of political power."[11] The Constitution,

---

[11] Max Ascoli, "Government by Law," in Max Ascoli and Fritz Lehmann, *Political and Economic Democracy* (1937), p. 233.

the Supreme Court, and democracy had increased in power and prestige at the same time. If the only function of the Court had been to review legislation and if, in doing so, it had uniformly adopted a strict interpretation of the Constitution, the Court would probably have been submerged beneath the rising tide of democracy; for its setup was intentionally far from democratic.

A stable reconciliation of democracy and constitutionalism involved something more than exhortation to the public or to the Supreme Court. The indispensable step was to take the strain off both democracy and constitutionalism.

THE CONSTITUTION, THE COURT, AND LAG

Studies of social trends had revealed various apparent lags; and to these lags were attributed some of our most serious strains and conflicts. Attention was called, for example, to the technological inventions and developments that had created problems faster than society had been able to solve them. The steam engine inaugurated modern industrialism, with mass production by machinery; but the nation had not yet solved the problems created by industrialism. Indeed, it seemed that society was not even keeping up with the additional and subsidiary problems that were continually being created by new technological discoveries and applications.

The existence of serious political lags could not be doubted. It did not follow, however, that all or many of them could be blamed on the Constitution. Political lag appeared in fields where government had unquestioned constitutional power to act. There was lag in legislation and in administration, lag in the exercise of the state police power, lag in the municipalities.

It was largely a matter of opinion whether, how, or to what extent constitutional law had lagged behind public needs. In certain spheres of governmental action, lag was inherent in constitutionalism. Constitutional development was brought about by two processes: amendment and interpretation. Only the latter could be employed by the Supreme Court. The scope of constitutional change by interpretation was limited to litigious cases. The Supreme Court had little opportunity to obstruct or develop the spending power or to block or encourage a reorganization of government. Even on the matters subject to judicial power, the American concept of a written constitution set both legal and moral limits to the possibilities of interpretation. Where these limits were no one could say; but, if the Supreme Court were to recognize no limits, we should have no constitution in the accepted American sense.

The Supreme Court had not been consistently hospitable to legislative innovations, to the new needs created by changing conditions, or to public demands. Few critics of the Court went so far as to assert that the power to annul federal and state legislation had always been used obstructively or unnecessarily. Legislation had not been invariably progressive; and few would denounce the Court for obstructing reaction. For example, the Court had checked numerous legislative attempts to abridge the civil rights of individuals. For its obstructive role in this regard, the Court was generally praised even by its most unfriendly critics.

With respect to economic and social legislation, it was asserted, the provisions of the Constitution were such that the Court could be progressive or reactionary as it pleased and with about equal reasonableness. Nevertheless, it was argued, the Court in recent years had tended to ignore the fact that the economic system was no longer local but national, that the various aspects of the system were intimately interrelated, and that it represented concentrations of power which, unless destroyed, curbed, or regulated by government, were inimical to the welfare of the masses.

The commerce clause had been interpreted broadly, but, the critics declared, not broadly enough or consistently enough. For one thing, the Court had drawn a distinction between intra-state commerce and interstate commerce. It had been reluctant to accept the view that commerce includes not merely transportation, but also the various steps from beginning to end involved in the production and distribution of goods and services. The Court had also been hesitant to give the broadest possible meaning to the congressional power "to regulate." Modern conditions demanded that commerce, that is, the economic system, should be governed. It followed from this point of view that the power should reside in Congress to take any action which it deemed advisable, not only to regulate, but also to promote or prohibit, any economic activity of an individual which affected other individuals.

The "due process clause," it was argued, had also been so interpreted as to protect vested interests and render government impotent. It had been construed by the Court as a restriction on legislatures as well as on the courts and as a protection to corporations as well as individuals. It is possible to cite other clauses of the Constitution which, allegedly, had been construed with the special design of protecting property rights.

The long-run effect of the Court's interpretations, it was charged, was to preserve the individualistic *laissez-faire* theory of economic enterprise, to maintain an unhealthy state of legal uncertainty, to give to the possessors of economic power a measure of immunity from democratic control, and, in general, to create serious lag between social need on the one hand and governmental action on the other.[12]

The fact seems to have been that, in its interpretation of the Constitution, the Supreme Court had been accommodating and constructive and it had also been inflexible and obstructive. For shorter or longer periods, its interpretations and its annulment of legislation had caused political lag. Some of this lag—we cannot say how much—should have been avoided; and it could have been if the Court had been ideally statesmanlike.

Lag in relation to public demands could be ascertained somewhat more precisely; but in this aspect of the matter, too, there was a wide margin in which conclusions could be little better than guesswork. One had to keep in mind that the American Constitution was intended to restrain public opinion. Nevertheless, the Supreme Court's interpretations of the Constitution, in general and in the long run, had complied with the popular will. Sometimes the compliance was prompt, sometimes regrettably tardy.[13] The politically appointed changing personnel of the Court insured its concordance, in the long run, with public opinion. In some specific cases, the delays occasioned by the Supreme Court compelled further and needed deliberation; but more important was the fact that judicial obstruction was implicit in constitutionalism.

Assuredly, in a real emergency delay is dangerous and prolonged

[12] See Edward S. Corwin, *The Twilight of the Supreme Court* (1934), and *The Commerce Power versus States' Rights* (1936).
[13] Dean Alfange, *The Supreme Court and the National Will* (1937), pp. 220-21.

deliberation impracticable. At all times and in all matters, legislative or administrative, promptness and decisiveness are of the essence of efficiency. Yet, speedy action is praiseworthy only when the necessary steps have been taken to insure its correctness. Wrong action is usually worse than no action at all; for it aggravates the situation it is designed to correct and increases the lag or tension it is intended to remove. In not a few instances, quick action—unsound because it was quick—has delayed constructive advance in the solution of public problems. In America, as in other countries, the tempo of discussion was quickening. The majority leadership appeared impatient of deliberation. We were failing to distinguish between reasonable and unreasonable delays.

PRESIDENTIAL ATTACK ON THE SUPREME COURT

The economic and social policies of the national government during the depression years were opposed to the economic and social purposes that had been uppermost in the framing of the Constitution and were equally opposed to those interpretations of the commerce and due-process clauses which, after the Civil War, had been applied by the courts to the protection of corporate enterprises. These policies demanded, therefore, that the Constitution should become more pliable than heretofore and perhaps proportionately weak, in order that the national government might be functionally equipped and powerful enough to be effective in the light of its enlarged purposes.

In the campaign of 1932 there had been a significant interchange with reference to the Supreme Court. In his address at Baltimore on October 25, 1932, Mr. Roosevelt said: "After March 4, 1929, the Republican Party was in complete control of all branches of the Federal Government—the Executive, the Senate, the House of Representatives and, I might add for good measure, the Supreme Court as well."[14] Commenting on that statement, Mr. Hoover asked the following questions: "Does it disclose the Democratic candidate's conception of the functions of the Supreme Court? Does he expect the Supreme Court to be subservient to him and his party? Does that statement express his intention by his appointments or

---

[14] *The Public Papers and Addresses of Franklin D. Roosevelt*, Vol. 1, p. 837.

otherwise to attempt to reduce that tribunal to an instrument of party policy and political action for sustaining such doctrines as he may bring with him?"[15]

In his first inaugural, Mr. Roosevelt spoke of the Constitution as follows:

Our Constitution is so simple and practical that it is possible always to meet extraordinary needs by changes in emphasis and arrangement without loss of essential form. That is why our constitutional system has proved itself the most superbly enduring political mechanism the modern world has produced. It has met every stress of vast expansion of territory, of foreign wars, of bitter internal strife, of world relations.[16]

President Roosevelt had no opportunity during his first term to recreate the Court in his or any other political image. Between 1902, when Holmes was appointed to succeed Gray, and 1932, when Holmes retired, a vacancy in the Court had occurred on the average approximately every eighteen months. In January 1937, about five years had elapsed without a vacancy. In the past, no full presidential term had ever gone by without the appointment of at least one justice. Taft, during his single term as president, had selected five members of the Court. In January 1937, two-thirds of the Court were beyond the retirement age of 70. Justice Brandeis, though the oldest in years, had rather consistently dissented in the past from the more conservative decisions of the majority; and he, with Justice Cardozo, one of the younger members in age and the youngest in service, would be expected to adopt an accommodating attitude toward New Deal legislation. Of the other seven, Chief Justice Hughes and Associate Justices Stone and Roberts could not be definitely allocated to any school of social or political thinking, but were apparently attached, more strongly than Brandeis or Cardozo, to traditional constitutionalism. The remaining four justices, Van Devanter, Sutherland, Butler, and McReynolds, represented that type of judicial thinking which had in general stood for the freedom of individual and corporate activity, limitation of the powers of the government, and the interposition of constitutional obstacles to economic regulatory and social legislation. These justices were all past 70.

[15] *State Papers and Other Public Writings of Herbert Hoover*, Vol. 2, p. 407.
[16] *Public Papers and Addresses*, Vol. 2, pp. 14-15.

During Mr. Roosevelt's first administration, the Supreme Court declared unconstitutional a number of congressional enactments. Other acts were upheld by the Court. Most of the adverse decisions were taken by a divided court; and in these cases dissenting opinions were rendered by the so-called "liberal" justices.

Following the annulment of the National Industrial Recovery Act in 1935, President Roosevelt declared that the decision was probably the most important since the Dred Scott case, imperiling a great part of the structure of national economic control that had been erected since March 4, 1933. The "big issue," he said, was this: "Does this decision mean that the United States Government has no control over any national economic problem?" Should the commerce clause of the Constitution, he argued, be adjusted to the conditions of the present day, when interstate commerce is affected by a wide range of activities which "in the horse-and-buggy age" were purely local? This "very, very great national non-partisan issue" had to be decided, the President declared, "over a period, perhaps, of five years or ten years"; and it might be decided, he thought, without a constitutional amendment.[17]

Thereafter, until his renomination, the President refrained from saying what plan he had in mind for effecting an adjustment between the Constitution and his policies.[18] The Republicans in their 1936 platform pledged themselves:

To maintain the American system of constitutional and local self-government, and to resist all attempts to impair the authority of the Supreme Court of the United States, the final protector of the rights of our citizens against the arbitrary encroachments of the legislative and executive branches of government.

Prior to his nomination, the Republican candidate, in a telegram to the convention, declared himself in favor of amendment, on certain specific aspects of social legislation, if needed reforms could not otherwise be achieved.

The Democratic convention noted in its platform that many national problems could not be settled by state action. An attempt

[17] President's remarks at press conference, May 31, 1935. *Public Papers and Addresses*, Vol. 4, pp. 200-22.
[18] On June 2, 1936, the President, questioned by reporters, refused to say how he expected to meet the situation. *Public Papers and Addresses*, Vol. 5, pp. 191-92.

would be made, it was promised, to meet these problems through legislation within the Constitution; but if this should prove to be impossible

... we shall seek such clarifying amendment as will assure to the legislatures of the several States and the Congress of the United States, each within its proper jurisdiction, the power to enact those laws which the State and Federal legislatures, within their respective spheres, shall find necessary, in order adequately to regulate commerce, protect public health and safety and safeguard economic security.

Thus, the platform declared, "we propose to maintain the letter and spirit of the Constitution."

Though the President "heartily" subscribed to his party's "brave and clear" platform, he remained during the campaign conspicuously silent on the question of amendment; and he suggested no other plan for assuring the constitutionality of New Deal legislation.[19]

No judicial retirements took place. The President, on the basis of his overwhelming re-election, believed that he had received a "mandate" from the people; and, immediately after his second inauguration, he proceeded to focus attention on the constitutional-judicial issue. During the preceding year, he told Congress, there had been "a growing belief that there is little fault to be found with the Constitution of the United States as it stands today. The vital need is not an alteration of our fundamental law, but an increasingly enlightened view with reference to it. Means must be found," he said, " to adapt our legal forms and our judicial interpretation to the actual present national needs of the largest progressive democracy in the modern world."[20]

Within a month, the "means" were found. On February 5, 1937,

[19] "As to the choice of a specific remedy to meet the undeniable fact that the majority of the Supreme Court was in fact legislating on the desirability rather than the constitutionality of laws, none was made during the campaign. There were several possible alternatives of method. . . ." (*Public Papers and Addresses*, Vol. 5, pp. 4-5.) "Some of the laws which were enacted were declared invalid by the Supreme Court. . . . I greet you in the faith that future history will show, as past history has so repeatedly and so effectively shown, that a return to reactionary practices is ever short-lived. . . . I have implicit faith that we shall find our way to progress through law. . . ." Greeting to Labor's Non-Partisan League, Aug. 3, 1936, *Public Papers and Addresses*, Vol. 5, pp. 280-81.

[20] Annual Message to Congress, Jan. 6, 1937.

he proposed to Congress a reorganization of the judiciary and submitted a draft bill for the purpose. In the absence of any retirements,
this bill, if enacted into law, would have meant the addition of six
members to the Supreme Court; and, in the future, the number of
justices would have been variable, ranging from nine to fifteen.

The purpose was to create immediately a majority in the Court
favorable to administration policies. This plan was represented by
its critics to be simply a scheme to intimidate or "pack" the Court.
In the President's view it was necessary to prevent calculated judicial obstruction and misinterpretation. His chief objective, as he
explained it, was "a modernized judiciary that would look at modern problems through modern glasses." If democracy was to function, a way must be found to make effective the will of the overwhelming majority that had spoken in the 1936 election. Moreover,
for the long-run salvation of democracy, speed was essential.[21] Constitutional amendment was represented to be too slow and too
doubtful.[22]

[21] The President asserted: "In this fight, as the lawyers themselves say, time
is of the essence. . . . If we would keep faith with those who had faith in us, if
we would make democracy succeed, I say we must act—NOW!" Address on Mar.
4, 1937.

He declared that ". . . time more than ever before is vital in statesmanship and in
government—in all three branches of it. . . . We can no longer afford the luxury
of twenty-year lags." Address on Sept. 17, 1937.

"To stand still was to invite disaster. Across the seas, democracies had even then
been yielding place to dictatorships, because they had proven too weak or too slow
to fulfill the wants of their citizens. Social forces in our day gather headway with
ever-increasing speed. It would have been dangerous to block too long the just
and irresistible pressure of human needs. Democracy here simply could not be
permitted to fail to function." *Collier's*, Sept. 20, 1941.

[22] "There are many types of amendment proposed. Each one is radically different
from the other. There is no substantial group within the Congress or outside it
who are agreed on any single amendment.

"It would take months or years to get substantial agreement upon the type and
language of an amendment. It would take months and years thereafter to get a
two-thirds majority in favor of that amendment in *both* Houses of the Congress.

"Then would come the long course of ratification by three-fourths of the States.
No amendment which any powerful economic interests or the leaders of any
powerful political party have had reason to oppose has ever been ratified within
anything like a reasonable time. And thirteen States which contain only five per
cent of the voting population can block ratification even though the thirty-five
States with ninety-five per cent of the population are in favor of it.

. . . .

"And remember one thing more. Even if an amendment were passed, and even
if in the years to come it were to be ratified, its meaning would depend upon the

Over the President's extraordinary proposal opposition developed in Congress, crystallized and increased by outside propaganda and by evidences of popular disapproval.

The discussion in its decisive aspects revolved in the main around the questions of judicial independence and presidential power. The Chief Executive had established his primacy in the legislative process. In January 1937 he had proposed an administrative reorganization which, if approved by Congress, would have greatly enlarged his control over administrative policy-determination. The Supreme Court, apparently the last remaining obstacle to presidential supremacy, appeared now about to be subordinated. The President's proposal was defeated.

THE RECREATED COURT

While the President's bill was still before the Senate, the Court already gave signs in its decisions of a change of attitude; and Justice Van Devanter retired. He was followed in January 1938 by Justice Sutherland. When the latter's successor was appointed, the formerly conservative majority was changed to a liberal one. Moreover, in July 1938 Justice Cardozo died; Justice Brandeis retired in February 1939; Justice Butler died in November of the same year; and Justice McReynolds and Chief Justice Hughes retired in 1941. At the beginning of 1940, President Roosevelt had already appointed a majority of the Court; and by the summer of 1941 he had named seven of the nine justices.

The President's appointments were consistent with the views that he had expressed. None of the seven appointees was an old man. Not one had previously been a federal judge. Only two[23] of the seven had held any judicial position; and in both cases it was relatively unimportant and the service brief. At the time of appointment, two were United States senators; one was a professor of law; and the other four were officials in President Roosevelt's administration. No doubt could exist with regard to the "predilections" of

kind of Justices who would be sitting on the Supreme Court bench. An amendment like the rest of the Constitution is what the Justices say it is rather than what its framers or you might hope it is." Address of Mar. 9, 1937. See also President Roosevelt's articles in *Collier's*, Sept. 13, 20, 1941.

[23] Justices Black and Murphy.

any of them. All were known to be in general accord with the President's policies.[24]

The change in the Supreme Court that can be dated from 1937 was not wholly due to the "infusion of new blood." The election of 1936 and the presidential attack in 1937 appear to have had a very considerable effect on the "middle-of-the-road" members of the tribunal. Since 1936, the Court has taken on a significantly different character, in its consistent refusal to hold federal acts unconstitutional, its frequent reversals of past decisions, and its approval of expanded governmental and administrative powers. The recreated court has shown little of Marshall's disposition to enhance judicial prestige. Rather, its policy has been to recognize the limitations of the judicial function. It is evident, too, that the Court has been increasingly reluctant to overrule administrative decisions. The conception of governmental power in the social sphere and national power in the economic, long obscured, now seems almost unreservedly accepted.

QUESTIONS FOR THE FUTURE

The latest movement against constitutional rigidity and judicial supremacy could hardly be adjudged, either from its origin or its results, a manifestation of a genuine and spontaneous democratizing impulse. It may better be characterized as a phase of crisis government, as an aspect of a struggle for political power, or as an effort to realize a conception of efficiency that is not necessarily related to enduring democracy.

Even if the changed attitude of the Court made government momentarily more responsive, it is not certain that the effect will be other than temporary or, if permanent, will in the long run strengthen democracy. The primary source of the change—a source which is manifestly transitory—is to be found in personalities.

Some of the immediate effects are not open to dispute. The Court became less legalistic than it had previously been and more inclined to take into practical consideration the needs of a dynamic society. It may be doubted, however, that the self-imposed limitations on

[24] Other presidents also had made appointments that were, in this sense, "political." It should be noted, moreover, that, on Chief Justice Hughes' retirement, Justice Stone, a former Republican, was appointed to preside over the Court.

the judicial function will be permanently observed. When further change comes in economic and social conditions, in public opinion and in governmental policies, the present "liberal" majority may prove as obstructive as its "reactionary" predecessor. Nor is it clear that the judicial function should be restricted even voluntarily and temporarily. A drastic revision of federalism and an ultimately high degree of centralization appear inevitable; but it may be questioned whether the movement requires a sudden or radical relaxation of judicial scrutiny of legislative acts. It is true that the Supreme Court cannot insure wise legislation or an integrated structure of policy; but it can, within the judicially fixed limits, prevent hasty legislative action and, in cases, compel constitutional amendment. The transfer in effect of greater responsibility to Congress for constitutional interpretation may conceivably have a sobering effect on that body, but it would seem as likely to intensify group pressures on the lawmakers, encourage political opportunism in legislation, and lower the quality and efficacy of public policy.

The tendency of the Supreme Court to withdraw measurably from the field of administrative control seems sound; but it by no means solves the problem of administrative responsibility. Because of this tendency it is all the more urgent that a solution be found. In the absence of a solution, it seems hardly possible that, so far as administration is concerned, the idea of democracy or that of government by law has been strengthened.

"Making democracy work" is more than a matter of power and policies: it is also a matter of process and mechanism. With regard to these latter, little has been accomplished; and no accommodating attitude on the part of the Supreme Court can change the constitutional structure.

It was probably desirable that the Constitution and the Supreme Court should be subjected again to public examination. Social rules tend to live beyond their time. The Constitution is not sacrosanct. Neither is constitutional morality. Any factor in government may be critically examined to find its utilitarian justification, if it has any. The question arises, however, whether it would not have been more logical in this instance from the standpoint of democracy and more fruitful in results to have attempted a solution through the amending process. To be sure, the process is difficult; but if government is being "planned" and if the idea is to "make democracy work," why should not an attempt be made to make the process of amendment more democratic and more efficient?

In conclusion, then, apart entirely from their inevitability or inherent logic, the events of the depression period, so far as they related to the Constitution and the Court, seem to have accelerated rather than retarded the questionable trend away from constitutional restraint. Chief among the more ponderable events were the early inflexible decisions of the conservative justices, the President's emphasis on the elasticity of the Constitution and his attack on the Court, the practical abandonment of the amending process, and the political adaptability, if not pliability, demonstrated at least for a time by the recreated Court.

CHAPTER XIII

GOVERNMENT AND WORLD CRISIS

International situations and foreign relations almost wholly account for our territorial expansion, largely explain the make-up and character of our population, and have contributed in important ways to the conditions and problems of American life. Yet, assuming the foundations and general setting, one can say that the determining factors in governmental evolution have been domestic. In the past, international crises and foreign wars might reasonably be viewed as incidents or episodes, which, in the light of our comparative or apparent isolation and vast national resources, had in this connection no major, continuing, or decisive influence.

The most recent crisis and the Second World War appear to have for us a different and greater significance. The Hitlerian revolution is aimed at the world-wide subjugation of peoples, destruction of democracy, and repudiation of civilized ideals. It is not a limited movement. With it no lasting compromise can apparently be made. No assurance exists that it will break down within the calculable future, unless stopped by superior military force. Hitlerian aggression is now aided by the productive resources of almost the whole of Europe, as well as by Japanese imperialism. Accordingly, the Second World War appears to be in a special sense a decisive struggle, as decisive for us as for other peoples.

Moreover, the long-run meaning of foreign relations and war, in terms of democracy, governmental efficiency, and political stability, has become larger, more vital, and more clearly permanent. The changed meaning is due, primarily, to the total effort called for by modern warfare, the long and comprehensive preparation required for it, the sudden and devastating methods of beginning a war, the range of air warfare, the speed with which aggression may be carried out, and the relative hopelessness of rebellion when once conquest has been accomplished.

It would be obviously futile to undertake in this chapter a definitive appraisal of contemporary developments or to venture sweeping predictions regarding the future. We shall tie the discussion as closely as possible to those general factors that appear to have basic and permanent significance. These factors fall into two divisions: (1) those associated with the conduct of foreign relations, and (2) those associated with military preparations and participation in war.

With regard to foreign relations, the American people may be assumed to have two general objectives: (1) that our foreign policies shall be democratically determined; and (2) that they shall be effective, both immediately and in the long run. In this connection, the questions to be dealt with are: Do we possess in general the essential conditions for democracy, or efficiency, or both? Have we in fact achieved either or both? Do recent conditions and measures tend to make either or both more likely?

With regard to military preparations and participation in war, the primary immediate need is for efficiency; and, when the issues are as grave as they seem today, efficiency is necessary even when it may mean the suspension of some features of the democratic process. We are concerned, therefore, with noting how our constitutional system works in time of war and whether the long-run trends that have appeared in the politics of democracy militate against the achievement of efficiency. Moreover, we are equally interested in the question whether war strengthens or weakens those trends that complicate in peacetime the achievement of democracy and efficiency. In this connection, then, the following questions present themselves: Are the governmental system and the broad recent trends in our political life favorable to an efficient war effort? Does a war effort help to realize democracy and efficiency?

Finally, we are concerned with stability. To the extent that the aims and power of the Axis threaten our existence as a free people and our form of government, we may be in a more precarious situation now than at any other time in our history. We assume, however, that we are not going to be defeated. On this assumption, are the elements making for stability in our government and in our political life being strengthened or weakened?

FOREIGN AFFAIRS IN RELATION TO
DEMOCRACY AND EFFICIENCY

The international system, based on the principle of national sovereignty, is an aggregation of independent states, with no superior central authority. The situation may be termed anarchic. In any case, it is unstable, characterized by competition and conflict as well as by much co-operation. In this situation, the ultimate means of deciding disputes is by the threat or employment of force. The system is undemocratic in the sense that it is not controlled in matters of general effect by a majority of the people concerned or by a preponderant world opinion.

From the beginning of the system, some nations have been aggressively expansionist or imperialistic. The larger present-day democracies, as well as autocratically governed countries, were characterized during the eighteenth and nineteenth centuries, not only by strong nationalistic feeling but also by expansionist or imperialistic policies. At the end of the nineteenth century, the democratic nations had become, generally speaking, "satisfied." The nations that still tended to be territorially ambitious and aggressively imperialistic were, again speaking generally, those that were powerful but had been retarded with respect to the acquisition of territory and the development of democratic institutions.

From these generalities, one might infer that if all nations were democratic and if territorial and economic needs were reasonably adjusted, assuming such adjustment to be possible, international relations throughout the world would be no more difficult and delicate than are, for example, the relations between the United States and Canada. Considering the state of affairs in the Eastern Hemisphere, however, it is evident that any political, territorial, or economic régime, no matter how satisfactory it may be in the beginning, subsequently requires maintenance by force or prompt readjustments. The conduct of foreign relations—or, let us say, world government—is not likely from this point of view to be essentially different in the future than it has been in the past.

We should also briefly note certain changes that have occurred in the spread of war. During the eighteenth century and until the final defeat of Napoleon in the early nineteenth, world wars were the rule. For a century after Waterloo, wars were localized. Since 1914, however, the most isolated conflict seems inevitably to drag in the whole world. The reasons for these changes need not here be examined; but it is apparent that the localization of war permitted piecemeal international adjustments at relatively low cost, and all nations did not have to bear the full strain of international instability. As an alternative to an attempt, which might now be deemed premature, to prevent war altogether, international statesmanship may conceivably find again a way to localize conflicts; but, if the United States participates in this enterprise, its responsibilities in the conduct of foreign relations will hardly be simplified.

It is safe to assume, therefore, that the task of government in the United States will in the future include international responsibilities no less exacting than they have been in the past. It may help to clarify the relation of these responsibilities to democracy and efficiency in government if we ask the following questions: Has public opinion and government in recent years actually functioned democratically and efficiently? Are international questions susceptible to democratic and efficient handling? Are democratic nations inherently inefficient in modern foreign relations? What is the effect of foreign relations on pressure groups and political parties? Are the organization and operation of government in foreign affairs democratic and efficient? Are steps being taken to make government in this field more democratic or more efficient?

*In foreign affairs, we have been
measurably democratic.*

Since the First World War, the American people have shown a greater interest in foreign affairs and have been supplied with a vastly increased volume and much better quality of information and interpretation.

During this period, the United States has had a public opinion on international questions, taking the form, until the Japanese attack upon us, of two general attitudes. The strongest and most widely held reflected the popular desire for peace and aversion to war.

Up to 1939, the organized peace movement was articulate and active. During much of the time, its propaganda, pressures, and lobbying practically dominated public opinion and powerfully influenced political leadership and governmental policies.

The second general attitude has been represented by isolationism, a belief that the security and welfare of the United States are best served by a policy of nonentanglement in the affairs of the Eastern Hemisphere, particularly in those of Europe, and nonintervention in foreign, particularly in European, quarrels. Isolationist feeling has been to a degree sectional, being strongest in the West. America's entrance into the First World War demonstrated the compelling premises of internationalism; but, after acquiescing in the rejection by the Senate of the League of Nations Covenant, the American people seemed steadily to become more isolationist in feeling and more decided against involvement in future wars.[1]

The European crisis, emphasized by the Munich settlement in 1938, marked with some clearness the beginning of a process of change in American attitudes, a process that was sharply accelerated by the fall of France in the summer of 1940. This change was primarily due to events abroad, specifically to the words and acts of Hitler himself. These, if Britain were to be crushed, meant a Nazi movement against or in this hemisphere, bringing at no distant date a direct menace to our own national security. Thus, an unprecedented military defense program was quickly accepted, if not anticipated and demanded, by the American people generally. Public opinion, not unanimously but preponderantly, followed, if it did not precede, a policy of "aid short of war." Public sentiment against American participation in war retained strength;

[1] Many factors contributed: the belief that we had been duped from 1914 to 1917 by foreign propaganda; the allegation that we had been maneuvered into the war by munition-makers and financiers; studies by American scholars showing that blame for the war was not wholly Germany's; gathering distrust of postwar Britain and France, heightened by their failure to pay their war debts to this country; and a marked revival of pacifist sentiment and of organized antiwar activity. The sharpening of economic competition among nations, the emergence of fascism in Italy and of nazism in Germany, and the sporadic outbreak of various undeclared wars served to confirm the feeling that the struggle which we had helped to bring to a victorious conclusion had totally failed either "to make the world safe for democracy" or "to end wars."

but, as an organized pressure group, the advocates of peace experienced disintegration and loss of influence. In general, a shift occurred from isolationism to internationalism.[2]

Fairly in accord with the more articulate public opinion, American foreign policy from 1929 to 1939, as in the preceding decade, sought to deal with an unorganized and unstable international system, charged with the potentialities and prospects of conflict, on a generally isolationist, pacifistic, moralistic, and legalistic basis. Acts of aggression on the part of Japan, Germany, and Italy were met with legal reservations, non-recognition of conquests, diplomatic gestures, warnings, public expressions of disapproval or of sympathetic interest, direct presidential intercession with heads of states, and "moral embargoes."[3]

[2] This shift is shown by the development of majority support for "full" or "all-out" aid to Britain, even at the risk of war, by an increase in the percentage of those favoring convoys, by the decreasing number of those who felt that it had been a mistake for the United States to enter the First World War, and by the growing proportion favorable to American membership in a new League of Nations.

In certain surveys, the Institute of Public Opinion asked the question, "Do you think it was a mistake for the United States to enter the last World War?" The answers are shown below in percentages:

	Mistake	Not a Mistake	Undecided
April 1937	64	28	8
November 1939	59	28	13
December 1940	39	42	19
April 1941	39	43	18

New York Times, Apr. 6, 1941.

In answer to the question, "Would you like to see the United States join the League of Nations?" answers in 1937 were: Yes, 33 per cent; No, 67 per cent. In answer to the question, "Would you like to see the United States join a league of nations after this war is over?" answers in June 1941 were: Yes, 49 per cent; No, 51 per cent.

Use has been made of surveys as reported in *New York Times*, Apr. 21, Sept. 15, 1939; Jan. 5, Mar. 31, May 10, May 29, June 9, 14, July 7, Aug. 19, Sept. 6, Oct. 13, 20, Nov. 17, 20, 23, 29, Dec. 1, 1940; Jan. 3, 22, 24, 29, Feb. 2, 7, 9, 12, 14, Apr. 6, 20, 23, May 21, June 4, 8, 15, 1941.

[3] Reference is to the following policies: co-operation with the League of Nations, but without assuming responsibility; participation in world economic conferences; reaffirmations of interest in the integrity of China; non-recognition of changes in title to territory brought about in violation of Kellogg-Briand Pact; passage of Philippine independence acts; enactment of the Hawley-Smoot tariff; President Roosevelt's effort in May 1933 to obtain "the complete elimination of all offensive weapons"; prohibition of private loans to foreign governments in default to the Treasury; mandatory embargo of implements of war

The crisis in Europe brought a change in policy, as it had in opinion. Gone, at least for the time, was faith in moral preachments and humanitarian appeals.[4] Three courses of national action were adopted: (1) a huge program of military preparedness; (2) international co-operation in the Western Hemisphere, under the leadership of the United States, for "hemisphere defense"; and (3) abandonment of neutrality and the giving of aid to nations at war with the Axis, involving finally naval participation in the "shooting" war.[5]

We can say, therefore, that our foreign policy, broadly viewed, has been determined democratically. Of course, there have been lapses and defects in the process, but perhaps fewer than in the normal process of determining domestic policy. Discussion has not been unduly inhibited by popular hysteria, by the demand for na-

---

to belligerent countries; the Neutrality Law of 1937; relative inattention to national defense; and repeated rejection of American adhesion to the World Court Protocol.

[4] "Since 1931 world events of thunderous import have moved with lightning speed. During these eight years many of our people clung to the hope that the innate decency of mankind would protect the unprepared who showed their innate trust in mankind. Today we are all wiser—and sadder." President Roosevelt in Message to Congress, Jan. 4, 1939.

[5] The outstanding congressional and presidential measures up to July 1941 were: (1) those in connection with the national defense program, including unprecedented appropriations, enactment of emergency tax bills, raising the debt limit, putting the National Guard on a war footing, enactment and enforcement of Selective Service and Training Bill, authorization of President to prohibit or curtail military exports, adoption of production priorities, building of plants for manufacture of war materials, introduction of price-fixing, prevention and settlement of strikes, seizure of plants, organizing of civil defense activities, co-ordination of petroleum industry, extension of training of selectees; (2) those in connection with "hemisphere defense," including inter-American conferences, declaration of non-recognition relative to transfers of regions in Western Hemisphere from one non-American power to another, adoption of the idea of collective trusteeship, steps to improve cultural and commercial relations with Latin America, loans to Latin American countries, setting up a Canadian-American Joint Board of Defense, acquisition of naval and air bases from Great Britain, establishment of Canadian-American economic committee; and (3) those in connection with the policy of aid to victims of aggression, including revision of neutrality law of 1935 as amended in 1937, substituting cash-and-carry provisions for the embargo, "freezing of funds," loans to Finland and China, use of the "moral embargo," passage of the lease-lend bill, appropriations for lease-lend operations, various retaliatory acts, seizure of foreign ships in American ports, opening of Red Sea to American ships, establishment of North Atlantic patrol, occupation of Iceland, the Churchill-Roosevelt meeting, aid to Soviet Russia, "shooting" orders to American warships.

tional unity, or by the necessity of suppressing subversive elements.

Moreover, the fact that dictatorship challenged democracy and placed democracy on the defensive no doubt helped to maintain a popular attitude in this country favorable to tolerance and the civil liberties. Like these liberties in general, intellectual freedom and the spirit and method of science are among the fundamental values menaced by Hitlerism and destroyed wherever Hitlerism has prevailed; and American intellectuals and scientists responded in various ways to this gage of battle. In 1933, the American Association for the Advancement of Science formally expressed "grave concern over persistent and threatening inroads upon intellectual freedom which have been made in recent times in many parts of the world."[6] In subsequent years protests and declarations issued from this association and from other organizations, groups, and conferences.[7]

The general course of opinion and policy represents ineffectiveness or serious lag.

World inefficiency, demonstrated by the recurrence of war, may be attributed to world conditions; but, so far as the United States has possessed opportunity and power to control these conditions, responsibility for them belongs to American leadership, opinion, and policies. Assuming that we have had opportunity and power, we may conclude that we have been ineffective.

Some of the major opinions and policies that the United States adopted between 1919 and 1939 were palliative and others constructive; but, on the whole and in the light of their underlying theory, they stand condemned for inconsistency, lack of realism, misapprehension of trends, absence of plan, and eventual failure. They were evidently ill adapted to a world in which nations still possessed sovereignty and commanded force, and in which cunning, ruthless, and powerful imperialisms were again on the march. Since 1938, American opinion and policies have been measurably adjusted to the immediate international realities; but we are now

[6] *Science News Letter*, Aug. 20, 1938.
[7] *Science News Letter*, May 7, Aug. 6, 1938, and Feb. 18, 1939; *Key Reporter*, Vol. IV, No. 2 (spring 1939); *New York Times*, June 1, Sept. 9, 1940.

compelled to employ at colossal cost (itself an evidence of in-efficiency) the very means that typify world inefficiency in order to avoid paying a more extreme penalty for our previous errors. Moreover, in view of the slowness with which a general reorienta-tion of public opinion could be brought about, prior to the direct and flagrant attack in December 1941, the adjustment necessarily took the form of piecemeal action, which, even at a very late date, resulted in lag, inconsistency, and confusion.

On the matter of neutrality, for example, the Secretary of State, as late as July 1939, pointed out that legislation then on the statute books encouraged "a general state of war both in Europe and Asia" and that the results were "directly prejudicial to the highest in-terests and to the peace and to the security of the United States."[8] The revised neutrality legislation of that year eliminated provisions that would have meant practical discrimination in favor of Ger-many, but imposed restrictions on the movement and arming of American merchant ships. The lease-lend law, subsequently passed, in effect abandoned neutrality for a policy of aid to the victims of aggression. It appeared, however, that the revised neutrality law was blocking the full effectiveness of the policy embodied in the lease-lend legislation. The Administration therefore proposed to Congress the repeal of those provisions of the neutrality act that prohibited the arming of American merchantmen; and the re-strictions both on arming and on movement were finally removed by Congress late in 1941.

International questions are intrinsically unsuited to democratic and efficient handling.

International problems are more remote and more imponderable than domestic questions, more complicated by irreconcilable claims. At the best, public information on international issues cannot be adequate. The conduct of foreign relations is of necessity partially cloaked with secrecy. Leadership of opinion and public expressions of opinion are subject, more or less in all countries, to a conscious

[8] Statement on Peace and Neutrality by the Secretary of State, appended to the President's Message to Congress, July 14, 1939. See also President's Message of Sept. 21, 1939.

or unconscious censorship. International communication must be largely diplomatic, bureaucratic rather than popular.

For any broad constructive results American public opinion must be synchronized with the public policies and opinion of other nations; but nationalism compels compartmentalized prejudiced thinking. Emotionalism is not only unavoidable; it is indispensable to the development and assertion of national power. But the emotional atmosphere required for defensive preparations or for war is in many respects seriously ill fitted to the task of settlement that immediately follows the crisis or the war. War is now the only effective preliminary to a thorough international readjustment; but the effect of war is to alter and complicate the problem of international readjustment, while aggravating domestic dislocations.

The long-run task of satisfying other nations as well as ourselves involves the adjustment and constant readjustment of complicated and obscure conflicts and imbalances—political, economic, commercial, financial, and psychological. Moreover, between World War I and II, stabilized and intelligent public thinking, as well as long-range and assured planning of foreign and military policies, became more and more difficult because of the sudden creation of new and unanticipated conditions that necessitated rapid alterations of policy and novel departures from previously held ideas. The world was becoming more unstable and more irrational, what would happen in it more unpredictable, and its problems less amenable to rational treatment.

An international system made up of various independent and competing national sovereignties creates a distinction, convenient but largely illusory, between domestic and international problems. Viewed with a long backward glance, opinion and policy in this country have been like a teeter board. Usually the domestic end is up; but occasionally, suddenly, and briefly, that end goes down and the foreign end comes up. The tendency at most times has been to emphasize one set of problems at the expense or to the almost total exclusion of the other, contributing to an accumulation of unsolved problems and to the difficulty of a uniformly sound and steadily constructive integration.

*The incompetence of democracies
may be inherent.*

In many essential respects, American public opinion and policy followed much the same pattern as that set by the British and European democracies; and the behavior of those democracies demonstrates that under contemporary world conditions popular governments, while possessing power to act decisively in international relations, have lacked to a dangerous degree the requisite foresight, intelligence, and will.

Where the institutions and dogmas of popular government are most durably rooted, they are associated with and apparently dependent upon a general condition of economic and nationalistic satisfaction. Hence, the democracies have naturally favored the international *status quo* and have been prepared in good faith to abandon war as an instrument of national policy. The psychology thus engendered in democratic peoples weakened their military power and consequently their diplomatic effectiveness. More than that, they have been disposed to retreat from reality, to lose both wholesome suspicion and genuine perception, and to meet developing aggression with a dilatory incredulity. Their preoccupation has been with the direct aspects of domestic economic well-being, not with power-politics.

Lack of balance, of integration, and of realism with respect to international problems has probably been most marked in the United States, where conditions on the one hand created a general and strong feeling of national security and, on the other, because of the size and resources of the country, emphasized internal problems. Moreover, the vast extent of the country, its huge interior insulated and protected, its frontage on two oceans producing divergent international viewpoints, its diverse racial composition enforcing a sort of tacit neutrality, and its historical traditions—these have been sufficient to impose on opinion and policy in foreign affairs a subordination and an inertia that could be swept aside only by aggravated grievances or overwhelming danger. No doubt, the United States, like the other democracies, has been in recent years not only "satisfied" internationally and preoccupied with immediate material ends, but also unduly confident in world culture and world morality. This over-confidence is quite natural and in the main creditable, since our social and political ideas rest on general assumptions of human dignity, freedom, rationality, law, and progress. American recognition of a moral obligation in foreign affairs became clearly evident at the end of the nineteenth century. It was a natural outgrowth of our mature acceptance of democracy and came to be identified with opposition not only to war but also to preparation for defense and even to the contemplation of the possibility of armed conflict. Thus, during the years immediately preceding war, the advanced intellectual and moral ideals that issue from and sustain democracy reduce the prewar international efficiency of democratic nations, however impressive may be the health and strength of some of them when conflict comes.

The disadvantages just mentioned are thrown into high relief by the manner in which modern dictatorships operate, their use of force, deception, and surprise, their complete rejection of the orthodox rules of international intercourse, their secret, shifting, and uncompromising diplomatic tactics, and their peculiar threat to national unity.

Pressure groups and parties retard foreign policy
and are confused by international issues.

In view of the fact that the so-called domestic questions are normally and for long periods given priority, the social organization is adjusted to the discussion of such questions; and, therefore, when international problems are uppermost, a partially new organization must be superimposed or substituted, new motivations called into being, and different objectives visualized. The process has to work against inertia, causes friction, and takes time.

In the meantime, the interest and specialized groups are unable to function in their customary way. Former groupings are cut across. Leaders formerly associated take opposite sides. Those once at odds find themselves in agreement. Even some of the special organizations that were actively concerned with questions of peace, foreign relations, and defense before 1938 were later practically replaced by new committees and associations formed on specific but transitory issues. Thus, international crisis changes the pressures that operate on the legislative mechanism. The new circumstances call for a shift of emphasis from distributive justice and restrictive economic control to a military allocation of resources and the stimulation of industrial military production. Large-scale public spending is necessarily resumed; budget-balancing, indefinitely deferred.

Confusion is similarly thrown into the party system. Additional cross-issues are introduced, further obscuring party lines and reducing party integrity. The party in power, because of the unifying influence of presidential leadership, is less affected than the opposition.

The minority has several courses that it can follow. It can unquestioningly support all administration policies. It can oppose all of them. It can support some and oppose others. Whatever its choice may be, its situation is one that calls for discipline and strong leadership. The position to be taken by the minority party is largely determined by the congressional leaders; but, generally speaking, the leaders and their colleagues in Congress are responsible to different constituencies. At a time when problems are most national and most closely identified with the general welfare, no leader of the opposition is in a position to claim national support or to discipline his followers. The effect is partly to neutralize and partly to weaken the opposition and thus temporarily to weaken the party system and suspend its normal operations.

As early as the spring of 1940, on the eve of the nominating conventions, the proposal was seriously made for a "political truce" between the major parties to preserve unity.[9] During the presidential campaign, it was felt with much reason that America should present a united front to the world, that the nation should have continuously an authoritative spokesman, and that it would not have one during the campaign if the presidency and its policies were contested, or between the election and the inauguration if the President were defeated. Since it appeared to be impossible for the

---

[9] See Arthur Krock, "In the Nation," *New York Times*, June 19, 1940. Also *New York Times*, July 14, 1940.

two major parties to nominate the same men for president and vice-president, it was suggested that the candidates get together and agree on foreign policies.[10] While they did not personally confer, they substantially agreed on the general questions. Frequently in the past international questions have either not been party issues at all, since the tradition is that politics stops at the oceans' edge, or these questions have been avoided on grounds of party strategy, since they cut across party alignments on other and more manageable issues. In this country since the Civil War, no clear-cut issue of foreign policy has definitely decided a presidential election, though such issues at times have been assumed to be decided by elections.

Intellectual and scientific leadership has been unquestionably influential since the First World War; but, on the central issue of isolationism versus internationalism, scientific study was unable to establish truths to which public opinion could hold fast and by which it might be permanently guided.[11]

*In foreign affairs, government shows shortcomings from
the standpoints of democracy and efficiency.*

In the making of foreign policy, the nature of the problems, the sources of official information, and the constitutional powers of the president require that leadership come from him.[12] While the president can create situations and, in this way as well as by propaganda, strongly influence public opinion, his power to determine policies is in many essential respects dependent constitutionally and formally on congressional action. Nowadays, the employment of economic and financial pressures, aids, and inducements in foreign affairs, together with the economic and financial aspects of defense, have increased the nominal power of the legislative branch

[10] *New York Times,* July 14, 1940.
[11] Some evidence on this point is supplied by the data shown in footnote 2, p. 410.
[12] "[Actual] practice under the Constitution has shown that while the President is usually in a position to *propose,* the Senate and Congress are often in a position to *dispose.* The verdict of history, in short, is that the power to determine the substantive content of American foreign policy is a *divided* power, with the lion's share usually falling to the President, though by no means always." Edward S. Corwin, *The President: Office and Powers* (1940), pp. 200-01.

to control the executive. Actually, the new aspects of international relations, combined with the domestic influences working for a strong executive, have made presidential domination of Congress as evident in external as in internal affairs. The general trend of legislation has been to give the President a freer and stronger hand in the determining of foreign policy. Some of his powers originate in the Constitution; others derive from laws that date from the First World War; a substantial portion appeared during the depression period; still others, provided for since 1938 to meet the menace of Hitlerism, represent novel and sweeping delegations of authority, extending practically to participation in a major war without a formal congressional declaration. More definitely than in any previous national emergency, the fate of the nation was placed by Congress in the president's hands. This result was in a measure unavoidable; but it was also in a measure attributable to the nature of Congress and to the system of separation of powers.

The election of members of Congress by districts and states encourages a local and provincial, rather than a national, point of view. It militates against adaptability and flexibility, especially when public opinion is itself in a gradual process of change. The numerous membership of Congress multiplies variations of opinion and makes possible minority obstruction.

With such a legislative body and with the system of separation of powers, it is essential that policies should be determined by the organ of government that can act speedily and from the national point of view. It is necessary that initiative should remain with the president, and frequently it is not "in the public interest" that executive information, action, and purposes should be reported to Congress. Nevertheless, it is highly desirable, from the viewpoint of future governmental leadership and effectiveness, that the legislative branch should participate in the planning process and that, without creating fatal delay or an injurious appearance of dissension, policies should be debated and acts of the administration criticized. Otherwise the formation of public opinion is hampered, the development of leadership discouraged, and opportunities for executive manipulation of policies and management of opinion increased.

*The concrete shortcomings are
not being remedied.*

For the most part and at most times Congress acts in an international crisis more than normally as a national body, rather than as a discordant collection of local delegates; but its organization and procedure remain substantially unchanged. The seniority rule still operates.

On the other hand, the question of a democratic check on foreign policy through Congress was raised in 1939 and 1940 by proposals for adjournment, and the fact that Congress remained in session doubtless served the ends of democratic as well as efficient policy-determination.

The constitutional provision giving the president power, "by and with the advice and consent of the Senate, to make treaties, provided two-thirds of the Senators present concur," remains unaltered. It has not been an important factor thus far in the contemporary determination of policy; but, whenever a treaty becomes necessary, this provision may either enable a minority to defeat the will of the majority or, by permitting obstruction, place a special strain on the democratic process. It may be added that, because of the situation of the Senate with respect to representation, even a majority of that body may reflect minority opinion.

The periodic election and fixed term of the president may also present an obstacle to the planning of foreign policy as well as to effective action. In 1940 the identity of the nation's future spokesman was more or less in doubt from some time before the nominations to the date of the election. Mr. Roosevelt's re-election prevented any longer or more complete interregnum; but, had Mr. Willkie been chosen, he would have been powerless to act for some two months and a half after his election, unless the Roosevelt administration had voluntarily retired.[13]

The issue of democratization, but with questionable implications, was presented by the Ludlow Resolution, which proposed a constitutional amendment providing for a national referendum on

[13] In the event of his election, Mr. Willkie could have been substituted for Mr. Roosevelt, if the latter had appointed Mr. Willkie secretary of state and Mr. Roosevelt and the Vice-President had then resigned.

declarations of war. The resolution received a considerable vote in the House of Representatives in 1937 and was said to be favored, as late as June 1941, by 56 per cent of the people questioned.[14] This proposal overlooked the fact that in foreign affairs, even more than in domestic, a mechanical application of the democratic principle, carried too far, may produce neither efficiency nor real democracy. As ex-Secretary of State Stimson pointed out, if the proposed constitutional amendment were adopted, its "greatest evils would be its psychical effects upon the people themselves," impairing those qualities of patriotism, unity, and loyalty, "inherent in our individual citizens, [which] have been fostered in time of war by our present system of leadership embodied in our system of representative government." "Instead of being trained," he continued, "to look forward in such a matter to the guidance of our responsible leaders, obliterating all thought of party and faction when once our President and Congress had spoken, we would be . . . distracted by the lower appeals and cross-currents put forward by every kind of selfish leader or faction for every conceivable political purpose." In conclusion, Mr. Stimson observed:

At best, when the referendum was over, the President would have behind him the support of a people temporarily delayed and distracted by irrelevant local appeals. At worst we might enter into the war with a popular support which had been openly divided and weakened in the face of our enemy. No more effective engine for the disruption of national unity on the threshold of a national crisis could ingeniously have been devised. On the most charitable supposition it could only have been brought forward in an atmosphere of complete detachment from the realities of the modern outside world and from experience with the necessities of a successful national defense.[15]

In foreign affairs, leadership must be predominantly governmental and governmental leadership predominantly presidential. It should be noted, furthermore, that in foreign affairs opportunities for manipulation and management for political purposes are considerably less than in domestic matters, since foreign policies almost inescapably appeal to and affect general rather than par-

---

[14] As reported by the American Institute of Public Opinion, *New York Times*, Feb. 5, June 20, 1941.

[15] *New York Times*, Dec. 22, 1937.

ticular interests. In this field, therefore, what might appear to be simply an elective dictatorship may not be essentially undemocratic. So far as efficiency is concerned, however, our method of choosing presidents does not as a rule give adequate assurance of special qualifications for meeting or foreseeing an international crisis, although the sense of responsibility created by such a crisis has usually induced or brought into play some of the necessary qualifications.

One danger is that a president, conscious of his power and convinced of the rightness of his program, may be inclined in a fundamental settlement to disregard until it is too late the constitutional arrangements for treaty-making, or even attempt in some manner to evade them. At their worst, these arrangements do make possible some measure of discussion, thus providing a check on presidential overreaching. Executive disregard or attempted evasion would be less likely if the arrangements were made, as they apparently might be, both more democratic and more efficient.

THE WAR EFFORT IN RELATION TO DEMOCRACY AND EFFICIENCY

A modern war effort is totalitarian. It involves all aspects of national life—military, economic, industrial, social, psychological, and moral. In such an effort centralization and concentration of authority, approaching temporary dictatorship, is unavoidable if efficiency is to be obtained. For the purpose of modern warfare, the primary need is for the industrial production of armament. In government, when the necessary appropriations have been made, administration must be almost exclusively emphasized.

The United States since December 9, 1941, has been waging war in the full sense; but for some time previously it had been making large-scale preparations, it had become an "arsenal" for the nations resisting Hitler, and it was participating to an increasing extent in actual belligerent operations.

In connection with the war effort as it developed before the formal declaration, we are here interested only in certain general questions that seem to have fundamental and permanent meaning. These have already been stated. Are the governmental system and the broad recent trends in our political life favorable to an efficient war effort? Will this war effort help to realize democracy and efficiency?

*Our governmental system is in some respects favorable
and in others unfavorable to war efficiency.*

American students of government have frequently praised our constitutional system for its adaptability to war conditions. It is pointed out that the system can provide for the necessary concentration of authority, at the end of war revert to its normal workings, and through popular elections remain at all times responsible to the people. The presidency, it is said, is an office readymade for the exercise of the new activities and their co-ordination with the old, while the constitutional war powers of the president are held to be sufficient in extent and elasticity.

The system, however, has three major weaknesses. First, it is possible for the president and Congress to be unco-ordinated, at cross-purposes, or deadlocked. In this respect, we have been fortunate up to the present; and, even if president and Congress were to represent different parties, circumstances attendant on the making of war tend toward co-operation. Nevertheless, war does not wholly eliminate jealousy or friction between the two branches. For example, during our major conflicts in the past, Congress has properly proposed to exercise supervision through its committees or through a special committee; but the president quite naturally has resented any action by Congress that might hamper his conduct of the war. In the English system, while parliamentary action or debate may be at times embarrassing, there can be no prolonged friction or deadlock.

The second weakness of our system, speaking generally, lies in the fact that the president, in whom the vast war powers reside, is not as a rule selected because of his qualifications to exercise these powers. Ordinarily, he is chosen because of his availability, his personality, and his stand or record on domestic policies, not because of his strategic skill or administrative capacity. He may be elected at a time when war is not expected. He may even win at the polls because he has "kept us out of war" or on a promise to keep us at peace. Once elected, if war comes he cannot be replaced, no matter how incompetent he may be, except by resignation, which cannot be forced, or by impeachment, which is a slow and difficult process.

In the English system again, it is possible to change the prime minister at any time. A change was made during the first world war and again during the second. In England, the Cabinet also can be changed as a whole or in part when parliament or public opinion is sufficiently aroused. The arousal, too, is more likely to come when the change is possible. In this country, because the president is to all intents and purposes immovable and because practically all power and responsibility are vested in him, public interest tends to focus upon him alone, and the men who advise him, possibly in the aggregate more important than he, are pretty much beyond reach and scrutiny.

The third weakness in our system results from the enormous burden it places upon one man. His several wholly different types of work must be done concurrently and more or less in co-ordination. If his peacetime jobs are nerve-wracking and back-breaking and if some of them are almost certain to be neglected, what shall we say of his wartime responsibilities?

Trends in the politics of democracy
work against war efficiency.

The inefficiency that characterized our war effort up to the end of 1941 may easily be attributed to personal or other factors that will not necessarily recur. Other causes lie in the constitutional system. Then, too, we had the concurrence of a presidential campaign with the beginnings of the effort. In this campaign, efficiency, industrial and administrative, was discussed; but the candidate who stood most decidedly for efficiency was defeated. In addition, the prompt achievement of a state of mind favorable to effective action was hampered by the piecemeal development of the problem and of our policies, the absence of a clean transition from neutrality to belligerency, the fact that for a long time it was not quite clear whether we were at peace or at war.

While various influences have been at work, a powerful contributing factor, if not a major cause, is to be found in several interacting and apparently deep-seated political trends and situations. These fairly long-run trends, determined in large part by the normal peacetime politics of democracy, have increased the strength of the president and the range and importance of bureaucratic authority, encouraged congressional delegation of power and presidential domination of Congress, emphasized distributive policies rather than those aimed at promoting production, stimulated group pressures for particular benefits, made political leadership group-minded and disposed to manipulate group interests, accentuated class and group divisions, and transferred electoral preponderance from the party primarily concerned with industrial production to the one primarily concerned with distribution.

National unity on certain essential aims and requirements is basic to the efficiency of a modern war effort, involving as it does a most extensive mobilization and control of industry, with widespread and profound changes in economic conditions. When such an effort is undertaken by a democracy, it is especially necessary that all groups should work together, and so far as possible should do so voluntarily. A general willingness to make sacrifices should replace expectations of "a more abundant life." Pressures for particular benefits and advantages inconsistent with the paramount national purpose should be postponed. Since in a modern war effort speed is vital, especially so under recent circumstances, it is necessary that national unity, in so far as it is essential to that effort, should be brought about without delay. The same can be said of legislative and administrative organization for war purposes. Otherwise, action may be "too little and too late."

Evidence appeared in 1939 and 1940 that, so far as the national defense program was concerned, public opinion already perceived and accepted the requirements of what constituted in large part a war effort. In general, it seemed that the majority interest had shifted from distributive justice to industrial productivity. More specifically, a majority of the people evidently favored such measures as increased taxation, elimination of strikes, reduction of nondefense expenditures, and the integration of the defense administrative organization under competent industrial direction.

In this process of readjustment for efficiency, government lagged behind public opinion. At first, the view was that the system of military-industrial production would be superimposed upon the normal peacetime system. Civil business would go on as usual. Economic and social policies previously established would not be disturbed.[16] Government also in large measure disregarded the judgment of economic, industrial, and administrative experts, as well as the experience of the First World War. Considerable planning had been done; but the plans were not carried out.[17]

Congress undoubtedly was more inclined than the President to act in accord with the new phases of public opinion; but Congress had formed subservient habits, or because of its own shortcomings was unable to take the initiative. It refrained in general from action unless or until the President indicated his wishes. Organization of war administration was entirely left to him.

This organization until January 1942 was characterized by headlessness (except for the President himself), multiplication and duplication of agencies, confusion and diffusion of authority and responsibility, and the employment of a system of separated powers and checks and balances. With respect to the last-named characteristic, the idea evidently was that labor or at least the social-justice viewpoint on the one hand and industrial management on the other should balance and check each other.

In consequence, inefficiency appeared not only in the quantitative and technical aspects of production but also in conditions basic to national unity. Industrial cleavage persisted. On one side industry was blamed; on the other, labor. Each suspected the other of pur-

---

[16] "[We] must make sure in all that we do that there be no breakdown or cancellation of any of the great social gains which we have made in these past years. . . .

"There is nothing in our present emergency to justify making the workers of our nation toil for longer hours than now limited by statute. . . .

. . . .

"There is nothing in our present emergency to justify a retreat from any of our social objectives—conservation of resources, assistance to agriculture, housing, and help to the underprivileged." President Roosevelt's radio speech, May 26, 1940, *New York Times*, May 27, 1940. See also his speech to the teamsters' union, *New York Times*, Sept. 12, 1940.

[17] Leverett S. Lyon and Victor Abramson, *Government and Economic Life* (1940) Vol. 2, pp. 1062-82; Carl B. Swisher, "The Control of War Preparations in the United States," *American Political Science Review*, Vol. 34 (1940), pp. 1085-1103.

poses that are identified with the struggle for power or profits, rather than with the success of a war effort. So far as political power and war policies are concerned, labor retained the upper hand. Under the circumstances, industry feared that government would use its opportunity to "socialize" the private enterprise system. In the presence of this conflict, particularly when the facts were more or less obscured, other elements in the population tended to take sides, to insist on their own prerogatives, and, in general, to doubt the seriousness and urgency of the war effort.

These unfavorable factors had been altogether too long in operation when on December 7, 1941, the Japanese attack produced a substantial unification of American opinion and established conditions for more efficient national action.

Does the war effort help to realize democracy and efficiency?

The question whether this war will in the long run promote democracy and governmental efficiency cannot be even approximately answered. We do not know its duration, what its eventual requirements may be, what political changes will occur during its progress, or what will be done in the immediate postwar settlements and readjustments. We can be guided in a measure by our experience in and after past wars; but the present effort is incomparably vaster than any we have undertaken in the past, and it has of course occurred at a later stage of the country's growth, in the presence of different economic and political conditions.

Assuming that the Axis will be defeated, democracy's opportunity to realize itself and work out its problems in its own way will at least be preserved; and we shall be spared for some time the complications due to Nazi infiltration and propaganda. If as a result of the war the world is so organized as to insure peace, freedom, and justice and to promote economic stability, prosperity, and progress, many domestic problems that have long plagued us may be advanced nearer a solution.

It is true that since 1938, public opinion, governmental responsiveness, and public leadership have to an encouraging degree vindicated some features of democracy; while the popular and governmental inefficiency that has come to light may not be fatal. Yet, public opinion and leadership have been reacting in the main to events that are concrete, sensational, and easily apprehended, and the problems of government, while immeasurably critical, have been to a degree simplified by the postponement of domestic problems as well as those of the peace settlement and postwar reconstruction.

War emphasizes regard for the general welfare, encourages unselfishness, stimulates co-operation, works for unity, and creates a certain exaltation of spirit. Unfortunately, the periods following the Civil War and the First World War would lead us to expect after this one a materialistic reaction, with an intensification of selfish pressures. Different conditions, however, may produce this time different after-effects. The huge debt, high taxes, lowered standards of living, and the aggravated difficulties of government or the conditions of the peace may serve to create a wider and keener popular interest in public affairs, bring forth an exceptionally courageous and intelligent type of leadership, and result in a new and more serviceable alignment of parties.

No American war effort has ever brought dictatorship, even temporarily, in the full sense of the word; but every such effort of necessity vastly increases presidential power. In this respect, the present situation represents no sharp break with that which existed in the early depression period. At that time, too, we had an emergency (it was in fact compared with war), the emphasis was on action and speed, and the range of economic and social policies, though by no means totalitarian, was vast and tending to become vaster. The essential difference between the two situations lies in the problem itself rather than in its handling; and the essential element of difference is in the present need of concentration on industrial production of armaments. But, as we have just noted, the full implications of that need have been very slowly accepted.

In the handling of the problem, governmental developments have for the most part conformed with previous trends.

With added authority, funds, and functions, the bureaucracy has continued rapidly to increase in size. Following the practice adopted in the domestic emergency, Congress has enlarged by delegation the discretionary powers of the executive and of administrative agencies. Many established agencies,[18] as well as new ones more directly concerned with the war program, have acquired an enlarged authority that extends beyond their immediate and specified jurisdictions into broad and undefined areas of economic control and social service.[19] Though the states are exercising important defense functions, the national bureaucracy has become more than ever a centralized one. The problem of administrative responsibility, made more important, remains in abeyance. Congress is more than ever dependent on the President for leadership and on the bureaucracy for information and advice.

Opportunity for political manipulation of policies and group interests has been restricted in one important way by the compelling need of emphasis on unity and sacrifice. In some other ways, however, the opportunity for management of opinion has been enlarged. Public personnel continues to increase. The national government is now even closer to individuals. The persons who feel that they are receiving or may receive benefits from government are probably more numerous; though the broadening and increase of taxation may serve to solidify a group concerned more with the control of government than with dependence upon it.

Additional publicity and information services have been established; and government propaganda has probably increased, been more systematically conducted, and advanced in standing as a recognized policy. This latter development is largely due to the employment of propaganda for strategic and diplomatic ends. Moreover, in spite of the apparent lack of co-ordination among the recently established information services, the control of such services both new and old is now more clearly centralized in the chief executive.

More direct measures for the control of opinion have heretofore been deemed unavoidable in time of war; but the measures

[18] At the end of 1940, a considerable number of the peacetime nonmilitary agencies had been given defense assignments. These included a number of bureaus in the departments of Agriculture, Labor, Treasury, and Justice, and in the Federal Works Agency.

[19] An interesting example is the Reconstruction Finance Corporation, which sets up subsidiary corporations and operates as investment banker in the foreign field, apparently for political as well as trade purposes, in both the foreign and domestic fields with respect to the acquisition of essential raw materials, and in the domestic field with reference to the construction of defense plants.

attributable to the present situation do not appear to have infringed appreciably any of the essential liberties.[20]

The major characteristics of war government, apart from its fiscal aspects, are: increase of national governmental power in general, extension of economic control, expansion of the bureaucracy, and enlargement of presidential authority. At the end of the First World War, there was, with respect to all these characteristics, a substantial return to prewar conditions, although the personnel of government remained at a higher level.

After the present war effort, a permanent retention of these characteristics would seem more probable than in the past; for, in the present situation, the prewar trends have been more distinctly and rapidly in the direction of what the war effort has produced. The war features of government are supported by political attitudes toward industry and by theories of economic planning that have long had a strong lodgment in officialdom. The public mind is now more thoroughly conditioned to the ideas of strong government and a strong executive and to governmental expansion in the economic sphere.

On the other hand, one can see the possibility of an unusually strong influence proceeding from fiscal conditions, particularly the huge national debt and the unprecedented burden of taxation. From this influence one might reasonably anticipate another and perhaps an extremely radical economy and efficiency movement.

FOREIGN AFFAIRS AND WAR IN RELATION TO STABILITY

The considerations just mentioned have a close relation to the stability of our system of government.

[20] A civil-rights unit was established in the Federal Department of Justice in February 1939, by Attorney-General Murphy. See report of Attorney-General Jackson's addresses at Annual Conference of United States Attorneys (*New York Times*, Apr. 2, 1940), at convention of New York State Bar Association (*New York Times*, June 30, 1940), and at annual meeting of American Judicature Society (*Journal of American Judicature Society*, Vol. 25, No. 1, June 1941, pp. 6-10).

For repressive legislation proposed and enacted and administrative action to the fall of 1940, see Carl B. Swisher, "Civil Liberties in War Time" in *Political Science Quarterly*, Vol. 55 (1940), pp. 321-47.

An unstable international system introduces into every nation a disturbing and unpredictable influence. If the result of the present war is to increase international stability and give to the American people a justified sense of national security, a contribution will have been made to our own stability. The stabilizing effect will be greater if postwar economic arrangements make for general and lasting prosperity. If the war is followed by a period of economic strain and instability, the result will be popular feelings of insecurity. Such a psychological condition will be more dangerous if inflation has impoverished and demoralized the middle classes.

No nation can be insulated against disruptive ideas and social upheavals beyond its borders. The American Revolution in part reflected radical English and French philosophies. After our constitutional reaction we were considerably influenced by French revolutionary thinking and by what might be called a French "fifth column" in this country. During the nineteenth century and into the twentieth the example and evangelism of democracy wrought profound political changes throughout the world. The Russian Revolution, too, conceived itself to be the beginning of a universal transformation; and communism has not lacked contagious features.

When fascism and nazism were seen in the guise of a political reaction to dictatorship, standing primarily for order, national unity, and efficiency, they were probably exercising as ideas and examples a growing influence outside Germany and Italy. When, however, these systems were understood in other and more abhorrent aspects and particularly when they were joined with military aggression, they lost effect as ideas and examples. Nevertheless, the war itself and the undermining and subjugation of European countries demonstrate again that what happens in one country may shake the whole world.

As revolutions produce wars, so wars hasten and occasion revolutions. If in Europe social upheaval and fundamental political experimentation follow this conflict, as they conceivably may, it is unlikely that we shall remain wholly immune to the contagion thus generated. Particularly if economic conditions in this country are such as to produce widespread and acute discontent and if government behaves in such a manner as to discredit itself, we may find our political way of life seriously jeopardized.

In this country during recent years, signs have appeared of renewed devotion to democracy. After 1933 and particularly as Hitlerism became more menacing, the problem of democracy received more discussion than at any previous time in American history. Books, articles, and speeches on the subject multiplied; organizations were established to propagandize the democratic way of life and to combat foreign "isms"; conferences were held to study the problem as a whole and specific aspects of it; distinguished groups met to restate the democratic philosophy or creed; others called for a program of action; and "crusades" were proposed to revive the idealistic fervor that had once animated the American people.

The movement to renew American faith in democracy and the measuring of public policy by the standard of democracy or of dictatorship has been, perhaps primarily, a defensive reaction to the challenge of Hitlerism. It was arguable that internal developments alone might bring dictatorship to this country; but it was certain that Hitler, if victorious, would bring it. An important element, undoubtedly, in American public opinion during the crisis has been a feeling that democracy must prove its superiority. If the power of the people is thus asserted, can be maintained, and is vindicated by eventual success, a substantial and perhaps lasting contribution may be made to the rehabilitation of faith in democracy. It is a question, however, whether the movement for rehabilitation has yet extended beyond forms and slogans to the essence of democracy.

Some believe that war as such is morally stabilizing, that the only possible and worthwhile stability is that attained in an environment of conflict. It is contended that the ideals of national security and peace lead to that moral deterioration which some have noted in our domestic life. Security and peace, it is said, are linked with materialism and promote it, while the demand for both springs from fear. Thus, it may be reasoned, the seeking for national or international security is akin to the movement for social security: both securities, one may argue, involve an abdication of individual responsibility to the state or to a superstate, a process which, if continued, may lead to the abdication of democracy in the interest of a paternalistically produced security.

The country has been experiencing, apparently, a further breaking down of traditionalism and popular habits. More precedents have been departed from. The causes have not been wholly internal. Hitlerism outraged the dignity of international intercourse and violated international law, treaty rights, and morality. The democracies have been compelled in a measure to fight fire with fire. It appears more than ever necessary that popular government should rest, as the President has wisely said, on "a responsibility guided by a common conscience."

Does war strengthen the authority and enhance the prestige of the Constitution? In a large sense, when war is critical, a temporary disregard or suspension of certain constitutional provisions may appear necessary to save the nation and thus to preserve the Constitution. This viewpoint is expressed in what Lincoln is reported to have said during the Civil War to his Secretary of the Treasury: "These rebels are violating the Constitution to destroy the Union. I will violate the Constitution, if necessary, to save the Union, and I suspect, Chase, that our Constitution is going to have a rough time of it before we get done with this row."[21] The Constitution did "have a rough time of it." Afterward, constitutionalism was stronger; for one important reason because the outcome of the war decided the question not only of union but also of constitutional authority. It would not seem under any other circumstances that stretching or obscuring of the Constitution can increase respect for it or strengthen habits of obedience to it.

One may conclude that, under modern conditions and in the light of probabilities for the immediate future, foreign relations and war do not contribute to democracy, governmental efficiency,

[21] Carl Sandburg, *Abraham Lincoln—The War Years,* Vol. 3 (1939), p. 397.

or stability. The critical complications that foreign relations and war introduce into government may be attributed to the nature of an international system that is based on the principle of nationalism, makes possible power-politics, militarism, imperialism, and war, and excludes democratic processes from world affairs. In this system, isolation is impossible. The obvious remedy proposed is some kind of super-government or world union. The discussion of any such proposal is beyond the scope of this study; but it may be pointed out in closing that, to judge from previous experience, no union, whether based on treaties, covenants, articles of confederation, or a constitution, can quickly eliminate or simplify the problems that confront government. Even the Constitution of the United States did not prevent inter-sectional conflict, though, it may be noted, it did establish a structure within which war has not repeated itself.

PART III
THE SITUATION REVIEWED

Since the American people became politically independent, they have wanted both free government and "good" government, both democracy and efficiency. These two basic ideals have not always been consciously held, clearly defined, or called by these names; but varying degrees of preoccupation with one or the other and shifts of emphasis from one to the other do much to explain our governmental evolution and present problems.

Over long periods and to a considerable extent at all times, we appear to have lost sight of both objectives; and, in consequence, government has been in large part a by-product of our collective living, a derivative or residual development. We have always been politically minded; but we have not always been government-conscious. Neglect or indifference was perhaps most marked when Bryce wrote his *American Commonwealth*. Then we were, as he said, "sailing on summer seas."

The situation was quite different during the 25 years that preceded the adoption of the Constitution. At that time, we were engaged in revolution and, of necessity, consciously appraising and fashioning the forms and principles of government. During the present period of stress or in the immediate future we may be forced to a similar outlook and procedure. Apparently we no longer enjoy "the glorious privilege" of "committing errors without suffering from their consequences." If something in the nature of governmental reconstruction should now be needed, our situation can be in one respect contrasted with that of the founding fathers. They did their work in a day when the idea of democracy had long been dominant but, in some directions and in many minds, had been discredited by its practice. We shall make our effort at a moment when the concept of efficiency has been for many years ascendant, but finally brought into question by its extreme implications and perversions in other countries, as well as by its over-emphasis here. Yet, obviously, America's goal is to achieve the maximum of both democracy and efficiency and to reconcile the requirements of one with those of the other.

The framers of the Constitution undertook in their day, with deep insight and remarkable success, to do that delicate task. The structure that they erected still stands. Over the years we have added to it, taken some things away from it, and made alterations. Inside the structure, we are doing vastly more and in some respects strikingly different things. We have installed complicated machinery to serve various and complicated purposes. Outside, the landscape and climate have changed. The people who mill in and around the plant are a different people, feeling and acting differently. We are now heavily mortgaging the edifice, which is becoming an ever more powerful citadel in the midst of war.

The original construction engineers were not greatly disturbed by the thought that eventually their handiwork might have to be torn down and rebuilt. It was not long, however, before it earned a deep and wide sentimental attachment, which, with conservative tendencies, made any hint of demolition and reconstruction a source of alarm. At present, signs of instability do justify profound concern; for government and people are now so closely inter-acting and inter-supporting that no meaningful political disturbance can be kept on the surface or localized.

Having sketched in our study the major changes in government, we shall now attempt to restate in summary form the trends of the past in relation to the problem of the present. Three chapters are given to this review. Chapter XIV deals with democracy, Chapter XV with efficiency, and Chapter XVI with stability. Chapter XVII states briefly the present problems of government as they are posed by these three essential objectives.

CHAPTER XIV

DEMOCRACY

Though the framers of the Constitution distrusted the impulses of the people, they also feared abuse and usurpation of authority by public officials. The struggle against despotism and fear of it had given a certain form, apparent or real, to the English, colonial, and state governments. This form independent America adopted and perpetuated in the system of separation of powers and checks and balances, a system that was expected to prevent dictatorship, by one man, by a legislature, or by a popular majority. Federalism and local self-government appeared naturally out of the conditions of the time; and they were expected, not only to give democracy a large field of action, but also to provide basic safeguards against either the concentration or misuse of national political power.

At that time, the suffrage was restricted; but as a result of extensions during the Jeffersonian era, after the Civil War, and again in recent years, the right of adult citizens to vote has been made practically universal. Compared with the way votes were cast and counted in the early years, elections are now notably free and fair. The democratizing of the suffrage took place partly because the earlier assumptions regarding sound and wise government were ignored, partly because of frontier equality and a sense of fairness, and partly because of an identification of democracy with efficiency, an acceptance of the idea that mass decisions promised in the long run the only assurance of right decisions. Also departing from the views of the founding fathers, three democratizing movements after the Jeffersonian era produced in the national government the party system, political control of administrative officers, and the practically direct election of president, vice-president, and senators. In the states, democratization produced first a multiplicity of elective offices, and later the initiative, referendum, and recall. The secret ballot and the direct primary system of nominations have affected both state and national governments.

Though in the past each democratizing change made government more responsive, the responsiveness did not satisfy the masses. Moreover, even when an organ of government had been apparently democratized, it passed for long periods under oligarchical or dictatorial control. Such was the fate of the city council, the state legislature, the political party, the nominating conventions, and the national House of Representatives. Yet, in most cases where the formal democratic process has experienced some form of reaction or concrete perversion, the evils have in due time been attacked and more or less eradicated.

The gross corruption that for a long period infected and discredited party organizations and legislatures has apparently decreased. A high degree of partisanship coincided with and contributed to corruption; and the increase of independent voting, most noticeable after 1900, has helped to make government more responsive.

In the beginning, the Supreme Court was intentionally an undemocratic part of the governmental setup. Yet it has fortified democracy, for example, through the protection of civil rights and the prevention of arbitrary administration. The Court's assumption of policy-determining functions has on occasion frustrated the popular will and contributed to political lag. It has been possible, however, by remaking the personnel of the Court, to adjust its judgments to progressive opinion. The depression period witnessed another judicial "revolution," without structural modification; and certain influences have been tending to "socialize" the law, the legal profession, and judicial attitudes.

While many of the developments just mentioned represent, on the whole, substantial progress in the realization of democracy, so far as the structure and mechanism of government are concerned, and suggest a widespread and enduring inner vitality, certain political changes have made a democratic operation of government more difficult.

The trend has been toward unlimited and
centralized governmental power.

The American constitutional system was based on a deep distrust
of governmental power, especially of concentrated governmental
power. The functions of the federal government were therefore
expressly enumerated; and, until the Civil War, the idea of a
minimized central government was pretty consistently followed.
Local self-government provided in general the needed controls
and services, and was looked upon as the cornerstone of the
democratic structure, since it kept government "close to the
people."

Changed conditions, the most important of which are population growth, industrialization, urbanization, and specialization,
have imposed on government added activities. Practically all the new
activities were first assumed by the state and local governments;
but, because the problems of the new age were increasingly national and because the states were unequal in need, leadership,
technical competence, and taxable resources, the functions of the
national government have also expanded. Expansion was quite
evident after the Civil War; it became more rapid after 1900;
and during the depression of the thirties it suddenly swelled
to a scale previously unimagined. In the nation as in the states,
and for much the same reasons, expansion has been accompanied
by centralization. The American people appear in effect to have
discarded the principles of minimized government and of a
federalistic balance.

Congress seems to be losing, rather than
gaining, power and prestige.

Until recent years the general make-up of American legislatures
was the most standardized feature of our political system. Uniformly, they consisted of two houses, each composed of members
elected by and from territorial units. Each house was set up
for debate and deliberation; its members were expected to lead
as well as represent.

In the English struggle against the king and the colonial

quarrels with the governor, the legislative body had represented the people and spoken for them, and in so doing had become in a real sense the embodiment and symbol of democracy. Before the adoption of the Constitution, the congress of the Confederation and to a large extent the state legislatures were not merely law-making bodies but governments; and, as such, they were already losing popularity. The federal constitution expressed a reaction from legislative shortcomings and excesses; and, later, in the states, extravagance, incompetence, and corruption produced constitutional provisions designed to curb legislatures. With this end in view, governors, like the president, were generally given the veto power.

In the federal congress, the Senate grew in course of time to an assembly of 96 members, and the House to 435. On the average, Congress has been superior to the state legislatures in membership, functioning, and output; but neither its representative character, its responsiveness, nor its efficiency has been such as to establish an enduring popularity.

During the last half-century Congress of necessity has increasingly delegated legislative powers to administrative agencies; while, during more recent years, legislative initiative has been largely exercised by the president and the bureaucracy. The tendency has been for members of Congress to be on the one hand delegates with localized interests and on the other rubber-stamps in the hands of the president. In many cases, some important, Congress has asserted its independence, more often of the president than of the localities and pressure groups; but in recent years the national legislature has shown, by and large, little capacity for popular leadership. In an age of radio and energetic private leadership, the functions of debate and of crystallization of opinion are no longer centered in the national legislature. The legislative situation appears to justify a fear that democracy is in danger of losing an ancient landmark, a strategic position, a valued symbol, and a real protection against personal government.

Growth of governmental functions and powers resulted in

administrative expansion. An increased legislative burden, along with the requirements of technical and flexible administration, has necessitated more and more delegation of legislative powers to administrative agencies and the chief executive.

Growth of administrative authority poses the
problem of bureaucratic responsibility.

As the bureaucracy grew in size, power, and capacity for authoritative leadership, administration, long more or less ignored, became an urgent and extremely difficult problem. To the extent that bureaucratic power might be or was political, its control evidently affected the realization of democracy. When administration was simple and largely entrusted to local officials, locally elected for short terms, democratic control and responsibility to the people were quite effectively arranged. In technological America the situation is different. The number of public officials and employees in 1940 probably equalled the total population of the nation at the end of the Revolution. Most of these officials and employees are administrative. Any one of several administrative agencies at Washington exceeds in personnel the population of the largest American city in 1790. Moreover, through subsidies, benefits, and other private-public relationships, millions of citizens have become *half-public* and *half-private*, closely linked to public administrative agencies.

The work of the national bureaucracy is now so extensive and varied that its ramifications and effects, even its objectives and general policies, are incomprehensible to the average citizen. Along with the discretionary policy-determining power that can be directly exercised, the national bureaucracy possesses great influence over the making and determination of policies by president and Congress. Administration is controlled in different measures and ways by scientific and professional standards, by public opinion, by groups, by the courts, by Congress, and by the president. It is not possible or desirable to democratize a modern centralized bureaucracy to the extent that local officials were democratized in the rural American township or county; but the varied partial supervisions applied to national administration do not, in the author's opinion, represent a satisfactory application of popular control.

The "strong executive," growing stronger, suggests an approach to one-man government.

Somewhat parallel with the growth of the bureaucracy and partly because of it, the prestige of the executive has grown as that of the legislature has declined. In the states the governor and in the nation the president have come to be looked to by the people for political leadership and the carrying out of the legislative program. Since 1900, three "strong executives" have appeared —Theodore Roosevelt, Woodrow Wilson, and Franklin D. Roosevelt, each more successful than any of his predecessors in dominating Congress. Before Franklin D. Roosevelt, it appeared that after a "strong executive" the weight of power would always shift back to Congress; but another complete restoration of the balance does not now seem by any means assured.

In recent years, powers hitherto unimagined have been delegated to the president. His office overshadows in prestige and influence all other institutions and organizations, public and private. The president can make national policies his own; and by means of these policies, as well as through direct propaganda, creation of events, and other tactics, he is in a position to win and hold a combination of groups that constitute an electoral majority, keep control of his party, and obtain renomination and re-election.

The president is held with much reason to be more representative of the whole nation than is Congress; but the circumstances of presidential nominations and elections and the make-up of a president's political strength indicate that he may actually be and frequently is the representative of a minority or of an unintegrated combination of minorities.

Opportunity for aggrandizement of presidential power no doubt has been supplied in part and the movement accelerated by the continuance or recurrence of crisis. In the past a close relation has existed between economic depressions and democratizing movements. During the recent depression, however, the theory of democracy appeared to have no broad popular sources and little application to the organization of government, but rather to have originated from above and been applied to the rationalization and enhancement of presidential power. Crisis seems to have become a chronic condition; and the president has power to create and prolong emergencies. The long continuance or frequent recurrence of crisis, domestic or international, combined with the accumulating power of the presidency, would seem to indicate the possibility of a future personal perpetuation in office that may have little relation in fact to the reality of popular control or of governmental responsiveness. The abandonment of the third-term tradition in 1940 may be viewed as symptomatic, though not conclusive.

*Government and public problems have become more
remote, more complex, and more urgent.*

Expansion of public services and controls have brought government at numerous points in intimate relation to the daily lives and vital interests of the people. Government has been humanized. It is felt by individuals more frequently and more widely. Because of rapid transportation, government and people are geographically less distant. Communication facilities make possible prompt, even instantaneous, contact between public officials and the electorate. Yet, when the present is compared with the past, government in sum appears more remote from the observation and understanding of the masses. In the case of any one individual, the present "closeness" of government to him is less all-embracing, less revealing of the whole, and more technical or more superficial. The reasons are to be found in centralization, in the size of government and its complex organization, and in the difficulty amid complexity of fixing responsibility and of knowing where one must press to get a response.

More significant, however, than the remoteness of government is the remoteness of public problems. To a relatively large extent, the families and communities of pioneer America were self-sufficient economically. Through industrialization and urbanization, Americans in the mass have become dependent for their livelihoods on the workings of a nationwide mechanism over which as individuals they can exercise little deliberate control. Control of this mechanism has become increasingly the subject-matter of public policies, which deal with forces and relationships distant from individual experience. Similarly withdrawn from the individual are the means of equalizing opportunity and income. Problems both of economic control and of social justice impose varied technical demands on those who would understand them; and most of the technical requirements for their solution are unavailable and in part unknown to individuals in the mass.

This is another way of saying that problems have become so complex that, as whole problems, they are beyond the understanding of individuals.

*Individuals in the mass may now have relatively
less capacity to control government.*

In practice, majority rule has never meant and cannot mean that every individual voter must fully understand every public problem that calls for solution and decide independently the details as well as the general principle of every proposed policy. In the formation of opinion, the individual is limited, not only by the nature of problems and policies, but also by his intelligence, his emotional make-up and fixed attitudes, his conceptions of group or sectional loyalty and interest, his willingness to subordinate conceptions of particular welfare to conceptions of general welfare, the amount and reliability of information at his disposal, the intensity of his desire to reach right conclusions, and, finally, the time and energy that he can devote to political information and thinking.

One cannot hope to appraise precisely such imponderable elements or to prove how and in what direction they have been changing. Americans now are perhaps no more intelligent and no less emotional; but they are probably less inhibited than in the past by fixed attitudes. The people are more generally literate. Information available to the electorate has vastly increased in quantity and improved in quality. Little doubt can be entertained that modern America possesses and exercises as much freedom of opinion as it ever did in the past. Sectional loyalty would seem to have diminished. On the other hand, feelings of group interest are apparently stronger. Contemporary opinion accentuates particular welfares at the sacrifice of the general welfare. The desire to reach right conclusions, except on matters of group interest, may be less intense. The political life of the modern American is probably subject to more distractions and diversions, almost certainly to more bafflement and discouragement. Modern propaganda makes possible wholesale excitation and manipulation of popular emotions. In any event, such inadequacies as individuals in the mass may normally reveal are rendered more serious than in the past by the increased complexity and remoteness of public problems and of government itself.

Those who hold that the people collectively are instinctively sound and wiser than any individual generally agree that the people need time to reach right decisions. Modern problems, however, owing to the increased speed of change, are more urgent, pressing, and critical. Lag is no doubt inherent in human nature, in the character of social problems, and in the democratic process. It is evidenced by delayed and imperfect solutions, by problems left without any solution at all, and by alternations of complacent drift with accumulated discontent and excited action. Since 1900 each release of political energy, each instance of exceptional governmental activity, has produced policies of wider range, of more complex character, and of more confused interrelationships. These periodic lags and surges may correspond rather closely to the actual movement of opinion; but both the lag and the surge seem to represent maladjustments in the process of forming opinion and creating leadership. Even if the American people were to be providentially supplied with a leader for every crisis, it might be better if the leader came in advance of the crisis; and it would be still better if the crisis did not come. Increasing difficulty in the realization of democracy is suggested by the fact that problems accumulate to the point where opinion cannot be formed and expressed upon them and by the recurrence of crisis for which public opinion is unprepared and the normal democratic process unsuited.

Popular dependence on leadership is greater than in the past. Some of the needed leadership must come directly from government; but exclusive dependence on governmental leadership is inconsistent with democracy, for popular control demands disinterested appraisal, criticism, opposition, and debate. Our intermediate leadership has come chiefly from the political parties and the pressure groups.

*The party system, though indispensable, is
partly ineffective, partly perverted.*

The political party has been as a rule primarily an organization for capturing public offices, and, as such, it has served an essential purpose. But this has not been its only function. It has provided leadership for inadequate and inarticulate individuals; and the two-party system, presenting divergent viewpoints on public questions, has offered to the electorate a certain definiteness and conclusiveness of choice. Thus, the party system has aided in the crystallization and expression of opinion. The winning party, moreover, is concerned with holding its majority, that is, in making government responsive.

For effectiveness, parties require discipline, cohesiveness, and unity; but, when they have had these qualities in greatest measure, they have been most amenable to undemocratic control and least adaptable to change. The professional politician seems to be an inescapable feature of the party system; but his loyalty to the party has contributed to the rigidity of the system.

The realization of democracy through the party was first frustrated by absence of democracy in the party, in the main because of the fact that politicians and party organizations, like other individuals and groups, are motivated by material interest. The fact that the politician is a professional has tended to restrict his qualifications to those of a broker or manipulator. Instead of retaining or developing a class, specially equipped by training and inherited standards to govern, America created and maintained a political profession, the requirements of which precluded adaptation to the complex and changing demands of a technological age; while the preoccupations of a "business civilization" practically excluded from politics much appropriate material for public leadership.

To a large and apparently increasing extent, the politician and his party have adopted followership rather than leadership. Contributing to this tendency were the materialistic demands of sectionalized pressure groups; the virtual transfer of leadership to specialized and interest groups; the system of state, district, and local representation; and the method of direct primary nomination. By making the elected representative a delegate from a local unit, peculiarly subject to local pressures, the party lost some of the essentials of unity and, consequently, much of its responsibility for government and capacity for speedy action.

Moved by demands and conditions that are essentially unprincipled, the major parties tend also to be unprincipled. The private possessors of economic power are now predominantly in the Republican Party; the wage earners and persons on relief seem to be durably attached to the Democratic Party. This difference is largely founded on considerations of material interest and on questions of the relationship between government and industry. Otherwise, the major parties appear to be losing agreement on basic philosophy and disagreement on questions of current policy.

The growing power and scope of government and the complexity and changing character of technological society have increased the number of questions that the party and electoral system are expected to decide. The blurring, disintegration, and devitalization of parties have been hastened by the accumulation of unsolved problems and by the recurrence of crises, each with its demand for national unity and the suspension of the normal workings of the party system. Because public questions are crisscrossed and confused and have varying appeals to different sections and groups, elections are apt to decide little or nothing except the attractiveness and manipulatory skill of candidates as persons.

Past history has shown that the party system may be made for a time a more vital and effective instrument of public opinion through a realignment, such as that which marked the death of the Whig Party and the birth of the Republican. It is more than eighty years, however, since that event; and any similar party realignment in the near future, except under a revolutionary impulse, appears improbable. As a matter of fact, the party system today, while still indispensable, is less important except as a mechanistic electoral vehicle. It is supplemented, partially controlled, and partially supplanted by the pressure-group system.

Pressure groups tend to produce
minority government.

The growing consciousness and more effective assertion of group voting power has helped to realize democracy. The achievement of a better balance among groups through the organized-labor movement has also been a democratizing effect. Pressure groups provide individuals with leadership and a measure of psychological security. They constitute a social organization more flexible than the political parties and in some ways better adapted to the complex and changing conditions of the technological era. They have taken over from the legislatures to a large extent the function of debate and to some extent the work of formulating laws. Those groups that possess substantial voting power and the ability to swing it from one candidate or party to another may either occasionally or continuously control the legislative mechanism.

It is commonly said that the prime function of the modern legislature is to mediate between opposing pressure groups. In practice, however, simple yielding to pressure appears to be more usual than mediation. When a legislator is elected from a territorial unit, as all American legislators are, even a small minority group holding the balance of power can impose its will on the legislators; and a minority of legislators so controlled are able, by working together, to impose their will on the law-making body, as it is at present constituted. The process by which pressures are translated into policies is extremely crude and results in a mosaic no single part of which or even the whole necessarily corresponds to a majority opinion; though the majority, made up of minority groups, may have acquiesced piecemeal in a combination of particularized benefits. From the viewpoint of interest, the process may be considered at its worst one of reciprocal bribery—of the legislators by the groups and of the groups by the legislators.

Society does not yet provide democratic substitutes for the
growth and concentration of political power.

Since 1900, the subject of group self-government, as well as the question of democratizing private economic power, has been much discussed, posing the problem of a democratic decentralization more suitable to the "great society" than the old system of local self-government. The lack of an adjusted decentralization doubtless explains in part the growth, concentration, and personalization of political power. It is impossible to say, however, that much progress has been made toward adjustment in this connection. It appears, rather, that developments with respect to political power have had the effect of discouraging any basic, more complex, and more difficult type of reorganization.

Does the international situation threaten inroads on democracy?

Fruit of the failure of Englishmen to solve on a new scale the problem of empire-building, independent America was born into an unorganized world of sovereign nations and of wars. The thirteen sovereign states were themselves an international, not a national, system. The first purpose of the Constitution was "to form a more perfect union"; that is, to create a nation able within its bounds to substitute peace, order, justice, and prosperity for international conflict and capable of exerting power effectively in the larger world of nations.

In this larger world, political independence and national unity never meant and could not mean absolute isolation, absolute immunity, or absolute security. In the beginning we were racially, culturally, institutionally, and economically an offshoot and a phase of European history. Later, we were measurably involved in European affairs by various sympathies and interchanges, by commercial relations, and by the ideologies and world policies of European powers, as well as by our own. In some of these ways, we became involved also in Asiatic affairs. Nevertheless, we promptly gained and, during more than a century, steadily solidified the feeling of American nationalism. During this time, our own nationalism appeared to be a primary and beneficent influence in our development; and the disorganization of the world seemed, on the whole, a secondary and almost negligible embarrassment. This secure situation enormously simplified the task of realizing democracy.

The principal reasons for this relative freedom and simplicity were five in number. The first was a traditional and well-founded fear of standing armies, embodied in constitutional arrangements for the supremacy of civil over military power. The second was our psychological antagonism to the "European system" of monarchical governments, alliances, and balances of power, establishing in our political leadership the principle of non-entanglement. The third was our real geographical isolation in times of comparatively slow transportation and communication. The fourth was the fact that the United States was the only actually or potentially great power in the Western Hemisphere. The fifth was, as it seemed to us, the cheapness of war and of preparation for war and the fact that it was ordinarily localized.

At the beginning of the twentieth century, when America was realizing its international "interests," feeling its power, and showing renewed imperialistic symptoms, science and technology were profoundly changing the situation. The first world war illustrated what was happening; the second piles proof on proof. In the new situation, the society of nations and empires is no more stable than formerly. The impulse to use force is less restrained than in the immediate past by law, morals, humanitarianism, and reason. The supplanting in great nations of the democratic idea by the idea of totalitarian dictatorship gives to the employment of force— a policy to which such nations are irretrievably committed—an unprecedented efficiency, universality, purposelessness, and endlessness. Science and technology have provided the aggressor with techniques and devices for creating domestic as well as international conflict.

Nationalism and national sovereignty in the technological era no longer delimit and protect areas in which democracy may develop and function. Nationalism is based on the principle of force, not of discussion and majority decision; it is identified with an armed and aggrandizing state, not with the dignity and freedom of the individual; and international legal disunity seems now inevitably to breed militarism and war, both consistent with dictatorship but as incompatible with political democracy as they are with economic progress. Future existence in the kind of world that produced the first and second world wars seems certain eventually to impose on the American nation a burden of insecurity and waste that will discredit democracy, and bring economic and political responsibilities that cannot be democratically discharged.

War or a situation just "short of war" increases for a time undemocratic operations in politics. It has been a commonplace that under such conditions we are compelled temporarily to suspend democracy, but, it is felt, we always restore democracy after the termination of the crisis. The fact that government has always in the past resumed its constitutional and democratic aspect may be due to specially favorable conditions that are not certain to recur. The two decades that followed the Civil War and the two that followed the First World War do not suggest that democracy is strengthened merely by surviving a crisis. The lesson seems to be that, when the crisis is ended, or seems to be, the problem of realizing or preserving democracy becomes at once more pressing and more likely to be neglected.

In the world's history, governments have essentially changed with little or no change in their forms or procedures; and the location of power has sometimes radically shifted with few outward signs of what has occurred. Over a period of years numerous factors, most of them imponderable, influence the operation and evolution of government. At any one moment, the appearance of a set of unfavorable factors may indicate a pessimistic conclusion; but, while these factors are at work, counteracting influences may be growing in strength and in course of time may prevail. Such a situation has occurred more than once in American history; and the fact that the development of democracy has had in the past its encouraging and its discouraging phases would suggest the danger of prediction and the needlessness of despair. No one can fully assess the intangible recuperative forces latent in the American people.

Nevertheless, our review of the behavior of American democracy points to at least two general conclusions: (1) democracy is not yet fully realized, and (2) its realization is becoming more difficult. The first conclusion is a commonplace: no perfect democracy is possible. The second points to a situation that may or may not be serious, depending on the resources that we have available for coping with the difficulties. It may well be said that the realities of democracy will dominate the forms and processes of government whenever the people *will to have democracy*.

CHAPTER XV

EFFICIENCY

The basic characteristics of the American legislative system—constitutionalism, federalism, limitations on the national government, separation of powers, checks and balances, bicameralism, and territorial representation—were adopted because of conditions, feelings, and philosophies that were controlling in 1787-89. Considerations of efficiency were important with respect to the allocation of powers to the federal government, the establishment of union, and the setup of the presidency and the Senate. But other influences were also compelling—demands of expediency, distrust of and concessions to democracy, fear of usurpation or concentration of political power, need of stability, and acceptance of individual freedom. The legislative branch, adjudged to be inefficient, was nevertheless understood to be supreme. From the beginning, however, policy-determining powers were possessed in a small measure by the state governors, substantially by the president and the courts, and to some extent by administrative officers. The idea of local self-government, going beyond federalism, took the form of an extreme decentralization within the states.

A century and a half ago government was in general predominantly concerned with the maintenance of internal order and with defense against external dangers. Apart from the punishment of criminals and disturbers of the peace, what we now call social service or public welfare was rudimentary and almost entirely local. Government, in relation to business, was mainly engaged in the assistance and promotion of private enterprise.

In assessing the efficiency of present-day government, let us note, first, how the work that it is called upon to do has grown in quantity and changed in character. Growth and change have been incidental to a phenomenal increase of the nation's area and population. It is simpler to govern a small country than a large one, one where conditions are fairly uniform than one where variety prevails. Keeping this general environmental transformation in mind, we shall now consider three aspects of the government's evolving task: the economic, the social, and the international.

Government has assumed a complicated, intimate, and critical relationship to a changed economic system.

Except for the problems of slavery, union, reconstruction, and foreign affairs, the idea of economic development pretty thoroughly dominated the nation's opinion and policies until the end of the nineteenth century. Before the Civil War, though banking, transportation, and growth of incorporated business were shaping the modern economic problem, government at no time established an integrated, consistent, or long-enduring structure of policy. In the meantime, private industrial enterprises grew to impressive and apparently oppressive proportions. Farmers and wage earners, lacking effective control over the new forms of economic power, demanded restoration of competition and regulation of industry in the public interest. Following more or less ineffectual attempts by the states to regulate railroads and prohibit monopolies, the federal government in 1887 and 1890 undertook both tasks. Thus, the great groups that felt weakness and distress were increasing their demands upon government and enlarging their established expectations from it.

Other forms of public economic control had preceded that type of regulation provided by the Interstate Commerce Act. In fact, promotional measures were forms of general economic control. So also were currency and debt management, supervision of banking, taxation and tariffs. From the beginning the promotional and fiscal policies of government were regarded and employed as overall instrumentalities for influencing the economic situation.

Since 1900 public regulation has grown extraordinarily. It has been applied in a greater variety of ways to additional segments of economic life and has been used for more and different purposes. One purpose has been to eliminate business practices repugnant to the moral sense of the community; another, to enforce fairness and reasonableness in charges and services. The accomplishment of these purposes was intended to represent a rather clearly defined minimum of governmental interference with private initiative. Private enterprise was to be left free to organize and manage its activities, on the theory that such freedom was economically desirable and in accord with the "American way of life." The attack on monopoly struck at some of the broader features of industrial organization, but, it was held, only for the purpose of restoring freedom. Yet, in general, regulation, like promotion, has been brought about by group political forces; and regulation, more than promotion, has had direct distributive or equalizing purposes.

Eventually, as regulation developed and as it was applied at various points to strengthen regulation at other points, government assumed in certain fields what amounted to a superior or supervisory managerial function, determining in constantly wider range the policies of private industry. Moreover, in certain special fields, as well as in the general field covered by the antitrust acts, public authority undertook to decide how private enterprise should be organized.

As the people came increasingly to hold government responsible for their economic condition, they were disposed to emphasize the obvious over-all controls more than segmentary regulation. For it was these controls that were considered to influence the levels of prices, wages, interest-rates, business confidence, and general investment and business activity. The expansion and refinement of public economic policy has been strongly influenced by economic instability, by the recurrence of economic crises and depressions. During the latest depression period, an unprecedented surge of economic legislation supplied the national government with additional controls to be employed at key points of the economic system. The international situation, the national defense program, and the war have brought more controls and the possibility of other and stricter ones, with a likelihood that much of the emergency structure of control will remain after the emergency has passed. With the expansion of the bureaucracy and the diversification and intensification of its activities, control has ramified in all directions, producing various effects, some obscure and others generally unanticipated.

From the beginning, government in the United States has owned and managed property and conducted businesses; but, aside from some costly experiments, the earlier tendency in general was not to expand the proprietary or business activities of government. The closing decades of the nineteenth century marked in this connection a reorientation of opinion and policy. Reaction from extensive, exploitative, and wasteful private development coincided with growing confidence in government. Conservation policies retained in public ownership and use vast properties in land, forests, parks, water-power sites, and mineral resources. In other directions and with varied objectives government added to its business functions. Recently, the movement has rapidly proceeded and has expressed itself in a wide variety of substantially new undertakings.

In the meantime, the expanded organization, personnel, and operations of government have augmented its importance as a purchaser of privately produced goods. In this capacity alone, it is able to exercise considerable control over private enterprise, and specifically uses its power as purchaser to reinforce its other controls. The war program has increased this particular power.

Agriculture was long the most individualistic sector of economic life; but the economic functions of government—promotional, regulatory, control, proprietary, or business operational—were in large measure due to rural pressure. Numerous regulations were imposed on industry specifically for the protection of the farmers. So far as the farmer himself was concerned, government intervention, for the most part, took the form of assistance and promotion. From the beginning, the farming population has had from time to time its peculiar discontents; and, after the First World War, agricultural depression appeared chronic and its problems so deepseated and so complicated as to defy traditional solutions. With the acquiescence of the farmers and in part with their administrative co-operation, government since 1933 has applied to agriculture a number of unprecedented controls designed primarily to raise agricultural prices.

"Social consciousness" and the movement for social justice has been primarily concerned with the lot of the industrial wage earner —his wages, hours, and working conditions. Labor, however, is a major factor in the industrial process. Workingmen, losing ownership of their tools and excluded from the direct management of industry, fell back in self-defense on unionization and the strike. The nation now accepts with little discussion of alternatives a productive process that embodies two opposing interests and forces, each of which has been tending through separation and conflict to intensify its class feeling. With this situation accepted and with government responsive to voting power, the tendency has been to relieve labor of public regulation, to regulate industrial management in the interest of labor, and to hand over to an increasingly monopolistic labor leadership, substantially protected by government, an increasing power in effect to interfere in the management of industry. Thus, through the strengthening of organized labor and the fixing of minimum wages and maximum hours, government has been led on the one hand to undertake the decision of highly critical questions involved in the organization and management of private industry, and on the other to readjust the balance of private forces both economic and political. International crisis, making efficiency the first consideration, has acutely emphasized the vital relationship of public labor policy to the problem of maximum production and effective national action.

Government has undertaken to carry out
the conception of social justice.

The groups that felt themselves economically underprivileged but politically powerful demanded, not only public control of industry, but also measures aimed at a more equitable distribution of the national wealth and income. Public services concerned with education, recreation, health, housing, care of the dependent, treatment of the delinquent, rehabilitation of the handicapped, and protection and improvement of child life, expanded with the growth of population, wealth, industrialism, urbanism, humanitarianism, technical skills, and specialized leadership. These services, supported by taxation, are distributive and equalizing in purpose and effect. Having the same purpose are many of the economic controls and governmental undertakings that have just been mentioned, particularly those relating to labor.

During the depression, large-scale relief of the unemployed was added to the familiar public-welfare services. With respect to the employable unemployed, government recognized an obligation, not only to give relief, but also to provide work.

Prior to the depression, grants of money had been given to individuals, chiefly to war veterans but also as maternity benefits, old-age pensions, and assistance to the blind. The practice represented by such grants has been maintained and expanded, and rounded out by a system of unemployment insurance. Thus, government endeavors to insure individuals against certain major hazards, to guarantee their social security, incidentally distributing national income.

*The international situation contributes complexity, delicacy,
and special urgency to the governmental task.*

The task of government in the international sphere has also changed and become more difficult. No longer in a position of relative isolation and security, America since 1900 and especially since the First World War has had as a part of its governmental burden the problem of using national power for the maintenance of stability and order in the world. Considering possibilities in the calculable future, this problem may involve the playing of "power politics," the maintenance of vast armaments, the occasional waging of total war, or participation in a new and more authoritative international organization. In any event, the questions presented are in themselves of the utmost complexity and delicacy, requiring quick decision and prompt action. Whatever may be said about governmental efficiency in the domestic sphere, it is quite clear that, up to the present crisis, we have not shouldered our full load or acted effectively in world affairs. Furthermore, inefficiency appears in a measure intrinsic in foreign relations, in the position of America, and in the democratic conduct of both diplomacy and war.

Thus, from the point of view of economic control, social action, and international responsibility, a revolutionary change has taken place in the kind of work that the government does or attempts to do.

During the earlier years of our constitutional development, the economic and social conditions of the country and the idea that governmental powers and activities should be limited acted as brakes on the tendency to increase public responsibilities. For some time after this tendency had gathered noticeable momentum, the restrictive idea was still widely held. It has now, apparently, lost most of its following and practical meaning.

For a century after the adoption of the Constitution, the organization and strengthening of government itself received and seemed to require little conscious effort. In technological America, however, it came to be realized that the adaptation of government to a changed society and to new and more difficult tasks presents a problem of extraordinary difficulty. Recently it has been feared, more generally than in the past, that it may be impossible to reconcile democracy with the requirements of efficiency. We shall now review briefly the major political developments in their bearing on governmental efficiency. First, we shall consider the adequacy of public opinion for sound and effective control of government.

Shortcomings of the individual relative to public problems make leadership more than ever necessary.

In rural America, when a larger proportion of the tasks of government were performed locally, the individual could act reasonably well on public questions. They were simple and close at hand, while he had varied interests and aptitudes and leisure for things political. He was equipped and able to understand a public problem as a whole problem. Local discussion, too, brought together in one place all who were interested in and informed about a problem. When state or national policies were under consideration, however, the individual was handicapped even in that simpler age. It was harder for him to get relevant facts and impossible to discuss matters personally with those of his fellow-citizens who had interests, viewpoints, and prejudices different from his. Naturally, his function as a democratic citizen became more difficult as public policies became more centralized in the nation, as problems became more numerous, complicated, and interrelated, and as he himself became more specialized or otherwise more narrow in his interests and outlook.

Mass education was expected to prepare citizens for the duties of self-government; and, as time passed, more of American youth completed each stage of the educational process. Incentives for and concentration upon technological industrial development produced in America, with respect to physical and mechanical things, a high degree and a wide and quick acceptance of special technical skills. In relatively narrow fields having to do with physical discovery, mechanical invention, plant organization, office management, and administrative operations, the individual capacity of Americans was notably developed and demonstrated. In the political sphere, however, private specializations and diversions worked against any similar adaptation and achievement. The situation was not improved by extensions of the suffrage and by the influx of millions of immigrants.

Individuals in the mass have always required leadership. They require it more than ever in the "great society," because of the complexity and remoteness of public problems and of government, the specialization of individuals, and the impossibility of integrated discussion in the locality. While America has had influential "free-lance" leaders, the leadership that has been most significant, outside of government itself and the party system, has come from groups.

*Group leadership fails to clarify
and integrate thinking.*

Associations and organizations have multiplied, reflecting the increasing specialization and differentiation that characterize a highly developed industrial and urban society. Religious institutions and associations dedicated to general moral or idealistic ends have come to play relatively, if not absolutely, a less important role. Social organization has been shifting from the abstract to the concrete, reflecting a general transition from faith to function.

From the viewpoint of governmental efficiency, the crux of the problem of private leadership is presented by two types of groups, the specialized associations and institutions and the interest-groups. The two types merge into each other and share each other's characteristics and motivations. Many organizations fall into both classifications.

Roughly speaking, the specialized groups are primarily concerned, not so much with direct benefits for themselves as with the good of people generally or of the underprivileged. The good that is promoted or the evil that is combated is generally narrowed to a specific, frequently professional, and usually technical objective or course of action. These organizations are predominantly middle class, and are concerned largely with social objectives rather than economic functioning. In the long run and quite generally, they press for additional expenditures by government for the purpose of carrying out their programs.

With respect to such organizations, integration has been achieved in a measure and for limited purposes by federation, conference, or other forms of co-operation among the specialties involved. On the other hand, the taxpayer interest, while offering a means of balancing specialized promotion with the national income, has not been consistently effective.

The interest groups are popularly held to be best represented by "business," "labor," and "agriculture"; but no one of these groups is completely or unitedly organized. Each is represented, or considered to be, by a number of organizations. The unemployed, the aged, and the veterans constitute three interest-groups that in recent years have played a peculiarly active role.

The specialized and interest groups together roughly correspond to what are known as social or economic classes. Judged by one criterion or another, classes have always existed in America; and they have generally been described as three: (1) the "upper" or "moneyed" class, "capital," aristocracy, or plutocracy; (2) the "lower" or "propertyless" class, labor, or the proletariat; and (3) the middle class or classes. No precise apportionment of the American population can be made; but the indications are that, tested by vertical mobility, by feeling and by solidarity, cleavage has been increasing between what may be called "capital" and "labor" or between the highest-income and lowest-income groups.

Whenever a locality, section, class, or group develops leadership through established or extemporized organization, such leadership is almost invariably partial, representing a particular rather than the general welfare or interest. The innumerable specialized associations supply indispensable leaderships and they are more likely to be concerned with an aspect of the general welfare and to reflect a general social conscience; but, because they are specialized, each of them deals with only a portion, often a minute portion, of a problem. Even if the individual were not himself specialized and joined by force of circumstances to a class or interest-group, it would be impossible for him to use, co-ordinate, and integrate the various leaderships that are offered him.

His difficulty is increased by the fact that the objectives of the various groups and organizations may be inconsistent or conflicting. With respect to capital and labor and the organizations representing them or allied with them, conflict is more serious than mere partiality.

If questions at issue were satisfactorily settled in the private sphere by discussion and adjustment—if all classes and groups were to "pull together," sharing sacrifices as well as profits—private leadership would obviously assume greater authority, and private control of the economic system would become more effective, thus removing a considerable part of public confusion and of pressure on government.

Until comparatively recent years, the holders, manipulators, and conquerors of private economic power, however much they may have contributed to industrial development, were lacking in a sense of social responsibility and in equipment for broad economic statesmanship. Ownership of industry, more widely diffused, has become superficially more democratic; but actually management has tended to be dissociated from ownership. On the other hand, the feeling that industry exists to meet social needs has become one of the governing conceptions of our time; and the private managers of industry, though still narrow in outlook, like most other men, reveal an increasing sense of social responsibility and are becoming better equipped for private economic statesmanship.

Though both capital and labor pay lip service to their mutuality of interests, they are in too large measure sharply opposing powers. Labor, itself divided, struggles for its share of the industrial output and intervenes, frequently by force and without informed responsibility, in the making of industrial policies. As mediating, balancing, and integrating factors, neither the stockholders nor consumers as such are effectual. The middle classes might conceivably be able, through the force of opinion, to impose co-ordination on the productive organization; but the middle classes are, ordinarily, more than any other portion of the population, victims of disintegration and confusion. A certain amount and kind of leadership is provided or attempted by the legal, engineering, and educational professions; but it falls short of producing an adequate integrating effect.

To be sure, many of the conditions that produce confusion, disintegration, and conflict are inherent in political democracy and in a competitive, free enterprise system. But we are speaking now of efficient government; and we assume that the processes of public opinion should be such as to make it unnecessary for government to add to its already heavy burden or, if government is to act, compel it to do so in accord with sound principles and consistently from the viewpoint of the general welfare.

Propaganda is employed for the formation of public opinion. Propaganda is large-scale discussion; and it is an inevitable phenomenon of the "great society." Its power has probably been exaggerated; but, because individual time and attention are limited, the tendency of mass propaganda is to apply high-pressure methods to the particularistic solution of a few problems that appear most urgent or sensational, and to stampede opinion on a low intellectual level of discussion. Furthermore, the fact that propaganda is met by counter-propaganda and exposure may have tended to induce a general skepticism of publicity and of leadership. The relative decline of face-to-face discussion has in turn magnified the question of control of the media of mass propaganda, particularly the privately owned and commercially conducted press and radio.

International crisis places overwhelming emphasis on problems that are even more baffling than domestic questions; and the organization and process by which public opinion is normally formed and expressed are ill adapted to international issues. Emotionalism and demands for unity partially inhibit discussion. While the general welfare becomes a primary consideration, this gain is usually transitory, achieved by postponing or neglecting domestic problems, with the danger of a complete shift of emphasis from the external to the internal once the crisis has passed.

The party system is inadequate and is largely
supplanted by pressure groups.

The theory is that campaigns and elections, held within a framework of fundamental agreement, will crystallize opinion and clarify issues, deciding by majority vote the persons and principles that are to control government and the general policies that government is to adopt. Theoretically, therefore, group aims and group conflicts should be integrated in the party system, which should also select, offer to the electorate, and carry into the government the nation's ablest leadership. When the successful party takes power, according to the theory, its leaders will hold the party membership to unified and disciplined pursuance of the principles and policies approved; while the opposition will give to the people the benefit of continuous, informed, and constructive criticism.

The party system in practice has failed to measure up to its theoretical possibilities. For a hundred years "politics" and the "politician" have been popularly considered, and not without reason, to be separate from and opposed to the forces making for efficiency.

A tendency, having manifold and deep-seated causes, has been to identify party leadership with personalized presidential power. Another and related tendency, representing also the interplay of complex forces, has been to divide popular support of the major parties along class lines. A result, it seems, of this latter tendency in times of peace is to emphasize in party strategy the appeal of distributive justice and to subordinate the problem of industrial productivity.

The party system still operates; but it is the pressure groups, not the parties, that play continuously the more vital, active, and effective role in the control of government. A disturbing characteristic of this control is its preoccupation with particularistic and often conflicting interests and objectives, its concern with partial and piecemeal solutions.

Government in turn, through the devolment of its power, manipulates pressure groups, as well as parties. The ultimate outcome of this association and interaction between government and the groups, if the tendency were to continue, would be to give to the pressure-group system a relation to government somewhat similar in certain respects to political parties and factions. The pressure-group system would still retain its independent potentialities; but, with the passing of its leadership to government, the latter would mold, influence, and from time to time control the groups, for opportunistic and tactical ends, with manipulatory means, and with particularistic effects. Thus, while the system remained apparently unimpaired, government would tend to be self-controlling; and any such tendency would seem to be reinforced by centralization and concentration of governmental power.

Means of improvement, not yet fully realized, lie
in intellectual and scientific leadership.

Apart from a quick and universal transformation of human nature in general, which cannot be expected, the chief hope of reconciling efficient government with popular control would seem to lie in intellectual and scientific leadership, operating more authoritatively and more democratically than in the past. Until Jackson succeeded John Quincy Adams, America had the semblance of a governing class that represented intellect, training, experience, and political dedication. Under Jackson, the national government felt the leveling influence of the frontier, with its confidence in the common man and its disbelief in superior education, expertness, and intellectual leadership. Thereafter, for almost a half-century, these values were by no means entirely absent from government and they were constantly growing in the country; but they had no accepted and close working identification with political leadership or the conduct of public affairs.

Extension of elementary education and increase of literacy did not appear sufficient to raise the intellectual plane of politics.

In some ways, industrialism seemed no more favorable than the agricultural frontier had been to informed and high-minded leadership. On the other hand, mechanical invention and physical discovery have been prime factors in America's economic and social progress. Technological industry, enlarging and perfecting its own research facilities, has supplied much of the motive power of industrial expansion. Increasing productivity made possible an extension of higher educational facilities; and constantly more numerous became a class interested in ideas with equipment and time for thinking, speaking, and writing.

The scientific spirit and method were most readily and fruitfully adapted to physical phenomena. Thus applied, the results were so numerous, so fascinating, and apparently so beneficent as to make science, in the minds of many, almost a new and sufficient religion.

In the early years of the twentieth century, conditions created by rapid material progress pointed to the critical need of intellectual and scientific leadership in public affairs. The process of social change appeared to an alarming extent merely a blind response to instinct and interest, resulting in social waste and accumulating problems. Technology and the physical sciences seemed to have created a world so complex, so rapidly changing, and so full of portents as to be quite beyond the possibilities of democratic, efficient, and stable direction.

In the face of this challenge, intellectual and scientific leadership in public affairs did develop and did produce effects.

Since 1900, public information has increased in quantity and improved in quality. Ideas are now more quickly and widely propagated. Information and ideas are more extensively and successfully popularized; and, in general, an enlarged opportunity has been given to those who are trying to deal with social problems in the spirit and with the method of science. In recent years, a widespread, organized, institutionalized, systematically directed, and more or less standardized effort has been made to apply the scientific spirit and method to social problems.

The social sciences, representing this effort, have enlisted since the turn of the century a constantly increasing number of workers. The published results are impressive and to an increasing extent successfully popularized. Moreover, social scientists personally have done much to dispel the notion that they are a cloistered, "academic," and "impractical" breed. In various ways and to an increasing extent, economists and political scientists have established working relationships with government and, in the case of the economists, with industry, labor, and agriculture.

They have encountered certain important obstacles; for example, the incompatibility of political processes with the scientific attitude, the infinite number and obscurity of social facts, and the lag of research behind the need of or demand for political action, the tendency, in part unavoidable, to specialize and to neglect or postpone synthesis, the difficulty of establishing with respect to social facts general "laws" and principles of universal and permanent validity, the difficulty of identifying a real social scientist, the human frailties of scientists, and the general lack of agreement, of unity, and consequently of authority among social scientists, along with the indispensability of absolute intellectual freedom.

The technical expert has made important contributions to the efficiency of plant and office management, administrative operations and procedures, and the organization of men and materials for limited concrete purposes. In rural America he had little political standing. After the Civil War intellectual leadership, reacting from partisanship and corruption, established the principle of the merit system. Thereafter, expertness became increasingly the characteristic and the test of American administration.

The mark of the expert is authority; but his authoritativeness does not extend to the larger and more critical aspects of policy determination. It has been difficult in practice to draw the boundaries of his appropriate jurisdiction. His growing prestige is a possible danger, because it permits him to act politically without seeming so to act, and because in certain fields the habit is to pay deference to "experts" where real expertness does not and cannot exist.

In spite of the signs of progress just mentioned, the tendency has been for the task of leadership, initiation, and integration to devolve upon government itself. We shall now examine indications and possibilities of efficiency within the governmental mechanism.

In the structure of government, the requirements of centralization and of decentralization are imperfectly adjusted.

In rural America, a relatively large measure of local self-government was reasonably satisfactory. When, however, the problems of government were seen to be regional or state-wide and their solution appeared to be beyond the financial and technical resources of the community, state centralization became necessary if popular demands for social service and economic control were to be effectively met. Within the states, elements of confusion soon entered into the centralizing movement and have persisted down to our own time.

Local self-government, identified with democracy, had developed a tradition so tenacious that it has thus far prevented any rational reconstruction of the territorial basis of state governments. The counties are in most if not all states still treated in theory as little states; and the effort, usually unconscious, to reconcile efficiency with localism has produced a system that seems neither efficient nor locally democratic. This state of affairs is attributable in part to the application of the idea of localism to the system of legislative representation. Another retarding factor has been the role played by, local units in the party organizations.

The cities, for reasons peculiar to themselves, have made a better showing with respect to the overhauling of traditions and the reconciliation of centralization with local self-government. But the role of the cities has been a paradoxical one. They have largely preserved, for themselves, the vitality of local self-government; they have, with industrialism, produced the need of governmental efficiency and the desire for it; but they have also been potent forces back of national centralization, which in turn accentuates the problems of both democracy and efficiency.

There was much reason in 1787 for a constitutional division of powers between the states and the federal government. Much might be said now for an absolute centralization of power, accompanied by a delegation downward of legislative and administrative activity. The system that we now have is neither one nor the other. It has come through no general policy or plan; and it has not been preceded or accompanied by any deliberate or reasoned revision of ideals and principles, or by any correspondingly far-reaching amendment of the Constitution.

The federal balance has never been a steady one. To its present situation, the inefficiency of the state governments has contributed; but more important factors are the economic and social changes that have regionalized and nationalized problems. With reference to those problems the states were and are unable to take effective action either singly, in co-ordination, or in co-operation.

Constitutionally, the opportunity for centralization lay chiefly, first, in the susceptibility of the commerce clause to expansion by judicial interpretation and, second, in the spending power of Congress, almost entirely free from judicial supervision. Thus, control over the centralizing trend is divided between Congress and the Supreme Court. We may say, with possibly some oversimplification, that centralization follows two directions and adopts a different method for each direction. One may ask whether the two methods and the two rates of progress are correlated. The recent accumulation of state trade barriers and of state and local promotional schemes, along with the relatively slight promotion by the federal government of normal industrial productivity, would seem to indicate considerable maladjustments in the territorial distribution of powers and responsibilities.

Before the depression, use by the national government of its spending power in connection with state activities was for the most part a result of federal surpluses, and its purpose in most cases was to stimulate the states. More recently, federal grants have emphasized support, rather than stimulation, and have rested on federal borrowing, thus largely sidestepping taxpayer resistance. Centralization through borrowing and spending appears to remove certain restrictions on the general expansion of government, and upsets the balance that constitutional federalism was expected to preserve between public and private responsibility. The power taken over from or shared with the states is exercised to a great extent by federal administrative agencies. Accordingly, the tendency seems to be for state legislation and administration to reflect any lack of co-ordination that may exist in federal policies and administration.

A further effect, it would seem, is to divide responsibility for state legislation. Finally, one may ask whether the present type of centralization does not bid fair to eliminate from government that varied experimentation and accumulation of experience that local and state initiative made possible.

The work and facts of modern government challenge the theory of separation of powers.

A system of separation of powers and checks and balances was supported on the theory that it would promote deliberation, prevent concentration or usurpation of power, protect individual liberty, and mitigate popular impulsiveness. Bicameralism was linked with the system and has also been theoretically though less strongly supported. The system presupposes an equilibrium that has never been continuously maintained. In the past, as a rule, we have had considerable periods of congressional dominance alternating with comparatively brief assertions of presidential leadership backed by exceptionally intensified progressive opinion. Correspondingly, periods of relative inactivity have alternated with sudden surges of legislation. From time to time, the system has produced deadlocks, as well as waste of time and energy through jealousy and maneuvering for personal or political advantage.

It is quite possible that the system never had any real justification except as a set of expedient contrivances to make a federal union possible. It may well be maintained that if social forces are in equilibrium, government will be equally so, whatever its setup may be. Be that as it may, the indications are that technological America is changing permanently the operations and effect of the governmental mechanism, and adding to it, without any conscious attempt to abolish or alter the original system. Various conditions have, in fact if not in law, augmented executive and administrative, compared with congressional, power.

The competence of Congress is, on the whole, unequal to its task.

Compared with its capacity and functioning in previous periods, Congress seems to have improved in some respects; in others, it appears to have become more incompetent and ineffective; and in still others, it is probably no better and no worse. At times when critical action is called for, it acknowledges its own impotence. In certain important fields of legislation, initiative is no longer expected from it. Though Congress continues to function and retains its constitutional powers, it has largely lost popular leadership; and its own resources appear insufficient for the planning and revision of policies with reasonable promptness.[1]

Bureaucratic power increases efficiency in details without insuring integration.

Delegation of legislative power to administrative agencies has relieved Congress of a part of its burden and increased the flexibility, adaptability, and effectiveness of technical policy-determination. The bureaucracy helps also by providing Congress with expert and experienced advisers. As delegation increases and the bureaucracy grows, the tendency is to make Congress more and more dependent on administrative counsel.

Group demands pass through Congress into the shape of laws with some filtering but with little focusing; and they finally imprint themselves on the shape of the bureaucracy. Thus, we find various administrative agencies representing, linked with, and sup-

---

[1] To judge the present and prospective inadequacy of Congress relative to the need for integrated and prompt action, one should recall the following conditions and developments: division of Congress into two chambers; the numerous membership of the House of Representatives; election of members by and from states and districts; the frequency of election of representatives; the leveling of members down to the popular average; unequal national distribution of leadership; transformation of representatives into delegates; the reciprocal and cumulative influence of material inducements on members and their constituencies; the effect of localized pressures, accentuated by the direct primary system of nomination, on personal independence and party cohesion; assimilation of policy with party strategy; shifting of pressures from state legislatures to Congress; reflection by the national legislature of intense and unintegrated minority pressures; rural overrepresentation and predominance of rural and "stand-pat" leadership, producing maladjustment to the conditions of an industrial-urban society and retarded adaptation to change; waste of members' time and energy; decline of congressional leadership in Congress and the country; the comparative futility of congressional debates; absence of co-ordination among the committees of Congress; the unsatisfactory features of committee investigations; and the lack of any strictly legislative machinery for the balancing and co-ordination of national and state policies.

ported by the very groups whose unintegrated pressures are brought to bear on Congress. Since the bureaucrats are not completely unified, co-ordinated, or controlled by Congress or the president, when they advise and press Congress or president they bring to that operation a considerable part of the disintegration and conflict that characterize both Congress and the social organization. Moreover, each administrative agency tends to become a special group concerned with its own perpetuation and aggrandizement and possessing a vested interest in particular policies.

Presidential domination accelerates the mechanism, without necessarily improving the output.

Executive leadership or domination, in its final stage, means that the president makes himself the focus of pressures, the leader of those groups that possess decisive voting power, the controller of the bureaucracy, the boss of his party, and dictator over Congress. Assuming for the president ideal moral and intellectual qualifications, he could conceivably bring about the needed integration. The American political system, however, gives no assurance that he will possess such qualifications. Besides, he has other engrossing functions.

Presidential domination may or may not resolve itself into a deliberate political manipulation of underprivileged groups, with policies and propaganda as the manipulating instruments; but in any case it is almost certain to emphasize distributive policies and the curbing of private economic power. The problem of industrial production is likely to be minimized or ignored or dealt with in such a way as to involve no appearance of sympathetic co-operation between government and industry and no postponement of the process of satisfying popular demands.

The actual formulation of policies will necessarily be left to the groups concerned and to the bureaucracy. In many instances, congressional leaders will be consulted. Such assistance and consultation will by no means insure integrated policies; and the president will have neither time nor ability to provide integration. The process will get action quickly and in quantity; but the resulting policies will suffer from group-mindedness, experimentalism, and lack of balance. In this process, furthermore, both Congress and the Constitution lose prestige, while governmental expansion and centralization continue.

Neither the efficiency and economy movement nor "planning" solved the problem.

Around 1910, governmental costs were rising and tax burdens growing heavier; administrative agencies were multiplying and diversifying, apparently without plan or reason; "strong" and administratively minded executives were appearing in the states and in the national government; the "short ballot" movement was gaining strength; in the cities, the commission plan first and the council-manager plan later seemed to be promoting efficiency through the separation of legislation from administration and the integration and simplification of administration; industrial corporations, apparently organized on similar principles, were held to be brilliant exemplifications of efficiency; and political science, developing the technique of governmental research, put itself at the disposal of legislative and executive commissions of investigation.

In the main, the results were: to promote expertness in administration; to introduce improved methods of budgetary and fiscal control, more economical purchasing systems, and many savings in detailed operations; and partially to integrate administrative organizations under executive control. The movement did not result in permanently reduced or stabilized governmental expenditures or, so far as the national government was concerned, in permanently sound fiscal procedure.

The key to basic efficiency lay in the legislative mechanism and in the political processes; and these parts of government seemed too extensive, too imponderable, and too much bound up with constitutions, traditions, and emotions for practical study or opportune action. The movement aimed at executive control of administration; but it devised no means either to qualify the executive for this function or to control him in the exercise of his added power. The purpose was to divorce administration from legislation; but the effect was to increase executive power over the legislature, leaving unresolved the dilemma presented by our dual-function executive. Executive control over administration and executive leadership in policy-determination were advocated in one breath as means to "make democracy work"; but no satisfactory evidence appeared that either proposal would insure efficiency or strengthen democracy.

The idea of "planning" stemmed from the elaboration and appreciation of social intelligence, scientific progress, extensions of technical expertness, and efforts to achieve efficiency and economy. The conditions that confronted America at the turn of the century emphasized acutely the need of order, systematization, co-ordination, and foresight.

Wherever engineering is involved, as in highway construction and the physical layout of cities, "planned" programs are possible and are to an increasing extent accepted and carried out. In certain other more critical areas, especially those that are predominantly economic, social, or political, the difficulties are those that inhere in the inadequacies of human nature, in the social organization, in the democratic process, and in the social sciences. The fact remains, however, that as additional governmental controls are applied to the economic system, an integrated scientific handling and appraisal of these controls becomes more and more necessary.

In any event, public administration has been attracting a larger number of men and women who are occupied with research and concerned with intellectual and scientific leadership. Their influence, compared with that of similar private leadership, seems to be relatively increasing.

These developments are on the whole encouraging, but they raise certain questions. Does the co-ordination of scientific men in administrative work restrict that open competition of minds which facilitates the testing of theories and discovery of the truth? Does political direction, as well as administrative requirements, abridge freedom of expression as well as freedom of thought? Does partial control of information and *ex officio* prestige give to administrators an unmerited authority? Are they in a position to intimidate other scientists, particularly those on the side of industry?

Most of the elementary and secondary schools and adult-education activities and a large portion of the higher educational institutions are included in government administration. They are still predominantly under state and local control; but the possibilities of increasing national control cannot be disregarded. It may be that academic freedom is as well protected in public as in private institutions; but the public institutions, as institutions, are not as free of actual or potential political control. Moreover, economic and fiscal conditions appear to have been strengthening the public institutions, compared with the endowed institutions and foundations.

Does judicial review and constitutional amendment contribute to efficient policy-determination?

The bearing of judicial power on democracy and stability is, at least, capable of a somewhat concrete appraisal. The question of its relation to governmental efficiency is in many respects exceedingly speculative.

Judicial review has involved a negative and restricted policy-determination. Because of its conservative tendency, it has slowed up legislation in some fields; but in the long run, the Supreme Court has yielded to public opinion, to presidential power, or to both. In some cases, judicial brakes may have had the effect of improving public policies. In other cases, the effect has probably been to complicate the legislative task and distort the structure of policy. Certainly, in the national government the Supreme Court, with respect to its political function, is, of the five separate legislative organs,[2] the least likely to be for any extended period coordinated with the others.

Legalism and judicial qualifications, as evidenced in the Court, proved to be inadequate for dealing with technical, economic, and social questions. In view of other judicial responsibilities, this inadequacy could not be entirely removed by professional education or by the "socialization" of jurisprudence. A more logical but still not wholly satisfactory solution of the problem of technical competence is coming through enlargement of the scope and finality of administrative adjudication.

[2] President, Senate, House of Representatives, Supreme Court, and the administration.

The recently reconstructed court seems to embody, on the one hand, a frank recognition of the Court's political function and, on the other, a substantial abdication of that function to Congress, the president, and the bureaucracy. Apart from the relation of this judicial "revolution" to the problem of stability, its effect is apparently to free Congress, at least for a time, from any substantial judicial restraint, to encourage governmental expansion and centralization, and further to increase administrative power.

The amending process has been so difficult and so seldom used that its efficiency is comparable to that of a stalled machine. Its chronic inaction has been both a cause and an effect of the extension of judicial power over policy-determination. Partly in consequence of the two phenomena—comparative abandonment of amendment and long-run judicial accommodation with respect to governmental powers—the structure of government, as distinguished from its powers, has been left unchanged and largely uncriticized.

*The general result in domestic affairs is an unduly
confused structure of policy.*

With respect to domestic policies involving economic control and social justice, the manner in which we are proceeding has been called piecemeal or gradual "collectivism." We have gone a considerable distance from the free enterprise system as it existed a century or even a half-century ago. We are still far short of state socialism, communism, or totalitarianism. But we show no signs of stopping where we are. While rapidly sloughing off the doctrine of economic freedom, we have adopted no reasoned collectivist objective. Nor have we defined an intermediate position, in terms that are adequate, generally accepted, and politically controlling.

Although the crux of the national problem lies in industrial production, the cumbrousness of the legislative system and the complexity of the problem necessitate a piecemeal approach. "Mediation" among pressure-groups takes the form of yielding one by one to the demands of the most powerful articulate interests. Thus, the recent tendency seems to be to overweight policy on the side of distributive justice and restrictive economic controls. Industrial productivity and expansion, central to the problems of economic progress and economic stability, appear either comparatively neglected or questionably treated. One finds little evidence of consistent effort to appraise and protect those practices, influences, and aspirations that appear to be identified with the growth and success of privately managed production.

In the development of policy, as of democracy, economic instability and recurrence of economic crises have been prime influences. The result has been periods of relative legislative inactivity alternating with sudden surges of more or less radical policy-determination. Economic instability may have been a necessary sort of political stimulant; but it has not been a continuous and measured stimulant. Among its effects have been political fatigue and legislative indigestion.

The structure of policy seems to be suffering a progressive distortion; and the problem presented to the legislator grows progressively larger and more complicated. Any substantial change in the trend of policy appears to become constantly more difficult, because of vested interests in beneficiary laws.

A conspicuous incident of developing policy is its division of economic power and responsibility between government and private enterprise and the scattering of power and responsibility in both public and private spheres. Management of this central function—production—is still preponderantly private. Public opinion, government, and private management presumably are or should be supremely concerned with this function; but, at periods in the past and in recent years for much of the time, government and business have been ranged against each other like hostile forces, each accusing the other of lack of vision, selfishness, incompetence, and immorality.

Absence of principle and of co-ordination is also noticeable among those policies that relate to politics and governmental organization. It is now generally held that the critical task of politics is the maintenance of democracy. To this end public policies have embodied the ideas that government should curb private economic power, distribute income among the people, and protect the nation against external aggression. Such policies may be sound; but, too often, their contribution to democracy is an afterthought, a rationalization, or pure speculation. With respect to other democratizing or stabilizing policies, one finds little conscious correlation and in many respects the effects have been quite different from those expected.

As was pointed out in the introductory chapter, the author is not judging the necessity, the merits, or the effect of specific policies. Nor does he assume that there is any standard of "right" policy or any ideal of integration to which government should, or under practical conditions can, conform. The processes of popular government would necessarily set limits to the attainment of a standard of perfect policy, if one could be established. Some of the defects or alleged defects just mentioned may be inevitable and inescapable.

The important questions in regard to governmental policies is not merely whether they lack integration or are wanting in balance, but whether disintegration and imbalance are increasing, whether these conditions appear in such form as to be dangerous to the democracy that encourages them, whether that democracy recognizes the conditions and the danger, and whether, if it has the recognition, it is really attempting democratically to solve the problem.

In foreign affairs, inefficiency seems inherent in democracy and nationalism and potential in our governmental organization.

The existence of national sovereignties creates a distinction between domestic and international problems, produces imbalance and lag, invites neglect, and promotes confusion, while the conditions that favor and characterize democracy render it incompetent in the presence of world instability. When war comes, because of the international disorganization that nationalism and democracy have encouraged, the vital prior need is for unity, for presidential leadership, and for strategic administrative and industrial efficiency. Strategy may be brilliantly planned and executed; but administrative and industrial efficiency lags, owing to factors that in large part seem to be inherent in the politics of democracy and in our system of government. Moreover, efficiency in the task of winning the war operates against efficiency in the peace settlement. The latter is complicated by other factors, including democracy itself, the feeling of nationalism, the constitutional system, the character of the presidency, and the attitudes and policies of other nations.

On the nature of the peace settlement depends the possibility of a long-run easing of the task of democratic government; but, whatever the settlement may be, the problem of governmental efficiency in domestic affairs will be for a time more rather than less serious.

As Plato summed up the matter long ago,

Until philosophers are kings, or the kings and princes of this world have the spirit and power of philosophy, and political greatness and wisdom meet in one, and those commoner natures who pursue either to the exclusion of the other are compelled to stand aside, cities will never have rest from their evils,—no, nor the human race, as I believe,—and then only will this our State have a possibility of life and behold the "light of day."[3]

Inefficiency will always be with us. Some of it is the price that we pay for democracy. If, as the author believes, the problem of governmental efficiency has become more pressing, we need to inquire whether inefficiency is approaching the point where it threatens the durability of democracy.

[3] *The Works of Plato*, Modern Library ed., p. 431.

CHAPTER XVI

STABILITY

It seems a fair assumption that no government can long maintain stability when it has become responsible for the general economic welfare and fails through its own action or inaction to meet the economic expectations of the people or of the groups that possess preponderant political power. A central issue is presented, therefore, by the apparent or imminent lag between governmental efficiency positive or negative on the one hand and governmental responsibilities and popular expectations on the other. If this lag is, or is believed to be, the fault of popular government, the psychological foundation of democracy in the absence of other types of support becomes subject to gradual undermining or sudden upheaval. It seems an equally reasonable assumption that economic expectations cannot be met if international disorganization and national insecurity impose on America an exceptional continuing burden of armament or the waste of recurring wars, while a changed international system or an altered American relationship to it may also profoundly affect our political stability.

Long-time trends seemed to assure stability; but
threats to it have never been wholly absent.

The doctrine of revolution contained in the Jeffersonian philosophy was based on the assumed necessity of a particular revolution, on the theory of natural rights, on fear of governmental power, and on confidence in the perfectibility and wisdom of the people. The framers of the Constitution did not attempt any absolute freezing of the *status quo*. They were aware that government, while maintaining its life and authority, would have to adjust itself to change; but they were primarily concerned not so much with adjustment itself as with the restraining and ordering of adjustment.

The Revolution produced independent American states; the Constitution and the Civil War, a united American nation. Events between the Constitution and the Civil War seemed to confirm

America's isolation from an unstable European system and likewise to preclude the establishment in this hemisphere of any similar system. From territorial expansion, as well as from individual opportunity and achievement, came a sense of national power and national security, confidence in the destiny of America. From the Revolution to the twentieth century, the fact and the feeling of American nationalism contributed to security from external dangers and made possible concentration of energy on domestic affairs.

American development has been marked by a sweeping alteration of the physical face of the country and by technological and scientific achievements that have repeatedly and profoundly modified the material life of the people. As time went on, the rate of material change accelerated.

The conditions of expanding and developing America met reasonably well the economic expectations of the people. Successive democratizations of government served to confirm the belief that popular rule could be and was being realized and provided a framework in which changed or enlarged expectations could apparently be met without violent upheaval.

For more than a century, hard work and saving in the presence of opportunity made equality a substantial reality. When substantially equal economic opportunities existed, which could be seized and converted into prosperity by industry and thrift, actual inequalities of wealth or of income were likely to be stimulating rather than discouraging. It was really good luck then to be born in a log cabin. During that time, the insulation of economic phenomena from psychological and political currents was supported and prolonged by certain moral standards—notably those related to or identified with religion, property, domestic relations, charity, work, saving, and self-reliance—and by certain principles—individualism, equality of opportunity, free enterprise, and minimized government.

The general effect was to create and maintain faith in American conditions and institutions and confidence in the future. This faith and this confidence reduced political strain while contributing to the success of the private enterprise system.

As national power grew, as constitutionalism established itself, and as the enfranchised masses intermittently or partially seized political control, American government came to mean in popular thinking democracy and order, both associated with national security and with an undefined conception of social efficiency that seemed to be proved by economic progress, increasing production, wide distribution of goods, and rising standards of living.

While democratization may proceed from economic interest, economic interest may also produce a reaction from democratic philosophy and an intentional paralysis of democratic functioning. The Constitutional Convention reflected the first reaction, a comparatively mild one, but having enormous effect on American political development. Another came from the southern slave-holding interest. During the decade before the Civil War, the basic tenets of the democratic faith—liberty, equality, government by consent of the governed, and confidence in the wisdom of the people—were widely disputed in the South and to some extent in the North; and the political representatives of the southern economic interest were able in effect to prevent a democratic solution of the slavery problem.

In addition to sectionalism, other real or imagined inroads on stability were at one time or another perceived by observers of the American scene—foreign entanglements; war, militarism, and the "man on horseback"; industrialism; monopoly; materialism in politics; corruption; debt; imperialism; presidential perpetuation in office; civic indifference; and class conflict.

The real threats have not produced revolution and the imagined ones have not materialized; and, in most outward appearances, American democracy now, compared with previous times, is in principle firmly established.

Accelerated economic and social change during the last half-century has introduced few new factors; but the aggravation of certain major factors already existing, the intensification of situations, and a rapid alteration of the popular attitude toward the function of government have greatly magnified popular expectations, increased popular demands, contributed to strain, and in other ways brought about what amounts to a substantial restatement of the problem of stability.

In the light of the present international crisis, which confirms the lessons of the First World War, it appears that American nationalism has embodied and exemplified a system that in Europe and Asia invited catastrophes which have increasingly threatened to doom us along with others. The two world wars have demonstrated that, internationally, the absolute principle of national sovereignty has not been and probably cannot be reconciled with morals, law, effective collective action, or enduring peace. Moreover, the present war effort, following an exceptional depression, brings what may prove to be an unprecedented interruption of economic progress and of the process of meeting the economic expectations of the people along with possibly serious inroads on the power of the middle classes.

The elements of the democratic spirit have been undergoing significant changes.

The democratic philosophy represented in its origins a revolt against religious, intellectual, and political authoritarianism. Actual concrete experience with oppression engendered a deep-seated fear of power; and, under early American conditions, this fear was, in the main, a fear of political power. Revolt against political power was coupled with and justified by theories that all men are politically equal and that they are equally possessed of certain in-born rights—the right to individual liberty and the right to self-government. These doctrines were further supported by a belief that the purpose of government was the happiness of the individual, not the power and glory of the state. The logic of the democratic creed was rounded out by faith in the perfectibility, good will, justice, rationality, and collective wisdom of men; and it was further practically supported by feelings of confidence in the effectiveness of a government whose forms and functioning were democratic.

Conditions in rural America served to confirm most of these familiar premises of democracy—individualism, liberty, equality, antagonism to authority, fear of political power, and confidence in the capacity of the people. Democratizing movements surged forward repeatedly from their agricultural breeding ground; but, little by little, with the economic and social transformation of the country, the elements of the democratic faith have appeared to lose much of their vital identification with the life of the masses.

As time passed, the Revolution, which in the minds of our ancestors had climaxed a long and deeply felt struggle against actual oppression, receded into history. Tyranny first became a fading memory; later a subordinated and diluted portion of the school textbooks.

While economic independence, self-sufficiency, or self-reliance did not at any time characterize all Americans or completely characterize any of them, democratizing movements originated in that part of the nation which, outside the South, was closest to the frontier. The rural population, however, has been growing relatively less numerous; a considerable part of its capacity for political initiative seems to have been drained away; and modern conditions make the rural regions less isolated, less individualistic, and more like the cities. Except for its relics, the direct frontier influence has well nigh disappeared from American life.

The city was once called "the hope of democracy." Its relation to and eventual effect upon political development are not yet clear. Up to this time, urban conditions appear to have contributed more to technical governmental efficiency than to the fact, the feeling, or the inspirations of democracy. Certain retrogressive changes in the basic elements of democracy that have marked American political evolution appear to spring from conditions that are characteristic of the cities. In any event, urban life has imposed a multitude of restrictions, many of them highly technical; and proper adjustment to such a life demands a very considerable taming of the spirit of liberty.

The beginnings of the American nation coincided with the abandonment of the "mercantile system" and the adoption, in its place, of the principle of *laissez faire*. Thus, economic freedom triumphed, at least in theory, over economic restriction. The new nation, embarking on the exploitation of a continent, centered its exuberant hopes and energies on the development of transportation and manufacturing. The corporation was popularly accepted as an appropriate form of industrial organization; and to it was granted in principle and largely in fact that relative freedom from regulation which was then the prized possession of individuals in general.

With the growth of industrialism, the relation between property and individualism changed both in fact and in theory. In revolutionary and rural America property as a right and a value was considered on a par with life and liberty. The importance attached to property had a meaning that extended beyond materialism or acquisitiveness. When property was largely conceived of as land, it meant substantial equality, family integrity, and an individualistic economy. Thus, landed property figured vitally in the Jeffersonian democratic philosophy; it was made a common aspiration through the abolition in this country of the rule of primogeniture; and the most pressing problems of government in rural America were problems directly or indirectly concerned with land.

The change, measured by relative importance, from tangible to intangible property, from individual to corporate ownership, and, to an increasing extent in recent years, from individual and corporate to institutional and governmental ownership, has had profound effects on the popular and legal concepts of property and property rights, the status of individuals, the relations of groups and classes, their attitude toward government, and the fact and the feeling of independence, equality, security, and responsibility. An important aspect of this change is the separation of the ownership of productive property from its use, a separation marked first by the growth of the industrial wage-earning class, and later by the substantial abdication of industrial control by the stockholders. Agricultural change has itself been characterized by increasing tenantry and a kind of absentee landlordism.

Among the results of the change in the form and meaning of property was an attenuation of the feeling of individual power and responsibility. Revolution against tyranny had necessarily emphasized rights, rather than obligations or responsibilities; and assertion of rights had been stimulated by frontier conditions. These conditions had, to be sure, compelled an extensive and continual community co-operation that had made the individual in practice responsible for the welfare of others; but the very naturalness and practicality of the co-operation and of the responsibility that flowed from it precluded the formation of a felt and propagated system of obligations to balance the system of rights. As the economic and social system became more complex and interdependent, as the groups engaged in production and distribution separated from one another, became group conscious, and demanded economic benefits from society, co-operation was no longer natural, and responsibility was no longer automatically and unconsciously enforced. Nevertheless, new rights gained social recognition, rights that had very tangible content. Government, rather than the private community, was looked to for the granting and enforcing of rights; but a democratically controlled government found it less easy to define and impose responsibilities. So an undue emphasis on rights having social significance and a tendency toward the creation of new and similar rights persisted.

Other changes brought by industrialism confused the meaning of individual liberty and reduced the intensity of its emotional quality. For the industrial wage earner, the individualism embodied in freedom of contract, in the absence of an equality of bargaining power, meant in practice the opposite of freedom. The farmer, too, found, not only that his liberty was circumscribed, but that the practical meaning of liberty was confused.

From time to time the agrarian or labor group or both groups have attacked the possessors, real or alleged, of private economic power. These attacks have been represented as struggles against oppression and therefore in behalf of freedom; but in these cases the opposition to oppression and the championship of freedom have been in the main simply means to compel a more equitable distribution of income among the groups. Moreover, the attacks have been on the whole justifiably directed against the liberties of the so-called privileged group; but the group thus attacked naturally became in turn on certain specific issues the champion of liberty. Apart from the social merits of free or of unfree enterprise, the tendency seems to have been, in the minds of the masses, to qualify liberty in practice and to discredit the term in theory. Freedom took on special meanings from special group interests and special situations, appearing to become less than formerly a constant and universal feeling, as well as a concrete and easily tested fact.

It is impossible to say that Americans on the average are actually less free than in the past; but it appeared until recently that large sections of the population were more disposed than in the past to accept restrictions on freedom.

At the present moment, an international crisis brings again to the fore the ideal of freedom, while subordinating materialism and the demands of group interests. One may hope that this experience may cause a more than transitory rejuvenation of the spirit of individual liberty. It is quite possible, however, in the presence of national danger, when democracy cannot be fully operative, for a people, losing opportunity for the practice of freedom, to lose still more of the desire for freedom.

*Concepts of social justice and social security
tend to replace liberty and equality.*

The demand for economic privileges is not a recent phenomenon in American history. Democracy has been long conceived to be government *for*, as well as *by* and *of*, the people. From the beginning, Americans have been materialistic; and the circumstances of national development have not only perpetuated materialism but also have created and maintained general and rising expectations of material progress. Religion, the presumed competitor of materialism, yielded in part to the prevailing spirit and steadily lost influence; and it is not certain yet that art and intellectualism are acting with any general effect as counter-influences.

For a hundred years, the almost exclusive responsibility for meeting the economic expectations of the people was located outside of government, in the private enterprise system. That system was competitive and subject to rapid changes and extreme fluctuations; but the changes and fluctuations more or less took care of themselves through the operation of "natural" economic laws and the conditions of expanding America. As technological industrialism developed, the "natural" economic laws broke down to an extent; production and distribution were governed more by the conscious decisions of industrial managers; and private economic power seemed to be increasingly concentrated. This situation in turn accentuated group and class conflict, which was not resolved by private integrative forces or by an adequate sense of social responsibility on the part of the private holders of economic power.

Liberty, expressed in terms of competition, class differentiation, or concentration of economic power, tended to create ever-widening inequalities.

The result was to give more and more importance to "social justice," in effect a more equitable distribution of income. Though the corporation is not property itself but an instrument for the productive use of property, the protection of property rights has come to be looked upon as protection of corporate selfishness. A distinction is drawn between "property rights" and "human rights," implying that property has little if anything to do with the general welfare.

Surrounded and profoundly affected by complex conditions and forces beyond their control, visited from time to time by depressions, deprived of a free market and of the opportunity for self-relief provided by free land, Americans in the mass have tended to substitute in their political thinking the ideal of security for that of liberty. Individual thrift, which had formerly served in most cases the purposes of security, no longer appears sufficient.

The substitution has come about, not only because of social conditions pressing upon the individual, but also, possibly, because of changes that have taken place in personal character. Personality in formation could hardly fail to be impressed by an environment in which the individual in many ways can function only with the help of machines and technicians, in which home life has been invaded, in which entertainment and recreation are in large measure standardized, mechanized, and commercialized, and in which the creative impulse can find few ready individual means of expression and development.

Confidence in governmental power has increased.

Demands for social justice and social security, arising from economic and social conditions and implemented by mass possession of political power, has had the effect of making government, specifically the national government, increasingly responsible for the efficiency of the private enterprise system and for the protection of the masses from its abuses. The resulting expansion of government has been accompanied by a radical change in the popular attitude toward governmental power, a change from distrust to confidence, from faith in individualism to practically unreserved expectations of public benefits. Thus, various brakes on the development and concentration of public power have been removed or weakened, reducing in turn the simplicity and automatic assurance of individual freedom in relation to government.

Much of the economic and social strain and burden on government might have been mitigated or eliminated had Americans in the mass been passive, "deferential," docile, fatalistic, ignorant, or devoid of materialistic ambition. Americans for the most part have not had such negative characteristics; and, up to this time, the whole tendency of American political life has been, on the whole fortunately, opposed to their development.

On the other hand, a patient attitude has not been encouraged. Such an attitude could be expected only from a recognition that the situation creating impatience is substantially just, economically desirable, or economically unavoidable. That recognition, if it were to be morally and politically salutary, could not come from political processes, as these processes had worked in the past: it had to come from the development and acceptance of scientific leadership on the basis of a philosophical and religious way of life.

The general result has been to sidetrack the democratizing urge.

Increasing reliance on governmental power for protection from private economic power has been accompanied, rationalized, and in part occasioned by a shift in the application of the democratic doctrine.

On the one hand, as an ideal and a hope "industrial democracy" tended to eclipse political democracy. Concentration of power in the hands of industrial managers, though they remain politically neutral, is looked upon as undemocratic; while concentration of labor power, even though politically unneutral, is considered democratic. In both cases the theory is that the ends of democracy are served by intensifying competition, by balancing forces, by qualifiedly encouraging private warfare.

On the other hand, while democratizing movements in the past made government more responsive to public opinion, especially to group opinions, it can hardly be claimed that these movements, particularly those after the Civil War, aimed to realize democracy purely for the sake of democracy. Their ultimate aim in general was distributive justice. Though both government and people fall considerably short of fully realizing democracy, the groups that possess voting power appear to think that they have found in the "strong" executive an adequate means of realizing popular control and in pressure politics and bureaucracy effective techniques for attaining economic ends without further trouble over formal political means. Such ideas were conspicuously absent from traditional democratic thinking.

Moreover, with the removal of brakes on the development and concentration of governmental power, governmental efficiency became more difficult and more necessary, and preoccupation with it more unavoidable.

The substantially new concepts—efficiency, distributive justice, and security—do not under the circumstances supply fresh nourishment to the democratizing urge. They are not emotionally or practically tied in with political democracy. All are possible of achievement in an autocratic régime.

Had they been continuously and habitually recognized from the beginning as inevitable accompaniments of industrialization, a less rigid, more feasible, more democratic, and more efficient political system, as well as a better correlation between politics and economics, might have developed. As it was, the unavoidable but belated preoccupation with these concepts seems to have had the result of eclipsing and partially discrediting the idea of democracy. The drive for efficiency concentrated on the less rigid parts of the governmental structure—the executive and the bureaucracy. These parts, however, like the concept of efficiency, are identified historically and logically more with autocracy than with democracy.

The earlier theories still embodied in our governmental organization assume that structural and mechanical equilibrium can be self-sustaining under the pressure and manipulation of organic forces. The expected balances have not been continuously maintained and certain recent trends suggest the possibility of a definite and lasting upset; but the effort to maintain them has contributed to disequilibrium in public policy and in the larger social organization. The final result of converging tendencies appears to be personal government.

Thus, the feeling, and to some extent the fact, seems to be that the function of preserving democracy, that is, of stabilizing it, has gravitated to the president. We might conceive of a president capable of performing that function through extraordinary gifts of intellectual, moral, and spiritual leadership, joined with rare humility and a supreme abnegation. But obtaining such a president in our system would be pretty much of an accident. As Abraham Lincoln said in 1837:

Is it unreasonable, then, to expect that some man possessed of the loftiest genius, coupled with ambition to push it to its utmost stretch, will at some time spring up among us? And when such a one does, it will require the people to be united with each other, attached to the government and laws, and generally intelligent, to successfully frustrate his designs.[1]

The presidency in the long run is unstable to the extent that it is personal; and, to the extent that the president dominates government, presidential instability becomes governmental instability.

Do the people still trust themselves?

The doctrine of government by consent of the governed was based on faith in the perfectibility, good will, and wisdom of men.

This faith in operation has not been an unmixed good. Flattery of the people has obscured the difficulty and responsibility of their task; while the tendency has been to make of legislators mere delegates and of executives leaders without popular control. A kind

[1] Carl Sandburg, *Abraham Lincoln—The Prairie Years*, Vol 1 (1926), p. 214.

of fatalism implicit in majority rule has tended to estop discussion and inhibit thinking with reference to certain questions on which the people are deemed to have spoken and other matters closely identified with popular prejudices. Progress in America may well have been due, less to the wisdom of the people politically expressed, than to private enterprise and uniquely favorable circumstances. Since 1900, however, while confidence in government has increased, self-criticism and distrust of popular capacity have apparently widened and deepened.[2]

The American people from generation to generation have been facing, without any "breathing-spell," a tremendously difficult problem of adaptation. In fact, one might say that America's governmental development has largely been determined by the capacity or incapacity of adults to adapt themselves to new situations, new ideas, and new demands.

In rural America, conditions facilitated the adjustment of the individual to society, while minimizing the necessity of adjusting society to the individual. For one thing, the times were slower; and, because the family or the community was measurably self-contained, the individual as he grew from infancy to manhood experienced at the appropriate stages of his development the successive responsibilities of social living. His final adjustment was reasonably satisfying because it was gradual and comprehensive.

In an industrial and urban régime, the process of personal adjustment during the formative period is blocked and distorted, while the rapidity of change imposes greater strains on adults. The

[2] Contributions to this loss of faith, if it is real, may have come from various sources—political fatigue; the repeated frustration of the popular will; the relatively low esteem in which politicians, especially legislators, came to be held; demagoguery; revelations of corruption and incompetence; the sham battles of political parties; the inconclusiveness of election results; increasing remoteness and complexity of public problems and of government; the success of selfish minority pressures; the fact that positive government in a technological society made constantly more exacting demands on intelligence; the new psychology, reflecting both on mass intelligence and mass rationality; the tendency to question all traditional assumptions; the belief that through propaganda the sources of public information were polluted; the doctrine of economic determinism; the collapse of idealism after the First World War; and finally a spreading suspicion that moral standards governing thought and speech were either insufficient or crumbling.

diminished integrity of the family and the community has reduced their stabilizing educative influence on the individual. Consequently, a heavier burden is thrown on the formal educational and corrective agencies which, in turn striving for adjustment, are confronted with the problem of instability.

In this process, individuals, communities, educational institutions, and various remedial forces doubtless increase their powers of adaptation. Moreover, social change seems to be in some respects slowing down. Nevertheless, the tendency toward political complication and political confusion is, if anything, accelerating. It would seem that for some time in the future individual Americans will be on the whole more unstable and psychologically more insecure, relative to their environment, than in the past. The social results are many. From the political standpoint, the possibilities include a more prevalent cynicism, or a more widespread disposition than in the past to escape from reality, to seek stability and security in illusion, to avoid individual responsibilities, and to depend on the more self-confident and reassuring types of leadership. On the other hand, one may reasonably infer the possibility of wider and more vigorous political interest, a fresh assertion of political individualism suited to the times.

While little doubt can be entertained that modern America possesses and exercises as much civil liberty as in the past, it has appeared for some time that freedom of thought is neither prized nor exercised in proportion to the need of it and that, for the protection of the civil liberties, Americans are more inclined than formerly to depend, as in other matters, on government. Finally, there has been justified fear that no successful stand would be made for freedom of opinion in the face of economic collapse, class warfare, or national peril.

At these vital points, the course of public discussion and of public opinion during the last two years has given a measure of reassurance.

Tolerance may not be a moral principle; but it is a social rule implicit in democracy and its exercise stabilizes as well as preserves democracy. Orderly adjustment demands tolerance by the minority of majority rule, tolerance by the majority of minority criticism, and general tolerance of inequalities and differences—cultural, intellectual, economic, racial, and religious. One cannot detect any long-run trend toward disruptive intolerance; but, in the presence of both economic and national insecurity, intellectual confusion, and dependence on personal leadership, increased possibility exists of a "whipped-up" intolerance.

Morality changes.

Changes in the ingredients of the democratic spirit and even a temporary eclipse of the democratic ideal might be viewed as phases of adjustment. A similar interpretation can be put on the breaking down of old moralities and virtues and the growth of fundamental skepticism.

The old moralities and virtues emphasized duties rather than rights and acted as restraints on the individual in his personal and public relations, while contributing to his feeling of security; but their revision was inevitable. New moral compulsions, seemingly better suited to the times, are expressed in such terms as "social conscience," "social justice," and "co-operativeness"; but they lack spontaneous generation, simplicity, and concreteness. They are utilitarian expressions of old radicalisms; and they have gained impetus from class and group conflict. In part, they are imposed by some groups upon others. Those that benefit from the *status quo* are usually most devoted to the old and more restraining moralities; and, therefore, when mass discontent presses on public opinion and government the conservative defense of past maxims helps to discredit them. Thus, to a large extent, the politically significant moralities are tossed about in the arena of political controversy.

Standards of honesty in their narrower and more tangible applications seem to have suffered little change. Progress appears to have been made in the control of gross political corruption and unethical business practices; and this progress has contributed to stability, as well as to democracy and efficiency. It has proved more difficult, however, to extend these standards to the relations between government and private groups; and this failure, one that may be inherent in democracy, presents one of the central problems of stability.

Constitutionalism, as a restraining factor,
appears to have weakened.

When certain social influences are ranged in opposition, orderly adjustment means equilibrium rather than transition. The legal system, popular respect for law, and obedience to it are obviously potent factors in maintaining order. In its gradual evolution through the centuries, law embodied the moral sense of the community; it was considered to be nonpolitical in origin; and its impartial development and execution were held to be major safeguards of liberty. In America, individualism and the democratic spirit bred a species of lawlessness; but the habit of law-abidingness persisted, and, on the whole, equilibrium continued between obedience to law and criticism or revision of it.

This equilibrium has been threatened and the sanctity of law obscured by various developments. Statute law expanded in response to economic pressures rather than morals or principles. This expansion was followed by the development of administratively made law, more technical and in intent even more variable than statute law. The courts were substantially assimilated into the political system. Politics became the source of law; and as a result law reflected whatever incompetence and inertia resided in the legislative mechanism. Difficulties arose in the enforcement of multitudinous technical laws. The courts and the legal profession were identified with unpopular economic interests.

The Constitution viewed as law and enforced by the courts was expected to stabilize the general form and functioning of government by placing restraints on the persons and groups that might win political control. The function of the Constitution—more especially the function of the Supreme Court as the guardian or interpreter of the fundamental law—has been to maintain a continuing equilibrium between conservatism and radicalism, between the forces making for restraint and those making for release. Incidentally, the Constitution contributed to the sense of historical continuity, to confidence in the future, and to psychological security. Until recently the question of political stability seemed to be answered by the extraordinary prestige of the Constitution and the prestige and power of the Supreme Court, along with the elasticity of the instrument and the accommodating attitude of its interpreters. At the present moment, the answer is not so clear.

The ultimate sanction of the Constitution has always rested in the feelings of the people; and these feelings are influenced by economic conditions and by the association of the Constitution and the Court with popular or unpopular developments. Moreover, neither the Constitution nor the Court could remain aloof from political controversy or the deeper conflicts that political controversy reflected. Owing to their inevitable lag, both the Constitution and the Court came to be associated with and championed by that private economic power which was popularly distrusted as power and as an assumed obstacle to social justice.

In the meantime, constitutional law has ramified obscurely, intricately, and massively away from the plain letter of the written document. Popular mastery and understanding of the instrument have been impeded by the difficulty and practical abandonment of the amending process. Finally, the rapidity of change and the pressure of political leadership for radical action makes the Court more than ever before a political organ and therefore less a self-stabilizing one. Incidentally, constitutional law is rendered more uncertain.

It does not appear, however, that the recent relaxation of constitutional restraints extends to the civil liberties. In this area, the maintenance of constitutional restraint may do much to further orderly adjustment through discussion and eventually, if intellectual freedom persists, through scientific leadership.

Areas of structural rigidity in government suggest instability.

In many important respects, the Constitution, as judicially interpreted, has facilitated, or at least has not prevented, an orderly adjustment of governmental organs and powers. In other respects its more conspicuous contribution has been to rigidity rather than to adaptation. In still other respects it has had little relation to or influence upon the matter of adjustment.

Since the time of Washington, of Jefferson, or of Jackson, the social environment and the task of government have undergone an extraordinary transformation. The terms that are now employed in the appraisal of government—efficiency, social action, positive functioning, power, personal influence—are almost the opposite of those used in rural America. Yet no comparable change has been made in the form of government, with reference, for example, to the setup of legislatures, legislative representation, the general legislative-executive relationship, and federal-state and state-county organization. This fact suggests that either these structural survivals have had durable validity or they have persisted because of governmental or popular inertia or both. When these features of governmental organization are examined from the standpoint of their actual operation, their present appropriateness seems at least open to serious question. The doubt persists when one notes certain striking major departures from the theories and expectations of those who established these institutions. Among such departures are the party system, the practically direct election of the president, the direct primary system of nomination, the pressure-group system in its political operations, the increase of governmental power, centralization, and executive domination of legislation.

Each of these phenomena constitutes an extensive and complex field of study but with regard to all of them one may make this generalization: they have come into being or attained their present importance for the purpose, express or tacit, of remedying defects in the original structure without its drastic or apparent alteration, without disturbing popular feelings, without running full tilt against popular theories and prejudices, and to avoid the trouble of amending the Constitution. Assuredly, they may be interpreted as means of adjustment; but they have done little to keep public interest and public discussion alive regarding the major principles, practices, and problems of government and have therefore had the effect of preserving basic maladjustment. Moreover, the new devices, along with the old institutions, have made government more complex and its structural problems less amenable to treatment.

The structure of policy reveals inertia, disequilibrium, and "runaway" tendencies.

One might afford to ignore maladjustments in governmental organization if the economic and social policies of government were properly adjusted to one another and had the total effect of promoting stability.

When responsibility for economic control and distributive justice has been assumed, the need increases for adjusting policy to changing economic and social conditions. Piecemeal additions to policy may be politically justified; but, from the standpoint of effect, every addition is something of an experiment. Nevertheless, however experimental the policy may be, neither time nor wisdom is available for its reconsideration, while popular feelings and economic interests rally to its support and demand its retention. Any errors or bad effects that may have become evident are sought to be cured by additional piecemeal action. Policies once adopted or laws once passed possess a power on the one hand to preserve themselves and on the other to produce offspring.

A developing body of policy is necessary; but in this development continuing balances are generally held to be essential, for example, between certitude and experimentalism, between the need of legislation and its enforceability, between expenditure and revenue, between centralization and decentralization, between considerations of the general welfare and particular demands, between the concepts of private enterprise and of public control, between emphases on production and on distribution, between ideas of competition and of monopoly, and between nationalism and internationalism.

Certain principles and conditions have acted as automatic limitations on popular pressure and legislative action; for example, state rights, minimized government, individual liberty and *laissez faire*, national security, war, industrial expansion, constitutionalism, budget-balancing, and taxpayer resistance. The manner and extent of their action have varied from time to time. They are not all inoperative at the present time; and it is not improbable that some may again be fully effective; but the legislative history of recent years seems to indicate extreme "runaway" tendencies.

Does increasing governmental economic control imperil democracy?

The structure of policy that has been erected in this country is still distant from a socialistic or totalitarian system. Many would say, however, that no economic system can work half free and half controlled, and that, when a government such as ours tries to occupy the middle ground, its choice are so many and so difficult that they are certain to have an adverse effect on a complicated and delicate economic mechanism. Thus, it may be argued, a government in this position is fated to disappoint the people.

It is objected further that fiscal collapse is an inevitable result of a middle course, in which government is unable to encourage industrial production but is compelled continually to increase its spending for social purposes. The day of reckoning, from this point of view, may be postponed first by a public works program, second by building armaments, and finally by war; but, sooner or later, public credit collapses and depression comes, with general confusion and profound feelings of insecurity. If the crisis of 1933 demanded "stronger" leadership than ever before, the next crisis, it is said, will make an even stronger leadership necessary and acceptable. If other crises have brought hints and appearances of a suspension of the Constitution, the next crisis may bring an actual and indefinite suspension.

Apart from this possibility, it is evident that, when democratic government goes into fields of service and control where no restrictive customs and principles operate, the result is an increasing bureaucratic paternalism. The predictable effects were portrayed by de Tocqueville when he sought in his *Democracy in America* "to trace the novel features under which despotism may appear in the world." In our day, one might profitably reread his observations, from which the following excerpts are selected:

. . . The will of man is not shattered, but softened, bent, and guided: . . . such a power . . . does not tyrannize, but it compresses, enervates, extinguishes, and stupefies a people, till each nation is reduced to be nothing better than a flock of timid and industrious animals, of which the government is the shepherd.

. . . .

. . . They . . . console themselves for being in tutelage by the reflection that they have chosen their own guardians. . . . By this system the people shake off their state of dependence just long enough to select their master, and then relapse into it again.

. . . .

. . . It is in vain to summon a people, which has been rendered so dependent on the central power, to choose from time to time the representatives of that power; this rare and brief exercise of their free choice, however important it may be, will not prevent them from gradually losing the faculties of thinking, feeling, and acting for themselves, and thus gradually falling below the level of humanity. . . . It is indeed difficult to conceive how men who have entirely given up the habit of self-government should succeed in making a proper choice of those by whom they are to be governed; and no one will ever believe that a liberal, wise, and energetic government can spring from the suffrages of a subservient people. . . . The vices of rulers and the ineptitude of the people would speedily bring about its ruin; and the nation, weary of its representatives and of itself, would create freer institutions, or soon return to stretch itself at the feet of a single master.[3]

On the other hand, many believe that it is possible for government, operating at key points and in selected segments, to control "booms," cushion the effects of depressions, correct maladjustments, eliminate abuses, regulate monopolies, stimulate desirable activities and discourage undesirable ones, alleviate poverty, and prevent accumulations of great wealth. These things can be done, it is argued, without destroying those incentives that provide motive-power for the private enterprise system. It is asserted, finally, that government has already done these very things, and possesses the instrumentalities for doing them efficiently, while the private enterprise system has been rapidly adjusting itself to this form of control.

Government, they say, is also making a satisfactory adjustment. It is admitted that the ideal of democracy is only partially realized in the political mechanism; but, it is argued, the essential procedures of popular government remain firmly bulwarked. Specific evidence may be cited to prove that democracy still operates. It is recognized that the functions assumed by government and the conditions of modern society demand more political intelligence; but, it is contended, the nation's intellectual resources are adequate for the task and these resources are rapidly being mobilized. It is pointed out further that those developments in our government that have been characterized as "dictatorial" have been accompanied by an increase of real governmental responsibility to the people,

[3] Alexis de Tocqueville, *Democracy in America* (rev. ed., 1900), Vol. 2, pp. 330-35.

and, through the alleged paternalistic enforcement of distributive justice, sources of popular unrest have been removed and popular faith in and attachment to democratic government have been restored.

Among both critics and defenders of public policies are many who see in them an irresistible movement toward state socialism or totalitarianism.

While socialism as a doctrine has not been up to this time an important issue or the announced goal of any considerable group and has been quite consistently and almost universally repudiated, nevertheless, it is noted, public opinion and public policies have moved, ever more rapidly, away from a substantially free economy toward a controlled one. Political forces, it is contended, may conceivably halt the movement, but only temporarily; for no middle-ground position can be fixed and held. Democratic government, to compensate for its own inefficiency or for that of the private enterprise system, necessarily proceeds from promotion to regulation, from regulation to participation in management, and thence eventually to a "planned economy." This progress or retrogression, whichever it may be, will be hastened, it is predicted, by economic and military requirements during and after the present war.

It is maintained that socialism will destroy democracy in one of two ways. Either democracy will be discredited and deliberately discarded because of its inefficiency; or the possessors of political and economic authority, while retaining the forms of democracy, will dispense with its essential procedures in order to obtain a modicum of efficiency or merely to perpetuate themselves in power. Perpetuation in power will be manifestly easier when all the people are directly dependent on government.

Those who feel that the more serious threat comes from the Right assume that the private enterprise system has failed, that its control must be socialized, that a class or group that possesses power will never give it up without a struggle, and that the private holders of economic power in America are essentially selfish, "Fascistminded," and in no way devoted to real democracy. They were willing, it is granted, to make concessions to the masses in the form of social services and economic regulation so long as expanding industry was producing an increasing national income; but in the future, it is argued, such concessions will be no longer possible. Accordingly, class feeling will become stronger and class conflict more irreconcilable, destroying that basis of common agreement on fundamentals indispensable to the resolution of differences by democratic means.

Thus, it is predicted, a stationary and decaying capitalism, with its back to the wall, will resist to the last with the obstinacy of the Bourbons. In this situation, a dictatorship of the Right may come through the election of a reactionary president who will also be a "strong" president and who will have at hand the means of perpetuating himself and his group in power. Or, partly because of divisions, confusions, and vacillations in the middle classes, partly because of the selfishness and obstinacy of the capitalists, partly because of recurrent strikes and violence by labor, partly because of the slowness and ineptitude of representative legislatures, and partly because of inefficient administration, the population, suitably prepared by propaganda, will finally turn with relief to centralized and in effect irresponsible one-man rule. The dictator in this case, it is supposed, will represent the positive desires of the capitalists aided and abetted by the manipulated acquiescence of the impoverished and insecure middle classes.

On the other hand, it is contended that the assumptions on which this line of argument rests are not warranted by the facts, that the economically powerful are as a class opposed not to democracy but to socialism, that in recent years industrial leadership has gained a larger and deeper sense of social responsibility, that the tendency is now toward a redressing of the balance and a more workable adjustment of the relationship between capital and labor, and that, instead of becoming more widespread and irreconcilable, industrial conflict will decrease as methods and habits of collective bargaining or joint management are perfected.

It is further urged that the conditions associated with class struggle, which have recently appeared more ominous, are not really worse than during or after previous depressions, and that a new adjustment and stabilization can be accomplished consistently with the preservation of both the free enterprise system and political democracy. Opinions may differ on the means of bringing about this result; but various approaches to it have been suggested, for example, reorganization of private industrial management, development of an "industrial constitution," assumption of greater social responsibilities by management, participation by labor and the public in management, growth of industrial statesmanship informed by economic research, further adoption by private industry of policies based on the capacity of technology to increase production and lower prices, education of labor and the general public in economic facts and principles, introduction of industrial leadership into politics and government, and preservation of competition through adequate enforcement of the antitrust acts.

Regardless of speculations and predictions, we may conclude that America has entered a period of precarious balance. Looking to a longer future, one may draw some consolation from the thought that, however unstable democracy may be, dictatorship is and always will be more so. If there is a cycle in public affairs, if human beings must from time to time experience despotism in order to appreciate the value of self-government and understand its methods, then, whatever happens, one can look forward with confidence to another "new birth of freedom," a re-birth not likely to be long delayed.

CHAPTER XVII

TOWARD POLITICAL READJUSTMENT

The preceding analysis of American government has brought to light certain adverse trends, indications of weakness and strain, and evidences of structural and mechanical defect; and we have come to the general conclusion that the realization of democracy has become more difficult, the problem of efficiency more pressing, and the question of stability more critical.

At this point, we naturally ask: What should and can be done to strengthen government and redirect political tendencies? While the purpose of this study has been diagnosis, not prescription, it must be admitted that the procedure of diagnosis, necessarily stressing symptoms of trouble, may create an impression that the patient's condition is beyond remedy or hope. It is proposed in this final chapter, therefore, to suggest that an unusually favorable opportunity for conscious and planned political readjustment may be at hand, to point out briefly some sources of strength and encouragement that America possesses, governmentally speaking, and to locate in a general way the prior problems and key questions around which constructive discussion might profitably revolve.

Opportunity for readjustment
appears to be at hand.

Democracy was long under the spell of what Bryce called the "fatalism of the multitude," which, he said, produced "a loss of resisting power, a diminished sense of personal responsibility, and of the duty to battle for one's own opinions, such as has been bred in some peoples by the belief in an overmastering fate." At the same time, confidence in democracy shifted its basis from the actual qualities and aims of freedom-loving men to such things as manifest destiny, the inevitability of progress, the magnitude of our material resources, and the assumed dominance of good in human nature. It was really felt, as Mencken observed, that optimism "is a virtue in itself—that there is a mysterious merit in being hopeful and of glad heart, even in the presence of adverse and immovable facts." On the other hand, between 1933 and 1940, the energy and apparent efficiency of dictatorship, its ability insidiously to subvert democracy, and, finally, the seeming invincibility of its military power appeared to spell a fate for free peoples both tragic and inexorable. Optimistic fatalism inhibited the individual will, bred complacency, and invited catastrophe. It is now pretty well shaken out of American life. So also is the later fatalistic pessimism. For the anti-democratic forces of today, when they chose military aggression, adopted the most effective way to shock Americans into a reaffirmation of their historic faith.

But democracy cannot be made durably vital merely by warring against the aggressive despotisms of Europe and Asia or by winning a military victory over them. The victory, when it comes, will be a truly decisive one if it is followed within our own country as well as throughout the world by measures of political readjustment, designed to safeguard the democratic way of life from both internal and external threats.

It does not appear that a democracy whether in peace or at war is paralyzed or weakened by self-criticism. Democracy gained its revolutionary impetus and consolidated its institutions in the seventeenth and eighteenth centuries, when it was compelled to challenge an almost universal denial of the right and capacity of peoples to govern themselves. Political discussion seems to have been most fruitful when carried on in "times that try men's souls."

We are living in such times. We are no longer paralyzed by fatalism, either optimistic or pessimistic. We are under the pressure of a vast movement against human rights and civilized values. We know that we must seek to remove the causes of such a movement. We realize that these causes are not all in other peoples and regions: some are in ourselves. We are now prepared for more responsible American participation in the maintenance of world order; and we understand that such participation will involve changes in national policies, perhaps also in certain features of government. Thus, the present juncture tends to make political readjustment possible and expedient.

*America has numerous sources of strength
and much reason to feel encouragement.*

The writer sees no reason to be unduly pessimistic about the outcome. The manner in which the American people have met serious challenges in the past may well contribute to confidence for the future. Undoubtedly, we have resources—geographical, economic, and intellectual—adequate to insure our national safety, our political freedom, and our economic progress.

The present situation with all its perils and losses has increased America's will to have democracy, sharpened the sense of individual responsibility, and emphasized the general welfare. Our ability to resist internal subversion and external aggression has again been demonstrated.

Apart from the international crisis, the ultimate effects of which are still obscure, the American people possess many undoubted political advantages. Without undertaking an extensive inventory, one may recall our vast educational plant and its potentialities with respect to intellectual leadership; the place that science occupies in the popular imagination; the number, variety, and excellence of our sources of information; the widespread dissemination of facts and ideas; and the recent rise of popular interest in government.

The decrease of political corruption in its cruder aspects, the freedom and fairness of election procedure, and the maintenance of liberty of opinion are to be counted as very considerable assets.

Especially encouraging is the improvement of municipal organization and administration since 1900. Experiments in this field have been so numerous, so intelligently studied, and so revealing that eventually trends in city government may suggest, if not determine, some of the main features of state and federal governments.

Equally encouraging are American achievements with respect to operating efficiency, both in industry and public administration. The abundance of our professional and technical resources and the strength of the merit principle seem to exclude any possibility that administration in America may fail because of technical deficiencies. The practice of delegating legislation to administrative agencies provides still another reassuring evidence of governmental ingenuity and adaptability.

From about 1900 to the Second World War, the concept of efficiency was ascendant in America and the democratizing objective pretty thoroughly obscured, if not discredited. But the American cult of efficiency was brought into partial disrepute by its narrowness and its extreme claims; fascism and nazism helped to restore the balance by showing what efficiency means in the absence of democracy; while totalitarian aggression has served to rekindle a more general concern for democracy and devotion to it. So at this moment America seems to be in an unusually favorable position, perhaps the best that it has enjoyed since 1787, to work out a system capable of achieving the maximum of both democracy and efficiency.

Under limitations that seem feasible, the two concepts are not basically or ultimately contradictory or incompatible; and, when both are embodied in government, they go far to assure stability. To a large extent, undemocratic and inefficient features of government are traceable to identical conditions; for example, the range, complexity, and remoteness of public problems; economic and international instability; the form and operation of the legislative mechanism; the lack of controlling principles with respect to the increase and centralization of governmental power; and the nature of both public and private leadership.

In governmental readjustment, the basic and prior problems are presented by economic conditions and international relations.

The major inroads upon or threats to the democracy, efficiency, and stability of government are economic and international.

In essence, the economic problem is, as always, one of increased production at lower prices, equitable distribution, and a generally rising standard of living; but, with the growth of industry, economics and politics have become more critically interrelated. Government has been extending its power more and more into the private economic sphere. Largely because of economic influences, public questions as a whole have increased and are increasing in number, range, complexity, urgency, and importance.

Politico-economic influences operate in a vicious circle. If this circle is to be broken and if political democracy is to be durably reconciled with a free enterprise system, we must fix the limits of private and public power in the economic sphere, possibly restricting the present area of public activity. To this end, the first essential is to solve the problems involved in making the private enterprise system operate in the public interest and to the general satisfaction. Along with the solution of these problems, we must understand more clearly and widely than we do now the value of free enterprise, the danger of indefinitely aggrandizing political power, and the need of restraint and patience on the part of the people with respect to their economic expectations and demands.

Related to the strictly economic questions and issuing from them are other questions that involve moral standards, social ideals, psychological motivations and reactions, and influences that extend directly or indirectly into the political sphere. Thus, we have problems created by concentrations of private power, diffusion of private responsibility, inadequate sense of social responsibility, conflicts between capital and labor, insufficient development of private economic statesmanship, and insulation of industrial leadership from politics.

The problem of opinion-formation derives most of its elements from situations concerned with industrial production and distribution. The major question with reference to integration of opinion and policies are presented by the predominance of specialized and particularistic organizations and leaderships; class differentiation and apparent stratification; cleavage between capital and labor; territorial segregation of industry, wealth, and leadership; persistence of sectionalism and localism; urbanism; diminished agricultural individualism; relative decline of local discussion; and weaknesses or lags in the classes, groups, and organizations having integrative functions or potentialities.

These various conditions are not mutually exclusive or precisely co-ordinate; but their general tendency is not only to scatter, confuse, and paralyze opinion with reference to the central problem of industrial production but also to subject government to the inordinate pressure of demands that are not sufficiently compromised or adjusted in the private sphere. Further scattering and unbalancing effects are produced by the division of the most effective leaderships between the social-service groups and the interest groups, the inability of the taxpayer interest to check or co-ordinate the former groups, and the inability of the consumer interest to co-ordinate and rationalize the latter. These situations emphasize questions of middle-class disintegration and confusion and of inadequacies in the party system.

The question of international organization, likewise central in the governmental problem, is, of course, tied in with that of industrial production and distribution; but the international problem, in its decisive features and ultimate form, is political. It is a problem of so organizing world affairs as to eliminate militarism, war, and threats of war, provide for the peaceful settlement of disputes and the establishment of law, and promote world-wide economic and social progress. What the problem involves in detail is now being widely studied; and the various questions under discussion do not need to be stated here. The importance of these questions cannot be overemphasized. How they are answered in the postwar settlement may in the long run tip the scales for or against durable democracy.

If the essentials of the international system are to be unchanged, those who desire a greater assurance of efficient and stable democracy will have to re-examine systematically the kind of situations that have rendered democratic nations ineffective and weak in the presence of emerging international dangers. How can a democracy co-ordinate and balance its international and domestic tasks? How can public opinion be kept organized for international action? How can the normal politics of democracy be prevented from complicating and delaying the operations of government in world affairs? How can military power be created and maintained at a high point of efficiency without militarizing or degrading the popular mind, infringing basic liberties, threatening civilian supremacy, and producing economic crisis or retrogression?

*Improvement of the human factor
presents continuing questions.*

Economic, social, and political conditions are created by people interacting with their physical environment. To an extent these conditions are simply ways in which people act and in which they reveal their merits and demerits. In the end, political freedom depends on the vigilance of the masses, and good government on their virtue; but how to make them vigilant and virtuous, how to shape their minds and morals to meet the changing and enlarging demands of self-government, has long been the hope or despair of civic leaders, educators, philosophers, and statesmen.

De Tocqueville, writing more than a hundred years ago, thought that

the first duty which is at this time imposed upon those who direct our affairs is to educate the democracy; to warm its faith, if that be possible; to purify its morals; to direct its energies; to substitute a knowledge of business for its inexperience, and an acquaintance with its true interests for its blind propensities.

In Bryce's opinion, the America of fifty years ago,

seeing nothing but its own triumphs, and hearing nothing but its own praises, [seemed] to need a succession of men like the prophets of Israel to rouse the people out of their self-complacency, to refresh their moral ideals, to remind them that the life is more than meat, and the body more than raiment, and that to whom much is given of them shall much also be required.

Two decades ago, James Harvey Robinson in his *Mind in the Making* pointed out:

If some magical transformation could be produced in men's ways of looking at themselves and their fellows, no inconsiderable part of the evils which now afflict society would vanish away or remedy themselves automatically. . . .
. . . The world seems to demand a moral and economic regeneration which it is dangerous to postpone, but as yet impossible to imagine, let alone direct. The preliminary intellectual regeneration which would put our leaders in a position to determine and control the course of affairs has not taken place. We have unprecedented conditions to deal with and novel adjustments to make—there can be no doubt of that. We also have a great stock of scientific knowledge unknown to our grandfathers with which to operate. . . . We have, however, first to create an *unprecedented attitude of mind to cope with unprecedented conditions, and to utilize unprecedented knowledge.* This is the preliminary, and most difficult, step to be taken—far more difficult than one would suspect who fails to realize that in order to take it we must overcome inveterate natural

tendencies and artificial habits of long standing. How are we to put ourselves in a position to come to think of things that we not only never thought of before, but are most reluctant to question? In short, how are we to rid ourselves of our fond prejudices and *open our minds?* . . .

Most of what de Tocqueville, Bryce, and Robinson said is pertinent to the present situation. We can be sure that popular intellectual and moral adjustment has been taking place, though it has lagged behind the requirements of government. Does democracy itself contribute to this lag? Political leadership in a democracy is prone, not only to cover up its own defects and failures, but also and more especially to maintain silence regarding the shortcomings of the people. In any form of government, men who seek preferment deem it desirable to flatter the sovereign, whether one or many. But constant flattery is unhealthful for a man or a people. Progress has probably been made toward the solution of this problem through the development of social psychology and of a critical private leadership independent of political control. The key question seems to be: How can people generally be better and more quickly taught to know their own minds, without creating too much psychological insecurity and destroying general confidence in popular government?

One could, if one wished, make a long list of our shortcomings as a people. These present an educational problem both broad and intricate, to be solved, not merely by the schools, but also through the influence of the whole environment. That encouraging movements are under way toward its solution cannot be gainsaid.

Readjustment is needed in the structure
and mechanism of government.

What has just been said of economic and international conditions and of the people tends to minimize the importance of the structure and mechanism of government. Some might dismiss the matter entirely, as in Pope's couplet:

> Over forms of government let fools contest;
> That which is best administered is best.

Nevertheless, it is quite clear from our own political evolution and experience that forms, while secondary, play a real and an increasingly influential role in the rise or decline of democracy and efficiency.

Government reflects the society of which it is a part; but political institutions and practices are by no means wholly chameleon-like. They develop a vitality of their own and profoundly influence the feelings of the people and the extra-governmental social organization. As the role of government enlarges and its power grows, the derivative characteristics become relatively less important and the contributory and basic features more important. At some point in the progression, government may cease to be the servant and become the master of society.

The ultimate test of the strength or weakness of any governmental feature is whether it contributes and may be expected to contribute to stability, efficiency, and democracy. When a weakness is recognized, the difficulty of finding a remedy for it or the doubtful wisdom of making a change does not alter the fact of weakness. The difficulty and the doubt may simply point to other and more fundamental weaknesses, for example, institutional rigidity, lack of political-mindedness, inadequacy of leadership, in short, absence of democratic and efficient over-all control.

Many of the numberless weaknesses that have been and are being pointed out by students of government relate to details that would presumably be corrected if the more fundamental weaknesses were remedied. Take, for example, the common and often well-founded criticism that we do not put our "best men" into office. If we do not ordinarily do so, it is quite likely because of weaknesses in the people, in economic and social conditions, or in the political system. Similarly, certain shortcomings in the party system are symptoms rather than the disease itself. The line between primary and secondary factors is not always clear.

It seems to the writer that the problems more directly involved in governmental structure, mechanism, function, and operation can be usefully segregated into five groups: (1) those concerned with fundamental adjustment; (2) those that relate to legislative organization, representation, and efficiency; (3) those involved in the increase of governmental powers and functions; (4) those concerned with the territorial distribution of public power; and (5) those presented by governmental leadership, the influence of government on social organization and opinion-formation.

1. Among the problems concerned with fundamental adjustment, the primary difficulty seems to lie in a general unbalanced position of the Constitution and the Supreme Court, produced by the difficulty of reconciling the utilitarianism of these features of government with their prestige or sanctity. More specifically, we have failed to employ a direct, candid, open, democratic, reasonably proportioned, or reasonably prompt method of amending the Constitution. We have shifted the function of constitutional development to the Supreme Court, without any real endeavor to adapt the Court to the function or to make the Constitution amenable to a proportioned readjustment by judicial interpretation. In the meantime, the Court, the country's political leadership, the legislative branch, and the people have been unduly preoccupied with certain rigid doctrines—separation of powers, federalism, and local self-government. The attempt to keep these doctrines inviolate, along with the limitations of judicial interpretation, has prevented a frank and educative discussion of the question of power and largely precluded open, direct, and constructive steps toward its solution.

2. Problems that relate to legislative organization, representation, and efficiency may be looked for from various points of view, depending on what is conceived to be the most serious defect, the greatest need, the highest value, or the most imminent danger. Some may be preoccupied, favorably or unfavorably, with executive leadership, localized representation, minority pressures, planning, lag, deadlocks, administrative responsibility, federal-state coordination, party control, or the "runaway" tendencies in policy-determination. Some may emphasize democracy; others, efficiency. One encouraging fact seems to be that more democracy in the legislative process is not irreconcilable with more efficiency.

The central question appears to be posed by the vast growth of executive power. How can the benefits of concentrated national leadership be obtained while avoiding the danger of personal irresponsibility and preserving the advantages of composite representative legislatures? In considering this question in the light of the general situation, it becomes necessary to re-examine the principles of separation of powers and checks and balances, including the basic assumption of our government that the Executive should be independently and popularly elected. Can his responsibility be better enforced in this way than through appointment by Congress? Whether or not Congress should be made solely responsible, certain features of the legislative mechanism present secondary but extremely difficult problems—bicameralism, territorial representation, unwieldy memberships, rural over-representation, weakness of leadership, blurred jurisdiction of legislatures, absence of effective means of co-ordinating federal with state legislation and legislation of one state with that of another, and, in general, the resistance of the legislative organization as a whole to change, complicated by the steady growth of bureaucratic power without a commensurate organization of responsibility.

3. Problems involved in the increase of governmental powers and functions cannot be solved solely by changes in government. Changes in the means of fundamental adjustment and in the legislative mechanism should contribute to a stabilization of the relation between public and private power and at the same time prepare government for a more efficient and more democratic use of power. These problems, in addition, are closely related to those concerned with the territorial distribution of public power.

4. Questions concerned with the territorial distribution of public power compel re-examination of the following: the appropriateness of the constitutionally established system of federalism; the desirability of a constitutional enumeration of powers granted to the federal government; the possible superiority of a constitutional centralization of power with a statutory decentralization of functions; the advantages and disadvantages of centralization through federal spending; the problem of assuring effective budgetary controls; and the relation of taxation and tax-consciousness to centralization, as well as to governmentalization.

5. The problems presented by governmental leadership—the influence of government on social organization and opinion-formation —spring primarily from the nature of the social organization and of the opinion-forming process; but they are in part directly derived

from the waning prestige of legislatures, the magnification of the Executive, growth of governmental powers and functions, and centralization. A vital problem is presented by the large number of citizens who are directly dependent on government for the whole or a part of their incomes. Democracy demands that a free public opinion shall control government and that elections shall be uncoerced. But when opinion can be manipulated or bought by officeholders so as to create and hold a majority, popular government is actually no longer operating and the moral standards essential to its revival and maintenance suffer widespread deterioration.

The questions to which we have called attention in this study are numerous, widely distributed, serious, and provokingly interrelated. Altogether, they constitute a problem of individual and collective adjustment. If every question had to be separately studied and specifically answered, the prospects would not be bright. But political progress is not made in quite that way. Conditions produced by the war or by its aftermath may bring extraordinary pressure at one point or another, compelling important changes, creating new and potent sources of influence, and more or less irresistibly rearranging the governmental pattern.

The suggestion of such a possibility does not mean that the rehabilitation of democracy is predestined and to be brought about without much individual effort or personal responsibility. To accept this view would be to exchange the defeatism of recent years for the earlier rosy-hued but anaesthetic confidence in an automatic progress toward the millennium. If democracy is to be saved, it can only be saved democratically, by the free minds and wills of free men. When these are moved by deep feeling, America can make the most of its fateful moment.

INDEX